PUBLICATIONS ON ASIA
OF THE INSTITUTE FOR COMPARATIVE
AND FOREIGN AREA STUDIES
Number 30

Chinese Politics
and the Cultural Revolution

DYNAMICS OF POLICY PROCESSES

Byung-joon Ahn

UNIVERSITY OF WASHINGTON PRESS
SEATTLE AND LONDON

Library of Congress Cataloging in Publication Data
Ahn, Byung-joon, 1936-
    Chinese politics and the Cultural Revolution.
    (Publications on Asia of the Institute for Comparative and Foreign
Area Studies; no. 30)
    Bibliography: p.
    Includes index.
    1. China—Politics and government—1949-
I. Title. II. Series: Washington (State). University.
Institute for Comparative and Foreign Area Studies.
Publications on Asia; no. 30.
DS777.55.A6735   320.9'51'05   76-7780
ISBN 0-295-95515-5

To Young-ja

Contents

Appendixes

Preface

When I began Chinese studies, I heard it said that China is so huge a
country and so rich a civilization that almost anything written about
her can be right and at the same time wrong. This comment lingered in
my mind during both the research and the writing of this book. In an
attempt to avoid both generalities and trivialities, I chose to study how
the Chinese leaders and people actually sought to solve the real human
problems they confronted in carrying out simultaneously their twofold task: political-social revolution and economic modernization.

The purpose of this book is to understand and explain the dynamics
of Chinese policy processes on its own terms. Specifically, I have
focused my work on the major choices that the Chinese leaders and
people had made in the period between the Great Leap Forward and
the Cultural Revolution. In so doing, however, I have been unable to
develop a general theory that can provide a comprehensive explanation
of the choice-making processes; nor do the data that I have been able
to collect provide a basis for such an all-encompassing theoretical
analysis. I have opted, therefore, for a methodological eclecticism and
an interdisciplinary approach for my analysis. The result of these
efforts may have come closer to a policy analysis in a crude form, for
I have tried to describe as best I can how the Chinese perceived a public
problem, defined alternative options to solve it, made an authoritative
decision, implemented it, and evaluated its consequences. Now that my
endeavors have led to this book, it is my remaining hope that I have

been able to avoid the same mistake of the blind man who after touching one leg of the elephant, tried to explain the entire animal.

This book is the result of almost a decade of work. I began training in political science and Chinese studies in the late 1960s at Columbia University, where I found much intellectual stimulation and encouragement from many professors, colleagues, and friends. More specifically, A. Doak Barnett, John N. Hazard, Victor H. Li, James W. Morley, Andrew J. Nathan, Michel C. Oksenberg, Richard Sorich, and C. Martin Wilbur aided my work with wise counsel and selfless assistance. Columbia also supported a year of my field study in Hong Kong in 1969-70, which brought me closer to Chinese reality; there, Sai-cheung Yeung in particular rendered valuable assistance in my research.

Various institutes have also provided financial support without which the publication would have been further delayed. The East Asian Institute and the Research Institute on Communist Affairs (now the Research Insitute on International Change) of Columbia University sponsored my work in 1970-72 so that I could work on a first draft; for this I am especially grateful to their directors: the late John M. H. Lindbeck and Zbigniew K. Brzezinski. The Research Council of Western Illinois University awarded me two grants to aid my research: one in 1973-74 and another in 1976-77. The Joint Committee on Contemporary China of the Social Science Research Council and the American Council of Learned Societies awarded me a grant that enabled me to take a leave of absence from my teaching duties in 1976-77. The Institute for Comparative and Foreign Area Studies of the University of Washington guided the final draft toward publication.

I am also in debt to those who read portions or the entire manuscript and made helpful suggestions: A. Doak Barnett, Parris H. Chang, John N. Hazard, Chalmers Johnson, Victor H. Li, James W. Morley, Robert A. Scalapino, Ezra Vogel, Allen S. Whiting, C. Martin Wilbur, and Edwin A. Winckler. Andrew J. Nathan and Michel C. Oksenberg in particular helped me with critical comments and questions ranging from the style to interpretations. James R. Townsend and Thomas W. Robinson provided me with further criticisms with regard to its structure and contents. Finally, Margery Lang of the Institute for Comparative and Foreign Area Studies of the University of Washington carefully worked the manuscript into its final publication. With the usual caveat that those who have taught me cannot be held responsible for my own imperfections, I extend my heartful thanks to all of them.

Finally, I should like to acknowledge the contributions of my own family. When I send this manuscript to press, the memory of my parents, now deceased, comes alive; they had raised me with love and faith before I knew China. More recently, my children, Catherine and Theodore, have also suffered the burden of my work. My special thanks, however, go to my wife Young-ja; her endurance, understanding, and cooperation have sustained me throughout the research and authorship of this book. I happily dedicate this book to her.

Byung-joon Ahn

October 1976
Ann Arbor, Michigan

PART I
The Chinese Policy Process
1949-1959

The responsibility of correctly knowing and changing the world has been placed by history upon the shoulders of the proletariat and its party.

Mao Tse-tung, 1937

In changing the world we cannot divorce ourselves from reality or disregard reality; nor can we escape from reality or surrender to the ugly reality; we must adapt ourselves to reality, understand reality, seek to live and develop in reality, struggle against the ugly reality and transform reality in order to realize our ideals.

Liu Shao-ch'i, 1939

We cannot hope to accomplish this [socialist] transformation overnight. We must proceed step by step in the light of the experience and political consciousness of the masses and in accordance with what is possible in the actual situation.

Liu Shao-ch'i, 1951

Make the high mountain bow its head; make the river yield the way.

Mao Tse-tung, May 1958

In doing anything there has to be a period of high speed and a period of low speed. . . . Hard battle and rest and consolidation are the unity of opposites. This is law. They are also mutually transformable.

Mao Tse-tung, 1959

1
Introduction:
The Context of the Processes

There has always been a gap between man's ideas and his reality. Yet only human beings, by virtue of their humanity, attempt to bridge this gap, trying to solve problems arising in their environment. A collective expression of man's efforts to solve problems for society as a whole is politics. If politics is to be understood as a process of making choices to solve public problems, there seems to be no escape from issues in politics. One of the crucial elements in Communist politics is the inter-action of ideology and practice, for all Communist political systems share one thing in common: their commitment to a particular set of ideas called Marxism-Leninism or "Marxism-Leninism-Mao Tsetung Thought" as it is known in China, as a guide for political action. Because of this commitment, any Communist system faces an acute dilemma when solving problems occurring in its changing reality without com-promising its ideological imperatives. A graphic manifestation of this was the unfolding of the Great Proletarian Cultural Revolution in China.

This book is an attempt to understand and explain the dynamics of Chinese policy processes that led to the Cultural Revolution. By dy-namics, I mean the changing relationships between policy, power, and ideology, the three most crucial variables of Communist politics, that have evolved in the Chinese policy process. The policy process pre-supposes three basic components: (1) alternative means and ends avail-able for solving problems, (2) alternative actors and processes seeking

3

the means and ends, and (3) alternative values justifying the ends and means.[1] It follows that conflict and cooperation are endemic in making authoritative choices. In Communist politics, the means and ends are defined in policies, the actors and processes are represented by the political leaders and their organizations, and the values are expressed in ideological pronouncements. When the leaders share consensus on policy matters, they enjoy a synchronized relationship between policy, power, and ideology. When they disagree, however, their policy differences are bound to turn into power and ideological struggles, for not only are their stakes high but they have to justify their differences in terms of ideological beliefs. How the relationship between these components actually emerges depends upon the context within which they interact.

The central problem to explore in this study is: How did the major substantive and procedural conflicts evolve in 1958-66 and how eventually were they linked to the Cultural Revolution? In exploring this question, I will concentrate on the causes and effects of the major issues that shaped the policy processes leading to the Cultural Revolution. This will enable us to understand *why* Mao and his supporters chose to violate established patterns of policy formulation in launching the Cultural Revolution in 1965-66. It should be pointed out here that I am concerned with both the content and the process of policy and especially with the linkage between them. Most American political scientists have focused their professional concern mainly on the *process* by which public policies are made but have little concern with their *contents*. But the content and process are inseparable in a dynamic relationship, since the process often depends on the content.[2] In studying the Chinese policy process, therefore, we must understand how the Chinese leaders and people have been grappling with real and difficult problems while trying to remain faithful to their revolutionary ideas.

A study of the Chinese policy process in 1958-66 is significant for several reasons. First, an analysis of this period is crucial to understand the Cultural Revolution, for the revolution resulted from a decision that Mao made in response to a series of policy and procedural conflicts occurring in the post-1958 period. The Cultural Revolution should be analyzed within the context of these conflicts *as perceived by Chinese leaders*. Indeed, one of the central themes I pursue in this book is that the Great Leap Forward (GLF) and the Cultural Revolution were the two most important events in post-1949 Chinese politics and that the diverse political trends emerging from the Great Leap Forward and its aftermath necessitated the Cultural Revolution. The Great Leap Forward of 1958-59 approximated a Maoist prototype for revolution and development, whereas the adjustment and consolidation policies that the Chinese Communist Party (CCP) effected in the subsequent years of 1959-62 widely diverged from the Maoist prototype. The deepening conflicts between Mao's efforts to reassert his cherished policies and his operational associates' attempts to restrain them in 1962-66 culminated in the Cultural Revolution.

Second, the 1958-66 period provides the historical context of the Cultural Revolution. The Chinese policy process prior to the Cultural Revolution can best be understood in the context of a transformation-consolidation cycle. In fact, another over-all theme of this study is that in the long run the consequences of the previous policy become the causes of the succeeding policy and vice versa. A salient feature of the Chinese policy processes since 1949 is that two distinct phases have alternated. In the first phase, the Party sought policies aimed at promoting revolution, that is, changing social structures and remolding human mentality, trying to enhance equality through a rational allocation of resources. In making and implementing these policies, the Party relied on political activists and highly decentralized and diffused structures geared to mass mobilization and participation. The Party justified these by emphasizing dialectical struggle. We call this phase "transformation." In the second phase, however, the Party sought policies designed to promote development, that is, increasing production and income, trying to enhance efficiency through an incremental allocation of resources. In making and implementing these policies, the Party relied on professional bureaucrats and highly centralized and differentiated structures geared to institutionalization and regulation. The Party justified these by stressing compromise. We call this phase "consolidation."[3]

Since any policy must be ideologically legitimized, the shifts of policy cannot be explained adequately in terms of "feedback" characteristic of the cybernetic model of problem-solving.[4] Rather, they can be better understood in terms of "self-fulfilling prophecy" and "reality-testing."[5] The Maoist ideology aims at transforming social structures and men's outlook. When Mao calls upon the Chinese people to uphold such an ideology, it becomes a basis for building consensus. In so doing, Mao initiates campaigns to implement his policies. Local cadres then seek to be "Left" even if this results in "subjective" errors of "commandism" and "communism." They often provide policy makers with inflated information about local situations; the new policy based on this distorted information is bound to produce many unanticipated results. Since policy makers respond only to information that confirms their beliefs, the policy process tends to be comprehensive and ad hoc mobilization.[6]

But once policy makers begin to realize the consequences of their activities, they attempt to collect more accurate information. When this happens, it marks the beginning of the consolidation phase. In this way the "self-fulfilling prophecy" goes through the process of "reality-testing." Now that information becomes the basis for reaching consensus, policy makers carry out extensive adjustments to solve the most urgent problems; they also restore the administrative machinery to implement policies. Local cadres seek to protect the interests of their localities even if this results in the "empirical" errors of "departmentalism" and "tailism." The policy process tends to be incremental and bureaucratic.[7] The shifting of these phases created different issues and conflicts that become cumulative over the years. The post-Leap Chinese policy process presents a clear example of these shifts.

Lastly, the Cultural Revolution and the data it produced reveal more about the process of Chinese policy formation and implementation in 1958-66 than any other period. More specifically, the inner working of the policy process involved interactions between one supreme leader, who called for mass mobilization, and the Party, which defended its bureaucratic processes. Despite the outpouring of new books on Chinese politics in recent years, few of these account for the policy process and the issues involved in a holistic analysis. For example, in order to understand the importance of the Cultural Revolution in Chinese politics. one must trace it to its origin by explaining how the consequences of the Great Leap gave rise to the adjustment policies in 1959-62 and how the latter caused Mao to initiate the Socialist Education Movement and encourage the political campaigns in the army, why he demanded reforms in the economy, education, health care, and culture in 1962-65, and finally how the conflicts attendant on these issues developed into the Cultural Revolution. The significance of these issues cannot be understood separately without explaining the over-all linkage among them. Only when they are analyzed in the context of the shifting policy patterns since 1958 can we understand their respective roles in proper perspective. The data made available by the Cultural Revolution shed new light on these issues, enabling us to put together a holistic account of the policy process shaped in 1958-66. This endeavor can, I am hopeful, improve on what are so far somewhat incomplete explanations of this period.

My aim in this study is not to break theoretical ground on Chinese politics but to understand and explain critically significant policy issues and processes in contextual and clinical (problem-solving) perspective.[8] For this purpose, I shall use whatever relevant concepts and insights developed in the social science literature insofar as they can help to clarify the issues and processes. In concluding each chapter, I shall make some general observation in an analytical perspective and then in the final chapter, I shall try to synthesize the contents of the book with several coherent themes.

The method of handling data will be both chronological and topical. I shall first extrapolate the major trends of policy processes in chronological order and then assess them in an analytical context. In so doing, I shall try to understand them in terms used and accepted by the Chinese themselves. I will pay special attention to what they call the "struggle between the two roads," not necessarily to agree with their interpretation but to understand the meaning they give to it. Following this, I shall try to translate their meaning into terms familiar to contemporary Western social scientists. The analysis may then be meaningful both to the agent of action and the observer.[9] In this way, I shall endeavor to explain the actual state of policy development, mindful that in reality there could have been more than the two roads. Admittedly, the analysis I present here is not the only one that can be offered, for it could be reversed by some yet unearthed data.

The study draws mainly upon the written sources originating from China and is based essentially on their exegesis. The use of Red Guard sources poses a problem because they present information out of context and therefore are distorted for political purposes. Hence, their accuracy must be suspect. I have crosschecked these sources, wherever possible, with other official sources. But the problem still remains. Perhaps their factual accuracy will never be known. The pertinent question, it seems to me, is not whether to use them but rather how to use them and for what purpose. I have tried to use them to illustrate certain processes rather than to ascertain facts. A judicious reading of them yields far more information about the Chinese policy process than any other available source.[10] In addition to the written sources, I shall also draw upon information gained from interviews with refugees in Hong Kong that I conducted in 1969-70. They provided me with further clarification of the written sources and, more importantly, brought me into closer contact with the reality of Chinese politics.

Finally, this type of inquiry brings the investigator to the edge of evaluation. Inevitably, I shall be evaluating, but in so doing, I will do my best to distinguish facts from value judgments. This is easier said than done. Therefore, as to the adequacy of my efforts, the text must, in the last analysis, speak for itself.

The book is divided into four parts. In Part 1, I set out to describe the evolution of the Chinese policy process in 1949-59. Chapter 2 surveys how the Party initially tried to collectivize the economy and to suppress its political enemies, how and why China adopted its First

Five-Year Plan on a Soviet model, and how and why Mao decided to launch the Great Leap Forward. Part 2 documents the process of retreating from and making adjustments in the Great Leap in 1959-62. Chapter 3 analyzes how the Party retreated from the Leap in 1959-60, focusing on the people's commune. Chapter 4 follows this with a detailed analysis of the adjustment and consolidation measures the Party effected in 1960-62. Part 3 comprises the bulk of the book by delineating the issues and the processes of conflicts that evolved in 1962-66, thereby illustrating the process through which the Cultural Revolution evolved. Chapter 5 describes how the Party carried out the Socialist Education Movement and chapter 6 how the army implemented its emulation campaign in 1962-66. I deliberately juxtapose these two institutions to contrast their respective performances. Chapter 7 analyzes the substantive policy conflicts between Mao Tse-tung and Liu Shao-ch'i by describing the divergence of their innovative efforts in the economy, education, and health care in 1962-66. Chapter 8 documents the cultural reforms Mao initiated in 1962-66 and how they were gradually transformed into the Cultural Revolution in 1966. Part 4 analyzes the Cultural Revolution and its aftermath in 1966-76. Chapter 9 describes the actual making of the Cultural Revolution in 1965-66. And, finally, in chapter 10, I conclude with an analytical overview of Chinese policy processes evolved in 1949-76, explaining the progress of the Cultural Revolution in 1966-69 and the legacies it left in 1969-76.

2
From Consensus to Debate:
The Road to the Great Leap Forward

In the first decade of Communist rule in China, which the regime later called "Ten Great Years,"[1] the CCP initially enjoyed a basic policy consensus on how to restructure and rebuild Chinese society, but as the consequences of its initial efforts became known, the Party was faced with increasing dissidence. Since the conflicts in the 1960s leading to the Cultural Revolution can be traced to these debates in the 1950s, we must analyze the pre-1959 Chinese policy process as our point of departure.

By and large, the Party shared consensus in the first half of the decade. This was based partly on the Chinese revolutionary experiences and partly on the exigency of emulating the Soviet Union. Before 1955, policy was basically Soviet and urban oriented, thus reversing the trend of the pre-1949 Chinese revolution. In the second half of the decade, however, the Party's policy consensus began to deteriorate as the leadership faced more difficult choices. Realizing that the Soviet model of revolution and development had undermined the legacies of the Chinese revolution as he understood them, Mao, from 1955 on, asserted a Chinese way to revolution and development by seeking a faster pace of social transformation, especially in the countryside. This gave rise to intra-Party debates as to what priority the Party should adopt in collectivization and industrialization, what institutional processes it should devise, and what ideological justification it should develop for a selected course of action. As time passed, these debates tended to

9

polarize between those Party leaders who sought to continue the same policy and Mao, who began to articulate a new set of "correct" policies. The so-called two-road struggle emerged from them. In the end, Mao's views prevailed and the Party accepted a series of decisions Mao initiated in 1956-58, thereby paving the road to the Great Leap Forward (GLF) of 1958-59, which presented a prototype of the transformation phase.

THE EVOLUTION OF POLICY CONSENSUS: CHINA'S INITIAL COOPERATIVIZATION AND FIRST FIVE-YEAR PLAN, 1949-55

When the People's Republic of China was proclaimed in October 1949, the task ahead for the new republic called for no less than a complete reconstruction of China, necessary after a century of internal disintegration and external humiliation. The immediate problem of the CCP was to consolidate its power and to rehabilitate the devastated economy. While coping with these problems, the Party also had to renew its revolutionary commitment, forcing it to carry out both transformation and consolidation simultaneously. As a result of the long and hard struggle, the leadership reached consensus on carrying out a gradual transformation to concentrate on consolidation as manifested by its policy on agricultural cooperativization and the First Five-Year Plan. But this gradual approach later generated a set of new dilemmas for the Party in the mid-1950s.

Transformation, 1949-53: Land Reform, Cooperativization, Marriage Reform, and the Suppression of Counterrevolutionaries

The CCP's revolutionary experience left more enduring legacies on its transformation programs. Within the Chinese revolutionary experience, however, there had been two broad policy orientations; both were socialism, but one was an urban model and the other a rural model. During the "orthodox phase" of Chinese communism in 1921-27, the CCP followed the urban model under the direction of the Comintern, but the policies of this phase turned out to be disastrous. It was during the "peasant stage" of 1927-35 that the Party was able to carry out a peasant revolution under Mao's leadership.[2] With the help of the Japanese invasion of China proper in 1936, the Party led this revolution to success by mobilizing nationalist sentiments during its Yenan phase of 1936-49.[3] The protracted Chinese revolution thus combined a social revolution against the old Chinese society and a national revolution against the foreign enemy.[4] During the revolution, Mao sought to adapt Marxism-Leninism to Chinese reality as he understood it, thus using the foreign doctrine as a tool (*yung*) to solve China's problems without forgetting the substance (t'i) of the Chinese identity.[5] But the ultimate triumph of a weak Party over the strong internal and external enemies, as Mao repeatedly pointed out, further reinforced the revolutionary legacies in the post-1949 politics.[6]

It is important to note that even after Mao assumed leadership from the "International Faction" at the 1935 Tsunyi conference, two somewhat different revolutionary experiences existed in the "red areas" and the "white areas." The former refers to the liberated areas (generally in the countryside) where Mao exercised leadership and the latter to the urban areas under Japanese or Kuomintang control, where Liu Shao-ch'i exercised leadership (Mao once called him the model of the white area).[7] The Communist movement in the red areas, also known as the "Yenan experience," involved protracted guerrilla warfare and violent class struggle among the peasants.[8] Wherever the Party and the Red Army "liberated" certain areas their cadres carried out intensive propaganda and thought reform to remold the peasants' identity through struggle meetings. They actively mobilized the peasants, thereby forging a direct organizational link between the Party and the masses. They also lived more egalitarian lives, often receiving no more than free rations for their service, and tried to build self-reliant economic bases.

The movement in the white areas mostly involved underground activities, led by secret agents, among workers, students, and intellectuals. The underground agents' work often required compromise and cooptation; they relied on tightly knit Party cells. The only link they maintained with the masses was the highly disciplined, professional, and elitist Party organizations they served. Depending on their functional contribution, therefore, the treatment of these cadres differed from their counterparts in the red areas, for their success depended entirely on their environment.

These contrasts were also manifested by the differing personalities and leadership styles of the cadres who led the two different areas. A crucial element in shaping the Chinese revolution was Mao's leadership after 1935, a leadership he had earned as a result of his experiences in peasant and guerrilla movements. His position was unique within the Party, enabling him to reign over the Party with ad hoc political maneuvering, often regarding the policy process as a series of ideological movements. When he needed support, he skillfully played one group off against another, forming a "minimum winning coalition."[9] Liu built his reputation in the white areas, for which his reward was, from 1942, the position of the Party's second ranking leader. The white area experience enabled him to become a good organization man, always operating within the confines of Party discipline, and regarding the policy process as a series of practical adjustments. Their contrasting outlooks were revealed in the Rectification Movement of 1942-44, when Mao stressed the need for changing one's outlook through struggle by "learning from past mistakes to avoid future ones," and by "curing the sickness to save the patient." Liu distinguished the two kinds of problem-solving and, although he accepted struggle for what he called "questions of principle," he favored compromise for those of a "purely practical nature."[10]

These two outlooks complemented each other during the Chinese revolution and on the basis of these a policy consensus emerged later in 1949. In fact, Liu first championed the "Thought of Mao Tse-tung" as the CCP's dogma in 1943.[11] The Seventh Party Congress in 1945, which Mao later called "the Congress of unity," produced Party consensus on policy matters and a winning leadership coalition of the red areas and the white areas, while weakening the International Faction. At the Second Plenum in March 1949, Mao put forth the plan to shift the Party's efforts from the countryside to the cities. In implementing this policy, Liu, retreating from his 1943 position, differed from Mao when he stressed compromises and organizations in the speeches he made in Tientsin.[12] But these differences could be submerged *at this time*. Mao articulated Party consensus in the major pronouncements he made in 1940-49 that culminated in the Common Program of October 1949.[13]

From these documents we can discern the impetus of the policy consensus. First, Mao declared at the Second Plenum that the period of the city leading the village began and that from the first day the Party took over a city, it would pay attention to production. For this purpose, the Party committed itself to a gradual transformation of the capitalist economy by restricting but not liquidating the capitalists, so that their experiences and talents could be used. According to this policy, the rich peasants were allowed to operate under the policy of gradual agricultural cooperativization. Second, the Party decided to form a coalition government, albeit under its leadership, so that even non-Communist minor parties could participate in the People's Political Consultative Committee. Thus, at the top as well as the bottom, the Party sought to form a "grand coalition" so that all elements opposing the Kuomintang could join it.[14] Accordingly, the new regime theoretically established democracy among "the people," consisting of the workers, peasants, petty and national bourgeoisie, but exercised dictatorship toward "the enemy"; hence came the People's Democratic Dictatorship. Third, the Party justified these policies in the name of New Democracy, envisioning a two-stage revolution: a democratic revolution in which socialism and capitalism would coexist, followed by a socialist revolution. Lastly, for the sake of national security and development, the new republic committed itself to leaning toward the Soviet Union as its protector and teacher.[15]

Under these principles, the Party implemented several programs in 1949-53 designed to transform the social and economic structure of the old society. First of all, the Party's Third Plenum resolved in June 1950 to carry out land reform on the basis of its early experiences in the liberated areas. By this time, however, about one-third of the Chinese peasants had already carried out some type of land reform.[16] Then Liu formally presented the Land Reform Law to the People's Political Consultative Committee. This law aimed not only at the redistribution of land but also at the political purpose of mobilizing the peasants, thereby forming the "worker-peasant alliance."[17]

The Chinese method of land reform differed considerably from Stalin's. As Mao later related, Stalin's method was merely to confiscate land and redistribute it to the peasants in a bureaucratic way. Mao, however, regarded land reform as part of the revolutionary movement; as he told the Third Plenum, without land reform there would be no class struggle.[18] As soon as the Party or the Red Army cadres entered a village, they organized peasant associations by recruiting activists from the poor peasants. These associations, in turn, classified the peasants into five categories: landlord, rich peasants, middle peasants, poor peasants, tenants, and rural workers. The poor peasants and their allies held "struggle meetings" through which they redistributed land. By October 1952 these processes had been completed.[19]

In December 1951 the Politburo adopted the Resolution on Mutual Aid and Cooperatives for Agricultural Production. Liu as the Party's ranking leader and Teng Tzu-hui as director of its Rural Work Department directed cooperativization. In the areas where the land reform had been completed, the Party organized "mutual aid teams" allowing a dozen peasant households to cooperatively assign labor and draft animals. At the same time the agricultural producers' cooperatives (APC) were formed, "lower APC s," to which forty or fifty households contributed land and tools, and drew certain dividends for their contributions. In December 1953 the Party decided to enlarge these lower APC s to higher APC s so that about two hundred households could hand over their privately owned land and tools, and receive pay only according to their work. By 1955 only 14.2 percent of the Chinese peasants had joined either of these two forms of APC s.[20]

While agricultural cooperativization was being carried out, the Communist regime also embarked upon a program for nationalizing capitalist enterprises and commerce under the leadership of Ch'en Yün. On the eve of the Communist takeover, the "bureaucratic capitalist enterprises" comprised 80 percent of China's industry and transportation, and "national capitalist enterprises" 20 percent.[21] The Party adopted the policy of "peaceful transformation" by placing these enterprises under a joint state-private management. With the exception of some capitalists who resisted, the original managers were allowed to participate in a joint board with the state-appointed cadres and even to receive certain "fixed interests" for their contributions. By 1953 joint enterprises came to control 28.5 percent while the private enterprises declined to 14 percent.[22] The Party also enacted a national system of purchase and supply for commodities to bring inflation under reasonable control. Another reform aimed at transforming society was the Marriage Law of May 1950, designed to emancipate women, thereby loosening family control over individuals.

While carrying out these reforms, the CCP also attempted to eliminate any source of opposition through mass campaigns. In May 1951 it started the Three Anti-Campaign directed at corruption, waste, and bureaucracy among the cadres. This was followed in 1952 by the Five Anti-Campaign aimed at businessmen who were supposedly engaged in bribery, tax evasion, thefts of state property, cheating on government contracts, and stealing state secrets. These were soon unified in the "suppression of counterrevolutionaries" campaign in which about 4 million people were investigated and 38,000 labeled counterrevolutionary.[23] Although Mao repeatedly stressed persuasion in contrast to Stalin's purges in the 1930s, 2 or 3 million people were either "controlled" or executed in 1949-53.[24]

Consolidation, 1953-55: The State Constitution and the First Five-Year Plan

With the completion of state control over the economy, the Party placed more emphasis on consolidating authority and production. For these tasks the leadership clearly looked to the Soviet Union as their model as shown by the 1954 state constitution and the First Five-Year Plan (1953-57) announced in 1955. After the Party established the State Planning Commission in 1952, it drafted the state constitution, which was ratified by the National People's Congress (NPC) in September 1954. The central government then abolished the existing six large military-administrative regions, where the old field armies functioned as the major loci of authority, and assumed tight control over both the economy and the military. As Tung Pi-wu, then chairman of the government's Political and Legal Committee, remarked, the Chinese Communists had in the past lived by movements, but from this time on they were supposed to live by the law.[25]

In March 1955 the Party formally adopted China's First Five-Year Plan, even though the plan was to have actually started in 1953. This plan gave priority to development over revolution, institutional processes over mass movement, and consolidation over transformation. First, the plan presented a sequential development very similar to Stalin's industrialization be placing emphasis in sequence on heavy industry, light industry, and agriculture, thereby striving to maximize efficiency even at the expense of equality. Second, the plan provided for a highly centralized and bureaucratic management. As a result, the Politburo in 1956-57 was always supplied with a fait accompli in a "heavy downpour" of reports by planning agencies instead of a "steady drizzle"; according to Mao, it therefore became a "voting machine" without a thorough discussion that would make it similar to the United Nations.[26] Yet the state constitution justified these policies in the name of New Democracy: "The system of people's democracy— New Democracy—of the People's Republic of China guarantees that China can, in a peaceful way, eliminate exploitation and poverty, and build a prosperous happy country."[27]

The performance of the First Five-Year Plan was quite impressive, with an average economic growth rate of 7 percent per year, but its consequences created a series of new problems. The emphasis on industrial production resulted in a remarkable record in industries, but its sequential approach gave rise to a host of perplexing inequalities between industry and agriculture, and the cities and the countryside. The centralized bureaucracy facilitated an orderly management but it also undercut Mao's power and his doctrine of mass line. The doctrine of New Democracy justified the gradual approach to transformation but it was tantamount to postponing the socialist transformation in favor of industrialization.

CHINA'S INDUSTRIALIZATION DEBATE
AND THE ROAD TO THE GLF, 1955-58

Beginning in 1955, Mao began to address himself to these dilemmas by proposing an accelerated pace of agricultural cooperativization and development. This caused intra-Party debates as to whether the Party should continue or change its current policies. The Party consensus that had derived from the pre-1949 struggle began to erode as these debates raged on in 1955-56. They were largely between the majority of the Party leaders who still adhered to an urban model of socialism and who stressed the consolidation of an industrial base before agricultural cooperativization and Mao, who again advocated a rural model of socialism that stressed the transformation of productive relations through agricultural cooperativization before industrialization. By treating these debates as part of class struggle Mao somehow made the Party accept his views. The impact of the Twentieth Congress of the Communist Party of the Soviet Union (CPSU) had the effect of temporarily moderating Mao's efforts. After the Hundred Flowers Campaign aborted in 1957, however, Mao refined his ideas as the GLF in 1958.

China's Industrialization Debate and Mao's Agricultural Cooperativization and Development Plans

A great debate occurred in 1955-56 within the CCP that was reminiscent of the Soviet debate following the New Economic Policy.[28] It revolved around the Party's general line during its transition to socialism, and more specifically, the question of whether the Party should carry out agricultural cooperativization *before* or *after* mechanization. The official Party line up to 1955 was stated in the Land Reform Law: only when the conditions are mature for mechanized farming will the rich peasant cease.[29] In 1951 Liu stated that since transformation could not be accomplished overnight, the Party should continue New Democracy as a transitional formula.[30] But Mao sought to end New Democracy when he proposed a new General Line in October 1953, stating that the period of socialist transformation had already started in 1949. Despite this new interpretation, the majority of the Party leaders still adhered to New Democracy as restated in the 1954 Constitution.

This difference was centered on the policy toward agricultural cooperativization. As Mao called for the transformation of lower APC s to higher APC s, advocating the thesis of cooperativization before mechanization, such Party leaders as Liu Shao-ch'i, Teng Hsiao-p'ing, Teng Tzu-hui, Ch'en Yün, Li Fu-ch'un, and Li Hsien-nien refuted Mao's view with the thesis of industrialization before cooperativization, citing the Soviet experiences. In 1955 Teng Tzu-hui actually dismantled two hundred thousand APC s to prevent unwarranted rashness.[31] These two views had to be defended by their proponents in Marxist terms. Mao contended that during the transitional period the Party should transform "productive relations" through cooperativization so as to release "productive forces" hitherto hampered by old social relations. His opponents maintained that the Party should develop the productive forces first through industrialization. In fact, Mao's supporters later accused Liu of having taken this line from Bernstein, Kautsky, and Bukharin.[32]

Mao's ideas were revealed in a series of policy documents he drafted

in 1955-56. The first of these was his speech "On Agricultural Cooperation," which he delivered at a meeting of provincial and district Party
secretaries, seeking their support. Accusing those who defended incremental cooperativization of "tottering along like a woman with bound
feet," he issued a stern warning: "On no account should these comrades
use the Soviet experiences as a cover for their idea of moving at a snail's
pace."[33] Characterizing the debate between himself and his opponents
as "a struggle between the two roads," he proposed that the higher
APCs be completed by 1960.

This proposal was met with strong opposition from central planners.
To overcome this Mao went directly to the leaders of cooperatives, who
produced a faster pace of cooperativization and production. He then
convened the Sixth Plenum in October 1955, which provincial and district leaders again attended, where he accused the planners of committing Right empiricism.   Instead of Teng Tzu-hui, Ch'en Po-ta made the
report on agricultural cooperatives and Mao eventually succeeded in
having the plenum decide to complete higher APCs by the spring of
1958. (After this plenum Li Hsien-nien and Ch'en Yün wrote their open
self-criticisms.)[34] To the participants of this plenum Mao distributed
120 model reports that he had collected from the rising cooperatives. In
December he edited these, and, together with a preface and notes,
compiled a book entitled *Socialist Upsurge in the Countryside*. With its
dissemination, Mao launched a mass campaign to "achieve greater,
faster, and better results."[35]

Mao then contended that the question of a speedy socialist transformation was already solved and that only the scale of construction
remained undetermined. The major stumbling block for this new task
was "rightist conservatism," a tendency among cadres to fall behind the
masses' enthusiasm.[36] To counter this trend he drafted a document in
January 1956 entitled Draft National Program for Agricultural Development, commonly known as the Forty Articles, and presented it to
a Supreme State Conference of which he was chairman. The Forty
Articles envisioned the completion of higher APCs by 1957 and the
basic industrialization of the Chinese countryside by 1967, to be
achieved mainly through self-reliance and mass mobilization.[37]

One of the themes Mao had pursued thus far was that problems
should be tackled with a comprehensive perspective. In April 1956,
after the CPSU concluded its Twentieth Congress, he drew up another
document, Ten Major Relationships, to "bring all positive factors
into play and mobilize all forces that can be utilized."[38] By positing ten
relationships in dialectical terms, he elaborated his views on cooperativization and industrialization. He also called upon the Party to fight

bureaucratization through decentralization of authority and mass criticisms. Addressing himself to the questions Khrushchev had raised at the Soviet congress in February, he suggested a new policy toward the intellectual community: Let a Hundred Flowers Bloom, Let a Hundred Schools of Thought Contend.[39] Finally, he renewed the Party's commitment to revolutionary change by declaring (and repeating in 1958): "We are poor and blank. . . . Because we are poor, we yearn for change, want to make revolution and rise in greater vigor. A piece of white paper is good for writing on."[40] It should be clear by now that Mao had already set forth the basic assumptions underlying the GLF that was yet to come.

When Mao was busy promoting these policies, the majority of the Party leadership were still wavering. In Mao's own estimate, those expressing the middle reaction were in the majority while those approving and opposing them were in the minority.[41] Among the opponents Teng Tzu-hui was most outspoken, calling Mao's programs a "reckless advance."[42] The editorial of the *People's Daily* on June 20, 1956, entitled "Oppose Both Conservatism and Rashness," which Teng T'o, then editor, drafted with the approval of Liu, stated that "reckless advance" was more harmful than conservatism.

The Impact of the Twentieth Congress of the CPSU on the Eighth Congress of the CCP, 1956

While these debates were raging on in China, there occurred an external event that greatly influenced its direction: Khrushchev's secret report to the Twentieth Congress of the CPSU. The impact of this report was revealed in the resolution of the Eighth Congress of the CCP in September 1956. Specifically, Mao was opposed to Khrushchev's description of Stalin's rule as "an attempt at the theoretical justification of mass terror policy"[43] even after class enemies have been liquidated. He also could not accept the enunciation of peaceful transition to socialism and of peaceful coexistence as the general line of Soviet foreign policy. The CCP Politburo discussed these points in March 1956, and presented its views in an April *People's Daily* editorial that claimed for the first time that the People's Democratic Dictatorship in China was identical to the dictatorship of the proletariat.[44] Asserting that even in a socialist society contradictions exist between the individual and the state, the editorial suggested the way to avoid falling into the Stalinist quagmire should be self-criticism and criticism. Based on a secret speech Mao made to a supreme state conference in May, Lu Ting-yi, director of the Propaganda Department, later explained Mao's thinking in this way: in correcting mistakes a clear line should be drawn between the people and the enemy; criticism of the former can be comradely and only for the latter should the method of "killing at a blow" be applied.[45]

Because de-Stalinization posed the danger of a Party split, its impact upon China was a moderation of Mao's domestic policies. First, the Second Five-Year Plan adopted by the CCP's Eighth Congress was to continue the same policy of the First Five-Year Plan, giving industrialization the highest priority. Liu's political report specifically reaffirmed the thesis of mechanization before cooperativization. Second, although the Congress adopted a program of drastic decentralization of economic management in the state bureaucracy, the new Party Constitution explicitly provided for Party discipline, centralization, and collective leadership. Unlike the 1945 constitution, which allowed the Party chairman to hold concurrently the chairmanship of the Secretariat, the new constitution created a separate Secretariat with its own general secretary, which Teng Hsiao-p'ing assumed, and deleted the "Thought of Mao Tse-Tung" from its preamble. Teng's report on the new constitution pointed out in clear terms that one lesson of the Twentieth Congress of the CPSU was to guard against the deification of the individual.[46] Except for the Kao Kang incident of 1954-55, which did not involve policy issues, Mao did not purge the challengers to his policies. As a result, the old Mao-Liu coalition still remained intact.

Liu was able to state in his political report and the Party resolution that the contradiction between the working class and the bourgeiosie in China had basically been resolved and that therefore the major remaining contradiction was between "the advanced socialist system and the backward productive forces of society," reiterating his early view that the Party's task was economic development.[47] Mao himself praised the Soviet congress by saying: "At its Twentieth Congress not long ago, the CPSU formulated many correct policies and criticized shortcomings which were found in the Party."[48]

The Hundred Flowers Campaign and Its Aftermath, 1957

Mao confessed in 1958 that two unanticipated events had occurred in 1956: the "antirecklessness" reaction and the Hungarian revolt. The circumstances were stronger than men, compelling him to face new problems.[49] The revolts in Hungary and Poland in October 1956 shattered the semblance of Party unity, for they were the type of turmoil Mao had feared would result from de-Stalinization. To cope with this situation Mao proposed the Hundred Flowers Campaign. Once again, the majority of the Party leadership balked, for the issue at stake concerned the Party's authority and the extent to which it could allow criticism by non-Party people, thus raising a central issue that was to re-emerge in the Cultural Revolution in the 1960s. But Mao manipulated support once again by going outside the Party's regular channels. When the campaign exceeded his original expectation, he skillfully maneuvered it into another antirightist movement, directed towards those who had challenged Party rule, and revived his agricultural policy.

The CCP's Central Committee discussed Hungary at its Second Plenum in November 1956, at which Mao stated that Khrushchev had thrown out two swords of communism: Lenin and Stalin.[50] To overcome the subjectivism, sectarianism, and bureaucratism that he believed were sources of trouble in Hungary, he called for the Hundred Flowers Campaign. The official response of the CCP to Hungary was published in a December *People's Daily* editorial. Seeking a theoretical compromise between Stalin's policy of terror (under the pretext that class struggle becomes acute as socialism nears) and Khrushchev's revision of it (that class struggle no longer exists after the means of production have been socialized), the editorial distinguished two kinds of contradictions: the antagonistic ones that arise only if any particular sector of the people challenges the fundamentals of Soviet experiences, and the nonantagonistic ones that arise among the people.[51] To apply this reasoning to China in a substantive manner Mao presented his thinking at a meeting of provincial secretaries called in January 1957. He said that Stalin's mistake derived from metaphysics and that, therefore, contradictions in China should be settled through dialectical struggle. Many of his associates did not share this view, believing that such a method would cause nothing but trouble. Mao urged them not to fear trouble, saying: "Remember we were trouble-makers before."[52]

By January 1957 two policy trends emerged between Mao, who wanted the blooming, and such associates as Liu Shao-ch'i and P'eng Chen, who tried to limit it. To rally support from non-Party leaders, Mao made his speech "On Correctly Handling Contradictions among the People" at the supreme state conference in February.[53] According to the original version, Mao went so far as to say that the Communist party could be strengthened by criticism from non-Party people.[54] Since he was opposed to "finishing people off with a single blow" he believed that the juxtaposition of two opposites could settle contradictions. He also repudiated the line of the Eighth Party Congress, saying that class struggle would continue even after the socialization of the means of production had been completed, for such struggle in the ideological field would be a protracted process.

Despite this speech, little had been done by March. Mao then held several discussions with provincial leaders and non-Party people in

April, but the press did not report them. At a Hangchow conference in April he reiterated the themes he had sounded all along: because one school of thought had dominated for so long, a deep ditch stood between the Party and non-Party people; therefore, to cleanse the minds of five million intellectuals the Party had to allow the airing of their grievances. His associates did not openly oppose this view but simply did not implement it.[55] In April Mao and his associates reached a compromise so that the campaign could proceed "as gently as a breeze or mild rain."[56] Nevertheless, some top leaders still entertained differing views on the cause of subjectivism and bureaucratism. Liu, for example, persisted in his stand that with the completion of socialist transformation the primary contradiction in China was one among the people, to be resolved by *compromise*.[57]

When the Hundred Flowers finally bloomed in May, it confirmed Liu's fears. The intellectuals first complained about their powerlessness, and then gradually shifted their attack directly to one-Party dictatorship. Chang Po-chün and Lo Lung-chi, both non-Communist ministers—of communication and the timber industry—pointed out that the State Council was always supplied with finished products. Chang went so far as to say that Mao's terms of office should be restricted. Chang Hsi-jo, minister of education, and Chu An-p'ing, editor of the *Kuangming Daily*, attacked the Communist rule as "Party kingdom." Sporadic industrial strikes and parades broke out in the streets. At Peking University, students raised big-character posters attacking the Party. A student named Lin Hsi-ling said that the very cause of bureaucratism was none other than communism itself and a lecturer named Ko Pei-chi said that the downfall of the Communist Party would not mean the downfall of China.[58] Alarmed by these developments, Mao made a speech entitled "Things Are Changing," condemning a large number of intellectuals who confused "journalism for reflecting the collective economy of socialist countries with journalism for reflecting the anarchic state of the economy in capitalist countries."[59] In June the Party signaled an abrupt shift from liberalism to an antirightist campaign. Chou En-lai warned non-Communist leaders they would be labeled as class enemies if they continued their attacks. Mao himself wrote an editorial saying: "Only when ghosts and monsters are allowed to come out into the open can they be wiped out."[60] Finally, when the revised version of Mao's February speech was published, he laid down six criteria for open criticism, banning any debate that was harmful to socialist transformation and the Party.[61]

In a way, the outcome of the Hundred Flowers Campaign also confirmed Mao's belief in social transformation. Hence, he used the antirightist campaign to revive the Forty Articles on Agriculture. In July 1957 he convened a meeting of provincial secretaries at Tsingtao to resurrect this document. In September he summoned the enlarged Third Plenum again attended by provincial secretaries, which approved the Forty Articles. Mao then accused the proponents of the antireck-lessness argument of seeing only one finger out of ten, calling for an ideological rectification among the intellectuals. The plenum also decided to implement a drastic decentralization of the economic admin-istration.[62] In November Mao went to Moscow to attend the Commu-nist parties conference, where he made the celebrated statement: "The east wind prevails over the west wind." During this trip he tried to per-suade Khrushchev to abandon the doctrine of peaceful transition and to secure more economic aid for China's Second Five-Year Plan. But he failed to alter Khrushchev's views. Recalling this trip in 1964, he said: "I haven't been there since 1957. They made fun of me then. I'll never set foot there again."[63] This trip further reinforced his quest for an independent Chinese way to communism.

The Hundred Flowers Campaign shared a characteristic with the Cultural Revolution in the 1960s in its invitation to non-Party elements to criticize the Party's errors. It also displayed once again the differ-ences between Mao and Liu when Mao cherished an extended campaign whereas Liu resisted this with organizational discipline. In this sense, as MacFarquhar points out, the aftermath of this campaign in the long run became one of the causes of the Cultural Revolution.[64] In the short run, however, it led to another grand endeavor to remake China: the GLF.

The Great Leap Forward, 1958-59:
Mao's Quest for Transformation

The policy debate over cooperativization, the Hungarian revolt, and the intellectuals' attack on the Party deepened Mao's concern about the possibility of a regression in China's revolution and development. The GLF was his attempt to prevent this possibility and to put China on an irreversible course toward a Communist society. The term Great Leap Forward actually consisted of three separate but closely interrelated movements encapsulated in the slogan Three Red Banners: the GLF, the General Line, and the people's commune. The GLF was a mass movement that resulted from a series of decisions Mao initiated after the Third Plenum in September 1957. These decisions, in turn, were incorporated into the General Line adopted at the second session of the Eighth Party Congress in May 1958. The aftermath of this session generated the people's commune movement.

As in previous cases, Mao launched the GLF by seeking support from provincial leaders against the wavering attitudes of central leaders. Soon after returning from Moscow in December 1957 Mao embarked upon a nationwide trip until May 1958, participating in over ten provincial Party meetings. About thirty provincial leaders were purged in this period for opposing Mao's agricultural policy. But K'o Ch'ing-shih, first secretary of the East China Bureau, who accompanied Mao, began the counterattack on the antirecklessness argument.[65] And then such leaders as Li Ch'ing-ch'üan of the Northwest, and T'ao Chu and Wu Chih-pu of the Central South joined K'o in promoting Mao's policy.

The first major meeting in 1958 was held in joint discussions of central and local leaders at Hangchow and Nanning in January. There Mao attacked those heading the finance and economic departments, specifically Ch'en Yün and Li Hsien-nien, for failing to inform the Politburo of their work. He proposed a faster rate of economic development so that China could overtake Britain in fifteen years, saying that it was better to "strike the iron when it is hot."[66] At Nanning he drafted a document called Sixty Work Methods, setting forth the policy of simultaneously developing both industry and agriculture. He argued that this could be accomplished by accelerating the rate of production and by aiming at higher targets per unit. Once again applying dialectical reasoning to problem-solving, he espoused the doctrine of "uninterrupted revolution," a wavelike process in which one battle follows another.[67] While expressing his wish to relinquish the chairmanship of the republic at this time, Mao firmly committed the Party to "basically transforming the entire country after three years of hard struggle."[68]

In March Mao called another conference of central and provincial leaders at Ch'engtu to refute the "superstition and inferiority complex" of high officials.[69] "It is strange for a person to fear the professors," he said, "while he does not fear imperialism."[70] To smash this fear and thereby make people dare to think and act, he directed Ch'en Po-ta to start a new theoretical journal, *Hung-ch'i* (Red Flag), and asked each province to have its own journal. With these exhortations he put forth several important decisions: (1) a proposal to amalgamate the existing APCs into even larger organizations, (2) Views on the Questions of Agricultural Mechanization, calling for a semimechanization of traditional tools on the basis of self-reliance, (3) a major decentralization of industrial management, and (4) an educational reform encouraging the combination of study and labor. By so doing, he urged "tide-watching" colleagues to support a "great industrial leap forward."[71]

These decisions were incorporated into the resolution of the second session of the Eighth Party Congress in May that year, which reversed the resolution of the first session in 1956. Mao explained at this session that the GLF meant a sudden change from past and by implication from the Soviet model of socialism. He stated that Stalin's two slogans—Technology Decides Everything and Cadres Decide Everything—were incorrect, for politics actually takes command and the masses really decided everything.[72] He personally guided the drafting of the new General Line, advocating a simultaneous development of all sectors. He stressed the importance of the peasants in this strategy, claiming that without the peasant there was no politics.[73] Reversing his report to the 1956 session, Liu's political report to this session spelled out the General Line as: "To build socialism by exerting our utmost efforts, and pressing ahead consistently to achieve greater, faster, better, and more economical results."[74]

This policy shift was also reflected by a change in the Party's leadership composition. This session added twenty-five alternate members to the Central Committee, most of whom were the provincial leaders who had actively responded to Mao's agricultural policy. Subsequently, the Fifth Plenum added Mao's other supporters to the Politburo: Lin Piao as its new vice-chairman and member of its Standing Committee, and K'o Ch'ing-shih, Li Ch'ing-ch'üan, and T'an Chen-lin as new members. Finally, Liu's report clearly stated that the doctrine of uninterrupted revolution was the Party's guiding principle, claiming that Mao had actually stated it in March 1949.[75]

After this session was over, many localities swiftly responded to the Party's calls for amalgamating APCs, close planting, building large irrigation systems, and eliminating four pests (flies, sparrows, mosquitoes, and rats).[76] Of these the most important was the emergence of the people's commune from the amalgamating cooperatives. By June 1958 about 789,000 APCs had merged into about 741,000 larger APCs. These enlarged co-ops performed multifaceted functions with different names. The Red Flag Co-op in Chekiang, for example, called itself "commune" (kung-she). In June-July Mao drew a conclusion from these co-ops in Honan and Shantung.[77] Having appraised the experiences in Hopei and Honan, Mao visited Peiyuan hsiang in Shantung on August 9. There he stated: "It is good to set up people's communes. Their advantage is that they combine industry, agriculture, commerce, education and military affairs, thus making the task of leadership easier."[78] The People's Daily reported this remark on August 13 and five days later publicized the Weihsing (Sputnik) commune in Honan, which was said to have been the first commune in China since April 20. In this way, when more than 99 percent of the peasants in Honan and 30 percent of all Chinese peasants had joined the commune, Mao convened the enlarged Politburo meeting at Peitaiho to authorize a foregone fact with a formal resolution published on August 28 stating: "the people's communes are the logical result of the march of events."[79]

The Peitaiho conference made two other important decisions. The first was to bombard Quemoy and Matsu Islands. The second was to produce 10.7 million tons of steel by building the backyard furnaces.[80] In October Mao praised the "tremendous energy of the masses" generated by these decisions when he attacked his critics who had characterized the energy as stemming from "irregular and guerrilla habits."[81]

THE GREAT LEAP FORWARD AS A PROTOTYPE FOR
MAOIST REVOLUTION AND DEVELOPMENT

The GLF, as it emerged in this way, presented a prototype for Maoist revolution and development, for it revealed Mao's innermost thinking on policy issues and processes more clearly than other situations had. In understanding Mao's ideas we now possess two invaluable pieces of his writing: *Critique of Stalin's "Economic Problems of Socialism in the Soviet Union"* (1959) and *Notes on the Soviet Union's "Political Economy"* (1961-62).[82] In both of these works Mao criticized what he considered incorrect in Soviet policy and sought to set forth the "correct" policy for China. In the first book Mao pointed out that Stalin had no single word on the relationship of the superstructure and man, meanwhile reaffirming his own belief in man's malleability, his belief in man's unlimited ability to know and change nature. In the second book he reviewed the experience of Soviet economic development. His argument can be summarized as follows: (1) the Soviet Union made industrialization the prerequisite for collectivization by concentrating on heavy industry at the expense of light industry and agriculture, thus favoring the cities and the workers over the countryside and the peasants, and relying mostly on material incentives and Western technology; (2) in administering these policies the Soviet bureaucracy controlled every aspect of the economy from the top, recruiting a large number of managers and professionals into its hierarchy without implementing a thorough ideological remolding; and (3) theoretically, these policies were based on metaphysics rather than dialectics, for they did not identify contradiction and struggle as the motivating forces of development. He then cited aspects of the GLF as the corrective measures to these negative examples. Three important themes can be discerned in this regard.

The Strategy of Simultaneous Development

This strategy stemmed from the basic premise that tackling both production and distribution simultaneously maximizes not only productivity but equality. This view also derived from Mao's perception of China's backwardness. By setting forth the General Line of *aiming at higher, faster, better, and more economical results*, Mao sought, in effect, a short-cut to communism and industrialism. Realizing that the sequential strategy of the First Five-Year Plan had increased social inequality, the best way to meet China's problems as he perceived them was to "walk on two legs": industry and agriculture, inland industry and coastland industry, modern technology and traditional technology, and so on.[83]

The slogan Great Leap Forward prescribed the method of implementing this policy. In many aspects, this endeavor presented Mao's deliberate efforts to apply his revolutionary experience to economic development. Time and again, Mao reminded his associates that the weak CCP had fought the strong enemy and won; so, he argued, can they in economic development despite China's inferior technology. This being the case, the more backward the economy, the easier the transition from capitalism to socialism, for the political consciousness and collective efforts of the masses could compensate for the lack of technology.[84] The attempt to mobilize potentially untapped resources and talents was thoroughly manifested in the idea of semimechanization based on traditional tools and of labor-intensive backyard furnaces. Theoretically, this approach approximates comprehensive rationality, the idea that it is possible to choose all desired goals first and then the appropriate means. The antithesis to this is incrementalism, that it is only possible to adjust the goals to the available means. In fact, there were some debates in China along these two views. Liu, for example, defended the policy of achieving goals in a comprehensive way when he refuted Chang Hsi-jo's advice to take incremental steps rather than to strive forward.[85]

The Process of the Mass Line

In formulating and implementing the GLF, Mao applied the mass line by encouraging mass mobilization and participation. He personally tried to reach out to the masses, and the masses were called upon to respond directly to him. The resulting political order was a highly decentralized one through which the Supreme Leader attempted to maintain constant contact with the masses. The ideal of this practice comes closer to that of mass polity.[86]

The policy process was highly erratic and irregular. Mao was in full charge in 1958, as he would confess at the Lushan conference the following year. He was the locus of power because he made all crucial decisions. He identified the pressing problems and articulated their solutions into correct policies. When he encountered opposition, he side-stepped the Party's regular policy-making bodies and went directly to local leaders for support. He relied upon informal ad hoc conferences, such as the Party's work conferences attended by provincial leaders, the supreme state conference, and the enlarged Politburo meetings. After he had manipulated these meetings to endorse his policies he usually had the Party's regular plenums ratify them. As a result, the regular bureaucracy and its professionals were put aside; in fact, he said in May 1958 that as a general rule nonprofessionals would lead professionals. He was particularly contemptuous of the intellectuals, saying that people with culture and knowledge were more stupid than the general populace, for in history people with a lower level of culture always triumphed.[87]

Policy making and impementation were inseparable processes in these mass movements. The Supreme Leader selected the cases that closely approximated his correct policies. Once he had legitimized these cases, the press popularized them and the masses immediatly responded. Ideology became a basis for consensus as Mao collected only the information he needed to confirm his policy; the decline of accurate information resulting from this practice led him to resort more and more to mobilization for implementing policy.[88] Organizationally, the people's commune encompassed all of these aspects.

The Ideology of Uninterrupted Revolution

This ideology sanctioned the contents and the process of Mao's policies. However strange it may sound to Western observers, Mao genuinely attempted to apply what can only be described as existential dialectics to problem solving. The central idea of uninterrupted revolution was the wavelike development of things: if all things are governed by the unity of opposites, the succession of unity and opposites becomes wavelike; hence one should seek to solve contradictions through uninterrupted struggle.[89]

Mao stressed the role of the superstructure in these struggles in a manner very similar to Weber's thinking: "Only a life guided by constant thought would achieve conquest over the state of affairs."[90] But the proletarian values in Mao's thought were not necessarily imbued in class or organization, but regarded as ill-defined transcendental forces to be held by anyone who practiced Mao's thought.[91] Mao also championed the role of the common man, egalitarianism, and self-reliance. In the Three Red Banners, for example, there was little differentiation of policy, power, and ideology. According to Mao, "a plan is an ideology, while consciousness is a reflection of actuality."[92]

What was lacking in the slogan was an operational code based on a compromise between the ends and the means. This ideological stand assumes in general that if any practice goes wrong, there must be something wrong with the practice, not with the ideology.

In short, the Three Red Banners became Mao's self-fulfilling prophecy, which was to undergo a process of reality-testing in the years to come. When Mao imposed such an ideological consensus on the Party, other leaders went along with him by taking a wait-and-see posture. Thus, Party unity at this time depended to a large degree on the actual outcome of the GLF. It is in this sense that the Leap itself contained the potential of an irreparable intra-Party dissension, for were it to fail, that would further undermine the post-1949 policy consensus and leadership coalition.

PART II
The Policy Process in Consolidation
1959-1962

Like a child playing with fire, without experience and knowing pain only after getting burned, we declared war on the earth, unfamiliar with the strategy or tactics. We must frankly admit such defects and errors.

Mao Tse-tung, 1959

Being basically unversed in construction, I knew nothing about industrial planning.

Mao Tse-tung, 1959

So long as it raises output, "going alone" is permissible. Whether cats are white or black, so long as they can catch mice, they are all good cats.

Teng Hsiao-p'ing, 1962

3
The Retreat
from the Great Leap Forward

The synchronized meshing of policy, power, and ideology so obvious during the GLF gradually went askew as the ideas of the Leap were confronted by a harsh reality. The transformation of 1958-59 had to be followed by the consolidation of 1959-66. The post-Leap consolidation policy process, however, produced a pronounced tendency toward sequential development, institutionalization, and practical compromise. The period of 1959-62 in particular was one of the most critical years for the CCP since its rise to power, for it was in these years that the Party weathered a severe economic crisis by retreating from and making adjustments in the GLF. But the consequences of these endeavors compelled the Party to confront another major political crisis in the subsequent years, which led to the Cultural Revolution. The aggregate outcome of the retreat and the adjustments in 1959-62 turned out to challenge the very assumptions of the GLF, resulting in an apparent divergence between the Party's official ideology and its actual practices. The inevitable conflicts between Mao's efforts to narrow this divergence and the Party leaders' resistance in 1962-66 culminated in the Cultural Revolution.

This theme can be ascertained by analyzing the consolidation measures of 1959-62 first. This will enable us to understand how the Party was involved in policy adjustments on the one hand while the Army was still encouraging mass campaigns. In this chapter we explore the process of retreat in 1959-60 to see how the CCP tested its self-fulfilling prophecy toward the GLF in the light of its changing reality. This will be followed in chapter 4 by an exposition of the two broad trends appearing between the Party and the army in carrying out policy adjustments in 1960-62.[1] The purpose is to explain the contents of policy reviews and debates, and to assess their legacies in the policy process leading to the Cultural Revolution.

We start with the process of retreat from the GLF. The Party steadily withdrew from the Leap programs in the two years between the Peitaiho conference of August 1958 and the Peitaiho conference of August 1960; during this period, the GLF underwent a process of change through the interaction between Mao's ideological and policy demands and the shifting environmental conditions of localities. Since the GLF programs were concentrated in the commune, the changes that took place in the commune provide the best illustration of the retreat process.

TRIALS AND ERRORS IN THE COMMUNE, 1958-59

During the four months of 1958 between the August Peitaiho Resolution and the December Wuhan Resolution (by which time virtually all Chinese peasants had joined the communes), the commune movement became a self-fulfilling prophecy. At this stage, ideology and practice were merged. A euphoric atmosphere followed the Peitaiho conference, exemplified by such conference statements as: uninterrupted revolution leads to a new society; people do not need money for food; communism is heaven and the commune the road to it; in the commune people become omnipotent, and so forth. It was this momentum that rushed the peasants into the practice of the commune. There were various reports about the commune in progress but the only comprehensive model was the twenty-six-article draft concerning the Weihsing commune publicized in September, which was too limited for application under different conditions.[2] Under intense pressure, the local cadres to whom communization was entrusted naturally showed excessive zeal even if this resulted in a "Communist style," because to do otherwise would have made them vulnerable to the charge of lagging behind the masses.

Soon after the commune program was launched, however, criticisms were voiced that the commune was established "too early, too quickly, and too crudely."[3] Writing in the first issue of *Ch'ien-hsien* (Frontline), Liu Jen, second secretary of the Peking municipal committee, characterized the efforts to include as many functions as possible in the commune as petty bourgeois thinking.[4] In November 1958 Chang Ch'un-ch'iao wrote an article advocating abolition of wages in the *People's*

Daily. Soon after this, Teng Hsiao-p'ing called a meeting at which he maintained that the right to wages could not be eliminated, for the wage system was actually less costly than the supply system. At the meeting, Hu Ch'iao-mu, director of *New China News Agency* (NCNA), defended Teng's view, quoting from Lenin's *State and Revolution* that such a bourgeois right was kept even in a socialist society. When Wu Leng-hsi, then editor of the *People's Daily*, entrusted the summing up to Chang Ch'un-ch'iao, Chang refused because Mao did not agree with the tenor of the discussion.[5] As for the slogan All People Smelt Steel, some people called it a "great mess in the world." Many intellectuals derided these slogans as blowing trumpets and indulging in empty talk.[6]

To investigate the progress and criticisms of the communes, the central leaders set out on another nationwide tour soon after the Peitaiho conference. During these trips, they began to confront some results of the commune movement. Subsequently, consecutive meetings were held to cope with the rising problems. In November, Mao convened a conference of central and provincial secretaries at Chengchow (that is, the "first Chengchow conference"), where the decision was made to rectify Communist style and slow down the pace of communization.[7]

Soon after the first Chengchow conference, Mao summoned another conference of provincial secretaries in Wuhan, and in December called the Sixth Plenum in Wuhan, which churned out the Wuhan Resolution, officially signaling that the commune was in trouble.[8] Talking to various local leaders before the full session of the Sixth Plenum, Mao pointed out that the main problems confronting the commune were coercion and false reporting. Despite these errors, he still anticipated that communes would be established in the cities as well.[9]

The Wuhan Resolution, notable for its ideological retreat from the doctrine of uninterrupted revolution, warned against the utopian dream of skipping the socialist stage and instead called for revolution by stages. Denying that the commune was already ownership by the whole people, the resolution stated that the transition from the collective ownership to that by the whole people was to be determined *not* by a mere wishful thinking but by the objective factors:

We should not groundlessly make declarations that the people's communes in the countryside will "realize ownership by the whole people immediately" or even "enter communism immediately," and so on. To do such things is not only an expression of rashness, it will greatly lower the standards of communism in the minds of the people, distort the great ideal of communism and vulgarize it, strengthen the petty-bourgeois trend towards equalitarianism and adversely affect the development of socialist construction.[10]

Unlike the Peitaiho Resolution, which envisioned three or four years for the transition, this resolution anticipated from fifteen to twenty years for such a change. It discouraged the free supply system because it dampened the working enthusiasm of the people, called for improved mess halls, banned overworking by guaranteeing at least eight hours of sleep and four hours of rest, and allowed certain small freedoms such as retaining personal belongings, pursuing side-line occupations, and establishing bank deposits. Specifically, it made allowances for exchange of commodities and warned against the slogan Getting Organized Along Military Lines. It also called upon leading cadres to "differentiate between the reality and false appearance of things and between demands that are justified and those that are not," and to be alert against being dizzy with success. Finally, the resolution designated a five-month period from December 1958, to April 1959, for *adjusting and consolidating* the commune.

The Wuhan Resolution, which clearly called for moderation, was a document designed chiefly to curb such excesses as disruption of family life, confiscation of private belongings, and unrestricted eating.

Still without precise guidelines, hsien and commune level cadres had to adjust the commune administrative machinery to the new directive. Actually, the adjustment began after the first Chengchow conference, and the Wuhan plenum officially sanctioned it. This process of reality-testing led to a compromise between the Center's demands and the localities' responses. Since actual situations varied, the whole country for a time seemed to have degenerated into fragmented units over which the central authorities had little control, as hordes of peasants were drawn to steel smelting and irrigation works.[11] Another problem was the organizational principle of "one, big and two, public."

To cope with these problems, Mao called another conference of central leaders in Peking in January 1959. From February through March, he then convened the second Chengchow conference, an enlarged meeting of the Poliburo, to which provincial secretaries were also invited. Mao contended at this conference that the broad masses of cadres had done useful work in the commune by showing great activism, but due to lack of experience they also had committed certain errors. He asserted nevertheless: "Whoever says that such a broad social movement can be free from any defect must be a wishful thinker, or a tide-wave-watcher or a bookkeeper, or simply an antagonist."[12] For "the relation between our achievements and our defects is, as we have often said," he continued, "that between nine fingers and the remaining one finger of both hands. Some people are skeptical about or negate the superiority of people's communes. This viewpoint is completely erroneous."[13] Labeling these skeptics as Right opportunists, he asked those cadres who had committed errors to undertake self-criticism and rectify "Communist and commandist styles." Under no circumstance, however, was the mass enthusiasm to be dampened on account of these leftist tendencies. The minutes of this conference together with Mao's speech became Party documents for study by the cadres.[14]

On the other hand, it appears that the second Chengchow conference dealt with some imminent problems that had risen in the communes. For the first time since the beginning of the GLF, Mao confessed at this conference that he was not clear about planned economic development. He conceded that tackling one side at the expense of other areas resulted in too many capital projects and in a waste of resources. "Like a child playing with fire," he continued, "we declared war on the earth. . . . We must frankly admit such defects and errors." In another talk made in February, he likened the practice of equalizing rich and poor brigades to piracy; hence he endorsed the principle of exchanging the same value. Already at this time, Mao recommended the brigade (*tui*) comparable to the former higher APC as the basic unit of ownership. To prevent the phenomena of inflated reports and coercion, he called upon all the provincial units to convene the six-level conferences of province, hsien, commune, brigade, and team without reporting them in the press. As a result of these conferences in Hupeh and Honan, Wang Jen-chung of Hupeh came up with the three-level ownership of the commune, the brigade, and the team with the brigade as the basis. Mao endorsed this idea through the Party's internal correspondences issued in March to the provincial secretaries.[15]

Following this policy shift, K'o Ch'ing-shih and T'ao Chu addressed themselves to lack of coordination when they put forth the slogan, The Whole Country as a Chessboard, the Whole Province as a Chessboard. Ch'en Yün went further by calling for a unified control of resource allocation on a national scale. He maintained that only after a national plan was formulated could regional and local projects be effectively carried out.[16]

While these central conferences were being held, the communes experimented at the local level with various methods of work assignments to cope with the unwieldy organizational problems that had resulted from their being too big and too centralized. From these efforts came the system of responsibility for fixed output quotas (*pao-ch'an-chih*) in the production brigade, the beginning of fixing output quota (*pao*). In Kiangsi the communes fixed the output quota, operating costs, and work assignments for the production brigade (*sheng-ch'an tui*); the brigade, in turn, fixed five items—land use, technical measures, production time, man power, and other minor production materials for the production team (called *sheng-ch'an hsiao-tui* or *hsiao-tsu*). In Fukien the communes fixed land use, technical measures, output, and cost for the brigades; alternatively, they fixed land use, man power, use of draft animals and farm implements; if the brigades fulfilled the quota beyond the fixed amount, they were awarded bonuses. Here were the beginnings of the four-fix and-one-reward system that spread throughout the country in the summer of 1959.[17]

A sort of contract (called *pao* or *ting*) concluded between the communes and the brigades characterized this system; with this the brigade became the unit of labor, if not that of accounting. Variants of this program were experimented with in Szechwan and Kwangtung. In Kiangsi a new format called "three guarantees and four fixes" (*san-pao ssu-ting*) was adopted by the Lu Chi commune. Under this format the brigade guaranteed output, work, and costs to the teams on the one hand, and on the other hand, fixed land use, use of draft animals, farm implements, and man power, thus giving rise to the contract between the brigade and the teams.[18]

The Party openly acknowledged that without a system of responsibility everyone managed to work as little as possible.[19] But a system that assigned laborers to the same task could take into account different terrain and skills. Once this system became widespread, three changes occurred: first, the unified leadership of the commune was transformed into a scheme of staggered-level management with the brigade as the base; second, the commune-directed labor troops were disbanded and labor quotas were set by the brigade; and third, labor payment on the basis of work hours gave way to a piece-rate system. With these changes, the production team emerged as the basic work unit even though the brigade made the actual work assignments. Since peasant wages were based on their labor, the brigades had come to regard wages, not free supply, as the main part of distribution. The Party rationalized this as the principle of exchanging equal value.[20] Thus, by legitimizing existing practices the Party accommodated itself to the changed situation.

After the second Chengchow conference, the Party identified the "styles" of exaggeration, commandism, and communism as the most serious problems. Teng Hsiao-p'ing proposed at a Secretariat meeting that the State Planning Commission and the State Economic Commission investigate the cause of these problems and collect materials for central work conferences. Accordingly, the NCNA collected information on them and published it in *Nei-pu ts'an-k'ao* (Internal References) circulated for the central leaders.[21]

The Seventh Plenum held in Shanghai in April 1959 reaffirmed its faith in the commune while making some adjustments.[22] It was at this plenum that P'eng Teh-huai raised opposition to Mao for discarding the Politburo in making decisions. Mao referred to this at a meeting of the Military Affairs Committee (MAC) in 1959:

They kept their silence at the Peitaiho Conference, at the Chengchow Conference, and at the Wuchang Conference. Though they mumbled something at the Shanghai Conference, we failed to hear anything. But when something happened later on (they thought that things had developed) they would again complain about such things as vegetables, pork, grain in some areas, soap, and even umbrellas.[23]

According to P'eng's explanation, however, Mao spent a good deal of time criticizing him at the Shanghai plenum. But Mao hoped that if the leaders could exercise forbearance, the masses would finally rise up to smash those skeptics.

In revising the ideology and practice of the commune, the Shanghai plenum seemed to have given approval to the practice of fixed labor. The plenum apparently produced an eighteen-article directive that promised, among other things, reimbursement to the well-to-do peasants when their properties were confiscated. After this plenum, many more brigades restored the work-point and piece-rate system. These work-point systems gave due consideration to differentials of labor productivity. The Party took cognizance of this by acknowledging that good distribution produced good production.[24] In allocating labor, too, the Party called upon the communes to put at least 85 percent of the labor force into agriculture, thereby modifying the earlier emphasis placed on basic construction and steel smelting. Thus the commune revived many elements of the former APC s; the difference was that the private plots and markets were still suspended. The only private undertakings permitted were small freedoms, such as planting fruit trees, setting up garden plots in homesteads, and pursuing side-line occupations.[25]

The typical Maoist solution to the problems arising in the communes was the method of sending cadres down to the productive units, that is, *hsia-fang*. As early as February 1959 cadres adopted the "three-together system" by which they were to eat, live, and work together with the peasants. Provincial work teams consisting of over ten thousand men also went down to the basic levels to carry out investigation.[26] Since these cadres were not allowed to dampen mass enthusiasm, however, such measures could hardly be effective in curbing excesses.

It should be noted here that Liu Shao-ch'i was elected chairman of the People's Republic of China (PRC) at the first session of the second National People's Congress (NPC) held in April 1959. According to the

explanation he offered in 1966, Mao stepped down from the first line
to allow Liu and others' prestige to be established before his death. He
did so, he further explained, to insure state security so that when "he
went to see God," the state would not be thrown into great convulsions
as was the Soviet Union after Stalin died. (In 1966, he was to regret this
decision.)[27] As far as Mao's role in the GLF was concerned, however, it
was not until after the Lushan conference that he really stepped down
from active leadership. In a speech at the Sixth Plenum in December
1958, which announced Mao's plan to retire, for example, he himself
said: "I am not withdrawing. I want to surpass the U.S. before I go to
see Marx!"[28] This he could not do when, externally, Khrushchev was
calling the commune reactionary and, internally, P'eng Teh-huai was
challenging his leadership.[29]

THE LUSHAN CONFERENCE AND ITS AFTERMATH, 1959-60

In all probability, the Lushan conference in June-August 1959,
marked the beginning of serious intra-Party struggles. Actually, this
conference consisted of two meetings, the Politburo meeting held in
June-July and the Eighth Plenum in August. The Politburo meeting was
originally engaged with the problem of how the Party could rectify the
malady that afflicted the commune. It was a work conference, but,
according to Mao's reminiscence at the Tenth Plenum, P'eng Teh-huai's
challenge jeopardized the proceedings, which turned into a forum for a
big debate.[30]

On the eve of this conference, however, Mao himself initiated drastic policy reversal. In several instructions he issued between June 29 and
July 3, which was the opening date of the Politburo meeting, he attempted to restore balance between agriculture and industry. In so
doing, he praised Ch'en Yün, who once said: "We should arrange the
market before we go into capital construction." Mao also recognized
that the masses had been demanding the fixing of output quota and the
restoration of market. Thus, he was opposed to equalitarian transfer of
goods and service without proper compensation. To prevent such semi-
anarchy in economic affairs, he called for a centralized and unified
Party leadership.[31] But P'eng Teh-huai's attack overshadowed these
proposals.

Although Mao had criticized some military leaders for their super-
stitious respect for the Soviet Union, calling for a critical study of
Soviet experiences instead of "eating ready-made food," and, although
P'eng had wanted to resign as minister of defense, the main issue P'eng
raised at the Lushan conference centered on the GLF.[32] After August
1958, P'eng had inspected the Northwest and other regions. In Hunan,

he had found, for instance, that production actually decreased as a result of the GLF. After traveling through Kiangsi and Anhwei, he made up his mind to speak out. Before the Wuhan plenum, he had composed a poem in Hunan that graphically depicted the situation:

> Grain was scattered on the ground, potato leaves withered;
> Strong young people have left for steel-making, only
> children and old women reaped the crops; how can they pass
> the coming year? Allow me to appeal for the people.[33]

Soon after the Shanghai plenum, from April 24 to June 13, P'eng led a Chinese military mission to the Warsaw Pact Powers. On the same day, Chang Wen-t'ien, vice foreign minister, also left for Warsaw as the Chinese observer to the meeting of the foreign ministers of the Warsaw Powers. During this trip, P'eng allegedly informed Khrushchev of shortcomings of the GLF, and Khrushchev encouraged him to oppose Mao's policies upon his return. At the northwest group meeting of the enlarged Politburo at Lushan held from July 3 through 10, P'eng did indeed speak out. He wrote an open letter of opinion to Mao on July 14 with "good motives." (On July 18, Khrushchev attacked the commune at Poznan, Poland.)[34]

First, alluding to Mao's uninterrupted revolution, P'eng pointed out: "We always wanted to enter into communism at one step" with the illusion that "communism was around the corner."[35] He called this a Left tendency caused by petty-bourgeois fanaticism, saying: "In our Party it has always been difficult to correct 'leftist' ones and comparatively easy to correct rightist mistakes. Whenever something leftist comes up, it always prevails over everything; many people dare not speak out."[36] As to the general line of socialist construction, he pointed out that there were only tasks and targets with neither concrete measures nor specific plans for achieving balances.

Secondly, P'eng questioned the way the GLF and the practice of the commune were being carried out. "Politics and economy have their respective laws," asserted P'eng, "Therefore, ideological education cannot replace economic work."[37] The capital construction in 1958 was too hasty, causing waste in precious resources and man power; a good example was the steel-smelting drive that led to "losses and gains but a relatively big loss." Some targets were raised level by level; the habit of exaggeration spread universally, which confused strategic planning with concrete measures, the long-term policies with immediate measures. "Everybody felt that the problem of food had been solved and that our hands could be freed to engage in industry," P'eng said, and continued: "We considered ourselves rich while we were still poor." Then, he specifically proposed a temporary suspension of the construction program to concentrate on agricultural production. As for the commune, he said it had appeared too early without the benefit of experimentation before the higher APC had been fully developed.[38]

Lastly, P'eng touched upon the mold of Mao's leadership in the GLF. In his view, the Party had suffered "a fever in the brains" [sic] since the anti-rightist campaign in 1957; it practiced bureaucratism after it had enjoyed prestige among the masses; with the GLF, however, the Party actually damaged its own prestige.[39] P'eng went so far as to say: "if the Chinese workers and peasants were not as good as they are, a Hungarian incident would have occurred in China and it would have been necessary to invite Soviet troops in."[40] He also derided the ad hoc method of implementing policy by pointing out that the collective leadership of the Politburo was ignored; that the State Planning Commission no longer planned; and that some techniques were popularized without evaluation. The most direct challenge to Mao was P'eng's stricture on Mao's leadership style:

At present, decisions of the Party Committee's collective leadership are ignored. Only decisions of individuals are valid. What has been decided by the First Secretary counts, but not that by the Second Secretary. Collective prestige has not been established. What has been established is only individual prestige. It is very abnormal and dangerous.[41]

Chang Wen-t'ien also confirmed in his July 20 speech that one could speak only positively and that the meetings of the Politburo were only large-scale briefings without any collective discussion.[42] Chang delivered his speech separately from P'eng's; only Chou Hsiao-chou and Huang Ko-ch'eng shared P'eng's views; hence this could hardly be the organized rebellion as charged by Mao.

Mao received P'eng's letter on July 18 and replied to it in his speech on July 23. Confronted with these challenges, Mao asked the Party to choose between him or P'eng, ominously threatening the "if the Chinese PLA [People's Liberation Army] should follow P'eng Teh-huai, I will go to fight guerrilla war."[43] He began his counterattack, presenting the image of a tireless worker, by confessing that he had to take sleeping pills to get to sleep. Mao regarded P'eng's challenge as one of class struggle, a product of bourgeois thinking. In the nine months after the first Chengchow conference, the situation as he saw it was one where Left tendencies had been largely rectified and the major danger confronting the Party was Right opportunism. He understood that P'eng was basically opposed to the Three Red Banners, despite his verbal support of them. Mao warned: "Suppose we do ten things, and nine of them are bad and are published in the newspapers. Then we are bound to perish, and should perish. In that event, I would go to the countryside to lead the peasants to overthrow the government."[44]

As for the Communist style, Mao blamed the middle-level cadres for not heeding Party directives. Therefore, he supported the mess halls; he even asked for a restoration of the disbanded ones. He admitted that he was responsible, together with K'o Ch'ing-shih, for the only partly successful steel-smelting drive; as for the commune, he said that he had only suggested it. He also acknowledged that he had shot "three big cannons": the commune, steel smelting, and the General Line; but he also held T'an Chen-lin responsible for "shooting big cannons." On the matter of GLF strategy, he said apologetically: "It seems to be impossible to judge the result if economic accounting is applied."[45]

As for final responsibility, Mao admitted that he should be held responsible for everything since August 1958, although K'o, T'an, and an unnamed person of the Ministry of Agriculture had to share some. Confirming that planning had ceased to function since the 1958 Peitaiho Resolution, he confessed: "Being basically unversed in construction, I knew nothing about industrial planning." He rejected, though, the argument that the Party's prestige was damaged: "You say that we have deviated from the masses but they still support us. I envision this as only temporary, maybe two or three months, about the time of the spring festival."[46]

He lumped together those who shared P'eng's views in what he called the "Military Club," or "Right opportunists." He was aware that the majority of the Party leadership opposed his policies when he lamented: "The fact is that you have all refuted me, though not by name perhaps."[47] By invoking the unity of the Party, he severely criticized those who were wavering as fellow travelers, charging that such an attitude was detrimental to unity. To convince further these skeptics he promised to convene a Party congress in the spring of 1960 or earlier (but this congress was delayed until 1969).[48]

Despite some Red Guard allegations to the contrary, Liu Shao-ch'i appeared to have kept silent and Teng Hsiao-p'ing shied away from the conference "on the pretense of ailing legs"; Ch'en Yün was not present; Li Hsien-nian agreed with P'eng in the beginning but disagreed later. Chou En-lai, Lin Piao, Ch'en Po-ta, and K'ang Sheng appeared to have defended Mao.[49] The fear of a Party split enabled Mao to dispose of P'eng Teh-huai with a test of strength. Under the facade of superficial unity, however, the Lushan plenum actually left the Party leadership badly torn apart.

There was evidence that Mao himself apparently agreed with some of P'eng's criticisms. In a letter sent to production teams soon after the

Lushan conference, he endorsed the system of fixing output quotas for the teams. He suggested that the teams should pay attention not to the instructions from a higher level but to the realistic possibilities, for "it is no more than trumpetblowing to say that the yield will amount to 800 catties, 1,000 catties, 1,200 catties and even more." He continued: "Many lies are told due to the pressure of a higher level. When the higher level resorts to trumpetblowing, applying pressure and making promises, it makes things difficult for the lower level." He ended the letter on a note of realism: "Compared with the high-flown talk that is in vogue at present, what I have said here is low-keyed. My purpose is to arouse enthusiasm in the true sense and to attain the end of increasing production."[50]

The Party also scaled down the target for production. The original goal for grain in 1959 was revised from 375 million to 250 million tons. The Lushan Resolution on the commune made the production brigade, consisting of some one hundred households, the basic unit of ownership under the name of "three-level ownership." This put an end to the "one, big, and two, public" principle, and the peasants were allowed to join the public mess halls "voluntarily."[51]

It is worth noting that at the Lushan conference Liu Shao-ch'i strongly criticized the exaggerated reporting of NCNA and *People's Daily*, which, he pointed out, helped create Communist and commandist styles. He said the NCNA reported his talk in Honan without requesting his approval and that it was inaccurate. The interesting development here was that although Wu Leng-hsi had made a self-criticism at that time, when he revealed this fact in 1967, he implied that Liu's attack on him was actually directed at Mao. Wu also confessed that he had immediately asked the head offices in Peking to locate those inflated reports and send them down to him; but after P'eng Teh-huai's case he asked Peking not to do so lest they be used by others against Mao.[52] This episode suggests that the Central Secretariat began to tighten its control over the flow of information from this time on. As Mao himself claimed in 1966, Teng Hsiao-p'ing thereafter sat far away from him at meetings and ceased to report to him about the Secretariat's work, while relying on P'eng Chen for his work.[53]

On the other hand, the communique of the Lushan Plenum emphatically stated that the General Line, the GLF, and the people's commune had been successful and that the principal danger was the emergence of Right opportunism. The Party resolution on P'eng Teh-huai, which was made public in August 1967, stated that P'eng's attack actually contributed to Party unity because it enabled the Party to hurl back in time the fierce onslaught on the Party line.[54] In September 1959, then,

Lin Piao replaced P'eng as minister of defense; later on, Chang P'ing-hua replaced Chou Hsaio-chou as first secretary of Hunan; and Lo Jui-ch'ing replaced Huang Ko-ch'eng as chief of staff. But by having launched the new antirightist campaign, the Lushan conference made it difficult for the local cadres to abandon particular disruptive aspects of the Leap. At one time after the Lushan plenum, the disbanded mess halls were restored; the mass line method was re-emphasized. A local newspaper bore testimony to this in its contention that the ownership scale in the commune must be transformed back from the current state into a larger unit. The Party exhorted the local cadres to learn from Wang Kuo-fan, who had built a model commune in Honan from what used to be called a pauper's cooperative.[55]

The Party gradually modified, however slowly, some of the GLF policies. Steel smelting had long been suspended; the multifunctional aspect of the original commune also had been put aside. The new slogan was Develop Multiple Undertakings with Grain as the Main. In October 1959 the Secretariat called a telephone conference to urge all communes to fulfill their targets of grain production.[56] In the communes, the actual control over the means of production had already been transferred to the production teams. The system of fixing labor (pao-kung) gave the team the right to organize labor forces through the three-fixes-and-one-reward and four-fixes systems. In some places these brigades or teams went so far as to fix the production quotas for the households (pao-ch'an tao-hu); but the Party strictly banned this practice as a Right opportunist trend. As to the ratio of supply and wage, the Party recommended 30 percent (but with a 40 percent maximum) for the supply and 70 percent (but with a 60 percent minimum) for the wage, a significant shift from the fifty-fifty ratio of the Wuhan Resolution.[57]

In the wake of the antirightist campaign, the spring of 1960 saw a resurgence of GLF policies. In March, Mao personally enacted the Constitution of Anshan Iron and Steel Company in opposition to the Soviet revisionist Constitution of the Magnitogorak Iron and Steel Company. He put forth five broad principles for industrial management comparable to the basic features of people's communes: (1) keep politics firmly in command, (2) strengthen Party leadership, (3) launch vigorous mass movements, (4) institute the systems of cadre participation in productive labor and worker participation in management, reform irrational outdated rules and regulations, and establish close cooperation among workers, cadres, and technicians, and (5) go full steam ahead with technical innovations and technical revolution.[58]

In April when the second National People's Congress was held,

Li Fu-ch'un upheld the Three Red Banners as the Party's three bea-
cons for the entire period of socialist construction. The congress
passed the Twelve-Year Agricultural Program into law, and T'an Chen-
lin claimed that the commune was the fundamental guarantee for fulfilling the program ahead of schedule. T'an also reported that by the
end of 1959, 3.9 million mess halls had been established, and 400 million peasants, about 73 percent of the entire rural population, had had
their meals there.[59] Externally, the CCP made it clear that it did not
share Khrushchev's idea of general disarmament. By this time Sino-
Soviet relations had considerably worsened. For example, after P'eng
Teh-huai was ousted, Khrushchev called P'eng "correct" and "best
friend."[60] Internally, the urban communes were being set up in the
cities, and the Party intensified the campaign for sending cadres down
to the grass-roots level.

From April 1960, most communes practiced the "two-five" system
by which the cadres attended to office chores for two days and worked
at production posts for five days a week. In this way they implemented
the policy of "four togethers"—eating, living, working, and discussing
together with the masses. These campaigns were directed at such practices as: brigades trying to cultivate only economic crops, peasants
caring for only their side-line occupations, and the individual relying
upon the collective for food but on himself for other needs.[61]

THE PARTY'S RESPONSE TO THE AGRICULTURAL CRISIS, 1960

The Party's initial response to the deteriorating situation in the
communes was the *hsia-fang* campaign (for details, see chapter 4). Ever
since Mao blamed the local cadres for not heeding Party directives at
the Lushan conference, the Party had maintained that its policies had
been correct but the cadres' errors in implementing them caused the
commune program to fail.

In the summer of 1960, the leadership identified five most prevalent
cases among such errors and called them "five styles": communism,
commandism, privileged behavior, blind direction, and exaggeration.
Communism referred to absolute equalitarianism such as confiscation
of properties and transfer of goods and man power at will. *Commandism* was a trend to impose any decision on the masses without consulting them. *Privileged behavior* was a bureaucratic attitude despising
physical labor. *Blind direction* was a manipulation of the masses by
force. And *exaggeration* was a trend to fabricate information without
seeking truth from facts.[62] Of these the most serious were communism
and commandism. The former was a result of excessive behavior by the
cadres in response to the ideological fervor accompanying the commune

movement. The latter was a result of unbridled activism called for by the leadership as characterized in the slogan Dare to Think and to Act.

Commandism in particular had been at the heart of the cadre problem during the GLF. The more the central authority demanded the local cadres to be activist, the more likely it was for them to commit commandism; but the less the demand for activism, the more they manifested "goodmanism" (*hao-jen chu-i*). By and large, the local cadres' behavior was a function of the central leaders' demands, for they generally did what they were told to do. Unless the Party changed the political climate within which the cadres had to implement Party directives, the *hsia-fang* campaign to rectify those errors would not suffice. Hence the general mood and lines at a time worked as policies as much as the lack of them.

It was during the late summer of 1960 that the full impact of the crisis began to be felt. An important external event that compelled the Party to change policy was the sudden pull-out of Soviet technicians in June. In the long run, this move forced the Chinese to pursue a strategy of self-reliance more vigorously and left the CCP with a legacy of bitterness toward the Soviet Union. In the short run, however, the immediate shock forced the Chinese leaders to re-examine their policies.

According to Liao Lu-yen, Mao had already put forward in 1959 the policy of Agriculture as the Foundation and Industry as the Leading Factor. Liao did not make it clear when it had been proposed by Mao, but certainly there had been a trend toward this. Ever since the Shanghai plenum of April 1959, the Party placed first priority on grain production. In his report on the 1960 economic plan at the NPC in April 1960, Li Fu-ch'un confirmed that the slogan was Party policy.[63] Now that the Soviets had pulled out their technicians so abruptly, once again the Party had to redirect its economic priorities.

From June through August, the top leaders discussed the consequence of the Soviet pull-out at a central work conference at Peitaiho, attended by first secretaries of provinces. In a speech made in June, Mao admitted errors in policy. At this conference, the Party decided to implement the new economic policy of Agriculture as the Foundation and Industry as the Leading Factor. The conference also decided to re-establish the Party's six regional bureaus to strengthen its central control over the provinces. In September, Liao Lu-yen explained this policy in a *Red Flag* article as a program to concentrate all man power and resources on the agricultural front. More importantly, on the question of when the transition from ownership based on the brigade to commune ownership would take place, Liao stated that it would be decided after 1965 in the light of the condition then prevailing.[64]

Thus, 1960 was a watershed year that spelled the end of the GLF. During the harvest of the autumn crops, it became painfully clear that a mere rectification of cadres could hardly alleviate the economic crisis. Nor could the summer reordering of priority accomplish this, for it came too late to bear any results; in addition, another year of natural calamities was a severe blow to the commune program. The regime attributed the failure of the GLF to these calamities, as well as the Soviet pull-out. In October, Mao directed the provinces to concentrate the labor force on agriculture.[65]

More than any others, the peasants suffered most and knew that the stopgap measures taken by the Party thus far were far from adequate. The Party was hard pressed to do something drastic. Responding to this need, the Central Committee, on November 3, 1960, issued in letter form its urgent directive on rural work, commonly called the Twelve Articles.[66]

This document provided concrete guidelines for the commune, free of the abstract ideological pronouncements characteristic of the former Party resolutions. As to labor organization and remuneration, it restated what was already in wide practice. The explicit endorsement of these practices suggests that they had not been fully enforced. The directive specified excessive practices to be the "one equalization and two transfers" (i-p'ing erh-tiao): equalitarianism in distribution and the transfer of man power and goods, the two salient expressions of Communist and commandist styles, were banned henceforth. This was an indication that the five styles had persisted and that now the Party clearly wanted to put a brake on them. The document also assured the commune members of as much a share of the income as possible and specified the ratio of supply and wage as three to seven; it also called for the "combination of rest and work."

The directive made the production team a unit of partial ownership, underscoring the importance of the team for using the means of production, if not owning it. Under the system of four fixes, the brigade owned land, man power, draft animals, and farm implements, but they were fixed for the teams to use and the commune could no longer withhold any of these. Under the three-fixes-and-one-reward system, the brigade entrusted output, cost, and man power to the teams. This was a compromise solution that maintained the centralized management of the commune while at the same setting quotas for individual households, which in effect would have restored private economy.

The team gradually came to own farm implements and draft animals and only the production plan was sent down by the brigades. It was allowed to dispose of most of its income through work points after deducting the share for the tax and compulsory sale as well as the collective funds. It eventually became the basic unit for organizing labor and production, for the brigades were not allowed to draw more than 5 percent of the total man power from the teams. These measures removed the uncertainty between the three levels in terms of ownership and production. In fact, the system of contract (*pao*) functioned as the crucial instrument in maintaining a semblance of commune structure, but once that much was granted, a number of cadres and peasants asked to fix output to household; and in some areas they apparently did so, arguing that such would bring about more production, only by a different method.[67]

In addition to this *pao*, the crux of the Twelve Articles rested in the restoration of private plots coupled with the family side-line occupation and the free markets. The enterprises run by the commune gradually restored economic accounting practices (even though the document did not mention this) so that they could be responsible for their own losses and gains. Only then did the agricultural crisis begin to abate. Finally, the directive further promised rectification and adjustment in the communes. But this time there was predictability: it was assured that the policy would not be changed for at least seven years.[68]

These twelve articles were the Party's urgent response to the deteriorating situation in the countryside. With the implementation of them, the GLF simply collapsed. But to straighten out the mess created by the collapse, the Party needed more systematic reviews and adjustments in the subsequent years.

4
The Adjustments and Their Legacies

The economic situation in China at the end of 1960 demanded some decisive policy measures. To meet this urgency, the CCP carried out policy reviews and adjustments in the two years between the Ninth Plenum in January 1961 and the Tenth Plenum in September 1962. The Party not only regularized existing practices into central directives and enacted new policies, but also allowed some debate and criticism about the state of the nation in the previous three years. What emerged from these was a policy direction entirely different from that of the GLF. Since this turnabout inevitably undermined Mao's personal authority, he attempted to regain his authority following the Tenth Plenum by appealing to ideological revitalization; but in doing so, he could not change the current policy and leadership of the Party. How did this development take place and what legacies did it leave after 1962? We now turn to these questions.

TWO DIVERGING TRENDS BETWEEN THE ARMY AND THE PARTY, 1960-61: IDEOLOGICAL CAMPAIGNS VERSUS POLICY ADJUSTMENTS

To put the adjustment features in perspective, it is necessary to take a brief look at their background. As to just how serious the situation was, the *Work Bulletin* of the People's Liberation Army (PLA) testifies. Peasant uprisings had occurred in some areas, mainly because of food shortages. Implementing a reversed policy after so much change within two years was quite complex, as the Party was faced with various difficulties in seeing that the basic-level cadres and the peasants understood and complied with the new policy. According to one PLA investigation, nearly 30 percent of the cadres and 50 percent of the soldiers were confused about the new directives because they had been told that the Three Red Banners were correct; yet, suddenly, they were told to do away with them. Therefore, they raised many embarrassing questions.

How do you interpret it now that you speak of only one, big, while in the past you had spoken of one, big, and two, public? As we no longer talk about one, big, and two, public, and five functions combined into one, do we still have ten superiorities of the commune or don't we? As the communes and brigades enter into contracts and the brigades resume distribution by work and private plots, what differences are there between the brigades and the advanced APC's?[1]

These were some of the local cadres' complaints about the Twelve Articles of 1960.

As to the situation in the countryside, the local cadres were of the opinion that it had been really worse before the Twelve Article directive:

The prices are too high and chaotic. The 7-grade or 8-grade labor is no better than growing a couple of onions [in terms of reward]. If things go this way, it will force all prices to skyrocket and the People's currency to depreciate; it may affect the development of socialist construction and at least the reform of peasants.[2]

These utterances begged the question of why such a situation came about. Here again, the peasants rebuked the official view that the Party's policies had been correct, and that in addition to the bad weather and the Soviet withdrawal the cadres' erroneous implementation of the five styles had caused the GLF to fail. They understood too well that such errors were the results of the correct Party policy when they asked: "Where do those 'five styles' come from? How come the 'Communist style' crops up all over the country? Isn't it true that without communization there would be no 'five styles'?" And these critics hit the mark again by pointing out: "Party policies are good but are unimplementable"; hence "it was inevitable for the cadres to make mistakes."[3]

Lastly, touching upon a solution to this situation, the local cadres clearly indicated that more material incentives would be the best remedy: "It is still material incentives that count in management; without it politics in command loses its soul. Material incentives and politics in command are both important, but the former is the basis for and superior to the latter."[4] While they aspired to receiving increased material incentives, these cadres were equally aware of their consequences. Once distribution according to labor was put in practice, those households who had a small labor force but large families to feed would suffer most; hence, the same polarization of the rich and the poor would occur; once family side-line occupations were introduced, commune members became more enthusiastic, but their energies were largely directed to developing private plots.

In coping with this unrest among the peasants, one can discern two broad trends in Party policy and practice, which in turn established the twofold orientation of Chinese political development in the 1960s. The first was to continue the policies of the GLF, that is, mass persuasion and mobilization; the second was to reverse this by restoring the pre-Leap practices of material incentives and regularized administration. By and large, the PLA under Lin Piao's leadership followed the former and the CCP under Liu Shao-ch'i's the latter.

Addressing himself to this problem, Lin Piao stated in December 1960:

Because of the great calamities of this year there are some difficulties in amassing grain food and some tensions in the supply of subsidiary food. The soldiers are the peasants and workers wearing military uniforms; hence whatever problems there are in the localities, they are to be reflected in the Army. In some Army units political incidents have increased due to the comparatively difficult situation of the current economic life.[5]

To assuage the troops and to insure that there would be no more such incidents, Lin stressed the need for ideological indoctrination within the Army.

On the other hand, it was under these circumstances that Liu Shao-ch'i remarked that the free market must continue even if it produced some capitalist elements; that without the interests of the individual there are no interests of the whole; and that therefore what is advocated is not public interest without private interest but public interest with private interest, although public interest takes precedence. In 1967, Mao's supporters labeled this posture a bourgeois outlook, a "theory of convergence of public interests and private interests."[6]

This is not to say, however, that Mao had already lost confidence in Liu Shao-ch'i. It appears that Mao truly trusted Liu Shao-ch'i, Teng Hsiao-p'ing, and P'eng Chen at this time. The three leaders went to the Moscow meeting of eighty-one Communist parties in November 1960; upon their return to Peking, Mao personally welcomed them at the airport, the only occasion on which he did so. The CCP's Ninth Plenum, held in January 1961, fully approved the Moscow Statement.[7]

The PLA: Read Chairman Mao's Works, Listen to Him, Do as He Instructs and Become a Good Soldier of Chairman Mao

Beginning with the PLA, the General Political Department (GPD) in

1960 embarked upon an intensive campaign of ideological revitalization among the soldiers to prevent unrest among their dependents and relatives. Lin Piao personally initiated this movement.[8] Lin presided over an enlarged meeting of the Military Affairs Committee from September through October and proposed the "four first" principles as the keynote to the political work: man first over weapons, political work first over other work, ideological work first over administrative work, and living ideology first over book ideology. The resolution of the MAC declared:

In an era in which imperialism is heading for collapse and socialism is advancing to victory, the Thought of Mao Tse-tung has applied the universal truth of Marxism-Leninism and creatively developed it in the concrete practice of the Chinese revolution and in the collective struggle of the Party and the people. It is the guide to the Chinese people's revolution and socialist construction, the powerful weapon for opposing imperialism and revisionism and dogmatism.[9]

Lin elaborated upon this resolution in an October article entitled "Hold High the Red Banner of the General Line and Mao Tse-tung's Military Thought," which criticized indirectly P'eng Teh-huai's military line and proposed a campaign for the study of Mao's thought.[10]

The October MAC resolution also quoted Lin's famous dictum: Read Chairman Mao's Works, Listen to His Words, Do as He Instructs and Become a Good Soldier of Chairman Mao. The resolution reaffirmed several themes of the GLF, such as the mass line and democracy in the three areas of politics, the military, and economics, and the "three-eight work style."[11] Pointing out that one-third of all companies did not have one, it also demanded the building of a Party branch in every company. It further called for intensifying youth work, training red-and-expert cadres, and increasing PLA participation in construction and militia work.

This was directed not only at the PLA but also at the whole Party. The Central Committee endorsed the MAC resolution and transmitted it to all regional bureaus and provincial and district committees. In December 1960, Lin discussed how to study Mao's works and to achieve quick results: "What is urgent for use must be studied first. In studying the thoughts of Mao Tse-tung, we must erect a pole to see immediately its shadow, that is, we must use the 'arrow' of Mao's thought to shoot the 'target' of our Army's ideological reality." He continued: "It is necessary to study with problems in mind, conduct living study and application, integrate study with application, study first what is urgent to yield prompt results and exert oneself in 'application.'"[12] Hsiao Hua, deputy director of the GPD, transmitted these words.

The political work in 1961 particularly stressed the need for education on the situation (*hsing-shih chiao-yü*). Lo Jung-huan, director of the GPD, revived Mao's theme that classes do exist in socialist society, and Liu Chih-chien, another deputy director, specified the method of the education as "two recollections and three investigations," that is, every cadre had to recollect his class and the nation's sufferings in the past while investigating his own viewpoint, his will to struggle, and his work.[13] Through this education, the cadres were told that the Three Red Banners had been correct and that the Party would overcome the temporary difficulties.

This education was accompanied by an intensive effort at simplifying administration. According to Lo Jui-ch'ing, Lin Piao ordered one-third of the cadres above the regiment level to go down to the companies while criticizing the "five many" (too many tables, documents, visits, general calls, and reports). Lo pointed out: "Some say that of so many figures only 30 percent is statistics and 70 percent guesswork; I say that all of them are guesses."[14]

In December 1960, the MAC decided to nurture "five-good soldiers" (who were to be proficient in politics and ideology, military techniques, three-eight style, fulfilling duty, and steeling the body); in 1961, the army followed this up with the "four-good company" (which was to be capable in politics and ideology, three-eight style, military training, and management of living).[15] One can determine the intensity of these campaigns from the rebuilding between July 1960 and February 1961 of 82 percent of all Party branches in the army. In one unit, at least, the effort induced three soldiers to commit suicide, prompting Lin Piao to issue a directive banning any methods so crude as to cause such harsh consequences.[16]

An important aspect of the PLA's political work was its special emphasis on youth. A noteworthy method of propagandizing for youth was the use of quotations from Mao's works. The GPD compiled Mao's quotations and arranged them according to several themes, such as overcoming difficulties in hard times, following the mass line, practicing self-reliance and frugality, and showing bravery and dedication to the people. These quotations were not intended to idolize Mao per se, for a few from Lin Piao and even from Liu Shao-ch'i were included. At the end of 1961, the GPD selected 18 out of the 158 pieces of Mao's four-volume *Selected Works*, drew upon 3 passages from "On Correctly Handling the Contradictions among the People," and edited them into *Quotations from Chairman Mao*. Then, the department issued the book to all military units for study. Lin Piao also instructed the army-run schools to shorten their school years.[17]

The GPD apparently took charge of the planning and operation of these programs. Lo Jung-huan and his deputies worked out the details; as the first vice-chairman of the MAC, Lin Piao personally supervised their work. As a result of this endeavor, the army produced two documents, Regulations Governing Political Work and Regulations Governing Company Guidance and Educational Work in 1960 and 1961, respectively. In sum, after P'eng Teh-huai's fall, Lin Piao assumed de facto head of the MAC and made the PLA a national model for political work. Yet it would be a mistake to suggest that Lin promoted political work at the expense of professional training; on the contrary, he advocated a professional-political ratio of seven to three for specialized units and six to four for other units. The important point, however, is that Lin was more steadfast than any other leader in marshalling Mao's thought during these difficult times, the others, in fact, openly displaying doubts about its use. In 1964, Mao himself recalled that except for army officials no one thought in 1962 that the situation was good.[18]

The Party: Readjusting, Consolidating,
Filling Out, and Raising Standards

The second trend in contrast to that shown by the PLA was evidenced by the CCP's policy review. In January 1961, the Party convened an enlarged Politburo meeting and subsequently held the Ninth Plenum.[19] This plenum adopted an operational ideology in tune with the actual situation, that is, Readjusting, Consolidating, Filling Out, and Raising Standards. Under this slogan, the Party scaled down the scope of capital construction and the rate of development, thereby putting an end to the General Line because rapid progress had been regarded as the soul of the General Line. The Party also readjusted the relationship between industry and agriculture by demanding the whole nation to implement the policy of "taking agriculture as the foundation of the national economy and of the whole Party and the entire people going in for agriculture and grain production." For this purpose, it raised a new slogan, Listen to the Party and Do According to Party Policies.[20]

In his speech to the Ninth Plenum, Mao set the tone of the Party's New Economic Policy by emphasizing realism. Declaring that 1961 was a year of "seeking the truth from reality," he called upon the Party leaders to investigate and study the local conditions before making decisions. He said that the 1959 Lushan conference did not deal with leftist deviations. Therefore, he stressed the importance of maintaining unity, preventing the five styles, and thereby restoring balance and quality in economic development. Once again admitting his own mistakes, he said "We cannot transform what we do not know about." The situation in Shantung, Honan, and Kansu was deteriorating; for the nation as a whole, 20 percent of the communes were collapsing. To cope with this trend, he promised that there would be no more new construction and that the fixing of output quota would be allowed. In short, Mao encouraged a drastic policy reversal to meet the imminent agricultural crisis.[21]

In the name of Readjusting and Consolidating, between the Ninth Plenum and the Tenth Plenum in September 1962, the Party's central machineries—mainly the Politburo's Standing Committee and Secretariat—carried out some sweeping reviews and regularized their findings into a series of comprehensive directives. This endeavor covered all five systems of policy, excluding only foreign and military policy: (1) agriculture-forestry, (2) industry-communication, (3) finance-trade, (4) culture-education, and (5) politics-law. Since agriculture, finance, trade, and political-legal matters concerned most of the population, policy adjustments in these areas stemmed from the interactions between the Center and the localities. Decision making involved frequent Party use of the central work conference (*chung-yang kung-tso hui-i*) format, which regional and provincial leaders attended. In contrast, for such specialized areas as industry, culture, and education, adjustments resulted from the interactions between the specialized Party-state organizations and the practitioners; for decision making in these areas, the Party relied on more specialized forms of the central work conference at which the Party-state officials as well as the practitioners were present.

The Sixty Articles on Agriculture

The first readjustment document emerging from such reviews was the Draft Regulations Concerning the Rural Communes, commonly known as the Sixty Articles on Agriculture. In March 1961, the Secretariat convened a central work conference at Canton and discussed the Sixty Articles. Evidently, the Secretariat under the aegis of Teng Hsiao-p'ing and P'eng Chen drafted this document without consulting Mao. When criticizing Teng and P'eng at the Canton conference, Mao reportedly asked: "Which emperor decided this?" and asserted: "Without investigation no one has the right to speak." As Liu Chih-chien explained, the Sixty Articles were written in the light of Mao's speech at the second Chengchow conference in 1959, the spirit of an intra-Party bulletin (*Tang-nei t'ung-hsün*) and the Twelve Articles, thus summing up three years of policy and practical experience.[22] In fact, the accumulation of the Party's incremental decisions made in these years culminated in this document.

The Sixty Articles comprised the first comprehensive manual for commune management based on a nationwide practice. Though quite similar in spirit to the Twelve Articles, they were more detailed and workable, for they stipulated with clarity what was permissible and what was banned in such a way that the communes could easily consult and apply them. The document specifically banned any coercive measures, discouraged enterprises except in slack seasons, allowed suspension of the mess halls if the commune desired, specified that private plots should not exceed 5 percent of the arable land, and prohibited commune authorities from interfering in family side-line occupations and daily necessities.[23]

To implement this directive, the Party Center transmitted it along with an explanatory letter to the Party branches, asking them to study these documents in April and May 1961 and to make suggestions.[24] The actual implementation fell into two categories: the general "plane" (*mien*) and some "spots" (*tien*) specially selected for further experimentation. On the plane level, the Party branches punctually took charge of its implementation; whereas on the spots level, central and provincial leaders of special task forces in the form of work teams (*kung-tso tui*) carried out investigation and experimentation, quite often "squatting" (*tun-tien*) there. Since Mao especially called upon central Party leaders to investigate rural conditions in person, most central leaders (including Liu Shao-ch'i, Teng Hsiao-p'ing, Ch'en Yün, and P'eng Chen) went on inspection tours. Teng, for example, went to Shun-i hsien near Peking, together with P'eng Chen and Liu Jen; during the Cultural Revolution the Maoists accused them of having collected "black" materials to attack Mao's policies.[25] To encourage investigation, the Center also dispatched Mao's 1930 essay "On Investigation Work" with an explanatory letter to the Party committees above the hsien level. The Party required its cadres to study them in hope of changing their work style.[26] Indeed, cadres began investigations and sent back many reports to higher levels. Based on these findings, the Center issued more instructions and regulations through central conferences.

As before, policy formulation involved a series of compromises between the Center's demands and local responses. But at this time, the process occurred under the direction and the approval of the Party Center, the regional bureaus, and the provincial committees. For instance, at the May-June 1961 central work conference, Liu Shao-ch'i pointed out that the peasants still had "no case of minds." At this conference, Mao apparently offered his own self-criticism for his responsibility in the GLF. In August-September, the Party convened the second Lushan conference to discuss further adjusting the communes.[27] As one report from PLA sources indicated, however, the local cadres maintained that the Sixty Articles were not good enough. To cater to these grievances, the Party could not but allow some experimentation exceeding limits imposed by the Sixty Articles. A poignant instance in this regard was the emergence of *san-tzu i-pao* (that is, the extension of private plots, free markets, and small enterprises, which conducted independent accounts with sole responsibility for their own profits and losses, and the fixing of output quotas for individual households).[28]

Ironically, Anhui and Honan, the very provinces that had set the pace for early communization, were at the forefront of the retreat.[29] An obvious explanation for the situation in Anhui was its widespread devastation by floods from the Yangtze River. To restore production, Anhui assigned output quotas in the fall of 1961 to individual households. In effect, this was a drastic measure, virtually abandoning collective farming; but elsewhere, too, Party organizations discussed fixing quotas for households or even dividing land among the households (*fen-t'ien tao-hu*). After Liu Shao-ch'i called an October meeting to discuss the prevention of commodities from flowing onto the black market, provincial authorities began to extend free markets and private plots.[30] Thus, illegal activities, in effect, were halted by granting them legitimacy.

For example, in June 1961, Liu Chien-hsün replaced Wu Chih-p'u as first secretary and made known that his purpose in coming to Honan was to provide a solution to the food problem. He encouraged diversity and experimentation, for, to him, "he who produces grain is a Marxist-Leninist, and sweet potatoes are as good as politics." In cooperation with Hua Yu-ch'un, secretary of the district committee, Liu promoted the cultivation of sweet potatoes in the Anyang special district. Elsewhere, he permitted Keng Ch'i-ch'ang, first secretary of Hsin-hsiang special district, to experiment with the renting out of land while letting Juang Lien-hsi of the Wuchiu hsien go ahead with fixing output quotas for households. In doing so, he swiftly put a halt to the zealous policies of Wu Chih-p'u, saying: "In recent years, many things have been done on impulse. They did not come from the masses. Instead of the movement being directed by the masses, the movement directed the masses." When he was accused in 1963 of being rightist for this kind of talk his answer was equally forceful: "You said that I was Right-inclined. I think the Right is good because I have work, and grain to eat. Some people said that I was an opportunist. If a favorable situation could come out of opportunism, why should I oppose it? If you search for my mistakes, get the big ones, not the small ones."[31]

This experimentation in rural policies spread into other areas as well, ranging from Shanghai to Szechwan. Following the Sixty Articles, Li Ching-ch'üan and Chia Ch'i-yun of Szechwan formulated an eighteen-article directive on the communes that made allowance for *san-tzu i-pao*.[32] The *Lien-chiang* documents also indicate that in Fukien the trend for dividing land and fixing output for households (also called "going it alone"—*tan-kan feng*) continued in 1962; in one brigade over 98 percent of teams engaged in it. The local cadres themselves pleaded for it to overcome difficulties. Peasant aphorisms caustically described Party opposition and their own attitude to *san-tzu i-pao:* "The government is afraid that the masses will eat too well, so they promote the collectives." But "there is not one Chinese with an unselfish public spirit"; hence "only under individual enterprise will he redouble his efforts."[33]

As the contract system of fixing output or labor for a small group of five or ten members or even for individual households prevailed, the brigade was found to be too big to handle their assignments. Besides, wide economic disparities existed among teams in the same brigade simply because of ecological differences. Eventually, the Party Center concluded it was unfair for the brigade to enforce a uniform distribution over the teams. The obvious solution was to make the team the basic accounting unit—the unit that determined the income of its members—which the Party officially did on January 1, 1962. In effect, this decision was a retreat to the level of collective organization under the lower APC s, since both the 1955 unit and the team had about twenty households.[34]

Returning to the Honan case, T'ao Chu, first secretary of the Central-South Bureau, who had been one of the vanguards in the commune movement of 1958 with Wu Chih-p'u, personally presided over a meeting of Honan provincial secretaries at Chengchow in April 1962 and worked out a document called the Six-Year Plan for Recovering and Developing Agriculture in Honan (1962-1967). This plan allowed the brigades or teams to devote a maximum of 7 percent, or in some cases 20 percent, of the arable land to private plots, to fix household output quotas, to divide land among the households, and even to rent commune land to them. In the Wutao hsien, over 63 percent of the teams assigned output quotas to individual households. About 12 percent of the land in the province was rented out. In July 1962, the Honan Provincial Committee instructed the production teams to extend the family side-line occupations. Chin Ming, secretary of the Central-South Bureau, supervised implementation of these measures. Liu Shao-ch'i allegedly commended Keng Ch'i-ch'ang for his involvement in these.[35]

As these experimentations at the local level increasingly turned away from the stipulated rules, they were bound to be reflected at the Center and to cause policy debates. By the Peitaiho conference of

August 1962, Mao had come to perceive that *san-tzu i-pao*, if adopted, would deny the very principle of collectivism all together. Therefore, at the Peitaiho conference he put a halt to the debate by invoking the ideological specter of class struggle and vetoed the current quest for *san-tzu i-pao*. In the light of these interactions between the Party's policy initiatives and the local responses, and between the Party Center's implementation and Mao's veto, the Party summed up the experiences acquired on the plane as well as the spots and amended the Sixty Articles into a revised draft. Finally, the Tenth Plenum in September ratified this revised draft of the Sixty Articles and adopted a Resolution on Collective Economy (discussed below in detail).[36]

The Seventy Articles on Industry

As for industry, in June 1961, Po I-po went to Shenyang to study the Twelve Articles on the Coalmine Work in Anp'ing, Fuhsin, which Sung Jen-ch'iung had drafted in April. Po and Sung worked together to formulate the Seventy Articles Concerning Industrial Enterprises and Mines, commonly known as the Seventy Articles on Industry. This document contradicted many aspects of Mao's 1960 Constitution of Anshan Steel Company. In July 1961, Po completed its first draft; in August, a central work conference presided over by Teng Hsiao-p'ing at Peitaiho revised it; and in September the Secretariat transmitted it throughout the country.[37]

This directive aimed at doing away with the mass-line method in industrial management. It restored the director responsibility system coupled with Party leadership, increased material incentives by adopting the piece-rate system of the three fixes and four guarantees from the readjusted commune, and restored bonuses for innovation and overproduction. It also provided for the technicians' and engineers' prerogatives in quality control and supervision, specifically banned any transfer of workers by the local authorities, and discouraged large-scale capital construction. Also new was the stratified "five-personnel" rank by which the duty and responsibility of the inspector, supervisor, custodian, procurement officer, and safety expert were specified. Yu Ch'iu-li was in the forefront of implementing these measures in the Ministry of Petroleum; in 1963 he himself formulated another directive on the petroleum industry.[38]

The Decision Concerning the Question of Commercial Work

As for finance and trade, upon Liu Shao-ch'i's instruction in March 1961, Li Hsien-nien formulated the Six Articles on Finance and Banking, which laid down the principle of vertical leadership, uniform planning, profit-making, and supervision by upper echelons. Through another directive on accounting, Li instituted a Western system of double-entry bookkeeping. In regard to commodity exchange, Li advocated the procurement of commodities through administrative agencies (*p'ai-kou*) so that the State Planning Commission could operate on a nationwide network of supply and demand. This unified transaction of commodities contrasted with Mao's policy of guaranteeing supply to the peasants; however, for this reason, a comprehensive directive on finance and trade was delayed until the Tenth Plenum when the Party adopted the Decision Concerning the Question of Commercial Work.[39]

The Eight Articles on Literature and Arts
and the Sixty Articles on Higher Education

A similar pattern existed in the cultural and educational systems as well. Particularly, the Party leaders in operational charge of this field were most critical of Lin Piao's promotion of Mao-study within the PLA. Chou Yang, deputy director of the Propaganda Department, stated in October 1960: "If everything is the peak, there will be no peak."[40] This was an allusion to Lin's claim that Mao's thought is the peak. As for the quotations from Mao popularized in the army, Chou Yang maintained that they were too simple and that while they might be suitable for the soldiers, they were definitely not for the cadres in the cultural field. At a work conference on science and technology held in 1961, Chou stated: "The Thought of Mao Tse-tung should be studied properly, but it must not be simplified or vulgarized." He then asked: "How can we ask one to put what he has learned to use on the same day? How can one learn something and then use it immediately?" And he continued: "The most serious crime in the world is the rape of the spirit! Literature should observe the spirit of the time, not the orders of an individual. . . . We must not harm people spiritually and throw them into a spiritual prison."[41]

Six years later in his acceptance speech of the sole vice-chairmanship of the Party at the Eleventh Plenum in 1966, Lin Piao confirmed that leaders such as Lu Ting-yi and Chou Yang had smeared the study of Mao's thought as "eating Hsüanwei ham, saying that one would get sick of it if they ate it every day!" Lin went on: "They smeared 'standing a pole on its shadow,' i.e., achieving quick results, by saying: 'Without the sun there will be no shadow.' "[42]

In the eased atmosphere of 1961, however, the Propaganda Department enacted several regulations. In February, Chou Yang and Lin Mo-han (also deputy director of the department in charge of drama and films) convened investigation meetings to examine six art forms:

(1) movies, (2) plays, (3) dialogue dramas, (4) music, (5) graphic arts, and (6) the press and literature. Representatives from each of the professional associations also took part at the meetings. In April, Chang Kuang-nien, secretary of the Chinese Writers Association and editor of *Wen-i-pao* (Literary Gazette), summarized the discussions in an article entitled "The Questions of Themes." In May, Yüan Sui-p'o, another editor of the *Literary Gazette*, and two leaders of the Propaganda Department drafted the Ten Articles on Literature and Art, which Lin Mo-han would revise several times. At a nationwide forum on literary work held from June through July, Chou Yang and Lin Mo-han explained the draft. As a result of these discussions, they revised it again, and circulated the original and the revised draft to the propaganda departments of the provincial committees to solicit further suggestions. In October, Lu Ting-yi took direct charge of the drafting. He instructed his deputies that the document should seek to eliminate political vulgarization in the arts and should embody the united front policy of all the intellectuals including the bourgeoisie. Under Lu's direction, the Ten Articles were revised in December into the Eight Articles. Lin Mo-han and Chang Kuang-nien added more revisions. Finally, the department dispatched it to all relevant Party units, including the various literary associations, not as a regular internal document but a draft, pending further consideration. At the NPC held in April 1962, Chou Yang circulated the draft to some concerned delegates and submitted it afterwards to the Secretariat and the Politburo's Standing Committee for approval. When it was approved, the Secretariat transmitted it as a Party directive to the Party units.[43]

This episode vividly revealed the inner working of the Party's decision-making process. In connection with this, Chou Yang reportedly retorted to a dissenter during the drafting of the document: "We are always nearer the Center than are you; therefore, we know the spirit of the Center."[44] Of importance here was that the central department not only sought opinions of the professional associations but also articulated their views and took them into consideration. The revised draft of the Ten Articles was a product of interplay between the Center's preferences and those of the practitioners, reflecting both the Center's desires and the intellectuals' wishes.

This document sought to establish some fundamental principles in literary and art work. In defining the relationship between politics and art, it recognized that art serves politics, but at the same time, it warned against a narrow interpretation of the relationship by cautioning that politics ought not to replace art or vice versa. Since art must improve and reflect reality, the Party appealed for high quality and refrained from using such a slogan as Opposing Simple Technical Views to deny the unity of political content and artistic form, style, and taste. Pertinent to the later Cultural Revolution, the document encouraged artists to seek inspiration from the literary and artistic legacy of Chinese history and folk culture, and to absorb the cultural achievements of foreign countries as well. It called for a guarantee of time for artistic work, correct standards of criticism, training of talent, spiritual and material incentives, unity of all active elements, and reform of leadership style.[45]

Besides Lu Ting-yi and Chou Yang, the highest Party official to further this new cultural policy was Ch'en Yi, a Politburo member and foreign minister. Propounding the spirit of the seven-thousand-cadre conference of January 1962 (see below), at the Canton Forum of Opera and Drama in March 1962, Ch'en Yi remarked: "If I fall into a net, I may seek survival by escaping through the net. [Even] if I have not fallen into a net but if everywhere there are invisible nets, how can I survive? Yes, the netless net is a big net. It kills people! . . . It is this that I must fight against today." He assured the artists that from that time on thought reform would not be implemented through a movement, nor would the Party force them to read Mao's works, for doing such things insulted their intelligence. He then asked; "What price is your goodness in politics? Can you sell it to me and can I weigh it for you?" As for literature, he had this to say: "Why shouldn't we write tragedies? The effects of a tragedy are greater than those of a comedy. . . . But now whatever is done, there is always a good ending and a victory, and nobody writes about failures." The reaction of the intellectuals to this Canton speech was best described in the bulletin of the conference: "After hearing Ch'en Yi's report, our hearts are filled with emotion, for we feel that the Party really is concerned for us and understands us. . . . As we were listening, we thought it too good to be true." And it was at this conference, too, that T'ao Chu joined Ch'en Yi in opposing forced and open thought reform by citing Tseng Tzu's credo: "Examine oneself in the quiet night."[46]

The Party Center soon publicized this policy in a *People's Daily* editorial of May 23, 1962, entitled "Serve the Broadest Masses of the People" written by Chou Yang in commemoration of the twentieth anniversary of Mao's talks at the Yenan Forum on Literature and Art. Naturally, this editorial encompassed the gist of the Eight Articles. It was this policy climate of liberalization that enabled Wu Han to write the historical play *Hai Jui Dismissed from Office*, and Teng T'o and others to launch the "Three-Family Village" column. Allegedly, K'ang Sheng once conveyed Chiang Ch'ing's disagreement with this policy to

Lu Ting-yi. Chiang Ch'ing herself talked with directors and ministers of the Propaganda Department and Ministry of Culture, but in her words, no one paid heed.[47]

A drastic reform was introduced in education as well. In January 1961, Liu Shao-ch'i instructed Lin Feng, vice-chairman of the standing committee of the NPC, to lead an investigation group at Peking University composed of Yang Shu, Wu Tze-ma, and P'eng Pei-yün. This group discovered many excesses of the GLF, particularly the extreme emphasis on politics and production (which caused the downgrading of teaching and learning) and too tight a control of schools by the Party branch (which disrupted academic activities). The first task was the restoration of regularized teaching. In February, P'eng Chen presided over a Secretariat meeting at which he asked all teachers to have a clearly printed copy of teaching materials before going to classes.[48]

P'eng placed Chiang Nan-hsiang, vice-minister of education, in charge of compiling the new teaching materials in science, engineering, agriculture, and medicine, and placed Chou Yang in charge of social sciences, literature, and art. In March Chiang convened a meeting at the Ministry of Education; in April Chou convened a similar meeting at the Propaganda Department. They found that during the previous collective scientific research, some people "only ran around to fetch material, tea, and water" and that, as a result, specialized training had been put aside. To rectify this, they proposed that experts be allowed to compile teaching materials. Teng Hsiao-p'ing approved this proposal. Lu Ting-yi also instructed Chou Yang and Chiang Nan-hsiang to exclude the Mao quotations from teaching materials, saying that Mao's thought was a new label that actually led the young to an ideological stalemate. Yang Hsiu-feng, minister of education, also maintained that there had been anarchy in education.[49]

The ministry convened a number of national conferences to readjust educational policies. In March 1961, Lu Ting-yi, Lin Feng, and Chang Chi-ch'un organized a task force for drafting a directive on higher education. Yang Hsiu-feng stayed at Tientsin University to investigate; later on, he asked Chiang Nan-hsiang to prepare a draft. In August, Teng Hsiao-p'ing convened a central work conference at Peitaiho at which P'eng Chen, Lo Jui-ch'ing, Po I-po, Wang Chia-hsiang, and Yang Shang-k'un were present. The conference discussed the Draft of Sixty Regulations Governing Work in Institutes of Higher Education, commonly known as the Sixty Articles on Universities. Teng in particular praised the draft as a good document and proposed to include in it a provision that the rightist teachers may also play a leading role in education. In September, the ministry put the draft into practice on a trial basis and in November with the approval of the Standing Committee, the Secretariat transmitted it as a Party directive.[50]

In January 1962, Chiang Nan-hsiang headed a one-thousand-expert group for compiling teaching materials, revising the curricula, and reforming examination systems. In February, the State Scientific Commission convened the National Conference on Scientific and Technological Work at Canton. On the basis of the discussions at the conference, the Ministry of Education drafted the Regulations Governing Work in Natural Sciences, commonly known as the Fourteen Articles on Science. At this conference, Chou Yang repeated his famous characterization of Mao study: "oversimplification, vulgarization, and dogmatism."[51] In June 1962, Chiang Nan-hsiang's group formulated the Regulations Governing Examinations that made examination the yardstick for evaluating the students' academic and political performances. In the latter part of the year, the ministry drafted two additional directives through similar processes: the Fifty Articles on High Schools and the Forty Articles on Primary Schools. These documents reversed the half-study and half-work system of the GLF into the full-time school system.[52]

Of these regulations the Sixty Articles on Universities typified the new approach. First, this directive did away with the excessive emphasis on political study, productive activities, and mass research; teaching and research were restored as the main task. Chiang Nan-hsiang spoke to this point when he urged a strengthening of the three fundamentals: fundamental theory, fundamental knowledge, and fundamental skills.[53] "The mistaken viewpoint of belittling book knowledge must be overcome," one article said and continued: "such phenomena as excessive production, scientific research, and social activities impeding and weakening educational work should be rectified." Another article gave top priority to restoration of normal educational activities: "Stability should be sought with efforts in the professional adoption of instruction projects, instruction plans and others, and teaching materials which should not be lightly altered."[54] As a result, by the end of 1962 all labor universities and agricultural universities run by the Ministry of State Farm and Land Reclamation (including the Communist Labor University in Kiangsi that Mao praised in a 1961 letter as the anti-Japanese Resistance University of that time) had all returned to being full-time schools.[55]

Secondly, the directive stressed excellence in specialized training. It stipulated that the redness of teacher and student should be manifested not only in politics and ideology but also in teaching and studying. An article specifically stated that "those who have achieved excellence should not be subjected to the limitations of qualification and experience."[56] Thirdly, where academic matters were involved, it increased the separation of teaching staffs from the Party committees. The university administration was still placed under the leadership of the Party committee, with the final responsibility vested in the school Party committee headed by the school principal. But the general branch attached to the academic department was to play only a supervisory role. On the theory that the Party was unqualified to exercise technological guidance, Lu Ting-yi called for a three-three system by which one-third of the university staff would consist of proletarian intellectuals, another one-third Left bourgeoisie and the last one-third neutral bourgeoisie.[57] Following this reasoning, in 1961 he appointed Chien Po-tsan vice-president of Peking University.

In journalism, too, there was a lessening of Party dominance. Upon an instruction from Liu Shao-ch'i and P'eng Chen, Lu Ting-yi sent a work team headed by Teng T'o in the spring of 1961 to the journalism department of the People's University. This team conveyed the principle of "truthfulness, objectivity, and fairness" in reporting. Liu again called upon the reporters to "maintain links with current reality while keeping a certain distance from it." This, as he saw it, was necessary to ward off sensationalism and to enhance service for the people.[58]

Resuming a Centralized and Collective Authority

The key to these adjustments was the way in which the Party carried them out. To restore the Party's tarnished prestige in the aftermath of the GLF, the Ninth Plenum sternly declared: "It is of the utmost importance to strengthen the ties of the Party and government organizations at various levels and all their functionaries with the masses of the people."[59] This plenum formally authorized the establishment of six regional bureaus so that they would act for the Central Committee to strengthen its leadership over the provincial Party committees. And Mao's withdrawal from the first line of the Politburo helped the collective leadership under Liu Shao-ch'i take a firm control of the Party's central machineries. In 1961, Liu assigned Ch'en Yün to lead a five-man group for reviewing economic policies; as for the cultural and educational systems, P'eng Chen apparently assumed a similar role, as did Teng Hsiao-p'ing for the political and legal systems.

From the Ninth Plenum on, the Secretariat extended special efforts to regularize the cadres' duties and responsibilities by issuing central directives.[60] Yet due to continued uncertainty and decentralization, the Party still faced numerous difficulties in trying to impose the unified leadership that was necessary for a coherent policy implementation upon the cadres. To cope with problems of dispersion in policy implementation, the Party convened an enlarged central work conference in January 1962 that some seven thousand cadres from five levels—central, provincial, special district, hsien, and commune—were invited to attend. Contending that the violation of democratic centralism was the basic cause of such dispersion, Liu Shao-ch'i went out of his way to stress the need for normalizing Party life.[61]

In response to this, Mao explicitly endorsed the need for eliminating separatism and strengthening centralized and collective leadership. He also gave approval to both the policy reviews in seven areas as he saw them—industry, agriculture, trade, education, the military, the government, and the Party—and the formulation of specific policies such as the Sixty Articles on Agriculture and the Seventy Articles on Industry. He actually conceded that the lack of such comprehensive guiding principles was an important cause in the failure of the GLF.[62] He also acknowledged that the Party had handled certain cadres improperly in the past.

Likewise, once the political mood at the Center shifted, Teng Hsiao-p'ing proposed in February 1962 to correct improper verdicts imposed on cadres in the previous antirightist campaigns, for over 80 percent of them had been subject to such action.[63] In 1967, Mao's supporters leveled a post hoc charge at this move, calling it a "reversal wind" designed to usurp Party leadership. But the evidence from 1962 reveals only a few instances of rehabilitation: Chang Wen-t'ien became a special researcher at the Economic Research Institute where he authored a book on socialist economy with Sun Yeh-feng. Huang Ko-ch'eng became vice-governor of Shansi, and Teng Hua, vice-governor of Szechwan. In June, P'eng Teh-huai was also allowed to go to the countryside for investigation; he brought back an eighty-thousand-word report this time, vindicating his previous views and saying allegedly: "I will not keep quiet any more. I want to be a Hai Jui."[64]

POLICY REVIEWS AND DEBATES: CRITICISM AND SELF-CRITICISM, 1961-62

It is important to note that these adjustments could hardly be possible without some measure of consensus at the Party's top level. In fact, while such reviews were being carried out, all sectors of the society were engaged in a process of self-examination about what went wrong and why.

Actually, Mao initiated the movement for such self-examination by offering his own in June 1961. This was revealed in his speech to the seven-thousand-cadre conference of 1962, though the exact content of his self-criticism was not made clear:

On June 12 last year, the last day of the central conference in Peking, I spoke on my shortcomings and mistakes. I asked the comrades to report what I said to all provinces and areas. Subsequently, I learned that this was not disseminated in many areas. It seemed that my mistakes could and should be concealed. Comrades, they cannot be concealed. For whatever mistakes are committed by the Central Committee, I bear direct responsibility and share the indirect responsibility, for I am chairman of the Central Committee. While I do not intend to encourage others to shirk responsibilities, nevertheless, I should be the first to bear responsibility.[65]

Following this, some provincial leaders also followed Mao's example. As Mao indicated, those who refused were forced to do so, as was the case in Honan, Kansu, and Tsinghai.[66]

The Peking Municipal Committee's Ch'ang-kuan-lou Affair: An Independent Kingdom?

While policy review was being carried out at the central level, similar processes also got under way at the provincial and local levels. A most conspicuous example, and one having a great bearing on the Cultural Revolution, was the Peking Municipal Party Committee. Responding to Mao's demand for investigation, P'eng Chen in May 1961 directed the standing committee of the Peking committee to investigate conditions in agriculture, industry, finance, and culture and education. Their most important conclusion was that many shortcomings at the local level had been the result of the Center's "blind direction."[67]

In November 1961 P'eng Chen instructed his closest deputies to review thoroughly central directives issued between 1958 and 1961. He said to Hsiang Tzu-ming, secretary-general of the secretariat of the Peking committee:

The Peitaiho conference [of 1958] talked about setting up a framework first for the people's commune. I do not know what exactly happened, but every place rose with a roar. In some provinces, the five styles are very serious. The Central Committee has a responsibility in this. . . . Some documents were issued with the comments of an individual, and it could not be guaranteed that they were free of problems. You had better organize some people to go through the documents issued by the Central Committee to see what problems there have been. See what those hotheaded people have done, and what are the documents of the Central Committee that have advocated the five styles. We must gain experience and learn lessons from them. For example, some slogans are things of subjective idealism.[68]

And he continued:

The proposition of "destruction before construction" is debatable. For example, the operation sequence left behind by the Soviet experts at the Anshan Steel Company was set aflame even before our own plan had been drafted. As a result, production declined; there was no order to talk about. Why should we act in such a hurry?[69]

P'eng Chen entrusted the supervision of this review to Teng T'o, secretary of the Peking committee. Teng, then, divided the work into several groups. In December 1961 this team gathered at a house called Ch'ang-kuan lou in the Western Suburb Park, Peking, and went through the central documents. What they found largely confirmed the views expressed by P'eng Teh-huai in 1959.

First, most mistakes were results of Left deviation instead of Right opportunism. Mao's decision for the GLF was hastily made and led to waste. To be sure, the individuals' initiative could have played an important role but to overemphasize it amounted to subjective idealism. For it was one thing to dare to think and speak, but it was something else to dare to act. As men were drawn to irrigation and steel smelting, the people's commune had become the "women's commune"; to rectify this, some cold water had to be poured on the mass movement.

Second, many GLF policies, such as rapid rate of development, simultaneous development, and political incentives, were all divorced from economic rules. Work accomplished by the efforts of all the people refuted by definition any division of work. There had been simply too many false reports that the Center had forwarded with approval.

Third, the Central Committee had changed policies so frequently that some of them contradicted one another. The Center received false information from the locale while the locale was not clear about the Center's intention; hence "nobody dared to tell the truth." Specifically, the indiscriminate enthusiasm generated by the Peitaiho conference and the Lushan conference simply contributed to the confusion. Liu Jen denounced the practice of issuing draft resolutions as a pretext for dodging responsibility for measures that the locale still had to carry out. Referring to Mao's defense of the GLF at the Lushan conference, he remarked: "The term of nine fingers and one finger cannot be used at random everywhere."

The Ch'ang-kuan lou review was a secret affair contained within the Peking Party apparatus. In fact, Hsiang Tze-ming specifically directed the participants not to divulge anything about it to outsiders. This review culminated in a two-thousand-word report to P'eng Chen. During the Cultural Revolution, it was alleged that Teng T'o had used the report in his jointly authored satirical "Notes from a Three-Family Village," and because the Peking committee had autonomously conducted such a highly classified review it was said to have become an "independent kingdom" similar to the Petofi Club.

Intellectuals: From Hai Jui to the Three-Family Village

In this new political mood of 1961-62, intellectuals also were allowed to air their views. But they could do so only in an esoteric language. For despite the changed atmosphere, the revised version of Mao's February 1957 speech precluded open discussion on any political subject; thus, the Party laid down the ground rule for literature and art: there was to be a clear separation between purely academic-artistic discussion and political-ideological contention, and freedom was granted only in the first area.[70]

Faced with these restrictions, writers nonetheless groped for better forms of expression. Some chose historical allegories as Wu Han did, or ghost plays as Meng Ch'ao did in his *Li Hui-niang*; others made comments via the newspapers as did Teng T'o. One thing they all had in common was a choice of ancient themes taken from the Ming or Sung dynasties, in which the emperors and ministers in their works spoke for them. In this way, they could couch political debates in terms of such academic issues as whether a particular Ming emperor (possibly meaning Mao) had improved the lot of the peasants.

The first and most important work along this line was *Hai Jui Dismissed from Office* written by Wu Han, a historian and vice-mayor of Peking, the very play that Yao Wen-yüan was to criticize in the first shot of the Cultural Revolution in November 1965.[71] Wu Han wrote the story "Hai Jui Deplores the Emperor" in the *People's Daily* of June 16, 1959, three days after P'eng Teh-huai returned from the Soviet Union and before the Lushan conference; he also wrote an essay "On Hai Jui" on September 21, 1959, while the Lushan conference was in session. He completed the seventh revision of the historical play, *Hai Jui Dismissed from Office*, on November 13, 1960, and published it in the *Peking Literature* in January 1961, which the Peking Opera troupe staged in February.

The story is worthy of brief account. Hai Jui was an honest and upright official of the Ming court. Of his various activities, Wu Han singled out his role in eliminating tyrants and returning the land confiscated by the tyrants to the peasants. The story took place when Hai Jui was serving as governor of Yingt'ing in Soochow (now Nanking) from June 1569 to January 1570. Wu Han's evil protagonist was a retired prime minister named Hsü Chieh. Hsü's third son, Hsü Ying, so the story went, encroached upon private land owned by a peasant called Chao Yu-shen; this caused the latter's only son to die of grief. On the Ch'ing-ming festival, Hsü Ying assaulted Chao and forcefully evicted his granddaughter, Chao Hsiao-lan. Infuriated by this, Chao Hsiao-lan's mother registered a complaint with the Magistrate Wang Ming-yu but Wang shielded Hsü at the court because he had been bribed by Hsü. Finally, Wang put Chao Yu-shen to death for lying. Dressed like an ordinary peasant, Hai Jui heard about this during one of his inspection trips. When Hai Jui made a courtesy call on Hsü Chieh, Hsü advised him to uphold the law vigorously. But when Hai Jui brought up Chao's case, Hsü flatly denied it. Later on, Hai Jui upheld the law by sentencing Hsü Ying to death. Only then did Hsü Chieh plead for mercy for his son, drawing on his old friendship with Hai Jui. Hai Jui rejected the plea. Hsü proposed to return the piece of land but Hai Jui rejected it. Finally, Hsü Chieh bribed a eunuch at the Ming court and had emperor Chia Ch'ing dismiss Hai Jui from office. Yet Hai Jui was scrupulously able to carry out the execution of Hsü Ying.[72]

Wu Han praised Hai Jui for his uprightness, farsightedness, and compassion for the people. In effect, he advocated the inheritance of old morality by saying: "the position of Hai Jui in history should be affirmed, and some of his good virtues are worthy of being learned by us today." Wu Han was not a professional playwright. Interestingly enough, he explained his motive for writing the play in Maoist terms: "Daring to think, speak, and act is a new style developed since the GLF. My script is also a product of daring to think, speak, and act."[73]

After Wu Han's play was published on January 2, 1961, Liao Mo-sha, director of the United Front Department of the Peking Municipal Committee, wrote in the *Peking Evening News:* "After the winter drums have sounded, the spring grass begins to grow. . . . An all-out effort will begin in spring." Liao also wrote a letter to Wu on February 16, which, it was alleged, congratulated him on "breaking through the door and dashing out" and proposed a division of labor between history and drama. Then, Wu replied to Liao: "May I suggest to you, brother, that you, too, break through the door and dash out." In March, Teng T'o, editor of *Frontline*, started writing a column, "Yen-shan yeh-hua" (Evening Chats at Yenshan) under the pen name of Ma Nan-ts'un because he was "compelled to mount a horse."[74] Between March 1961 and September 1962, Teng wrote 152 of these columns in the *Peking Evening News*.

On October 10, 1961, Wu Han, Teng T'o, and Liao Mo-sha launched together another column of commentaries in *Frontline* called "San-chia-ts'un ch'a-chi" (Notes from a Three-Family Village); this time the pen name was Wu-Nan-Shing, that is, Wu Han, Nan denoting the middle character of Teng T'o's pen name Ma Nan-ts'un, and Hsing, the last character of Liao's pen name, Fan Hsing. Thus came the formation of the "Three-Family Village"; they wrote, in all, sixty-seven pieces, from October 1961 through 1964.[75] According to one explanation given in *People's Daily*, Teng T'o chose the title from a poem written by Lu Yu who wrote in 1196: "Lost by chance the Marquis of ten thousand households, still can get hold of Three-Family Village."[76] Written during hard times, these columns, called "random comments" (tsa-wen), were mostly social criticism couched in ancient anecdotes or foreign fables. Thus, the formation of the "Three-Family Village" lent an aura of high purpose to their venture. Of three writers Teng T'o stood out as the most biting critic of the GLF in general and Mao's leadership in particular.

First of all, these writers questioned the ideological underpinnings of the Three Red Banners. Hitting at the basic premise of the GLF, Teng T'o castigated the idea of realizing communism through the development of the commune as substituting illusion for reality.[77] He narrated Mach's fable, which, incidentally, was also quoted by Lenin in his *Materialism and Empirical Criticism*, to satirize the Machian school's antiscientific theory:

Followers of Ernst Mach exaggerated the role of what they called the "psychological factor" and talked boastfully to their heart's content. Is this not the same as the titlark's nonsense about boiling the sea dry? Nevertheless, the *Machians imagined that through reliance on the role of the psychological factor they could do whatever they pleased, but the result was that they ran their heads against the brick wall of reality* and went bankrupt in the end.[78]

Commenting on Mao's accent upon thought reform, Teng implied that its overuse could be counterproductive: There was a strong energizer called "three-seven mountain medicine and field medicine"; if properly used, it could be very effective, but if overused, it was fatal.[79]

Equally critical was Teng's stricture on Mao's populism as reflected in the mobilization of labor. There was a passage in the *Book of Rites*, "One should use people's labor for no more than three days in a year," that Ch'en Ha, a scholar in the Yüan dynasty, interpreted to mean the use of labor for building walls, roads, ditches, palaces, and temples. Teng claimed that even the rulers during the Ch'un-ch'iu and the Warring States had discovered that corvée labor should not exceed 1 percent of the total labor force. He continued: "We of the 1960s in the twentieth century should understand it more clearly and should draw enlightenment from the experience of the ancients and take care to do more by all means to treasure our labor power."[80] Alluding to Mao's "poor and blank" thesis symbolizing change, Teng asked "If we are only satisfied with change as our purpose but do not care about what sort of change we want, it means that we only want change and take all changes as good. What sense does this make?"[81]

Perhaps the most humorous comment Teng offered was on the slogans of the GLF. He bluntly referred to them as "trumpet-blowing" and caricatured them in old stories. One of these was "A Fortune Built on One Egg," a story from the Ming dynasty.[82] This seems to have touched upon Mao's call that China must overtake Britain in fifteen years (during which time the fifteen years depend on the first five years and the five years the first three years, and so on). A poor peasant picked up an egg and made up his mind to make a fortune by raising chickens; the chickens would multiply over the years and he would buy cows; and finally, in ten years all the necessary steps would be taken and he would become rich. When he divulged this idea to his wife, he just could not help telling her that he would then be able to have a concubine. She was so angry at this that she crushed the egg. As the anger of the peasant's wife caused the whole dream to collapse, so it was suggested that the anger of the Chinese peasants had caused the GLF to collapse.

As for the commune, Teng, as did Wu Han, recommended that land be returned to the peasants.[83] In one column, he suggested two approaches in coping with problems: one was to block the path of the movement and development of things, and the other was to guide them actively so that they could proceed smoothly. The first was doomed to failure; therefore, he proposed to take the second attitude. As Yao Wen-yüan charged, this could have meant his support for facilitating, instead of blocking, san-tzu i-pao. As regards the half-work and half-study program, Teng implied that it destroyed individuality. For all people have individual identities that education should not weaken but develop.[84] In "Welcome the 'Miscellaneous Scholars,'" Teng praised those scholars in the Ch'un-ch'iu and Warring States era, saying: "It will be a great loss to us if we now fail to acknowledge the great significance of the wide range of knowledge of 'miscellaneous scholars' [tsa-chia] for all kinds of leadership work and scientific research work." Since the division of labor was clearer and more scientific in modern times, he asserted: "We need specialized knowledge and some general knowledge as well."[85]

Intellectually, these men of letters cried for a measure of freedom even within the framework of Communist ideology. The issue centered on historiography, and more specifically, how to evaluate past events and figures. Are they to be judged in the context of their times, or in the context of contemporary affairs? Are present standards to be applied to past acts? The problem was one of evaluating "middle characters" in history who made contributions to human progress but whose ideas were considered conservative by present standards. For example, Chien Po-tsan wrote: " 'Let theory guide history' is a slogan that is one-sided and wrong because it signified that historical research must proceed from theory or concept instead of from historical facts,

nor does it put the question in terms of classic Marxism-Leninism."
Historical study must reflect the spirit of policy, but this is not to say
that ancient history must be mixed up with present-day policy. Therefore, Chien asked: "How could we compel the ancient people to do
what we consider should be done today and prohibit them from doing
what we consider must not be done today?" Quoting from Marx,
Engel's *Anti-Düring*, Lenin, and Mao's *Selected Works*, he contended
that a Marxist historian should evaluate history from the proletarian
viewpoint; but at the same time, a historian should adhere to "histori-
calism." In this perspective, Chien was also known for the view that the
landlords in the feudal society did, in point of fact, make some concession to the peasants, and Fung Yu-lan also shared this view.[86]

Teng T'o's chiding of Mao's foreign policy was more straightforward. He characterized the statement about the East Wind prevailing
over the West Wind as great empty talk. "Some people are very elo-
quent and can talk on without stopping," he wrote. "After listening to
them, however, we always do not remember what they have talked
about." Recognizing that in certain special circumstances such empty
talk is inevitable, he went on: "It is rather terrible that such talks are
ubiquitous." As an example, Teng cited a poem allegedly composed by
a child in his neighborhood:

> The Sky is our father,
> The earth is our mother,
> The sun our nurse,
> The East wind our benefactor,
> The West wind our enemy.

The more high-sounding phrases like these are repeated, Teng claimed,
the greater the confusion. And he offered the following advice: "Read
more, think harder, and talk less. If you do want to talk, first take a
rest."[87]

In another column, Teng said that some people would not unite
with those who were stronger than they were. Citing the advice of a
scholar in the Sung dynasty, he wrote: "We should be pleased if a
friend is stronger than we are."[88] He made his point more explicit elsewhere: "If a man with a swelled head thinks he can learn a subject with
ease and kick his teacher out, he will never learn anything." In Yao
Wen-yüan's words, this was a "vicious attack" on Mao's struggle against
Soviet revisionism and "a demand that we ask the revisionists in and let
the wolves into the house."[89] More interesting was the article, "Gold
on a Golden Tortoise's Body." It seems more than just a coincidence
that the word Khrushchev in Russian (Хрушев) also means "May
tortoise." When Teng said that there was gold on this tortoise's body,

he apparently implied that the Chinese economy was so bad in 1961 that it needed Khruschev's aid.[90]

As for Party rule, Liao Mo-sha, writing in"Jokes about Being Afraid of Ghosts," praised Confucius for being democratic and welcoming criticism of his theories. He then derided some contemporary braggarts who claimed that they were not afraid of ghosts but were actually frightened.[91] Teng T'o also touched upon this in "The Royal Way and the Tyrant's Way." Even in ancient times the royal way (*wang-tao*) was superior to the tyrant's way (*pa-tao*) because the people could see at a glance how those who wished to be tyrants made enemies everywhere and became unpopular. By the *tyrant way* Teng meant the subjectivist and arbitrary way of thinking and style of work, bent on acting willfully. In another anecdote, he related:

By the time of the reign of Dowager Empress Ming Su, the Sung government was daily growing more corrupt. There was no intelligent and capable prime minister at the top with responsible assistants to take charge of personnel and administration, while the local officials lower down did exactly as they pleased.[92]

In "Is Wisdom Reliable?" Teng further elaborated this point by quoting from a scholar of the Sung dynasty:

When a man plans everything himself, flatterers will seize the chance to say things to please him. Some people always like to present their own ability and intelligence but look down upon the masses. No matter what they may do, they always regard themselves as important and try to achieve success with some original ideas but do not accept the masses' good advice from below. If people having this kind of shortcomings do not realize them and correct them, they will finally suffer a great blow one day.[93]

More vehement than this was Teng's depiction of such a man as suffering from amnesia. In "A Special Treatment for 'Amnesia,'" he wrote: "A man suffering from amnesia quite often forgets what he has said and forgets his promises by going back on his own word." "This will not only cause him to forget," he continued, "but will also cause him to experience abnormal pleasure or anger, causing him to have difficulty in finding words to express himself, making him lose his temper, and finally making him insane." A person with this disease must take a complete rest, should not talk or do anything, for if he insists on talking or doing something, he will run into trouble.[94] Perhaps addressing himself to Lin Piao's call for Mao study, Teng wrote these lines in "We Must Not Shout to Read Books":

Some people set aside days with plans to read books and teach others how to read them. In many cases they talk enthusiastically about the importance of reading. But if so much time and energy are spent in doing such things, it will result in fooling others and themselves. One needs not shout to read, nor will it do to make others read at any place. If one feels that he needs some knowledge, he can just go to a library and take the book he wants.[95]

It should be clear from reading between these lines that the intent of *Hai Jui* and the "Three-Family Village" was not so much their quest for artistic quality as their critique of GLF policies. Behind these writings lurked the profound disillusionment of these alienated literati with the way Mao had led the GLF. This is why the Maoists later labeled them "academic authorities" or "ghosts and monsters," charging that they attemped to form public opinion before undertaking a comeback through "peaceful evolution." It seems no exaggeration to say that the substance of those writings amounted to a de-Maoization of sorts, for, clearly, these intellectuals were no longer attached to Mao's ideology. That their veiled criticisms did not provoke a successful Maoist counter-attack *at that time* explains the circumstance under which they were written. There is little doubt, however, that Mao and his supporters were aware of them. As noted, not only did Chiang Ch'ing try to stop them but in March 1962, Yao Wen-yüan also attempted a counterattack. But Lin Mo-han dismissed Yao's critique as being oversimplified and rude.[96]

As soon as the political wind at the Center began to shift, however, there had to be a change in the literary circle as well. On the eve of the Tenth Plenum, Teng T'o wrote the last article in the "Evening Chat at Yenshan" entitled "Thirty-Six Stratagems" in which he declared: "Of all the thirty-six stratagems, to depart is best."[97] And in October he announced the suspension of the column altogether.

Party-State Leaders: Struggle Between Two Roads?

Although all aspects of the GLF except military and foreign policy had been reversed by the end of 1961, the specific direction and permissible extent of them was yet to be clarified. In 1962, this uncer-tainty led the top Party leaders to engage in debates.

Some of these debates occurred at the seven-thousand-cadre confer-ence of January 1962. In a written report to the conference, Liu Shao-ch'i set the basic tone of the debate. The point of departure was the appraisal of the current situation. Basically, Liu contended that the GLF was a failure: "In the last several years many shortcomings and mistakes have occurred in our work. The cadres and members of the whole Party and even the great majority of the people all have had personal painful experience of this. They have starved for two years."[98] And two months later, Liu concluded that the economy was still on the brink of collapse, for it could be hardly rehabilitated in seven or eight years even at the prompting of a decisive administration.[99] In May 1962 he again argued that the Center had not yet accurately assessed the gravity of the situation. On this point, Wang Kuang-mei admitted in 1967 that her husband had overestimated the difficulties in 1962.[100]

In contrast, Mao asserted at the seven-thousand-cadre conference that the difficult years were over. But Liu interpreted Mao to mean that the political situation was improving, for Liu saw no sign that the economic situation was better. In addition, Liu disagreed over how the Party should account for the depression. For the Party had given the masses only a partial explanation by attributing the crisis to climate, for fear of causing the cadres to lose their confidence in the Party. He saw in this neither genuine courage nor a Leninist attitude.[101]

Hence, a debate arose over why such a grave situation had come about. Again, Liu was quick to point out that the Center had to take the primary responsibility. To put this in perspective, he cited the peasants' views he had heard in Hunan: 30 percent of the difficulties were brought about by natural calamities and 70 percent were man made, an inversion of the official explanation.[102] He told the seven-thousand cadres that the Party had set up too many communes at one stroke, for attention was given only to faster and greater results and not to better and more economical results, and that things would certainly have been better without the communes.[103]

In response to this, Mao conceded that the prime responsibility lay with his leadership. He confessed that he had not really known as much about economy as he had told Edgar Snow in 1960. He argued, however, that the whole Party had lacked experience in construction and therefore was still groping for "our way without clear vision." Then he stressed a new theme: just as the Party had learned revolution in twenty-eight years, so had it to learn construction from practice. In stark contrast to 1958 when he had urged the Chinese to surpass Britain in fifteen years, he reminded the cadres of his talk with Marshal Montgomery in 1961 when he said that China needed at least one hundred years or more for industrialization.[104]

These questions led inevitably to another: what to do about the situation? Liu's prescription apparently was to do everything possible to restore a sound material base. He revived his thesis of 1956: "During the transitional period we may employ every possible means contributing to the mobilization of the productive enthusiasm of the peasants. We should not say that such and such a means is the best and the only one."[105] Concurring, Teng Hsiao-p'ing most succinctly stated this view at the Seventh Plenum of the Third Young Communist League (YCL) Central Committee in July: "So long as it raises output, 'going alone' is permissible. Whether cats are white or black, so long as they can catch mice, they are all good cats."[106] Liu and many others seemingly accepted *san-tzu i-pao* at least as a temporary measure.

The question of leadership was also raised as a main topic of the seven-thousand-cadre conference. Liu told the cadres:

We stirred up the "Communist style," thereby violating the principle of pay according to labor and the principle of exchange of equal values. . . .We arrived at decisions rashly and implemented them in wide areas. Moreover, things were done in short order. This was a violation of the principle of democratic centralism in Party life, the life of the State and the life of mass organizations. This is the basic cause of the serious mistakes which we committed in certain fields of work over the past several years.[107]

This cut to the core of the problem by suggesting that Mao's personalized decision-making disrupted democratic centralism and resulted in commandism among the local cadres. Liu allegedly went so far as to say that to oppose Mao was only to oppose an individual.[108] If true, this marked Liu's first open attack on Mao's leadership.

In answer to these criticisms, Lin Piao and Chou En-lai were said to have defended the GLF at the seven-thousand-cadre conference. Lin argued that since the Three Red Banners were unprecedented, the Party lacked experience in carrying them out, and that it was inevitable to have problems. Insisting that they were nevertheless correct, he championed again the Thought of Mao Tse-tung as "the soul and root of life"; hence the Party had to act according to Mao's instructions. Chou delivered a speech to "sum up the great achievements" of the GLF but what he said has not been disclosed.[109] In his speech on democratic centralism, Mao largely conceded the points Liu raised. He upheld the principle of collective leadership, saying that he did yield quite often to the majority view of the Politburo whether it was correct or not! But he placed more emphasis on democracy than Liu did. In the name of democracy, he had Liu's written report circulated among the cadres to seek their views. On the basis of their suggestions, the twenty-one member committee under Liu prepared the second draft of the report. He also warned that the word *separatism* should not be used indiscriminately. Perhaps this was a veiled critism of Liu, for he said that he was actually criticizing "some comrades without naming anyone."[110]

Lastly, Liu and Teng put a brake on "brutal Party struggle." Liu stated: "We fear that if we go too far, we may again label many as dispersionist. This time we must not do the same thing again, nor must we do so in the future."[111] He maintained that the anti-rightist struggle after the Lushan plenum had gone too far. As a result, there was no exchange of opinions between the top and the bottom and many issues had remained unresolved. Then, he decreed that anyone who had views similar to P'eng Teh-huai's but no illegal relations with a foreign country might have his verdict reversed, and that those who spoke at Party meetings would not be punished. In reference to this, Mao admitted that certain cadres had been handled wrongly, but he contended that demotion could be beneficial at times to temper revolutionary will.

In February 1962 the Party Center convened an enlarged meeting of the Politburo at the *Hsi-lou* building of Chungnanhai to deal with the direction of the new economic policy. Reporting on the findings of the Five-Man Finance Group to the meeting, Ch'en Yün pictured a bleak state of the economy. Due to the decline of agricultural production, food and goods were in short supply. Millions of *mou* of fertile soil were wasted; pigs could not be raised because of inadequate feed; farm implements had become unusable; and even seed grains were in short supply. Yet the efforts in industrial construction were still excessive; the stock of materials and labor declined. This led to inflation as money flowed from the cities to the countryside, causing speculation there. Worst of all, the government's financial deficit had soared to two billion yüan in the previous four years. Liu Shao-ch'i, Teng Hsiao-p'ing, and Li Hsien-nien agreed with this appraisal. The Party Center approved of the report and disseminated it to the provinces.[112]

As for the remedy, Ch'en Yün went farther than any other leader by saying that Teng Tzu-hui's idea of fixing output quotas for households was not enough. He asked that land be redistributed to the households. When someone asked him how he would justify this in terms of Mao's Thought, he replied: "After all, the People's Republic will last ten thousand years! We can try once more later." Teng Hsiao-p'ing agreed with Ch'en Yün, arguing that there was really no difference between fixing output for the households in Anhui and private farming. Teng regarded the practice of going it alone as a necessary step for going a step forward later.[113]

Against this background, the revised version of Liu's *How to Be a Good Communist* appeared on August 1, 1962. The new edition distinguished itself in its severe criticism of dogmatism and its emphasis on the need for different opinions within the Party.[114] Liu deplored such dogmatism in the following way:

Under any circumstances it is necessary to carry out an inner-Party struggle, and the fiercer it is, the better. They raised everything and anything to the "plane of principle," and they blame any small shortcomings on political "opportunism" and the line. They do not appropriately and concretely carry out the inner-Party struggle in accordance with objective needs and the law governing the development of objective things. Rather, they carry out the struggle mechanically, subjectively, rudely, and without regard for consequence.[115]

Liu stressed this point by adding an entirely new sentence: "The Left opportunists were clearly wrong in their attitude toward an inner-Party struggle." As in 1941, he distinguished questions regarding the plane of principle and questions of a purely practical nature: the former were questions of class struggle and the latter were questions of right and wrong in objective reality. And he was adamantly opposed to raising questions of principle for a purely practical problem. He also called upon the cadres to be good pupils of Marxism-Leninism, stating that the Communist must be able to make timely change in strategy and tactics to meet changing circumstances.[116] In 1967, Liu rejected the Maoist charge that he revised the book to usurp power by pointing out that the revision was actually made by someone else.[117]

Mao was well aware of these trends of ideological erosion, *san-tzu i-pao*, the "Three Family Village," and the "reversal wind," but not until the Politburo meeting at Peitaiho in August 1962 did he interfere with the way in which these issues had been handled. A passage in Liu's self-criticism made in 1966 threw more light on the relationship between Mao and Liu:

In the summer of 1962, at the Peitaiho conference, I committed the error of leaning toward the rightist line. After having returned to Peking, the Chairman undertook drafting the decision on further developing and consolidating the collective economy and the decision on commerce. Also at this conference, he brought up class struggle and contradictions. In September, the Tenth Plenum was held and it passed the decisions and a communique; only then were my errors corrected and the situation changed fundamentally.[118]

The Peitaiho conference was a work conference, lasting a month, which discussed problems of agriculture, commerce, industry, and Party unity. Ch'en Po-ta reported on agriculture, Li Hsien-nien on commerce, and Li Fuch'un and possibly Po I-po on planning. The conference also discussed the expansion of the control commission and the transfer of cadres.[119] When Li Hsien-nien advocated the unified supply of commodities under state control, Ch'en Po-ta voiced his opposition because it was against the mass line. Then, Mao criticized the spread of *san-tzu i-pao* and its supporters, such as Ch'en Yün and Li Hsien-nien. He derided the Ministry of Commerce as "Ministry of Destruction" and the State Planning Commission as well as the State Economic Commission as "independent kingdoms," asking them to go down to the countryside to make revolution.[120]

Clearly, Mao was questioning the current course of policy, but on the other hand, he presented no alternative. In a speech on the current situation, contradictions, and class struggle, he instead raised an ideological specter. He sternly warned the Party to never forget class struggle, and reiterated his enduring theme on this issue:

Socialist society is a fairly long historical stage. During this historical stage, classes, class contradictions and class struggle continue to exist, the struggle between the road of socialism and the road of capitalism goes on and the danger of a capitalist restoration remains. It is necessary to recognize the protracted and complex nature of this struggle.[121]

With this as his rationale, Mao called for socialist education. By suggesting that the current intra-Party debates were a struggle between the two roads, he began a counterattack upon his critics.

In September 1962 the Central Committee called its Tenth Plenum in Peking to transform the minutes of the Peitaiho conference into the Party line. In his speech to this plenum, Mao repeated a number of themes from his Peitaiho remarks. The communique of the plenum stated that class struggles inevitably find their expression within the Party due to the pressures from imperialism abroad and bourgeois influence at home. The prevention of capitalist restoration required the Party to be continuously vigilant against various opportunist ideological tendencies in the Party.[122] Mao also perceived the Sino-Soviet disputes as part of the class struggle, that is, the problem of struggle between Marxism-Leninism and revisionism.[123]

Mao then put an end to the reversal wind. First, he made some conciliatory remarks to the rightists:

I welcome several of the comrades here. . . .I wish to advise our comrades that even if you have conspired with foreign countries, if you will expose everything and speak out truthfully, we would welcome you, and also give you work to do and never take the attitude of apathy. Nor would we adopt the method of execution.[124]

He hedged this, however, with a warning: "The recent vogue of rehabilitation is not correct," for only individual rehabilitation could be made. The communique of the Tenth plenum reaffirmed the notion that the Lushan Plenum correctly smashed attacks by Right opportunism, that is, revisionism.[125]

As for the intellectuals' criticism of his policies, Mao had the following to say:

Isn't the writing of novels very popular now? To utilize novels to engage in antiparty activities is a great invention. In order to overthrow any political power, one must first create public opinion and engage in ideological and philosophical work. This applies to the revolutionary class as well as to the counter-revolutionary class.[126]

Lastly, the communique was insistent that "the broad masses and cadres of our country have always believed in the correctness of the general line for socialist construction, the big leap forward, and the people's commune—the three red banners."[127]

While the Tenth Plenum reaffirmed the bulk of Mao's ideological line, it also legitimized most of the adjustment policies by adopting three documents: (1) the resolution on strengthening collective economy, (2) the revised draft of the Sixty Articles on Agriculture, and (3) the decision on commerce. Unlike Mao's Twelve-Year Agricultural Program, the resolution anticipated that the basic completion of technical reform in agriculture would require four- or five-year plans; it also promised to stabilize the ratio of agricultural tax and procurement at an appropriate level. Although the decision on commerce has not been made available, according to the resolution on collective economy, the Party apparently adopted Ch'en Yün and Li Hsien-nien's idea of unified supply of commodities.[128]

The revised Sixty Articles clearly designated the production team as the basic accounting unit, made allowances for smaller communes, discouraged commune enterprises, increased the scope of private plots from 5 to 7 percent of the arable land, and sanctioned the fixing of output quotas to small groups. These measures made it clear that Mao only succeeded in arresting the drift toward *san-tzu i-pao*, thus preventing it from further slipping into private farming; but in doing so, he accepted all other practices of the commune, even beyond the 1961 commune charter. The 1962 charter further stipulated that the refurbished team should not be changed for at least thirty years![129]

Finally, the Tenth Plenum endorsed the Party-state authority structure that had taken shape in the course of adjustment. Its resolution stated that agricultural development must be carried out under uniform Central Committee policies and uniform national planning. Indeed, in the two years after 1960, the State Planning Commission almost doubled its size by adding seven more members. The plenum also strengthened the Party control commissions, the Central Control Commission in particular, by establishing a new standing committee and tripling the membership of the commission. The plenum elected Lu Ting-yi, K'ang Sheng, and Lo Jui-ch'ing as new members of the Secretariat while dismissing Huang K'o-ch'eng and T'an Cheng.[130]

THE ADJUSTMENTS AND THEIR LEGACIES, 1959-62

Since these adjustments were necessitated by the collapse of the GLF, a comparative study of the GLF and accomodations to it will illustrate how the practice of the adjustments diverged from the GLF and the legacy it left in the subsequent years, particularly the appearance of three major trends, which seem to be juxtaposed to those of the GLF: the application of sequential development, the appearance of an institutionalizing polity, and the rise of an operational ideology that justified the policy changes.

Policy: From Simultaneous Development to Sequential Development

As the Party became preoccupied with increasing agricultural production, the GLF strategy of simultaneous development gave way to that of sequential development: Agriculture as the Foundation and Industry as the Leading Factor. To cope with the economic crisis facing it, the Party was forced to re-evaluate its priorities and thereby to focus only upon the most urgent goals; it could only service a hierarchy of goals in sequence, thus incrementally adjusting the goals to the changing reality. The direction of adjusted communes provides a vivid illustration of this change: the five functions they had combined in 1958 (agriculture, industry, commerce, education, and the military) became redifferentiated as they concentrated their administrative energy upon grain production.

The basic goal of adjustment policy was·to make the communes more efficient and productive. Such management practices as awarding work points, providing material incentives, and establishing differential work assignments, stemmed from the quest for efficiency. From this fact, the CCP learned a lesson: intensive mobilization programs and organizational inputs can compensate for the lack of other resources in production but there are limits to the endeavors beyond which only the increase of material and technological inputs can raise productivity. As the promotion of productive forces was given the foremost priority, revolution—changing attitudes and developing productive relations—had to be put aside at least for the time being, and economics, rather than politics, took command. In 1966, Wang Jen-chung, first secretary of Hupeh, aptly recalled this period: "It was principally in 1961 and 1962 that we did not do a good job in putting politics in command or did nothing to put politics in command." And at the Eleventh Plenum in 1966, Mao himself asserted that a Right deviation had existed in this period.[131]

Policy Process: From Mass Polity to an Institutionalizing Polity

In the course of making such adjustments, the Party Center gradually turned away from the erratic mass polity of the GLF and consolidated the institutional arrangements of the policy process developed in the post-Leap period. In many ways, the policy apparatus had the qualities that Huntington attributed to an institutionalized polity: it was coherent, autonomous, complex, and adaptive.[132]

There were several key elements in this authority structure. First was the recentralizing of authority, for in order to give coherence to the adjustments, especially from the Peitaiho conference of 1960 on, the

Party Center re-established a firm grip over the policy process. Subsequently, the Ninth Plenum legislated guidelines to make adjustments take place under central direction. Since then, the Party Center has carried out policy reviews and codified their findings into central directives. The loci of decisions was the Politburo's Standing Committee and Secretariat. These higher level machineries functioned under a collective leadership headed by Liu Shao-ch'i and Teng Hsiao-p'ing. Mao seemed to have withdrawn from operational decisions after the Peitaiho conference of 1960; this made it easy for the Party Center to adjust policy in a more regularized manner.

A second characteristic of the national policy-making mechanism was a growing specialization, for a division of labor at the Center had become apparent by 1962. In economic affairs, the reactivated Ch'en Yün headed the Five-Man Finance Group, which carried out an over-all review; Li Fu-ch'un and Po I-po resumed their leadership in planning; T'an Chen-lin, Liao Lu-yen, and Ch'en Cheng-jen took charge of agriculture; Po I-po and Yu Ch'iu-li, industry; and Li Hsien-nien and Yao Yi-lin, finance and trade. As for culture and education, P'eng Chen led the team comprised of Lu Ting-yi, Chou Yang, Hu Ch'iao-mu, Yang Hsiu-feng, and Chiang Nan-hsiang. As for the Party and security operation, Teng Hsiao-p'ing led the team of Liu Lan-t'ao, An Tzu-wen, Hsieh Fu-chih, and Yang Shang-k'un. Each of the ten secretaries of the Secretariat also assumed a special task.[133] It would seem—and Mao's supporters certainly later argued—that this specialization introduced a note of autonomy to the policy process, with each system of specialists having a measure of independence in their realm.

A third aspect of this policy process was that decisions were reached through a complex process of consensus building. In fact, two slightly different types of policy processes evolved, one for general problems embracing all localities (such as general economic policy, agriculture, cadre problems, and ideology), and the other for specialized policy areas (such as industry, culture, and education). Both processes involved the Party's use of a forum called the central work conference that came into prominence during this period. Formulating policies for general and nationwide problems necessarily involved compromises between the Center's demands and the locale's capabilities and responses. For example, the policy of Agriculture as the Foundation evolved out of such processes when it was adopted at the central work conference at Peitaiho in August 1960, which the Peking conference in January 1961 further discussed, and the Ninth Plenum formally ratified. Participants in these general conferences seem to have varied but may have included members of the Politburo and the Secretariat, responsible heads of the central departments and the State Council, first secretaries of the regional bureaus and the provincial committees, and representatives of the PLA commands.[134]

The Party also used such conferences to make existing practices legitimate by issuing directives approving them. Directives on communes were a case in point. In November 1960 the Party Center issued the Twelve Articles ratifying the measures that had sprung up in the countryside. Then, the Canton conference of March 1961 expanded the Twelve Articles into the Draft [ch'ao-an] of Sixty Articles on Agriculture. The Politburo's Standing Committee apparently initiated the ideas and the Secretariat then convened the conference to prepare the draft. At these conferences, substantive discussions were held, regional and local activities were coordinated, and conflicts were resolved. The results of the conference discussions were summarized, with policy recommendations; they were then submitted as a draft report to the Standing Committee for its approval. If approved, the Secretariat transmitted the draft through the Party's regular policy apparatus. Unlike the GLF, the press did not play a major role in this; in fact, it reported very little about this draft. And implementing policy by such stipulated rules and procedures tended to be a routine matter rather than a means of mobilizing support for policy.

Policy making and implementation were closely related in this process. Indeed, policy was also made in the course of its implementation. Once a draft was transmitted, local cadres were in a position to judge its feasibility. Thus its implementation was constrained by local conditions. This process fell into two categories. First, the localities in general, that is, the plane, more or less evenly implemented the draft—a practice known as "running on the plane" (p'ao-mien); second, the Party Center selected some special spots and allowed those places to carry out calculated experimentation under central or provincial direction or by squatting some work teams there—a practice known as "squatting on the spots" (tun-tien). With respect to the Draft of Sixty Articles on Agriculture, Anhui and Honan experimented with variants of san-tzu i-pao. The combined efforts at the plane as well as the spots provided the Center with more accurate information. On the basis of a prediction of risks and costs made available by the new information, the Center amended the draft into the revised draft (hsiu-cheng ch'ao-an) in September 1962. In contrast to the situation during the GLF, where the policymaker (Mao) resorted to an erratic pattern of formulating policy and mobilizing support, responding only to the necessary information (and as a result, needing less consensus), during this adjustment period the policymakers somehow resumed a more regular process as they could acquire more accurate information and reach a greater consensus. The CCP learned another lesson that in order for organizational changes and mass mobilization to be effective they must be properly implemented in light of local conditions.

But local variations in implementation and diverging outlooks among the leadership invariably caused policy debates at the central level. For example, when many localities hankered for *san-tzu i-pao* and some central leaders supported them, Mao decided the situation was getting out of hand. Since such policy differences could only be resolved at the highest level, the Party convened another central work conference for this purpose. It was at this level that ideology was one of the most important constraining influences on policy, although the final outcome was predicated upon the relative power of those involved. At the Peitaiho conference of August 1962, Mao vetoed the current quest for *san-tzu i-pao* by making an ideological appeal for class struggle. And the Tenth Plenum ratified the revised draft of the Sixty Articles.

Another variation of the policy process occurred in a more specialized manner, where localities or functional organizations were concerned. Here policy was shaped through interactions between the Party-state authorities and the relevant constituencies. The Secretariat or the concerned central departments usually initiated ideas and organized task forces to investigate the policy options through such devices as squatting at the spots—in factories, schools, and so on. In preparing draft regulations, the Party Department convened more specialized central work conferences, attended by the relevant Party and state functionaries and representative practitioners such as managers, educators, and writers. After having implemented the draft for a certain period, the department solicited more suggestions from such functional organizations as schools or such professional organizations as the Writers Association, and then incorporated them into a revised draft. In this way, the Peitaiho conference of August 1961 produced the Seventy Articles on Industry and the Sixty Articles on Higher Education. In similar fashion, those conferences sponsored by the Propaganda Department in 1961 produced the Ten Articles on Literature and Arts, and their revision into the Eight Articles. Thus, the policy process involved constant and incremental adjustments among the participants in it.

The sum total of these developments was that intricate policy-making and implementing institutions were interposed between those at the pinnacle of power and the masses. It was almost impossible to obtain the kind of direct mass participation that Mao had urged in the GLF. The masses could participate only in a differentiated manner, more on some issues and less on others, and indirectly through a hierarchy of specialized organizations. What emerged then was an institutionalizing polity; its distinguishing feature, in contrast to a mass polity, was the institutional links that, to a degree, stabilized the relationship between the elite and the masses. In case these institutions failed to meet expectations, the architects of the recovery would seek a remedy through organizational reforms rather than ideological rectification, and would move to coopt diverse elements into such organizational frameworks rather than to train political activists.

However, where Mao's influence in the arena of policy making was concerned, it should be noted that approximately from this time on, Mao exerted, for the most part, a veto power on existing policy by challenging rather than redefining it, for he was divorced from the realm of operational decisions and their implementing instrumentalities. Hence even the new policy Mao upheld had to go through the Party's regular institutional frameworks, were it to be implemented. This, however, occurred neither through a conspiracy nor through a usurpation of the Party leadership by Liu Shao-ch'i, for, as he confessed in 1966, Liu's responsibility at the Center was such that he let others propose policy innovations at the central conferences he presided over while Mao was absent in Peking. Mao himself acknowledged his own responsibility because he voluntarily proposed the division of the Politburo. Hence, he could not entirely blame Liu Shao-ch'i and Teng Hsiao-p'ing in 1966. He was aware, perhaps correctly, that, since the division of responsibility, the central leadership had been scattered and the leaders at the first line, particularly Teng Hsiao-p'ing, no longer consulted him on vital issues and had set up independent kingdoms.[135]

Ideology: From Uninterrupted Revolution to Stage-by-Stage Revolution

The Party's ideological pronouncements had to justify the changes in its policies and institutional processes. As the ideology of the GLF was confronted by harsh reality, it perforce underwent internal adjustments. The Wuhan Resolution of December 1958 had already made an ideological retreat from uninterrupted revolution to revolution by stages, by warning against the Utopian dream of skipping the socialist stage. The antirightist campaign in 1959-60 saw a brief revival of the commune movement, but with the enactment of the Twelve Articles in November 1960 the original form of the commune ceased to exist. From that time on, the practice in commune management so diverged from the Party's official ideology that few cadres and peasants took it seriously. In 1961, not only did the local cadres voice open complaints

but some outspoken intellectuals went so far as to vilify Mao's ideological exhortations as being empty talk or vulgar. As soon as Party
leaders began to question the basic premises of the GLF, ideological
erosion became apparent among the peasants, the cadres, the intellectuals, and the top Party leaders.

It was against this background that the Ninth Plenum adopted the
slogan of Readjusting, Consolidating, Filling Out, and Raising Standards. This slogan served as an operational ideology that enabled the
Party Center to pursue its goal of restoring economic order with whatever means it had at its disposal. Faced with this crisis, the CCP had to
shelve the goal-oriented programs of the GLF in order to concentrate
its efforts on solving pressing problems simply to survive. At this point,
its operational code for the adjustments ceased to be useful for defining
long-term Communist ends; for it sought to ascertain the most effective
means for solving current problems, choosing ends appropriate to available means. The operational leaders at the Center under Liu Shao-ch'i
apparently stressed the integrative, legitimizing, and control function of
ideology rather than stressing such functions as orientation, motivation,
and socialization. Basically, they approached problems pragmatically: if
external changes forced practice to depart from ideological imperatives,
they adapted the ideology to the practice.[136]

Clearly, what emerged from these adjustments was the antithesis of
the GLF. The policy reversal, the loss of Mao's authority in the policy
process, and the ideological erosion left a profound legacy in Chinese
politics after 1962. Nevertheless, at the Tenth Plenum, Mao reasserted
his ideological beliefs. Thus, of the two trends that had emerged in
1960-62—the ideological revitalization movement promoted by Lin
Piao within the PLA and the policy adjustments by Liu Shao-ch'i within the Party-state apparatus—Mao gave more impetus to the former. Yet
Mao could not change either the existing policy practices or the current
cast of the Party's top leadership, for his GLF had turned out to be a
colossal failure, while the adjustments carried out under Liu's leadership proved to be successful in weathering the crisis created by the
GLF. These contrasting developments led to a widening gulf between
Maoist ideology and Party practice in the policy process. In the long
run, the ensuing divergence of ideology and practice became a focal
point of the adjustments in the subsequent political development
eventually leading to the Cultural Revolution.

PART III
The Policy Process in Crisis
1962-1966

Leading the mass movement must take place within the framework of the Communist Party and must not be left to the hands of bad elements. Those who oppose us can do so from the Right as well as from the Left. You must bear this problem in mind.

Liu Shao-ch'i, 1964

In the final analysis, all truths of Marxism can be summed up in one sentence: Rebellion is justified.

Mao Tse-tung, 1966

5

The Party's Socialist Education Movement

The adjustments in 1959-62 inevitably had many consequences that increasingly undermined Mao's version of Chinese communism. In an attempt to reverse some undesirable results as he perceived them, in 1962-66 Mao initiated the Socialist Education Movement (SEM), endorsed the army's emulation campaigns, introduced a series of reforms in education, health care, and culture to promote equality and self-reliance. As the Party Center tried to preserve the policy course harnessed in 1959-62, the conflicts between Mao's efforts and the Party's responses intensified in 1962-66. The Soviet Union's pressure in 1965-66 to form a united action with China in response to the American escalation of the Vietnam War enhanced Mao's fear of revisionism. As his final resort to fight these internal and external challenges to his authority in 1965-66, Mao decided to carry out the Cultural Revolution.

Thus, Part 3 is devoted to explaining the policy process through which the Cultural Revolution evolved in 1962-66. We shall first analyze how the Party carried out its SEM and the army its emulation campaigns in two separate chapters, contrasting their diverging approaches. In the following two chapters we shall delineate the substantive issues at conflict among the Party leadership, focusing on the policy differences between Liu and Mao in the areas of the economy, education, health care, and culture to see how these conflicts developed into the Cultural Revolution.

As was the case in 1959-62, the Party and the army again sought diverging orientations toward the solution of the problems created by the adjustments. Following the Tenth Plenum, two approaches—the institutional and the mobilizational—acquired organizational identity in adapting to changes generated by the consolidation measures of 1959-62. In response to Mao's call for the SEM, the Party adopted the institutional approach, trying to cope with the problems through organizational processes. But in the army-initiated emulation campaigns, the army's leadership was still relying upon mass persuasion and campaigns. Evaluating the Party's performance, Mao noticed a trend toward the bureaucratization of policy processes. To counter this he championed the army's campaigns. To explain this development we start with an analysis of the SEM.

THE BACKGROUND, 1962-63

After Mao called for a widespread adoption of the methods and aims of socialist education at the Peitaiho conference in August 1962, which the Tenth Plenum reaffirmed, the Party soon launched the Socialist Education Movement. In accord with this movement Mao formulated two documents: the first in May 1963, and the last in December 1964. The Party Center also formulated two documents: one in September 1963, and the other in September 1964. In the course of formulating these documents and revising them, it became apparent that Mao and the Party Center had different orientations toward the SEM.

In the fall of 1962, provincial Party committees convened "three-level" conferences of their own staff, the special districts, and the hsien to transmit the decisions of the Tenth Plenum. During the winter of 1962 and the spring of 1963, hsien committees in turn held three-level conferences of their own staff, commune cadres, and brigade cadres to transmit and explain the decisions. These decisions were aimed at strengthening the communes and making them observe the revised 1962 commune charter to its letter, thereby curbing the drift toward *san-tzu i-pao*. They also called for carrying out investigations on rural conditions.[1]

The Party acquired alarming information as a result of these investigations. First and foremost were disclosures about ideological erosion among the local cadres and the peasants, coupled with their loss of confidence in the Party. When the Tenth Plenum reaffirmed the correctness of the Three Red Banners, few cadres took it seriously. To them, the agricultural situation had not yet been restored to pre-GLF levels, and recent improvements, if any, were primarily due to the reintroduction of "four treasures": private plots, private reclamation, the family side-line occupation, and the free market.[2]

The investigations also revealed that former landlords and rich peasants were taking advantage of a difficult situation. In the Lienchiang hsien, Fukien, the poor peasants were told: "You work so hard but get so little food. If you go to work on your own, you will be rich in one or two years."[3] Some of them actually either assumed leadership positions in the production teams or formed intimate ties with the cadres. Besides the emergence of this old bourgeoisie, the reports disclosed that a new polarization among the peasants was developing, mainly due to the rise of well-to-do middle-class peasants (*fu-yü chung-nung*). The work-point system enabled households with a larger labor force—usually middle-class peasants—to earn more income, while those with aged dependents became poorer. Some of the cadres recruited during the land reform, cooperativization, and communization drives had become just the upper middle peasants.

The surveys of rural conditions indicated that all these factors undermined the collective economy. Probably the majority of the cadres and of the peasants (including the poor peasants) wanted temporarily even more small freedoms to help solve the food crisis. In a survey of the Ha-wu brigade of the Lien-chiang hsien, 57 percent were vacillating, and only 25 percent opposed the practice of these "freedoms."[4] And over 70 percent of team land in the Chengpei communes near Shanghai was held by the rich and well-to-do peasants in 1963.[5] Another report from Fukien's Lien-chiang hsien listed these arguments for individual farming: (1) it facilitated business operation and management; (2) it increased production and hence overcame difficulties; (3) the masses wanted it; (4) it stimulated labor enthusiasm; and (5) it meant less trouble for the cadres.[6]

The investigations of 1962-63 also discovered that the rural leadership was in shambles. The local cadres themselves shared the above views about private farming; more generally, over half of the cadres in Lien-chiang were found to have problems of one kind or another. These problems included such acts as misappropriation of work points and public funds, throwing of dinner parties, building houses with public funds, speculation, and even arrangement of marriages by sale. Most perplexing of all, many people refused to become cadre members because a member did not earn extra income legally and faced constant trouble and sacrifices.[7] The basic-level cadre members were caught, then, in a crossfire between the Party and the peasants. They had few incentives to act, but if anything went wrong, they shouldered the blame. Therefore, once the Party's pressure eased, they were prone to complacency.

Basically, the cadres were responding to the Party's instructions after 1960 to eliminate all Communist and commandist styles. In fact, they even rebuffed their erstwhile allies. For example, when the poor peasants protested against individual farming, the cadres threatened them: "If you do not agree [with individual farming,] we will be asking you for food to eat when production decreases." To many cadres, individual farming was not a class struggle but simply a way to eat well.[8] The basic-level cadres were indeed muddling through the crisis in a pragmatic way. A passage in the report on the rural situation in Hunan (which Mao endorsed in February 1963) described this atmosphere succinctly: "Some comrades have put it well in saying 'How can we achieve socialist construction when everywhere peaceful coexistence prevails in politics, the prevalent attitude is of muddling through in organization, and of doing things so and so (ma-ma-hu-hu) in economics?'" After reading the report, Mao warned: "If things were allowed to go on this way, the day would not be too far off. . . . when the resurgence of a nationwide counterrevolution becomes inevitable." He then went on to say: "the Party of Marxism and Leninism would turn into a party of revisionism and of Fascism. The whole of China would then change color. Let all fellow comrades give it a thought. Isn't that a most dangerous situation! "[9]

To study these reports from the rural areas, the Party convened a central work conference in February 1963. As Ch'en Po-ta intimated in 1967, Mao tried to return to the fore at this February meeting.[10] He personally read each report and made class struggle the quintessence of the SEM. While introducing the experience of Hunan and Hopei, he commented: "Once class struggle is grasped, miracles are possible."[11] In May 1963, another central work conference at Hangchow studied more rural reports, this time twenty-two documents submitted by various units ranging from the communes to the regional bureaus. Mao selected representative examples of rural work from these documents and directed that they be incorporated into a document called Draft Resolution of the Central Committee of the Chinese Communist Party on Some Problems in Current Rural Work."[12] By issuing instructions on the Socialist Education Movement in May 1963, Mao urged the Party to undertake "the first great struggle since land reform." He planned to carry out such a struggle from within the Party to the outside, from the top to the bottom, and from the cadre to the masses. Thus, the target of this new movement as Mao saw it was the Party's leading cadres at the hsien and communes. In a speech he made at the Hangchow conference, Mao also revealed that the need for "four cleanup" was found by the Paoting Special District Party Committee in Hopei during its investigation between February and May. When the committee went down to the basic level in order to investigate distribution problems, the masses asked for such cleanup to weed out corruption and complacency among the local cadres. If these errors were unchecked, Mao contended that the Communist cadres would not be different from the Kuomintang's *pao-chia* leaders. To make these cadres serve the masses instead of the authorities, Mao called for the SEM by drawing the Draft Resolution.[13]

<h2 style="text-align:center">MAO'S FORMER TEN POINTS</h2>

The May 1963 document, known later as the Former Ten Points, set forth Mao's correct line on rural work. It professed to summarize the thirteen years of practice and particularly the three years of experience since the appearance of the twelve-article directive in 1960. Thus, the Former Ten Articles represented Mao's analysis of those pressing problems confronting the Party.

The preamble of the document embodied Mao's essay, "Where Do Correct Ideas Come from?" According to Mao, correct theories and policies can only come from repeated practice and from dialectical interaction between ideas and existence. But many cadres did not understand this theory of knowledge. To educate them in the dialectical method of analysis was the main problem, for "once the correct ideas characteristic of the advanced classes are grasped by the masses, these ideas turn into a material force that changes society and changes the world." Nothing can better explain the goal of the SEM than this underlying assumption of Mao. From it derived his evaluation of the rural situation. The situation had greatly improved due to the Party's correct policy; the pessimistic views of some were ill-founded. Repeating his Tenth Plenum injunction that classes exist in the transitional period, Mao saw the manifold rural problems as indication of severe and sharp class struggle; yet some comrades had not fully understood the seriousness of such a hostile situation.[14] He regarded the SEM as "a struggle that calls for the 're-education of man,'" a struggle for reorganizing the revolutionary class armies. In lieu of the Three Red Banners, he laid down another theme: "class struggle, production struggle, and scientific experiment are the three great revolutionary movements that build up a powerful socialist nation. They are a guarantee for the Communists to do away with bureaucratism, to avoid revisionism and dogmatism, to stand externally invincible."[15]

As to the correct method and policy for carrying out the movement, this document clearly reflected Mao's preferences.[16] After some spot-testing, the SEM was to be universally carried out in all areas to demarcate antagonistic contradictions between friends and foes and nonantagonistic contradictions among the people. To restore the peasants' confidence in the Party, the Former Ten Points called for intensified education about Party resolutions and regulations. The directive commended the Honan experiment for encouraging the peasants to write their own "four histories"—those of their own commune, brigades, land reform, and collectivization. This was intended to demonstrate to the younger generation that the fruit of revolutionary struggle did not come easily. As for the comeback of former landlords and rich peasants, and the subsequent rural polarization, this document urged the Party to set up organizations of poor and lower-middle peasants, following the lead in Hopei. The committees of these organizations were to attend the meetings of the commune management committees as observer. And to curb individual farming, the directive called for strict execution of the 1962 Revised Sixty Articles on Agriculture.

The May 1963 directive also dealt with basic-level cadre corruption. It sanctioned the four cleanup campaign, to correct cadre abuse of account books, warehouses, property, and work points, emulating the example of Paoting Special District in Hopei. This campaign intended to unify over 95 percent of the mass *and* the cadres against the estimated 5 percent of "unclean" cadres, for the great majority of the cadres were considered good. It recommended education and persuasion rather than punishment for the erring cadres so that they might "wash hands and bodies." In addition, the directive instructed local cadres to participate in collective production, and, following the example of Chekiang and Shansi, to go down to the villages to remain there for a prolonged period (termed "squatting at a point") and to carry out investigation. The Party demanded that local units give top priority to the four-cleanup campaign. It asked them to plan activities well in advance, expecting the movement to be successfully completed in three years and to produce revamped basic-level organizations. In short, the SEM was to be a large-scale movement of the masses.

Comprehensive as it was, the Former Ten Points were framed in general terms and lacked an operational strategy or specific leadership and organizational guidelines concerning precisely how the directive was to be implemented. The document was transmitted to the communes, but it failed to trigger a large-scale mass campaign, for, since the anticommandist campaign in 1960-62, the local cadres had become cautious and were on their guard against excesses. The May 1963 directive was *not* the object of special study at the basic level, as was sometimes the case with important directives. The class education begun after the Tenth Plenum continued, however. In Kwangtung, many brigades began to organize the poor and lower-middle peasants' small groups under the direction of the Party branches. They stepped up the movement to unify the peasants, recalling past sufferings and comparing them with the current life, lest their past be forgotten. In the model Shengshih brigade in Chungshan hsien, for example, a special room exhibited all traces of the peasants' bitter experiences with their landlords before 1949.[17]

Through this class education, the Party hoped to stem the tide of assigning work to households and of redistributing land. A much tougher problem was the rectification of the unclean basic-level cadres. The results of spot-testing in the first half of 1963 showed that the movement had not penetrated the basic level because of its lack of leadership and organization.[18]

THE SECRETARIAT'S LATER TEN POINTS

The lack of organizational strategy in the Former Ten Points had to be supplanted by more concrete measures if they were to be implemented. Four months after Mao's first document, the Party put forth the Later Ten Points entitled Some Concrete Policy Formulations of the Central Committee of the Chinese Communist Party in the Rural Socialist Education Movement.[19] The editorial of the *People's Daily* for November 23, 1967, stated that this was drafted by "another top capitalist roader in the Party," a designation for Teng Hsiao-p'ing. However, Liu Shao-ch'i's first self-criticism made in 1966 stated that some leading comrades of the Central Committee had prepared the document on the basis of a report P'eng Chen had submitted to Mao. Wang Kuang-mei also confirmed that after the distribution of Former Ten Points, P'eng Chen set up experimental spots in some provinces and, on the basis of the results he obtained, had formulated policies.[20] Since P'eng Chen was regarded as deputy general secretary and the Secretariat often formulated a directive such as this, it is safe to assume that the

Secretariat drafted the Later Ten Points under the direction of Teng Hsiao-p'ing and P'eng Chen.

The Contents

According to the Maoist charges, this document was in direct opposition to the first. It indeed diverged substantially from the first document in the very way it defined the problems and the strategies to attack them, if not in its stated goal and contents. This is an important point to bear in mind when the two documents are compared.[21] In principle, there was little significant difference, for the second document was based on the first. It reiterated the five aspects of the SEM stressed in the first document: class struggle, socialist education, organization of the poor and lower-middle peasants, the four-cleanup campaign, and participation of cadres in collective labor. Of these, class struggle was the most basic. It also stated that the key to correctly launching the movement was the study of Mao's Thought.

The first distinctive feature of the Later Ten Points, then, was the more precise delineation of ascertainable goals. In the name of Mao's Thought, the Later Ten Points reordered the problems Mao had raised. While reaffirming the principles of the Former Ten Points, it omitted four topics included in the first document: (1) the situation, (2) the existence of classes, (3) the case of "severe class struggles," and (4) the cadres' lack of understanding. Instead, it enumerated twelve specific tasks concerning the direction and content of the movement, including such new items as: (1) organizing and training work teams, (2) convening three-level cadre meetings at the hsien and cadre meetings of the commune, (3) meeting production plans and fulfilling the state procurement, (4) readjusting the basic units of the Party, the YCL, and other mass organizations, (5) electing and transferring the basic-level cadres and improving management of each level.[22]

Secondly, the Later Ten Points differed in its description of operational strategy. On the premise that the key to the effective execution of the movement rested in leadership, the document called upon the leaders of the Party units to "wash their hands" first before asking others to do so. The whole movement was to be directed by the Party units in charge; the organization of the poor and lower-middle peasants and the dispatching of work teams were placed under the leadership of the local Party organizations. The work teams were *not* allowed to brush aside the basic-level organizations but to work as staff. The work teams were supposed to remain at the spots where more problems occurred, relatively speaking, whereas Party committees had to lead the movement on the plane. In either case, important decisions had to be referred to the immediately superior Party organization. This stress on the Party's direction and organization, the Maoists later charged, was a tutelage (*hsün-cheng*) that stifled the initiatives of the masses.[23]

Thirdly, the September 1963 directive—unlike the earlier May edict—specified in detail the range of action to be taken in dealing with concrete problems. It sought to curb excesses and exaggerations. It warned against setting up organizations of the poor and lower-middle peasants in a hurry, and required any commune unit to obtain approval of the hsien committee for waging mass rallies. As for the peasants' pursuit of private incentives, it drew a distinction between the actual attempt at a comeback by the class enemy and the backward masses who were used by the enemy, between common speculation and legitimate marketing, and between spontaneous capitalism and legitimate family side-lines. In handling these cases, the Party was to adopt an attitude of practicality and to "deal with a problem as it is, without exaggerating or minimizing its importance."[24]

On some topics, the Later Ten Points did not differ with but sought to deal with problems created by the Former Ten Points. Noting that in many places the poor and lower-middle peasant associations existed only in name, the September 1963 directive established somewhat clearer guidelines about their operation, placing them under Party leadership but granting considerable autonomy to lower levels to decide their tasks, powers, and relations with other organizations.

Another legacy of the May 1963 directive was its ambiguity concerning the question of middle peasants. But the September directive stated that in classifying the upper-middle peasants, neither their living standard nor their political attitude was to be the yardstick, but the extent of their ownership of production means as well as their degree of exploitation. No general reclassification was envisioned. The upper-middle peasants were not to be indiscriminately attacked; only their ideology and activities counter to the collective interest were subject to criticism. With regard to the four elements, the directive only called upon the masses to heighten their regular supervision, warning against any unauthorized arrest or confiscation of their properties. But the directive did include a new article on the offspring of the landlords and rich peasants, who constituted about 10 percent of the rural youth. Since they had never directly participated in exploitation, the directive allowed them to become members of the commune but prohibited them from marrying Party or League members.[25]

On cadre policy, the Later Ten Points restated the primary goal of the Former Ten Points: to win over 95 percent of the cadres. The directive distinguished corruption from "excessive eating"; if a cadre acquired property through corruption, he had to reimburse it in full; if he committed the mistake of "excessive eating," he was only to be criticized. To insure a good job in organizational management, the directive restricted the number of the punishable cadres to a maximum of 2 percent of the total, with the hsien as the unit, and called for a double check of the materials collected in handling such cases. The document continued to exclude the old upper-middle peasants and the offspring of landlords and rich peasants from serving as cadres.[26] To ensure that the cadres would participate in labor, the directive also stipulated that the local Party units set rules about fixing the cadres' basic labor days in a year, the percentage of work points they get for their administrative work and the place where they participate in production. The subsidiary work points for the cadres were limited to 2 percent of the total points of the production unit. Finally, the document had a separate article on the rectification of the Party's basic-level organizations, stressing the need for strengthening a routine organizational life. Rectification meetings were to be held first within the Party, after which activists among the poor and lower-middle peasants were to be invited. Where punishment was involved, all cases were to go through the proper procedure of approval by higher levels.[27]

The Implementation

The Maoists later charged that this document tied the masses' hands on the pretext of setting criteria for implementing specific policies.[28] Its many provisions give credence to this charge, for they were designed to nurture the Party's barely restored authority and agricultural production. The means the Secretariat prescribed in this document severely limited the end that Mao had prescribed in his Former Ten Points. After warning against the disruption of Party life, the September 1963 document stated: "At no stage of the movement should production be affected."[29]

When the Later Ten Points were transmitted as one of the Party's internal documents (according to Liu Shao-ch'i's self-criticism, it was on November 14),[30] hsien committees convoked the three-level cadre conferences to explain the document; this was followed by similar meetings in the communes. It should be noted from the outset that these local units communicated *their own understanding* of the central policy, just as the Secretariat had formulated the second document on the basis of its own understanding of Mao's preferences in the first document. Before the document reached the basic level, therefore, it had to be reinterpreted by the intervening units. A former cadre in the Kwangtung Provincial Council explained this process as follows:

The cadres, particularly the basic-level cadres, might hear about the Party Center's directives. Concretely, however, they still explain them to the masses or other cadres according to the transmission measures of their immediate superior Party committee, quite often saying: "This is a combination of our local situation and our study of the decision made by the province (or special district) and hsien." And they also used to say: "We do this according to the spirit of the Center's directive."[31]

There was also a time element involved in all of this. It took from two weeks to two months for a decision from the Center to reach the production teams. In Kwangtung, the hsien three-level cadres' conferences began in the winter of 1963; the commune followed them up with their own "transmission education" among the basic-level cadres. Only then did the cadres of the brigades and teams call the general assemblies of their members. They read the document article by article to the assemblies and then interpreted it. The SEM, spurred on by the Later Ten Points, was then implemented according to two different patterns. The first pattern was to "squat on the spot" (*tun-tien*), and the second "to run on the plane" (*p'ao-mien*). In general, only after the experimentation on a spot did the movement shift to a plane.

The Party adopted a different approach at specially selected experimental spots. The Party Center sent work teams, composed of high-level cadres chosen from various central departments, to the basic levels with a leader assigned to each team. They squatted there for a specified period, investigating and researching. The work teams by-passed the regular channels of the Party apparatus by going directly to the basic levels, but they usually notified the Party units of the areas in which they stayed. Nevertheless, they reported directly to the Center. In sum, the Center acquired rare firsthand information about the rural situation and about how a policy initiated by the Center got implemented at the grass-roots level. The information led the Center to formulate a new policy in the form of revised directives.

Special offices were established at each level to direct the movement. For example, in Kwangtung, the provincial committee set up the ad hoc Four Cleanup Office (*Ssu-ch'ing pan-kung she*) led by the Four Cleanup Office Leading Small Group and headed by Chao Tzu-yang, first secretary of the Kwantung Provincial Party Committee. The special districts and hsien committees established the four cleanup work corps (*ssu-ch'ing kung-tso-tuan*) while the commune committees had their four cleanup work teams (*ssu-ch'ing kung-tso-tui*). The provincial office organized the work teams with the cadres recruited from the provincial, the district, and the hsien levels. Among the team members were Party cadres, government cadres, and PLA soldiers. After receiving some training at the provincial office, they were sent to selected spots at the brigades or teams; while they were squatting, they all drew their salaries from their original posts.[32]

According to one interview, a work team assigned to a commune comprised some thirty members but at a spot where serious problems existed, a bigger team of over one hundred members was sent. Within the production brigade or team, there was usually a work group (*kung-tso-tsu*), comprising three or five members. As soon as this group entered a brigade, it got in touch with the brigade Party branch. The work group first convened a closed meeting limited to Party members, and raised questions about the situation. As time passed, each member of the work group established a more intimate relationship with the cadres and the peasants. After spending a considerable time in ferreting out unclean cadres, the work group gradually narrowed down the inquiry to a few blatant cases. If the accused admitted the charge and agreed to pay compensation, he could avoid mass criticism. Only if he resisted was he confronted with open criticism by the poor and lower-middle peasants. Even if they had a struggle meeting, the work group and the Party branch worked out in advance whom and how to criticize, and chose the critics. The actual struggle meeting amounted to no more than a rehearsed show. If the work group felt that it found some noteworthy cases, it reported to the superior authorities and with their approval invited the other brigades to the spot.[33] If the work group found it advisable to dismiss or punish some cadres, it always referred the case to the cadres' immediately superior level. Rarely did the work group brush aside the local Party organization. But since the basic-level cadres and their superiors were interdependent, the next higher level tended to protect its basic-level cadres and only rarely approved severe punishment.

In places where work teams were not dispatched—the plane—the local Party committees directly carried out the movement. The brigade branches first convened the general meetings of Party members and non-Party cadres in order to have Party lessons (*tang-k'e*).[34] At these meetings they discussed study documents (*hsüeh-hsi wen-chien*)—Party directives and important editorials of the *People's Daily*, *Red Flag*, and local Party papers. After having these meetings among the cadres themselves, they then convened the team congress. At this congress they did not present documents but conducted an oral education. Following this, the Party members organized a series of lecture meetings (*hsün-hua-hui*) held before gatherings of the four elements; for their offspring the Party offered a separate education.

And then, the *People's Daily* and the *Southern Daily* began to

report detailed cases of how the peasants recollected their past hardships. The Party urged the commune members to compile histories of
their own commune, brigades, teams, and villages, to compare the
present with the past. The local Party held meetings for recollecting the
old hardships and thinking about the present joy (*i-ku she-kan*) among
the poor and lower-middle peasants. In any case, the Party branch
always controlled any organized activities, including the reorganization
of the poor and lower-middle peasants.[35]

As for the four uncleans, the Party branch required the production
teams to make all the accounts public periodically. In instances of
irregularities, it employed pressure on the unclean cadres to reimburse
the amount they had taken. If it was found they were unable to repay
at once, they were allowed to pay in installments; only if they refused
to comply did the branch subject them to public criticism. But rarely
did the campaign reach this stage, however, because most of the local
cadres had obtained their posts through the Party branch, and the
branch usually found a solution before it came to the open.

The case of the Shingshih brigade in Kwangtung illustrates the
extent to which these methods had been effective.[36] In 1964, the
Shingshih brigade of the Shachi commune, Chungshan hsien, was
publicized as a model brigade in Kwangtung, equivalent to the Tachai
brigade in Shansi. When the slogan Learn from Tachai gathered momentum in the spring of 1964, the Kwangtung Provincial Committee called
upon all the brigades and teams to "learn from Shengshih."[37] As was
true of Ch'en Yung-kuei of Tachai, Ch'en Hua, secretary of the Shengshih brigade Party branch, came to be idolized for his good leadership.
He participated in meetings of activists for socialist construction held
in Peking. A poor peasant of Shengshih brigade, however, informed
the Kwangtung Provincial Committee of Ch'en's manifold crimes. He
told the Party that Ch'en not only expropriated the brigade's public
funds for his own use but also showed moral decadence by raping a
peasant's wife. Ch'en even had maintained an escape route to Hong
Kong and was said to have had contact with Kuomintang agents there.

When these startling accusations surfaced, the provincial committee
ordered the Chungshan hsien committee to dispatch a work team to
investigate this matter. But as soon as the investigation team completed
its inquiry and left the brigade, Ch'en's henchmen attacked and severely
injured the informer. Later on, when a four-cleanup work group arrived,
the informer was so frightened that he did not dare to talk. The group
at last succeeded in persuading him to appeal directly to the Center.
When he did, a central work group led by Liu Shao-ch'i's wife Wang
Kuang-mei secretly came to the brigade and Ch'en's case was laid bare.

It was only then that the Kwangtung committee ordered the Public Security Agency to arrest Ch'en. Hearing of this in advance, Ch'en attempted to flee to Hong Kong by a motorboat but was arrested before he made it. Fearing his punishment, he took his own life in jail.

The *Southern Daily* did not report this incident but the Party cadres at the provincial level were informed about it and even some low-level cadres came to know this story through "little broadcasts" (*hsiao-kuang-po*), a person-to-person medium of communication. Embarrassed with it, T'ao Chu (first secretary of the Central South Bureau) and Chao Tzu-yang both admitted that the squat during the four-cleanup campaign had been superficial. Interestingly enough, some refugees who related this episode suggested that it was in no way exceptional.[38]

This story reveals a facet of the SEM in action. What Mao had hoped would be a large-scale mass movement became a very ritualized affair, whether implemented by the work teams or by the regular Party organizations, and hence fell far short of his expectations. In either case, the movement relied on the basic-level Party organizations because they were not only best informed about the locality but had organizational links with the peasants. It could hardly be expected that the Party branches could struggle against the cadres with whom they had connections, nor could the work teams effectively scrutinize the local cadres if they collaborated with the Party branches. And the very open way in which the work teams led the movement made it difficult for the peasants to air their grievances against their own cadres. By and large, the provisions of the Later Ten Points were so restrictive that those who implemented the document had to err on the side of caution. Furthermore, the leadership's attitude toward the SEM facilitated this trend. Chao Tzu-yang urged the work team to evaluate the cadres on their merit, stressing that the four-cleanup campaign must be realized in production and construction. The provincial Party committee actually put forth the principle that the campaign should help the "poor countryside become a wealthy socialist countryside."[39]

In short, most local cadres sought to temper the campaign according to the exigencies of their own situation. In fact, interviews with former cadres encountered one common theme: the local cadres invariably loathed the periodic campaigns, for their immediate security was at stake. In reference to the SEM, one former cadre explained the situation as follows:

Throughout the four-cleanup movement, the Party first placed emphasis on the spot; the spot came first before the plane and from there the movement expanded to the plane. With this method it combined the spot and the plane; it developed work at the spot while undertaking general measures on the plane, held big and important meetings at the spot to which the cadres of other production teams on the plane were invited. This way of combining the spot and the plane by shifting from the former to the latter became a spiritual burden for the basic-level cadres. The cadres of the plane adopted the experiences gained on the spot but they also learned how to accommodate to them. Therefore, after the movement shifted from the spot to the plane, some cadres reported false figures, avoided struggles, and tried to delay organizational cleanings until the last moment of the movement. The so-called active participation of the basic-level cadres in the campaign was untrue; they were still forced. Activism was false; accommodation (*ying-fu*) was true.[40]

The majority of the cadres below the commune level had been recruited during the mass campaigns for land reform, cooperativization, communization, and during the antirightist campaign and the anticommandist rectification. Despite some turnover during the years, many of these cadres had survived those campaigns before the SEM came. Naturally, those who survived learned to play the game; they responded to the SEM in the light of their accumulated experiences. Through their long tenures, these cadres had developed mutual trust and friendship among themselves. When some outside force such as the work team directed a campaign at them, their initial reaction was to defend themselves by mutual assistance against the common hazard of being purged. They could do this by withholding information about their colleagues or by intimidating the peasants not to divulge their mistakes. In 1967, when the Maoists accused the Later Ten Points of "removing the burning brands from under the boiling cauldron" (*tsou-kou-ch'ang*), they might have referred to these phenomena.[41]

The Expansion of the Movement

Evidence shows that Mao was aware of the superficiality of mobilization in Party implementation of the SEM. In March 1964 Mao concluded that the test points in the movement had failed and some work teams had struck at innocent people. Yet he still recommended that Party leaders read the two documents to grasp the nature of class struggle. In May, he again urged them to go and stay at selected spots.[42] Yet the more he found his ideas blocked by the Party apparatus, the more he became committed to them and had to expand the campaign. In 1964-65, Mao went out of his way to enforce his ideas and policy but this led him into open confrontation with his associates at the Party Center. When such clashes did occur, they exposed the two different approaches of Mao Tse-tung and Liu Shao-ch'i on the method of carrying out the SEM.

The first sign of the expanded SEM was the rapid pace in the establishment of the poor and lower-middle peasant association (PLMPA).

At a June 1964 meeting of the Standing Committee of the Politburo attended by the first secretaries of the regional bureaus, Mao laid down six goals for the SEM: (1) truly to mobilize the poor and lower-middle peasants, (2) to solve the four-unclean problems, (3) to have cadres participate in labor, (4) to establish a good leadership core, (5) to discover whether the four elements have engaged in sabotage, and (6) to increase production.[43]

To meet the first goal, the Party issued in June 1964 the Organizational Rules of Poor and Lower-Middle Peasant Association (draft). While this document reflected most of Mao's preferences, it also embodied some organizational practices that the Secretariat had been using. Unlike other documents, this document was not labeled revisionist during the Cultural Revolution. The main tasks envisaged for the association were: (1) to respond to the calls of the Party and Chairman Mao, (2) to struggle against capitalism, (3) to unite with the middle peasants and with all others who could be united, (4) to assist and supervise the management organizations in the commune, (5) to train cadres in production, and (6) to carry out class education.[44]

The committees of the association were to parallel the management committttees at each level of the commune, serving as assistants to the Party committees. They were to report to the Party committees about the work of the management committees; and their cadres were not allowed to serve concurrently as the cadres of the management committees. The commune representatives congress had to mediate any conflict between the association and the management committees. If necessary, however, the higher level Party organization could intervene.

Prior to this directive, the PLMPA emerged mostly from a revival of the peasant association that had existed during the land reform.[45] Now that the Party had formally issued a directive, the poor and lower-middle peasants were emboldened somewhat to voice their grievances about the cadres and the middle peasants. (They challenged, for instance, the argument that land reform relied on the poor peasants but production had to rely on the middle peasants because the latter knew better how to manage the collective.) Despite the efforts to establish the PLMPA in the second half of 1964, it was not until after the Twenty-Three Points were sent down in 1965 that the formal structure of the association began to take shape.[46]

LIU'S REVISED LATER TEN POINTS

Dissatisfied with the Later Ten Points, Mao asked Liu Shao-ch'i to revise them so as to reflect more mass mobilization. To collect information for the revision, the Secretariat dispatched a number of work teams throughout the country. Joining one of these teams in November 1963, Wang Kuang-mei went to the T'aoyüan brigade of Lu-wang-chuang commune, Fu-ning hsien, Hopei, and squatted there until April 1964. Despite opposition from others, Mao personally approved of the idea of Wang's going down to the countryside, as she had done in Yenan.[47]

The T'aoyüan Experience

Before her departure, Wang Kuang-mei asked Liu Shao-ch'i what to do there. Liu stressed that it was not necessary for her to have any preconceived notion because she had to solve whatever problems there are. Liu told her that through secret contact she could rely on a few peasants for collecting information. She arrived at T'ao-yüan, disguised as Tung P'u, a secretary of the Hopei Provincial Public Security Agency. She led a work group of three men and one woman.[48]

Upon arrival, she scrutinized all brigade cadres without using pre-conceived criteria such as their class status and political activism. The work group first "linked up with and struck roots" (*cha-ken ch'uan-lien*) among the peasants. Then it singled out some typical peasants and lived, ate, and worked with them, thus doing the "three together." Gradually it forged more intimate relationships with them so that they would freely reveal the cadres' corruption. Soon after the work group reached this stage, it took over the brigade Party branch and management committee to "examine the root" and to weed out ruthlessly whatever errors the cadres had committed. The Maoists later derided this method as a cold dictatorship of the work team imposed on the masses at the expense of mass line, "hitting at many in order to protect a handful."[49]

Wang Kuang-mei relied upon linking up and striking roots instead of the open investigation favored by Mao. She was convinced that such investigation meetings could no longer reveal the real problems with the cadres, for they had created a screen of self-protection. From this experience Madam Liu concluded that practically all basic-level cadres were suspect, saying: "T'aoyüan brigade has changed its color into white; basically it is not red." She found the cadre problem much more serious and complex than was generally imagined. It was not simply a case of pinpointing who were the enemy and the friends as such, because all cadres had practiced some form of the four unclean. For instance, twenty-nine of the principal cadres in the brigade had mis-appropriated funds.

To cope with this situation, the work group first put pressure on those unclean cadres to confess their crimes, thus "hitting the surrounding first before attacking the strong." When a cadre under review refused to admit the charge, he was subject to a mass rally. In this way, 40 of the 47 cadres in the brigade—85 percent of the total—were struggled against, and 155 peasants made self-examinations. Then, the group dismissed the unclean cadres, including the secretary of the Party branch and the chief of the management committee, and replaced them with a new team. Wang Kuang-mei stated: "We must reform the 'four unclean' with the 'four clean.' " (In 1967, Wang was accused by Mao's supporters of selecting for the new team a former cadre, Kuan Ching-tung, who was able but who also had been corrupt.) To assure that no reversal would be made, the consolidation group remained at T'aoyüan until April 1965, a year after Wang's departure. As late as December 1964, in fact, three cadres in T'aoyüan received nationwide praise for emphasizing collective hog-raising at the expense of their own hogs.[50]

Wang Kuang-mei's work at T'aoyüan does resemble that of an underground agent in the white area before 1949, which represented Liu Shao-ch'i's leadership in microcosm. Liu used this T'aoyüan experience as the basic data for revising the Later Ten Points. In July, after disseminating this experience in Peking and Tientsin, Liu called on various provinces to send representatives to Peking to discuss the experience. In August, he and his wife traveled through the East China and the Central South regions to discuss the experience further. It was during this trip that a tape of Wang's speech about the T'aoyüan experience was circulated.[51]

In their speeches, Liu and Wang expressed views about the nature of the SEM that were in stark contrast with those held by Mao. First, their appraisal of the basic-level cadres was much more pessimistic and their appraisal of the problem nonideological. Liu contended that at least one-third of the cadres were not clean; in Hopei 60 or 70 percent were actually "under the control of the enemies." He maintained that the SEM thus far had failed, for the calamity-stricken peasants were still directed by corrupted cadres.[52]

The immediate goal of the four cleanup was to eliminate corruption and to rectify the relationships between the cadres and the peasants. But it was by no means simple to clarify such relationships, for complex problems also existed among many interwoven elements. Problems existed between the four elements and the other peasants; problems within the Party branch were interwoven with problems among the non-Party people; some of the four elements also forged connections with the cadres. This was why Liu shared his wife's description of the problems: "There are contradictions between the four cleanup and the non-four cleanup, the contradictions inside and outside are crisscrossed, or the contradictions between the enemy and ourselves are crisscrossed with those among the people."[53]

The ideological point at issue here was profound. Mao had always argued that the first step in analysis is to identify the principal contradiction and to delineate a sharp line between friends and enemies. Liu, however, was arguing on pragmatic grounds that this could not be done. Rather than contradictions between friends and enemies in the countryside, what existed in the countryside were crisscrossed problems that had to be solved. In 1966, Mao accused this view of being "Left in appearance but Right in essence."[54]

Second, Liu derived from his assessment a different method of handling the problem. He was keenly aware that the unclean cadres had numerous devices to evade the brunt of campaigns, and indeed that in some cases the Party's techniques were lagging behind theirs. To match their skills, the Party needed stronger measures. For instance, Liu opposed the open investigation meetings, for he believed:

Today, under many circumstances it won't do to hold a forum first because the basic-level cadres do not report on many conditions in the course of struggle. . . . Today, in investigating the conditions in rural areas and factories, we rely on reports. But we are supplied with false figures and reports about conditions. The poor and lower-middle peasants have a lot of misgivings and they are reluctant to hold investigation meetings.[55]

On another occasion, Liu warned against pseudoactivism among cadres as follows:

Some people pretend to be active but can turn out to be a mess in the end. This sort of people might well be among the basic-level cadres, at the commune level, and even at the hsien. They do not really want revolution but think of only one point, i.e., being "Left." *Leading the mass movement must take place within the framework of the Communist Party and must not be left to the hands of bad elements. Those who oppose us can do so from the Right as well as from the Left. You must bear this problem in mind.*[56]

To cope with such pretentious activism, he advocated a Party-controlled organizational approach rather than mass campaigns, by sending down strong work teams led by the higher Party units and having them squat at the basic level.

Instead of touching all areas and being unable to complete the movement within half a year, Liu also favored a sequential approach by making the work teams squat first and link up and strike root at some selected spots, and then use that experience to spread into other areas. This he said was a more satisfactory method of doing away with bureaucracy, for he believed: *"To do things one by one might look as if they are slow but in practice it is faster."*[57] This sentence strikes a

familiar note of the Western incrementalist approach in policy implementation: "In a system in which policy making is frankly recognized
to be serial or sequential, the whole system may be tailored to rapid
sequences so that, though no one policy move is great, the frequency of
small moves makes rapid social change possible."[58]

Liu was not alone, however, in taking this position. Teng Hsiao-
p'ing felt that it was easier to open a big meeting; P'eng Chen quickly
implemented Liu's method in Peking; T'an Chen-lin warned against the
"double trick" of the local cadres; and Li Hsien-nien praised Liu's
problem-solving approach.[59] Indeed, even before the revised directive
was formulated, various provinces began to comply with Liu's method.
In Hopei, for example, Lin T'ieh and Liu Tzu-hou, first and second
secretary of the provincial committee, respectively, organized work
teams of some 120,000 people; each special district team was made up
of over 10,000 people. These teams were no longer staff organizations
but representatives of the higher Party organizations that carried out
secret investigations in the countryside. In Kwangtung, after the Shengshih affair, T'ao Chu drafted a document entitled Introducing a Four
Cleanup Experience, based on Wang Kuang-mei's recorded speech; he
circulated this to all members of the work teams. T'ao himself squatted
for a while at Hsinho brigade of Hua hsien.[60]

The Revised Later Ten Points

Against this background, Liu at last completed the revision of the
Later Ten Points in September 1964 and transmitted the newer document in November.[61] The Maoists commonly called this the Revised
Later Ten Points (hsiu-cheng hou shih-t'iao) and attacked it for being
"Left in appearance but Right in essence." But the document itself
professed to have been based on Mao's Former Ten Points as well as the
Secretariat's Later Ten Points.[62] Moreover, it emerged from a Party
consensus built up through extensive experimentation, tempered by
results and by consultation with regional leaders.

On the premise that the SEM was more meaningful even than land
reform, this document stressed the seriousness of the cadre problem
and provided some concrete policies to remedy the superficiality of the
current SEM. It divided the movement into two stages: first, solving
the problem of the unclean cadres and, second, reorganizing the basic-
level organizations.[63] The basic difference between Mao's Former Ten
Points and the Later Ten Points on the one hand and this Revised Later
Ten Points on the other was that the former two directives both assumed
that over 95 percent of the basic-level cadres had been good and only
less than 5 percent bad, but the latter took the opposite posture that

the majority of those cadres had committed mistakes; hence only after over 95 percent of the peasants had been consolidated would over 95 percent of the cadres have a sound foundation of operations.[64]

To cope with the cadre problem, the September 1964 document reversed the cadre policy of the Later Ten Points, which specifically prohibited the work teams from taking over the rural organizations: "To launch the Socialist Education Movement at any point requires the sending of a work team from the higher level. The whole movement should be led by the work team. The missions of the work team include: mobilization of the masses, execution of policies, and completion of various items of work of the Socialist Education Movement."[65] By vesting more power in the work team, it hoped to enable the representative of the central authority to penetrate the protective net spun by both the basic-level and the middle-level cadres, for the "enemy's method" of evading the Center's directives was so cunning, even using certain articles of the documents, that the Party was said to be ill-prepared for the class struggle under these new conditions.[66]

To unearth the unclean cadres, the document recommended the mobilization of the poor and lower-middle peasants *under* the direction of the work team. It stressed organizational purity by demanding that the poor peasants become the backbone of the association. But the directive had few new provisions for the middle peasants.

The directive focused on two defects of the SEM. First, the masses had not been mobilized and as a result, the seriousness of the cadre problems had been overlooked. Second, after such mobilization, no distinctions had been made between conflicts between friends and enemies and conflicts among the people. Under the current circumstance, the first was said to be the major danger. (Thus Liu actually noted class distinction from a Maoist perspective but, in doing so, he relegated it to a status of secondary importance.) The document then suggested ways to avoid these pitfalls:

Before the masses are mobilized, we should stress the mobilization of the masses; after they are mobilized, we should stress practical handling of the problems. This is a question of experience in controlling the mass movement, and [of] the art of leadership. Provincial, special district and hsien committees, and all leading functionaries of work teams should master this art.[67]

The work teams were instructed *not* to worry about hurting cadres' feelings, for such an attitude would lead to a false cleaning. If the team found any economic expropriation, a full compensation was called for. All matters regarding punishment including those that needed approval of the higher level organizations had to be concluded while the team remained at the basic level, for some basic-level cadres maintained protection from "certain cadres of higher level organizations."[68]

The key feature in this third document was the increased power it gave to the work teams. It eliminated many of the constraints in the Later Ten Points. Basically, Liu advocated a sweeping, punitive purge of basic-level authorities, which he believed to be rotten to the core. Thus, the goal of the SEM had been significantly revised. The class education Mao had envisioned in the first document had given way to instructions for shaking up the basic-level cadres. In other words, the movement was directed at those who implemented policy. Interviews confirm that the Party carried out the SEM along this line after the summer of 1964. The work teams had almost unlimited authority in disposing of unclean cadres. The emphasis was on the side of remedy and punishment.[69] Because of this policy, the normal cadre-peasant relationship was somewhat disrupted and as a result, the morale of the cadres was at low ebb. In the six months following August, while the work teams seized power, a substantial number of cadres had been dismissed. In Kwangtung alone, one report had it that 147 cadres were purged. In some places, this enabled the poor and lower-middle peasants to take over (tang-chia) the management of production teams.[70]

Even the model Tachai brigade was no exception. In December 1964, a work team, composed of the cadres from the Shansi Provincial Committee, the special district, and the hsien, came down to the brigade. It scrutinized the brigade's production record, which had been nationally acclaimed. While the team remained there, Ch'en Yung-kuei, secretary of the branch, went to the Third NPC in Peking as a delegate from Shansi; he was reported to have had an audience with Mao. Soon after Ch'en returned, the work team withdrew.[71]

This episode suggests that Mao must have gotten conflicting information from Ch'en about the current SEM. A similar incident occurred in Peking at this time. On December 2, 1964, Peking's *Rural Four Cleanup Bulletin* published a report that Liu Jen, second secretary of the Peking Municipal Committee, had made at a forum of the poor and lower-middle peasants in T'ung hsien. It so happened that Ch'i Pen-yü was a member of the work team squatting in the hsien. Ch'i found Liu Jen's speech "aristocratic" and wrote a protesting letter to the Center. Subsequently, the letter was published in the Party's *Nei-pu ts'an-k'ao* (Internal Reference), a bulletin circulated among high officialdom. At the Hangchow conference (an enlarged Politburo meeting convened to discuss the SEM) a central leader read Ch'i's letter. Angered by this, P'eng Chen ordered the Propaganda Department to censure Ch'i.[72]

Another incident also suggests how the work teams were used in late 1964. During the four-clean campaign in the winter of 1964, some "heroic" people in Kweichow dared to attack Chou Lin, first secretary of the provincial committee, on the ground that he had opposed the study of Mao's Thought. This time Liu Shao-ch'i and Teng Hsiao-p'ing rushed a central work team to the defense of Chou Lin.[73]

MAO'S TWENTY-THREE POINTS

As these incidents indicate, Mao came to realize by late 1964 that the Party's policy on the SEM as defined by Liu was, in effect, opposed to his policy. In his report to the NPC convened in December 1964, Chou En-lai provided the first clue about Mao's discontent with the SEM. The premier revealed that the scope of the four cleanup had widened to include four broad areas: the political, economic, ideological, and organizational, instead of the narrow four cleanup in books, warehouses, property, and work points. Chou also made it plain that the newly expanded SEM would encompass profound class struggle.[74]

This decision, in fact, was made at the Hangchow conference before the NPC. For, at this conference Mao approved a document, commonly known as the Twenty-Three Points, that superseded the previous documents, and stipulated the expansion of the four cleanup.[75] At the Hangchow conference, apparently, a great deal of debate occurred between Mao and his associates. For example, Mao brought up Wang Kuang-mei's squatting experience in Hsin-ch'eng hsien, Hopei. Deploring the big work team of 15,000 people in the hsien of 280,000, Mao pointed out that the Chinese revolution had not been carried out in such a cold-blooded (*ning-ning ch'ing-ch'ing*) fashion. Instead, he recommended a smaller rally of 1,000. After listening to this, Wang Kuang-mei could not wait until the meeting ended. She left midway in the talks and headed for Hsin-ch'eng that same night. On arrival there, she convened a meeting of 1,000 people and wrote a report to the Center in the name of the Paoting Special District Four Cleanup Work Corps. As soon as Liu received the report, he forwarded it to Mao for approval.[76]

The discussions at the Hangchow conference led to the Twenty-Three Points, for the document was called a summary (*chi-yao*) of Politburo discussions, instead of either decisions (*ch'üeh-ting*) or regulations (*kui-ting*) as were the previous documents. The Party transmitted this new directive throughout the country on January 14, 1965.[77]

By then, Mao concluded that his method of mass mobilization had been upheld by the Party apparatus in principle but sabotaged in practice. He apparently perceived that the principal responsibility for this rested with those who had assumed the operational leadership of Party policy, particularly those who had directed the apex of its central machinery. He further reasoned that without major changes in the interlocking bureaucracy that intervened between him and the masses (ranging from the Secretariat to the basic level) his policy could not get through to the masses. In this sense, the Twenty-Three Points became the crucial document that lead to the conflict between Mao and his opponents during the Cultural Revolution.

In speeches he made to the Hangchow conference in December 1964, Mao sought to correct the Party's policy concerning the SEM. He insisted the SEM was a class struggle aimed at resolving contradiction between two factions within the Party—the socialist and the capitalist— but not one between unclean and clean officials. He argued that even clean officials in the old dynasties were pernicious. Hence, he pointed out that from the outset the SEM should have focused on power holders within the Party, that is, policy makers rather than implementors. Since some provincial Party committees, especially in Anhui, Kweichow, Tsinghai, and Kansu, had become "rotten," he continued, the movement should have caught wolves first and then foxes. In another speech he made in January 1965, he severely criticized the bureaucratic way in which the Party had implemented the movement. According to his charges, a county had spent forty days to study the documents and numerous work teams had been sent down, yet the peasants still did not understand the documents and there was no result. For example, one of his bodyguards had studied them for forty days but it was not till he entered a village that he began to understand its problem. So, he contended, the masses will do what they want to do in the struggle and will create their own leaders. To those who had led the movement, he said: "Now that you have formed a party, entered cities, and become bureaucrats, you are no longer adept at launching mass movement."[78]

Commenting on a report about the SEM in January 1965, Mao indeed regarded bureaucracy as a class-forming agency by saying that the bureaucratic class was becoming bourgeoisie and opposed to the working class. Since these people were the target of the struggle, Mao continued, the revolution could not rely on them.[79] In October 1966, Mao recalled the situation of January 1965 with these words: "It was I who proposed a struggle against the Secretariat. Furthermore, we had too much confidence in others. Our vigilance was aroused when the Twenty-Three Points were drafted. At the time neither Peking nor the Central Committee could find any means to cope with the problems that arose."[80] Chou En-lai later confirmed that by early 1965 Mao was no longer confident with the way Liu had handled the SEM, and that from that time on Mao had criticized Liu at meetings as well as in writings. According to Edgar Snow, Mao was already proposing the Cultural Revolution to overthrow the Party bureaucracy, but Liu remained defiant; it was only at a decisive meeting on January 25, 1965, *not before*, that Mao decided to purge Liu.[81]

The Twenty-Three Points

The Twenty-Three Points were framed in the same mold as the Former Ten Points. Starting with the premise that the current situation was "a new high tide of the socialist revolutionary movement," this directive reverted to the old view that the existing problems in the cities and villages were none other than an expression of acute class struggle, thus repudiating Liu's analysis that the problem was essentially one of corruption among local cadres.

The Twenty-Three Points also revoked three conclusions reached by the T'aoyüan experience and the Revised Later Ten Points. First, it rejected the analysis of the nature of the contradiction between "four clean" cadres and "four unclean" cadres. The document asserted that this was not simply reflective of organizational problems, but represented a continuation of class struggle in the countryside, for unclean cadres continued to harbor capitalist or bourgeois values. The remedy therefore could not be sought through organizational means—simple purging, improved reports, and surveillance by the work teams. Rather, thorough and ongoing class struggles with an emphasis on attitudinal change and education were called for. Second, the January 1965 directive condemned the T'aoyüan experience and the Revised Later Ten Points for blurring distinctions between "the enemy and us." Especially serious, the Maoist pronouncement stated, had been the earlier assertions allegedly made by Wang Kuang-mei and Liu Shao-ch'i that antagonistic contradictions (that is, those between the enemy and the CCP) contained nonantagonistic contradictions and could therefore be handled as such. Equally serious, the directive observed, was that although the contradictions between the local cadres and the masses were nonantagonistic contradictions, the Party still treated the local cadres as an enemy and subjected them to struggle meetings. Third—and most serious if Liu aspired to succeed Mao as guardian of ideology— earlier directives were condemned for not clearly stating the nature of the epoch or the fundamental characteristics of the SEM. Liu had offered no justification for his theory of overlapping contradictions crisscrossing friend and enemy, and the Party and non-Party people.[82] In short, the SEM policies associated with Liu were said to be devoid of ideological meaning.

In the Twenty-Three Points, Mao claimed to be most forthright on these matters. He saw the essence of the problem as the contradiction between socialism and capitalism.[83] The major contradictions remained the same as those enunciated in 1949, the contradictions that existed during the transitional period. According to Lin Piao, Mao defined the target of the SEM for the first time as follows: "The main target of the present movement is *the Party persons in power taking the capitalist road.*"[84] Lin contended that with this Mao had corrected the course of the SEM and determined the orientation of the Cultural Revolution as well. The Sixteen-Article Decision launching the Cultural Revolution indeed declared that its objective was also to overthrow the "Party persons in power taking the capitalist road" (*tang-nei nei-hsieh tsou-tzu-pen chu-yi tao-lu-ti tang ch'uan-p'ai*).[85] The Twenty-Three Points expressly indicated that "of those people in positions of authority who take the capitalist road, some are out in the open and some are concealed. Of the people who support them, some are at lower levels and some are at higher levels. . . . Among those at higher levels, there are some people in the communes, districts, hsien, special districts, and even in the work of provincial and Central Committee departments, who oppose socialism"[86]

The January 1965 document restated the six goals for the movement that Mao had stipulated in June 1964 (see above, page 104). It revived the emphasis on class education and on proceeding from correct theory to practice. It suspended the "human sea" tactic of saturating an area with a large work team. Instead of the work team taking over the whole movement, it suggested a three-way alliance of the masses, cadres, and work team. Rather than the secret linkage of the work team with the peasants, it demanded the Party organs immediately explain the movement to the cadres as well as to the masses once the movement got started. The movement was neither to be quiet and mysterious nor to be confined to a small minority but to be a bold unleashing of the masses. It clearly disowned Liu's method of secret squatting and revived open investigation meetings. If squatting were necessary, it had to be done in an open way.[87]

Some provisions in the Twenty-Three Point directive were designed to correct the harsh handling of local cadres. Instead of placing all the basic-level cadres under suspicion, the directive noted that cadres be classified into four categories: those who were good, those who were relatively good, those with many problems, and those who had made mistakes of a serious nature. In general the first two types of cadres were said to constitute the majority. The work team was not allowed to pit the cadres against the masses. Even cadres who had committed serious mistakes were to be educated and transformed. Only when the leading core had been taken over by "alien classes" could their authority be seized, first by struggle and then by dismissal. The leniency of the directive was also highlighted by its permitting, if the masses agreed, local cadres not to pay back funds they may have stolen or squandered.[88]

Unlike the previous three documents, which had been internal directives issued to the commune level, this one was sent down to the production teams. Interviews indicate that the Party directed the teams to put it on public display. This unusual measure was intended to insure its transmission and implementation. After its transmission, the Party recalled the work teams, easing the pressures placed on the basic-level cadres. A considerable number of the dismissed cadres were rehabilitated and the brunt of the struggle shifted from the basic level to the hsien Party committees.[89] In practice, however, it was impossible for the hsien or communes to change their methods suddenly. Still lacking a clear-cut direction from the Center, they had to comply as usual with their superiors' instructions and enforce them in accordance with their own judgment.

At the higher level as well, some central and provincial leaders were delaying enforcement of the new directive. In July 1965, Wang Kuang-mei was still "linking up and striking root" in Kao-chen brigade; T'an Chen-lin decreed that Liu's Revised Later Ten Points and the Twenty-Three Points could simultaneously be implemented; and T'ao Chu maintained that the Twenty-Three Points were not to be used to correct past deviations. But Lin Piao was said to have written a letter to Mao pledging a firm implementation of Mao's directive within the PLA.[90]

Specifically, it proved difficult for the masses, cadres, and work teams to form a three-way alliance without undermining the regular Party authority. When Peking University carried out the SEM in 1964, the work team sent there made an alliance with dissident students and struggled against the University authorities—Lu P'ing, first secretary and president, and P'eng P'ei-yün, deputy secretary. In this case, Teng Hsiao-p'ing and P'eng Chen had to protect the accused. After the Twenty-Three Points had been transmitted, Teng called upon the work team to form an alliance with the cadres of the university. When Chang P'an-shih, head of the work team, and the dissidents continued to attack the university authorities, P'eng Chen replaced him with Hsü Li-chün, deputy director of the Propaganda Department. The work team and the students still refused to comply with this decision, at which point Teng Hsiao-p'ing ordered all the parties involved to negotiate at the International Hotel. This negotiation lasted from July 1965 to March 1966. Finally, Wan Li of the Peking Municipal Committee reversed the verdict on Lu P'ing. Stressing Party discipline and state law (tang-chi kuo-fa), Lu then sent some of the dissidents to the countryside. In protest, one of them wrote a letter to Mao but it was diverted to the university authorities.[91]

As this event demonstrates, when the work team acted in defiance of those university authorities backed by the Party Center, the campaign was likely to get out of hand. Hence, Mao's reversal of Liu's SEM policies exposed the lower-level cadres to the existence of grave leadership conflicts at the Center. Thus, the expanded SEM changed the tone, if not the substance, of political life in China after January 1965. The rapid pace in organizing the poor and lower-middle peasant associations was indicative of this change. In Kwangtung, the Party committee admitted that the cadres had been lethargic in consulting the poor peasants, but in June 1965 the Kwangtung Provincial PLMPA was organized, with some military cadres also taking part.[92] For the first time, the association took shape at the provincial level in such places as Kwangtung, Shanghai, Chekiang, Hopei, and Peking. At least in three provinces—Anhui, Hunan, and Kiangsi—the association only came into being in the spring of 1966. In any case, the provincial Party committees directly organized them from above; in Hunan, Chang P'ing-hua, first secretary, became chairman of the association; in Anhui, Li Pao-hua, first secretary, did the same.[93]

These responses were a far cry from the instant reaction to Mao's calls shown during the GLF. Except for the organization of the PLMPA, the local Party committees and their cadres remained unchanged. Insofar as the organizational arrangements were concerned, the three-way alliance did not materialize after the work teams withdrew from the basic level. In the summer of 1965, communes made some efforts to emulate the PLA's political campaigns, as the last item of the Twenty-Three Points recommended. These efforts concentrated on discussions about the relationship between politics and production. The argument invariably led to the conclusion that the poor and lower-middle peasants should never forget for whom they produced. In order that the peasants would not forget their past sufferings in comparison with the present situation, communes again compiled their past histories.[94] While these debates were going on in the countryside, an open debate flared up within the Party leadership on cultural reforms and Sino-Soviet relations. At the September-October 1965 central work conference, Mao asked to start a criticism against Wu Han and raised the specter of revisionism at the Center.[95] After this conference, the SEM took a sharp turn toward a more virulent ideological compaign, following the example of the PLA's campaigns.

Revolutionization of the Hsien Committees

From the summer of 1965 on, the SEM expanded from the basic level to the hsien level, from policy administrators to policy makers, and also from the rural areas to the urban areas. In accordance with the Twenty-Three Points, the movement placed its emphasis on persuasion and education. After the PLA initiated the Learn from Wang Chieh campaign in September 1965, the Party embarked upon a campaign to "revolutionize the hsien committees" as part of the SEM. This campaign took on the appearance of a nationwide symposium for discussing the many problems facing the hsien committees and then culminated in January 1966 with the campaign for emulating a model hsien secretary, Chao Yü-lu. The *People's Daily* led this symposium from October through December 1965 by publishing over thirty reports and "short comments" (*tuan-p'ing*) about the investigation meetings that had been under way at hsien and communes.

These articles revealed some important facts about the intricate relationships between the basic level and the middle level of the Party hierarchy. The basic-level cadres conceded that they had been only looking to the higher levels, mainly the hsien committee, for instructions, and responding to them. They had no plans of their own.[96] The hsien requested so much information that commune cadres had little time to care for the masses. The Ch'ih-li-ying commune in Honan, for example, received calls from seven hsien units in one day, inquiring about the same question, the drought. "For a long time our work has been passive month after month," complained a secretary of the commune, "for we have been busy responding to the higher level requests for reports, questionnaires, and returns."[97] Some of these requests so complicated that they could not even be answered. Depicting this routinism (*shih-wu chu-yi*), the local cadres attributed its root cause principally to the leading organs of the higher echelon.[98]

The hsien cadres themselves acknowledged this fact. But they asserted that they also had been passive, without any long-range plan. They, too, did whatever the higher echelon asked them, always starting but never ending anything. One cadre said: "This year we do not know what to do next year. We only treat the head when we feel headache and treat legs when we have sore legs."[99] The search for stability and peace had been the guiding ideology of the hsien committee, yet many cadres called upon others to learn from Tachai while they themselves did not.

Some hsien cadres attributed this bureaucratic lethargy to their preoccupation with production. According to T'eng T'ien-chieh of Ninghan hsien, Heilungkiang, most cadres believed that as long as production

rose, other things did not matter. Many hsien strived to acquire maximum state aid, the Party's urge for self-reliance notwithstanding. In
Fukien, some cadres used to say that many wanted to cut flowers but
few wanted to cut thorns.[100] The hsien cadres were most concerned
with figures about production because they believed that if production
was good, politics had to be good, too, for, whenever production rose,
they received praise but whenever it turned bad, they got criticism for
being bad in politics.[101]

As a result, the hsien cadres became engrossed in administration but
alienated themselves from the masses. Instead of serving the masses,
they were serving the higher echelon, giving only lip service to going
down to the countryside. As Wei Chiu-ch'eng of Yungkow hsien,
Liaoning, succinctly observed:

The idea that we became "official" still existed in our mind, though in different
degrees; we used to think that the leaders are different from the masses, for they
are a grade higher. . . . We one-sidedly think that the hsien leads the communes;
the commune leads the brigades and teams. Hence it is natural that the lower levels
serve the higher levels and the lower levels must be responsible to the hsien level;
when the hsien requires them to provide tables and reports, they must submit them
even if they are unnecessary and irrational.[102]

He also revealed that the leading cadres of the hsien spent, on the
average, about two-thirds of their time at the higher levels in a year—the
special district and the provincial levels. The hsien committee issued an
outline (t'i-kang) directive to six or seven departments of the hsien a
day; then, twenty-four hundred units of the communes, the brigades,
and the teams had to work for them. Even if a hsien cadre squatted at
a team, he picked up an advanced one, avoiding poor teams. This
prompted the peasant to say: "Birds fly where light is."[103] The standing committee always met behind closed doors; rarely did they invite
the poor and lower-middle peasants. Still, the cadres were afraid of
committing errors; they usually were content with marginal progress no
matter how small it was. The catch words for this trend were: "The
upstream is adventurous, the middlestream insured, and the down-
stream dangerous": hence the majority wanted to stay in the middlestream.[104]

One common point all these criticisms reveal about the Chinese
political system is the trend toward bureaucratization. The hsien functioned as a conveying center (ch'uan-yün-chan): it mainly conveyed the
tasks to the lower levels that had been assigned by the province and
reports from them to the province.[105] The provinces also performed a
function similar to the hsien; hence the source of this bureaucratization
rested with the Center, from which all important policies and campaigns

originated. Yet in checking bureaucratization, Mao's approach was not to devise another countervailing hierarchy or organizations such as work teams but to transform the cadres' attitude and behavior by inculcating them with revolutionary ethics. Therefore, the local cadres were in a position to blame their own ideological laxity. The economic base had been changed, the argument went, but there still remained the same old thinking; therefore, to transform the "feature of objective nature," one had to change the "feature of his subjective nature" first—the mental state.[106] To change their mentality, the local cadres were asked to put the Thought of Mao Tse-tung in command, for it was like food and air, energizing all other activities. As Kuan Feng, a young theoretician, argued, all work ought to be done for revolution. To live up to this ideal, the hsien cadres were supposed to learn "three great styles": the linkage of theory and practice, the linkage of self-criticism and criticism, and the linkage of the cadres and the masses.[107]

The model hsien cadre who had epitomized these styles was Chao Yü-lu, secretary of Lankao hsien, Hopei. Chao went to the hsien, carrying with him only Mao's works. He initiated thought reform among members of the hsien standing committee by studying Mao's works, investigated the situation, and consulted the masses. Despite his worsening liver illness, he worked night and day to improve a sand hill. When his illness kept him at the hospital, he asked his colleagues to bury him in the sand after he died because he could not fulfill his duty while alive. He died in 1964, his last words expressing regret that he had not completed the duty the Party had assigned to him. Beside him were Mao's *Selected Works* and Liu Shao-ch'i's *How to Be a Good Communist!*[108]

In the tradition of the army's Lei Feng and Wang Chieh, in January 1966 the Party launched the campaign, Learn from Chao Yü-lu, a Good Cadre of Chairman Mao.[109] As a *Red Flag* commentator explained, the message of this campaign was that Chao was a good example of properly studying and applying Mao's Thought.[110]

The Chao Yü-lu campaign gradually changed the political atmosphere within the CCP. But as Mao's supporters escalated the campaign, they ran into conflicts with the Party bureaucracy, leading to the eventual Cultural Revolution, which had already surfaced in February 1966 behind the scene. In January 1966, T'ao Chu promptly sensed this shift and "suddenly" put forth the Decision of the Profound Study of Mao's Works at the plenum of the Central-South Bureau. (Exactly one year later, he was under attack for the political speculativeness manifested in that decision.)[111] Despite this shift of political mood, Liu Shao-ch'i maintained that the current trend substituted the four cleanup with a

Mao-study campaign; Teng Hsiao-p'ing apparently sensed that excessive study of Mao's works would lead to spiritual oppression. Commenting on a report by the CCP's Finance and Trade Political Department, P'eng Chen noted that it was full of Mao quotes but made no reference to finance; Li Hsien-nien called the report "Chiang Wei-ch'ing," a derision for excessive use of Mao quotes in public documents because Chiang Wei-ch'ing, secretary of Kiangsu, had been criticized previously by Liu Shao-ch'i for doing just that. A year later, all these leaders were to confess their errors for downgrading Mao study, as Ch'en Yi did, saying: "Owing to pressures of work, we had no time to study Mao's works. I am not lying."[112]

THE INSTITUTIONALIZATION OF POLICY PROCESSES AND MAO'S QUEST FOR MASS MOBILIZATION

The CCP's performance during the SEM reveals a growing degree of institutionalization in the policy process. The conflicts between Mao and the Party apparatus can also be explained in this perspective. When Mao formulated the Former Ten Points in May 1963, he made it clear that the SEM would concentrate on ideological education to be carried out through mass movement. But the Party's operational *means* for implementing the SEM gradually transformed the initial *end* of the movement from class education to organizational rectification. This change stemmed from differing perceptions within the Party of rural problems. Mao saw them as expressions of sharp class struggle as stated in the Former Ten Points, but the Party Secretariat regarded them as questions of four-unclean cadres as stated in the Later Ten Points. In the Revised Later Ten Points, Liu Shao-ch'i defined the problem strictly in terms of problem solving by describing the current difficulties as overlapping contradictions that crisscrossed the Party and the masses, and even friends and enemies. Liu's analysis, in effect, amounted to an alteration of Mao's theory in the guise of Maoist phraseology. After having witnessed all these digressions, Mao used the Twenty-Three Points to resurrect the original goal of class education.

These interactions between Mao and his associates at the Center, and the Center's demands and the local responses, resulted in a "rule of anticipated reaction" typical of all bureaucratic politics.[113] For example, when Mao formulated the Former Ten Points, he must have done so in anticipation of the Party Center's reaction; then the Secretariat formulated the Later Ten Points in the light of its own understanding of Mao's intentions expressed in the Former Ten Points and in anticipation of Mao's response to its formulation; so, too, did Liu Shao-ch'i in formulating the Revised Ten Points; and finally with the

Twenty-Three Points Mao vetoed the internecine two documents in the light of his understanding of the implementation by his associates and in anticipation of their reaction to his reversal. Apparently, Mao's associates sought to accommodate Mao's policy demands by avoiding consultation with him on details of policy implementation. To a certain extent, this was inevitable because those administering policy had to devise operational measures on the basis of their own perception of the policy intent. But it also means that the institutional mechanisms of policy execution—particularly the Secretariat—developed an autonomous life of its own—what Mao later called an "independent kingdom." For example, in the name of Mao's Thought, the Secretariat attempted to fill the deficiency of Mao's Former Ten Points in its Later Ten Points. But Mao found that the new directive lacked measures for mass mobilization. Aided by the T'aoyüan experience, Liu then came to regard work teams as the best way to mobilize the peasants, as expressed in the Revised Later Ten Points. Likewise, after two revisions had been made of Mao's original document, the emphasis upon class education and mass movement had yielded to a program for reshuffling the basic-level cadres through organizational control.

Similar processes took place in the two-way interactions between the Center and the localities. When the Center demanded that localities carry out Party directives, the localities also sought to accomodate them. Variations in local conditions made this inevitable. And the local cadres also learned how to survive Party-initiated campaigns with the experience they had acquired through previous campaigns over the years. As these cadres became capable of using many provisions of Party directives to protect themselves, the campaigns themselves were bound to be ritualized and ineffective, for a rule of diminishing return had existed. The more the revolutionary political system in China became institutionalized, the more its local political subsystems—the masses and local cadres—also became capable of evading (perhaps countermobilizing) the source of mobilization—the Party and its cadres. This means that, despite the frantic efforts by the regime to mobilize the population, government authority did not sufficiently penetrate into the rural population. Througout the SEM, Liu came to realize this problem, and he wanted to organize strong work teams precisely to make Party authority effectively penetrate into the protective network of the local political subsystems.

Thus, Liu and Mao differed significantly from one another in their approaches to coping with local cadre problems and their bureaucratization. Basically, Liu's approach was practical, remedial (and punitive), and organizational; whereas Mao's was ideological (and moral), affective, and educational. To obtain more accurate information, Liu relied more upon the method of squatting at a spot long enough to conduct calculated experimentation, investigate the situation, secretly if necessary, and link up and take roots among the peasants. This was necessary, Liu contended, because the usual method of open investigations and mass rallies could no longer reveal the really unclean cadres. Only by sending down relatively large work teams led by high Party cadres could the sinister cadres be exposed. The aim of this strategy was to rectify irregularities among cadres and to coopt able peasants and cadres into the local leadership. Thus, he sought to rectify the errors of policy administrators. To control corruption and bureaucratic power in this manner, Liu, in effect, advocated setting up a hierarchy of countervailing organizations under the Party, that is, the work teams would act in opposition to the existing local apparatus. So long as this principle was enforced, any ad hoc alliance of Party-state cadres, work teams, and the masses outside Party direction was untenable.

This institutionalized policy process actually undermined Mao's quest for mass mobilization and participation. Mao's approach was to mobilize as much mass initiative as possible. He preferred to collect information directly from those activists at the basic level who had actively responded to his calls. Since he wanted to arouse class consciousness through mass persuasion, he naturally favored open investigations and rallies. Instead of saturating communes with large work teams through "human sea" tactics, he suggested making an alliance of local cadres, work teams, and the masses so that the masses could criticize Party leaders. By so doing, he identified the target as policy makers themselves at higher levels. Essentially, Mao resorted to the "moralizing" effects of ideological persuasion and education to curb the unclean cadres and their abuse of power, for the aim was to transform rather than to control their behavior.[114]

Because of these divergencies, Mao and the Party bureaucracy ran into conflict. The more Mao attempted to impose his policy on the Party, the more he realized that the entire Party bureaucracy was blocking his efforts. Finally, at the Hangchow conference of December 1964, Mao came to perceive "those Party persons in authority taking the capitalist road," that is, the Party establishment, as the target of the SEM. To overthrow this, he resorted to the Cultural Revolution in 1966.

6
The Army's Emulation Campaigns

While the Party ritualistically mobilized the masses in the SEM, the PLA was actually mobilizing its troops in a series of emulation campaigns during 1962-66. This contrast, in fact, had existed in 1959-62 when the Party under Liu Shao-ch'i's leadership was involved in sweeping policy adjustments in the aftermath of the GLF while the army under Lin Piao carried out ideological indoctrination at the company level to overcome demoralization among its troops. The army's emulation campaigns gained further momentum after the Tenth Plenum and eventually became a nationwide movement in themselves. Both the Party's SEM and the army's emulation campaigns were directed at the basic-level cadres, and in principle, both aimed at class education and mass campaigns. In practice, however, these two organizations yielded somewhat different results in implementing their respective programs. The differences were particularly salient in the leadership style and the method of each organization. Because of these differences, it became apparent that in the SEM the entire Party bureaucracy was resistant to Mao's leadership style and policies, while in the army's campaigns the leadership and the rank-and-file were more responsive to them. Therefore, while Mao sought to struggle against the Party bureaucracy, he held out the army as the model for emulation by the entire nation.

THE LEADERSHIP

To begin with, the leadership of the PLA's top machinery proved to

123

be more amenable to Mao's ideas and policies than to the Party's. According to the 1956 Party constitution, the MAC was under the Central Committee, but after 1960 it apparently operated outside the executive bodies of the Central Committee: the Politburo's Standing Committee and Secretariat. After Lin Piao became minister of defense and first vice-chairman of the MAC, he continuously asserted his leadership as Mao's alter ego in the MAC's standing committee.[1] The only source of dissent within this committee turned out to be Lo Jui-ch'ing, secretary-general of the standing committee, but Lo had not seriously challenged Lin Piao before 1964; he was accused of having by-passed the MAC, reporting directly to the Party Secretariat of which he was a secretary primarily after 1964.[2]

Where military policy was involved, the standing committee of the MAC corresponded to the Standing Committee of the Politburo. And where political work within the army was concerned, the GPD took charge of political work within the PLA. After Lo Jung-huan died in 1962, Hsiao Hua became deputy director of the GPD, together with Liu Chih-chien.

Ever since the Ku-t'ien conference in 1929, when the CCP attempted to eradicate a purely military viewpoint by establishing the political commissar system within the Fourth Worker-Peasant Red Army (Mao Tse-tung was its first commissar and Chu Teh its commander), PLA units have had a dual leadership: the Party representative and the army commander.[3] When the Party adopted the Draft Provisional Regulations Governing the Political Work in the Chinese Worker-Peasant Red Army in 1932, it made the political commissar a permanent institution. A generation later, in March 1963, especially after it had undergone intensive political campaigns in 1960-62, the PLA revised the old draft (which was once revised in 1940 after the Red Army was placed under the Kuomintang command) and put forth a new document, Regulations Governing the Political Work in the Chinese People's Liberation Army.[4] Significantly, this document identified the study of Mao's writings as the central part of the army's political education. Article 2 of the document underlined this by restating the core of the 1960 enlarged MAC's resolution: "The Thought of Comrade Mao Tse-tung is the guide to the Chinese revolution and socialist construction; it is the guide to the construction of the Chinese People's Liberation Army and the political work of the army."[5]

The army had its own chain of command for such political work. Under the GPD, each service had its own political commissars and political departments. At each unit there were the political officers who usually led the political departments in the command unit: political commissars in the military regions, the provincial military districts, the divisions, and the regiments and battalions; political instructors in the companies and the squad; and political fighters in the platoon.[6] As far as political work was concerned, they operated independently of the commanders and in some cases could overrule the commanders' decisions. Most of the Party secretaries in the provincial and hsien Party committees served concurrently as first political commissar of the military command in the regions; for example, T'ao Chu was first political commissar of the Canton Military Region of which Huang Yung-sheng was commander, and Chao Tzu-yang first political commissar of the Kwang-tung Provincial Military District, of which Huang Yung-hai was commander. As these Party leaders were engrossed in their territorial Party affairs, the bulk of PLA political work was left to the second political commissar (Liu Hsing-yuan in the Canton region) or the director of the political department. These commissars often were dedicated veterans with long experiences in political work during the Yenan period. The PLA's political institutes (*cheng-chih hsüeh-yuan*) periodically retrained them while absorbing new blood into their ranks from the young activists.[7]

THE EMULATION CAMPAIGNS

In January 1963, the GPD promptly transmitted the "four-first" principle that Lin Piao had enunciated in 1960. The PLA had several organizational advantages over the Party in implementing a central policy like this one without undue delay and distortion. First of all, the army was less affected by local variations. As Lin Piao once said, discipline was more necessary in the army than in any other organizations since it had to retain combat effectiveness.[8] This made for great differences between the army barracks and the factories or villages. Not only were there more mobility and transfers among the soldiers but their length of service also was limited: three years in the army, four years in the air force, and five years in the navy. All this made it difficult for the military units, particularly those at the basic level, to develop their vested interests. In peace time the army's functions were simpler than those of the Party. While the Party was increasingly involved in the multifunctional work of government and administration, the army could devote itself to single tasks, such as political work. The Yenan experience in this regard remained a source of inspiration, for veterans of the period still held leading posts in the army extending to the company level. The informal relationship between the officers and the men that had been so valuable in the old guerrilla wars was still regarded as a virtue.[9]

The method of recruitment made service in the PLA a highly respected and coveted position. Legally, the army conscripted draftees between the ages of eighteen and twenty-two, who had to report whenever they were called. In practice, however, the draft was oversubscribed in most places by volunteers. Only one out of about twenty applicants were chosen, depending on the areas involved; only one or two in a commune could get such an opportunity at each call.[10] The local Party committees made recommendations about the candidates' political standing and other qualifications but the hsien military affairs department made the final decision. Not only did this selectivity make the draft appear attractive, but more important were the prospects for future livelihood opened up in the army. Without question, life in the PLA was better than in the villages—not just in material well-being but in other fields as well. The enviable PLA soldier was eligible for education that he could not afford in the villages. If he did well, he could remain beyond the stipulated years of service; if he was discharged with a good record, his chance for an appropriate civilian job increased. While in service, his family was generally taken care of. No wonder that those youths unable to enroll in the high schools or universities coveted the draft and that draftees wanted by all means to remain in the service.[11]

All these special attributes made the army better prepared for carrying out mass campaigns, as shown, for instance, by the "four-good" company movement that the GPD initiated at the New Year of 1961. After that time, many companies developed different methods of approximating the four goals. In April 1962 the GPD laid down seven guidelines for the campaign. The key point was that the leading organs above the company level must put forth some broad principles but must not interfere with the concrete method the companies adopted. The cadres of the divisions and regiments were asked to go down to the companies but no more than three cadres could squat within one company.[12] In contrast to the Party's policy in the SEM, the PLA made these efforts at preventing the higher organs from directly controlling the campaigns at the basic level so that the soldiers could criticize their own cadres.

A company was composed of about one hundred twenty soldiers and led by the company chief (lien-chang) and the political instructor (cheng-chih chih-tao-yuan). Within the company there was the soldiers congress for discussing general affairs and the soldiers club, which was divided into several committees, charged with a specific task such as displaying wall newspapers, undertaking military study and political study, and providing programs of athletics and recreation and for hygiene and economic cooperation.[13] As for political study, the political instructor assumed an over-all leadership; he often served as secretary of the company Party branch. Party members comprised the majority of the political study committee; they served as leaders of small groups comprising eight or twelve soldiers. The study session was conducted in small groups; it usually began with what was called "situation education" (*hsing-shih chiao-yü*), which was the group leader's explanation of the Party's evaluation on the current domestic and international situation. The participants compared the situation with that of the old period. The veterans, reminiscing about how hard it had been, often told the young soldiers their revolutionary stories. The "two recollections and three examinations" (*erh-yi san-ch'a*) continued to be a major part of this study: by recollecting the sufferings of the proletariat and the Chinese nation in the past, the soldiers were supposed to re-examine their own standpoint, their will to struggle, and their work style.

These study sessions then concentrated on the study of Mao's works. The group leaders or someone else read Mao's quotations or the full text of the "three constantly read articles": "Serve the People," "The Foolish Old Man Who Moved Mountains," and "In Memory of Norman Bethune." Each member offered his comprehension of the readings, trying to relate it to his own experiences. Sometimes they expressed their comprehension (*hsin-teh*) by way of written essays. Through these studies, they selected those activists they thought had shown best comprehension, and gave them the title of Five-Good Soldiers, that is, Chairman Mao's Good Fighter. In this manner, the four-good company and the five-good soldiers went hand in hand.[14]

In 1962, there were numerous conferences of these activists. In the spring of 1963, the GPD singled out a public security force company in Shanghai and gave it the title of Eighth Good Company of Nanking Road as a standard bearer (*piao-ping*) for emulation. Despite its urban environment, this company was noted for its good work style and for having produced a maxim in studying Mao's works: First Read, Second Discuss, Third Compare, and Fourth Act.[15] In February 1963 the GPD convened the all-army political work conference to sum up the experiences of the four-good company campaign. Hsiao Hua delineated twelve experiences; of these the two most tangible were the reorganization of the army's basic-level Party organizations and the recruitment of activists.[16]

A conspicuous example of these emulations was the Learn from Lei Feng campaign. No sooner was the diary of Lei Feng, which had been compiled by the GPD, reported in the press in February 1963 than the

Learn from Lei Feng campaign engulfed the whole country. After the *People's Daily* of February 7, 1963, first revealed Lei Feng's life, Mao personally gave his blessing to the campaign by writing the inscription, Learn from Comrade Lei Feng.[17] The YCL and the general head-quarters of the Chinese Trade Union promptly responded to this by calling upon their local organizations to emulate Lei Feng.

Lei Feng was a platoon leader of a transportation company in the Shenyang Military Region. A poor peasant's son, his family had experienced unspeakable sufferings under the old landlords. Relating his past, he wrote:

Thinking of the past I feel intense hatred for the "three major enemies" [imperialism, feudalism, and bureaucratic capitalism]. Thinking of the present I feel I owe unbounded gratitude to the Party and Chairman Mao for their kindness. Looking into the future, I feel full energy and confidence. I am determined to fight to the bitter end for the cause of communism.[18]

It was this commitment that made Lei Feng worthy of emulation. Furthermore, his life story, as recorded in his diary, was the epitome of Maoist virtues. He was born in a peasant home, but later became a worker in an Anshan mine, and then volunteered for the army to be Chairman Mao's Good Fighter. With great repose, he was constantly steeling himself, guarding against all possible temptations, to become "a steering wheel of revolution." He wrote in his diary: "A screw has to be regularly cleaned so that it may not rust. The same is true of a man's thought. It must be regularly examined so that it may not go wrong.[19] To become such a "rust-proof screw," he was said to have studied Mao's works faithfully and followed every line of them.

Lei Feng died August 15, 1962, at the age of twenty-two. While directing the truck driven by his assistant, he did not see a big wooden post standing by the roadside. The truck bumped into the post and then crashed on to Lei Feng. Five months later, the Ministry of Defense gave his platoon the title of Lei Feng Platoon and posthumously called him Chairman Mao's Good Fighter. For Lei Feng had "read Chairman Mao's works, listened to his words, worked according to his instructions, and had become his good fighter."[20]

All Communists were called upon to "regard Lei Feng as a mirror in life to see himself in that mirror, as a flag in production to lash himself, as a model (*fang-yang*) in study to encourage himself, and as a standard bearer in ideology to measure himself."[21] What counted was less the authenticity of the story than the message the campaign tried to convey. The GPD made Lei Feng a hero to demonstrate that possession of the correct ideology—which came from studying Mao's works—would result in such an exemplary life. Using Lei Feng as a model, the PLA also aimed to train successors to the basic-level cadres, claiming that it produced a maxim, Problem-Study-Practice-Sum Up.[22]

The use of a hero like Lei Feng provided the young with an example they could emulate. In this sense, the campaign had a moral and educational utility. Lei Feng also served as a direct linkage between the masses and the Supreme Leader in whose image he was projected. Such an example, if followed, was to function as a policy just as any other Party directive was. In 1963 and 1964, PLA drama units made plays and films about Lei Feng and widely circulated them across the country.[23] But as an officially sanctioned example, the use of these idealized symbols risked lower credibility.

LEARN FROM THE PEOPLE'S LIBERATION ARMY

The PLA-initiated emulations culminated in the Learn from the PLA campaign of 1964. Apparently, Mao was gratified with the army's performances, for he called upon the whole country to learn from the army in December 1963.[24] He also asked Party members to overcome conservatism and complacency by learning from one another, for some people within the Party had become arrogant by neglecting the might of the people and their subjective understanding lagged behind the development of objective reality.[25] Despite this warning, the Party leadership's response was still negative. But Lin Piao seized upon the occasion to step up political indoctrination by the army whose GPD promptly responded to Lin's instructions.

In January 1964 Hsiao Hua made a report on some problems of political work in the PLA. In it he set forth three new tasks for 1964: (1) an education against modern revisionism, (2) the training of successors to the basic-level cadres, and (3) the reforming of leadership style.[26] On February 1, 1964, when the *People's Daily* editorialized on "The Whole Country Must Learn from the PLA," it made the PLA's experiences a national model in accordance with Mao's instructions. The four-first principle was expanded to have universal meaning. To learn from the PLA, other sectors were, as the slogan went, to Compare, Learn, Catch Up With, and Help.[27]

In January 1964 Mao issued another directive urging all Party units to learn from the PLA and the example of the Tach'ing oilfield, to set up political departments, and to emulate the four-first and the three-eight work style.[28] Thus he raised the slogan, In Industry Learn from Tach'ing Oilfield and in Agriculture Learn from Tachai Brigade.[29] Lin Piao then called for a swift and decisive work style both in transmitting central directives within the army, stressing the importance of newspapers for doing this, and in reflecting local situations. Lin also urged the PLA units to use the dialectical method of taking hold of both ends of things such as subject and contents, theory and practice.[30]

The GPD and some members of the *Red Flag* editorial staff had already begun to coordinate their activities at this time. From March through May 1964, "Commentator" of the *Red Flag* wrote four articles, each commenting on one aspect of Lin Piao's four firsts. The first article dwelt on the role of ideology, making a strong plea for ideological work by asserting: "Work is done by man, and man's activities are governed by his ideology."[31] Then, it noted that a tendency to place less emphasis upon ideology had occurred within the Party:

Some people may think that to fulfill their tasks it seems enough merely to rely on authority and orders, and organizational leadership; that it is enough to be engrossed in economic work, with no need to pay special attention to ideological work, to care about the ideological conditions of the cadres and the masses. Or they may think that it is enough to do some ideological work only when a political campaign is on, and there is no need for day-to-day systematic work in this field.[32]

The central point of this passage was essentially identical with that of an article Ch'en Po-ta had written in 1958 to criticize the opponents of the GLF.[33] Although one cannot say for sure the Ch'en actually wrote this, one thing is clear: it restated Mao's emphasis on ideology. Equally clear is that it was a veiled attack on those unspecified people within the Party who did not pay as much attention to ideological work as the PLA did.

The second article, commenting on political work and reminding the Party of Mao's dictum delivered at the Ku-t'ien conference, castigated people who thought: "Once the proletariat took power, politics can no longer take precedence over economics, because the major task of the era is to carry out economic construction, and politics must serve the economic base that has been already established; hence economics should command politics and not the other way round."[34] Clearly, the commentator was counterattacking the prevalent views within the Party leadership voiced in 1961-62. By doing so, he was reviving another precept Mao had espoused in 1956: Political Work is the Life Line of All Works.[35]

For the third principle of the four firsts, that is, living ideology over book ideology, the commentator championed the PLA's experience in the study of Mao's works. The commentator then listed ten cases of the "living study and application of the Thought of Mao Tse-tung."[36] Finally, touching on the relationship between man and matter, he held man to be the decisive factor, claiming that such a position was a fundamental viewpoint of Marxism-Leninism.[37]

These articles urged the non-PLA units to emulate the PLA in the four aspects and implied that the Party had not sufficiently grasped them. Hence, the Party had to respond. Then, a host of attempts to emulate the four-good fighters occurred in communes, enterprises, and mass organizations. Among these were five-good communes, five-good workshops, five-good workers, five-good youths, five-good women, and so on.[38] A more direct way of learning from the PLA was the establishment of political departments in the Party-state apparatus, modeled after the army's political departments. In February 1964 the finance and trade systems first set up the political departments, and some cadres were actually transferred from the PLA to organs of finance and trade. The industry and transportation systems also followed suit. By June, all six staff offices of the State Council instituted political departments, and that same summer in 1964, the provincial agencies also followed suit.[39]

When Mao asked the Party to Learn from the PLA, he also endorsed two other emulations directly affecting the SEM: In Industry Learn from Tach'ing and in Agriculture Learn from Tachai. The Tach'ing oilfield as a model revived the multifunctionalism characteristic of the 1958 commune: the Tach'ing Spirit denoted combining industry and agriculture, the cities and the countryside, and mental labor and manual labor.[40] The Tachai Spirit meant self-reliance and hard struggle, for the Tachai brigade demonstrated that it could overcome natural hazards, yet achieve a high-yield farm by relying on itself and mobilizing its revolutionary enthusiasm. In addition, the communes emulated the PLA's "two recollections and three investigations" by compiling four histories—a history of the commune, the brigade, land reform, and collectivization. Thus the editorial of the *People's Daily* commemorating the fifteenth anniversary of the Chinese People's Republic saw all these emulations—Learn from the PLA, Learn from Tach'ing, and Learn from Tachai—as the integral part of the SEM.[41]

Another important aspect of this campaign was the PLA's method for the struggle against modern revisionism and for training revolutionary successors. After the CPSU rejected, in July 1963, the CCP's General Line of the international Communist movement, the CCP published all of the Soviet responses. On the premise that truth develops in struggle between two opposites, the PLA used these polemics as "teaching materials by negative example" (*fan-mien chiao-tsai*). The Party also required its cadres to read these materials in contrast to Mao's writings so that they could master the true Marxism-Leninism against modern revisionism.[42]

To fight modern revisionism, which was allegedly benumbing the revolutionary will of the Chinese youth, Mao called upon the entire

Party in June 1964 to pay more attention to military affairs and to cultivate and train revolutionary successors. Asserting that the third generation in the Soviet Union produced Khrushchev and to prevent such happening in China, he laid down five conditions for these successors: (1) they must be genuine Marxist-Leninists; (2) they must be revolutionaries who wholeheartedly serve the overwhelming majority of the people of China and the whole world; (3) they must be proletarian statesmen capable of uniting and working together with the overwhelming majority; (4) they must be models in applying the Party's democratic centralism and mass line; and (5) they must be modest and imbued with the spirit of self-criticism.[43]

The most important legacy of the campaign Learn from the PLA, therefore, was the study of Mao's works. In May 1964, the *PLA Daily* published the first version of *Quotations from Chairman Mao Tse-tung*. In July, following the 1961 version of the GPD's *Quotations*, the Party's editing committee for selected readings from Mao's works put out two volumes: *Selected Readings from Mao's Works A* and *Selected Readings from Mao's Works B*,[44] the former intended mainly for the cadres and the latter for the youth. Particularly where youth were concerned, Yao Wen-yüan argued in a *Red Flag* article that power seizure by the proletariat was not the end of revolution but the beginning, and that revolution therefore had to be handed down from one generation to another.[45] Noteworthy about this development was that the PLA's political work provided initiatives for Mao study not only within the army but also for the Party as well.[46] The PLA led the work in this Maoist indoctrination, thus usurping to a degree the role of the Party.

This is not to say, however, that the army led the Party organizationally. To the contrary, all campaigns emanating from it had to go through Party organizations, since Party committees set up the political departments and prescribed how to study Mao's writing. Even the PLA cadres who were transferred from the army to civilian posts were placed under the thumb of the Party committees. A case in point was the Political Department of Agriculture and Forestry staff office. The Party committee under T'an Chen-lin had exerted its control over the cadres in the department (who had come from the PLA) so tightly that when the Cultural Revolution came they first revolted against T'an Chen-lin.[47]

There is reason to believe, too, that the majority of the Party leadership were apprehensive of the way the army had been conducting the Mao-study campaign. For example, in September 1964, Liu Shao ch'i wrote a letter to Chiang Wei-ch'ing, first Secretary of the Kiangsu provincial committee, criticizing the excessive use of Mao's quotations in public documents. He had this to say in his letter:

This involves a question of principle—the question of whom we should learn from. We should learn form those who know the truth among the masses within or without the Party regardless of whether the positions they hold are high or low, but not from those who hold high posts. . . .We cannot regard the doctrines of Marxism-Leninism as dogma, nor can we regard Mao Tse-tung's writings and talks as dogma.[48]

Liu disseminated this letter to all provinces. In 1966, Mao himself referred to it: "Liu Shao-ch'i criticized Chiang Wei-ch'ing, saying that Chiang was stupid. Is he himself clever?"[49] In 1964, however, T'ao Chu of Kwangtung praised this letter and Liu Chien-hsün of Honan specifically restricted the use of Mao quotations in documents.[50] Besides, in February 1964 the Propaganda Department decreed that no publication of Mao's works would be permitted without prior approval from the Center. In August 1964, when the Propaganda Department convened the National Conference on Political Theory Class, Lu Ting-yi, director of the department, characterized the vogue of Mao study as "oversimplification, pragmatism, and formalism"; he went so far as to say that those who overstudied it would become "mummies" or traitors if war came.[51] Chou Yang, deputy director of the department, enjoined the New China Publishing House from printing more Mao books. P'eng Chen directed NCNA not to use such slogans as: The Thought of Mao Tse-tung Is the Peak of Marxism-Leninism or Chairman Mao Has Fully Developed Marxism-Leninism, because they "simplify and vulgarize" Mao's Thought. And Wu Leng-hsi, director of NCNA, also instructed that since the workers, peasants, and soldiers could not get quick results from such Mao study, it must not be done with "a big hullabaloo." As for the PLA's emulation method, Wang Kuang-mei, for example, maintained that it might be suitable for the companies in the army but was not applicable to the villages in the countryside.[52]

This resistance from Party leaders made Mao turn to the army for ideological revitalization. When he formulated the Twenty-Three Point directive in December 1964 to repudiate the Party's SEM, he specifically called upon the communes to learn from the PLA. While the responses of the Party leadership were still lukewarm, the PLA leadership continued its exemplary adherence. The 1965 New Year editorial of the *PLA Daily* called for putting politics in command of everything. On June 1, 1965, the army abolished all the military ranks and insignias; in June, some PLA units carried out the military training of college students;[53] in August, the GPD published a revised edition of *Quotations from Chairman Mao* with a new preface proclaiming that Mao's Thought was the Marxism-Leninism of the era. While the September-

October 1965 central work conference was in session, during which Mao issued the warning against revisionism at the Party Center, the PLA initiated the Learn from Wang Chieh campaign.[54] In the wake of this campaign, the momentum for studying Mao's Thought culminated in Lin Piao's November directive for the "living study and application of Mao's Thought" in 1966.

In September 1965, the GPD presented to the public another PLA hero, Wang Chieh, who had sacrificed himself to save a trainee in July while training a militia contingent of a commune in Kiangsu. He was hailed for his "single-minded devotion to revolution" (*i-hsin wei-ke-ming*). Like Lei Feng, Wang Chieh had pledged to become "a docile tool of the Party and a good fighter of Chairman Mao."[55]

In November 1965, Lin Piao ordered the GPD to popularize Wang Chieh's spirit of "fearing neither hardship nor death" (*i-pu-p'a-ku erh-pu-p'a-ssu*). Shortly thereafter, Mao had personally commended this spirit.[56] At the same time, Lin also issued the five-item directive for political work in 1966. The five items were: (1) the living study and application of Mao's works with the emphasis on application, (2) the promotion of the four firsts with the emphasis on living ideology, (3) the transfer of the leading cadres to the basic level for the four-good company movement, (4) the recruiting of able commanders for responsible posts, and (5) training for close fighting and night combats. (Chief of Staff Lo Jui-ch'ing sought to evade implementing this directive by taking up only the last item while downgrading the rest before he was purged.)[57]

With the campaign for the Living Study and Application of Mao's Thought, Lin Piao again held out the PLA as the national model. In December 1965 Lin cleared a final hurdle to this campaign within the army by removing Lo Jui-ch'ing from his post. By this time, the PLA-initiated campaigns were not confined to the basic level but extended to the higher levels. As the army intensified these actions at the end of 1965 and more so in early 1966, the synchronization of Mao's wishes and the army's responses drastically transformed the over-all mood of political life in China and eventually created a "public opinion" for the forthcoming Cultural Revolution.

THE ARMY LEADS THE PARTY?

In contrast to the Party bureaucracy, the army proved to be more amenable to Mao's approach to problem-solving, as shown by the various campaigns within the army that were patterned upon the Maoist method of mass movement. Accordingly, the kind of goal-replacement procedures that occurred in the Party's SEM did not take place in the army's emulation campaigns. With the exception of Lo Jui-ch'ing, the top army leadership under Lin Piao closely implemented Mao's policy. The MAC made the study of Mao's writings the core of the army's political work, and the GPD made every effort to ensure that all military units would implement that policy. Hence, unlike the Party, there was no communication gap between the initiator of policy and those who implemented it within the army.

Central directives of the army were also less affected by local variations, and the basic-level organizations could implement them without much distortion. Unlike the Party's SEM, higher military units were *not* to control activities at the company level insofar as political work was concerned, since an informal relationship still existed between the officers and the men as in the Yenan days. Two additional factors helped maintain the army as an organization conducive to mass movement: first, it could devote itself to single-purpose tasks, and second, its recruitment was highly selective and its soldiers were more ideologically motivated than any other sector of the population. These factors made it easy for the army companies to conduct small-group discussions and to adopt emulation in their political indoctrination. The model of behavior for such emulation—as exemplified by Lei Feng and Wang Chieh—then served as a policy guideline, linking the leadership and the basic level, so that all other units could take uniform actions. Therefore, in controlling the military in general and its lower units in particular, the Chinese PLA used the method of subjective control through politicization instead of an objective control through professionalization. Thus, the army increasingly utilized ideology while the Party relied on cooptation.[58]

This endeavor led to a basic reshuffling of Party organizations within the army. Although the army did not plan it in advance, the army-initiated campaigns, in effect, became a training exercise for the forthcoming Cultural Revolution. Since the PLA's performance in its campaigns came closer to what Mao had been urging the CCP to follow, naturally, Mao sanctioned the army's emulation campaigns while repudiating the Party's SEM. In 1964, he even called upon the entire nation to learn from the PLA. But as the advent of Mao study spilled into other sectors outside the army, the Party Center tried to curb some politically harmful aspects of such campaigns. Particularly after the September-October 1965 central work conference, at which Mao raised the specter of revisionism in the Central Committee, Lin Piao purged Lo Jui-ch'ing and further intensified the army's quest for Mao study with the campaigns: Learn from Wang Chieh and the Living Study and Application of Mao's Works. When the Party bureaucracy still resisted these pressures, Mao turned to the army as an alternative source of support by mounting the Cultural Revolution; subsequently, the army was to become a most formidable force in Chinese politics.

7
Policy Innovations and Conflicts in the Economy, Education, and Health Care

The Socialist Education Movement produced differences between Mao Tse-tung and the Party bureaucracy over policy implementation. The analysis of the movement in chapter 5 revealed *how* such differences came into existence. A corollary question involves *why* the differences occurred. This chapter studies policy innovations and conflicts within the CCP's top circle during 1962-66 to provide a partial answer to this question. Liu Shao-ch'i and Mao Tse-tung, for example, not only addressed themselves to somewhat different problems in this period, but their innovative concerns also differed from one another. Liu introduced certain innovations in the economy, whereas Mao proposed particular innovations in education and health care. As in the SEM, Mao's policies generated a degree of tension between his demands for change and the responses of the Party "persons in authority" (*tang-ch'uan p'ai*), the Party establishment.[1] While Mao's demands were to stress equality, instant action, and comprehensive programs, Liu's responses were to stress efficiency, adequate preparations, and step-by-step progress. These tensions became gradually intensified in such areas as economic management, education, health service, and cultural activities, and finally culminated in the Cultural Revolution.

LIU'S POLICY INNOVATIONS IN THE ECONOMY

The basic trends in economic policy set in 1959-62 continued until 1965, at which time the Third Five-Year Plan was readied for initiation in 1966. Specifically, the Sixty Articles on Agriculture and the Seventy Articles on Industry had remained in effect since 1962; however in 1964, Liu Shao-ch'i introduced a number of other innovations to enhance efficiency in the current economic management, further consolidating the trend of 1959-62. He did so in three areas: agricultural mechanization, industrial management, and labor and education.

State-Financed Mechanization

In agriculture, the refurbished commune and the concept of agriculture as the foundation and industry as the leading factor continued to be Party policy. Liu introduced changes in the agricultural mechanization policy, however. Originally, the tractor stations had been centrally managed before the GLF. It is pertinent here that in March 1958, at the Chengtu conference, Mao formulated the document, Opinion Concerning the Question of Agricultural Mechanization. This document set forth three basic directions for the mechanization program: (1) that it be a mass movement for reforming farm implements, (2) that it emphasize semimechanization based on the small-scale improvement of traditional tools, and (3) that it be undertaken primarily by local funds and initiatives in line with the principle of self-reliance.[2] Apparently, during the adjustment period and thereafter, the Party Center not only failed to implement this directive but even ignored it by re-establishing the tractor stations. According to one report, Liu had not transmitted the directive until July 1964; only then was it circulated in the Eighth Ministry of Machine Building.[3]

In 1958, under the principle of mass line, the peasants were asked to improve farm implements upon their own initiative, since the communes owned most of the existing tractors. By 1962, however, the Party Center had reversed this policy. From 1963 on, the central ministry—the Ministry of Agricultural Machinery—directly took charge of the mechanization program, and the Agricultural Machine Stations (AMS) got back 88 percent of the tractors formerly owned by the communes. In 1964 there were 1,488 AMS in the country. For the management of the tractor stations, Liu proposed in early 1964 that "trusts" of the tractor stations and the tractor repair stations be set up under the Eighth Ministry of Machine Building. At the provincial level, this plan envisioned that the provincial departments for mechanization would become the agricultural mechanization companies so that they could centralize the management of the AMS.[4] This was designed to lower the cost of mechanization. The government could achieve this goal by improving technical maintenance, planning, technical reform, and rational adjustment in the management of the existing tractor stations.[5]

In 1964-65, Liu made some concrete plans for the formation of these trusts. Together with P'eng Chen, Liu planned to form a chain of the tractor stations in one hundred key hsien so that these stations would eventually lead to a national trust. Consequently, the state was to concentrate funds on these selected stations to make their mangement financially viable. At the end of 1964, this program led to the creation of the China Tractor and Internal Combustion Engine Parts Company. T'an Chen-lin also supported this plan. In February 1965, following a directive from Liu recommending that he use economic methods to run the economy characteristic of the trust, T'an enacted the Draft Regulations on Reforming the Management of State Farms. With this, he introduced the work-point system into the state farms in lieu of the existing wage system. Finally, in July 1965, a national conference on mechanization decided to set up the China Agricultural Machine (Service) Company because the trust of only spare parts was considered insufficient. In October, Liu made a trip to Heilungkiang to report on the plan. But because these measures ran counter to the mass-line principle of mechanization, Mao did not approve of them. And Mao's opposition kept the plan from materializing.[6]

As for the production of tractors, too, the Party Center gradually shifted the emphasis from the policy of semimechanization to that of producing large-scale modern equipment. In 1962, the Ministry of Agricultural Machinery suspended its efforts to improve farm implements by abolishing its Bureau for Farm Implement Improvement. On the premise that agricultural mechanization must keep pace with industrialization, in October 1964 Po I-po merged the production of automobiles with that of tractors by entrusting both tasks to the First Ministry of Machine Building. He asked the Eighth Ministry to turn over the task of agricultural mechanization to the First Ministry. He expected that the Eighth Ministry would be eventually placed under the staff office for the agriculture and forestry department.[7] But these measures did not mean that the state entirely suspended the program for semimechanization. According to Hsü Pin-chow, vice-minister of agricultural machinery, while the state promoted mechanization as well as semimechanization, semimechanization was always to have priority.[8]

Lastly, unlike the 1958 program, all these innovations were based on the principle that the state should assume responsibility for financial investment and support. Liu suggested the idea of trust precisely to cope with the financial problems faced by the tractor stations. Even after the AMS took up the operation of tractors, they ran in the red.

In 1963, leaders of the agriculture and forestry systems proposed to close down those deficit-producing stations within two years.[9] But the National Conference on Semimechanized Farm Equipment and Implements in October 1964 reaffirmed the self-reliance principle of the communes.[10] These facts suggest that by the end of 1964 Liu's policy for mechanization encountered a series of challenges from Mao's supporters.

Industrial Trust

Originally, the idea of trust was put forth by Liu for industrial management. The Seventy Articles on Industry of 1961 established a regular, uniform model for the management of enterprises. But the principles of decentralized enterprises started during the GLF continued: with the exception of those enterprises directly run by the central ministries, constituting some 10 percent of the total, the rest were still run by the provincial and local governments under diverse local conditions.[11] Not only did this practice cause a great deal of overlapping and waste in manpower, resources, and capital, but it also led to confusion in specifications and supply.

In an attempt to alleviate this situation, Liu proposed in late 1963 to organize what he called socialist trusts in several key enterprises. At first, a few pharmaceutical plants in Tientsin and Shanghai began a trial operation as a trust. In the fall of 1964, Po I-po selected four more industrial trades (*hang-yeh*) as experimental units; later on, they were extended to twelve trades, most of which were concerned with transportation and consumer goods such as pharmaceuticals, rubber, aluminum, motor vehicles, tractors, internal combustion engines, tobacco, salt, and textiles. In the meantime, preparations were being made to expand this to the steel and petroleum industries as well.[12]

The central idea of the trust was to organize all enterprises belonging to an industrial trade into a single nationwide company. In this way, the company could manage the manpower, resources, capital, and supply through a unified chain of command. The approach to the pharmaceutical enterprises illustrates how a trust was organized and what it set out to accomplish. In 1964, the central government set up the China Pharmaceutical Company and incorporated virtually all the existing pharmaceutical plants into the national network of this new company. A Western scholar who visited China to study the industrial management confirmed that this company was operating under the Ministry of Chemical Industry.[13]

First, Liu contended that the trust must be independent of local Party and government's intervention. He regarded this as vital to ensure that the principle of using economic method to run the economy be observed. As he saw it, the current way the Party and the government ran the economy was feudalistic: they meddled in every aspect of economic affairs, thus violating economic principles. Liu suggested, therefore, that a monopolized trust be empowered to tackle all the economic problems while the central and local government organizations assume only supervisory functions, collect the national taxes and the local surtaxes, and act as arbiters when disputes arose between individual enterprises.[14]

Each plant belonging to the China Pharmaceutical Company indeed was allowed to purchase the raw materials it needed and to dispose of its products, thus becoming an "end user" in itself, directly dealing with its suppliers as well as its consumers without going through the government's commercial departments. Teng Hsiao-p'ing maintained that the head office of a plant must concern itself only with such matters as plans, technology, finance, marketing, supply, and price. He noted that such a practice was being adopted in East Germany.[15] The head office of the Shanghai branch of the China Pharmaceutical Company indeed was allowed to dispose of its commodities, allocate its funds, and assign its personnel. However, this undercut the power of the basic-level Party and YCL branches, because the plant Party committees exercised a unified leadership over the personnel, ranging from the top mangement to the workers. In Tientsin's People's Pharmaceutical Plant, the trade union also was placed under the plant Party labor committee.[16]

Second, the trust was a highly monopolistic, unified, and centralized organ. According to Liu's explanation, "trust meant getting organized." A major shortcoming in the current enterprises, Liu believed, was their dispersion due to lack of organization. To rectify this, he advocated efficiently organized monopolies that could lower costs and raise quality and labor productivity. He maintained that China must learn even from the capitalist countries whose managerial ability exceeded that of the socialist countries. But he also urged learning from the Soviet Union, for the socialist economy must be more monopolistic and centralized than the capitalist economy. The purpose of monopolization and centralization was to maximize rationality; in the long run, the trust would facilitate a rational geographical distribution through better plans and organization, though it might look disadvantageous to the localities for the time being. Po I-po elaborated that a unified direction of enterprises in such areas as management, planning, finance, supply, and marketing was essential to rationality.[17]

To meet this requirement, considerable readjustments had to be made in the structure of each plant. A case in point was the Tientsin plant cited above, which renovated two buildings to emulate the Shanghai Hsin-i Pharmaceutical Plant. Within a few months in 1964, about 40 percent of the old pharmaceutical plants in China were shut down. The Shanghai branch of the China Pharmaceutical Company shed more light on this. The management ruled that plans must be set even for requisitioning matches, and specified six unifications, that is, unifications in six areas: supply, marketing, transportation, storage, procurement, and accounting; later on, they were increased to eight unifications with unified overhaul and unified examination added. As a result, the workers had to act only as the management specified.[18]

Third, the trust provided for increased specialization and specification. According to Po I-po, the trust was geared to organizing specialized production to avoid the irrational phenomena of duplicating the same product. In every plant, a clear-cut specialization took place. In Tientsin, many plants made only one product; for example, the tablet unit in a pharmaceutical plant turned out only tablets. The People's Pharmaceutical Plant had produced one hundred kinds of medicine before but after having been incorporated into the trust, it produced only five kinds with nine specifications. Also at the Shanghai branch, strict regulations were drawn to specify the range of responsibility for those who participated in the production process. Department heads were solely responsible for their own departments, and technicians and inspectors were put in charge of quality control and supervision. With this change, multifarious procedures requiring more forms and tables proliferated. Since the head office of the company branch decided upon plans and profits, and kept them in secret while each plant had only some say over the cost of its products, the technicians and the workers knew only what they were supposed to know. They followed the stipulated system of rules (*küei-chang chih-tu*) and produced according to its specifications.[19]

Lastly, the trust was geared to profit making as its main goal. Liu cogently argued that a factory must make money or stop paying wages to the workers. He stressed the importance of material incentives in promoting production, for the workers worked honestly when they were offered good wages. Since the China Pharmaceutical Company had a monopoly over the production and sale of medicine, most private and small-scale local plants were banned: about 100 of the nation's 283 pharmaceutical plants were closed down because they had made no profit. In order to increase profit, the surviving plants also were asked to improve the quality of their products.[20]

In defense of these measures, Liu was of the opinion that the question of trusts was one of seeking truth and not one of who estab-lished it.[21] He seemed to have probed for solutions that would enable the Chinese economy to attain maximum productivity, gain experience in the application of technology and management, and train skilled workers.[22] Management of the Chinese enterprises was far more decen-tralized than other socialist industrial systems, including the Soviet *sovnarkhoz* (with perhaps the exception of Yugoslavia), and involved more small enterprises; yet there was no administrative network for integrating the scattered enterprises. The Chinese managers themselves acknowledged that the enterprises were suffering from inefficiency under such a dispersed system of management.[23] The trust was con-ceived to enhance efficiency in the use of scarce materials and capital.

Not everyone was enchanted with the spread of trusts, however. Some Party officials were opposed to the function of the basic-level Party organizations being circumscribed. Apparently, low-echelon cadres and the workers also complained about the change. Ch'en Pei-hsin, first secretary of the Shanghai Municipal Committee, told a 1965 meeting of Party secretaries that since the direction of trusts was sound, they must not criticize its defects because innovations are always defec-tive at first. Furthermore, the accent on unification and centralization forced many plants to alter their work schedules. The principle of unified management put the management in control of everything; as a result the workers were said to have lost contact with the cadres. The requirements for specialization brought about so many forms and speci-fications that the workers became "tools" or "accessories of machines." Personnel in charge of supply, marketing, finance, and materials no longer had to meet every day as the management handed down all pre-determined schedules and specifications. The workers found the new procedures cumbersome, often causing more accidents than before. Finally, the emphasis on profit making failed to take into consideration the urgent needs of hospitals or local demands for special medicine, which had to be satisfied, however unprofitable.[24]

The local units also resented the great emphasis placed on quality. After the China Tobacco Company was set up under the Ministry of Light Industry in 1965, a local Party secretary in Honan reported to Li Hsien-nien, minister of finance, that the peasants had been complain-ing about the collection of only good quality tobacco. Li advised him to emphasize the positive aspects of Liu Shao-ch'i's directive, instead of reporting such negative cases.[25]

These complaints were all brought to light during the Cultural Revolution, however. And the Maoist accusations about the trusts also were raised ex post facto. They followed a familiar line: With the trusts enforced, Liu attempted to usurp Party leadership by setting up an industrial Party along the model of Khrushchev's 1962 reorganization in the Soviet Union. Liu extolled economics in command instead of politics in command; his call for centralization and monopoly went contrary to the mass line; and the emphasis on expert and material incentives was aimed at restoring capitalism. Therefore, the trust was a hotbed of revisionism, a device concocted for peaceful evolution in China.[26]

Despite these invectives leveled against Liu, there is little evidence either in the official press or Red Guard papers that Mao opposed the trusts at the time of their inception (except for the tractor company), in contrast to his opposition to the way Liu handled the SEM and educational policy (see below). Nor did Chou En-lai mention the trusts in his report to the third NPC of December 1964. There is evidence, however, that in 1964 Mao intermittently criticized the State Planning Commission for being an independent kingdom.[27] Because the Learn from Tachai in Agriculture and Learn from Tach'ing in Industry campaign did get under way, the trust concept as projected by Liu seemed to run counter to the trend of mass campaigns. Liu expressed apprehension about the Tach'ing campaign when a number of factory workers were sent to the countryside in the name of integrating the workers and the peasants. He maintained that such action could cause more problems in the long run by disrupting the production process in the factories, for skilled workers were in short supply in China.[28]

The Economic Region

Closely related to the industrial trusts, the experiment with the concept of an economic region at T'angshan showed a comparable innovation in commercial practices.[29] Although Liu was not identified with this reform, its essential feature accorded with the principle of organizing the trust, that is, to use economic methods to run the economy.

Like the trust, the rationale for the economic region was to achieve maximum rationality in commodity circulation in accordance with the natural marketing processes and transportation arrangements. From December 1963 to February 1965, the T'angshan Special District experimented with a plan to set up an economic region with five market towns along a major railway, crisscrossing several hsien in the area. The finance office of the North China Bureau and the Hopei Provincial Committee supervised this experimentation.[30] This was to prevent double shipping of commodities between cities, hsien, and production brigades, which often used the same route. For example, in the past a brigade near T'angshan city that was under the jurisdiction of a hsien had to ship its products to the hsien, which was far away, at which point the hsien shipped the merchandise back to T'angshan city over the same route. In the economic region, the basic-level Supply and Market Cooperatives in brigades and teams directly transacted commodities with the cities near them, thus bypassing the hsien authorities, and consequently getting better deals by reducing unnecessary duplication.[31]

As in the trust, the economic units within the economic region were granted a measure of autonomy. Not only in the transaction of commodities but also in the acquisition and management of personnel, the industrial areas and the agricultural areas in the same region apparently cooperated with each other, depending on seasonal demand and supply. Actually, the region promoted this as a Party policy. The Decision Concerning the Question of Commercial Work adopted at the Tenth Plenum of 1962 allowed each industrial city to have its own economic region.[32] Besides T'angshan, this system spread into other areas as well. In April 1965, the Kwangtung Provincial Party Committee also decided to set up such regions to promote a unified socialist market.[33]

This reform had certain profound consequences. The emphasis on the economic principle led the leading cadres in commercial organizations to concern themselves more with commodities and professional techniques at the expense of politics and ideology. A more tangible result was that the hsien Party committees and administrative agencies lost power. When several villages and a city made, in effect, an alliance against the hsien, the hsien lost power, causing demotion of its cadres. And as these economic regions provided new and greater opportunities, the migration of workers and peasants also increased between the city and the villages. This gave impetus to the worker-peasant (*i-kung i-nung*) system, for the unemployed workers in the city were able to work either in the city or in the villages.[34]

Two Kinds of Labor and Two Kinds of Education

In the search for rationality, a more comprehensive problem awaited resolution: the problem of employment and education. In China, jobs were still scarce; yet as the economy progressed, an increasing number of skilled workers, technicians, and administrators were required to run the economy. This was a dilemma, for the regime had anticipated in 1964 that under the Third Five-Year Plan, industries could only accommodate five million workers, while six million would still remain unemployed.[35] The current Chinese enterprises also were overstaffed—a form of disguised unemployment that caused lower productivity.[36] Moreover, this situation raised the question of how the regime should educate students for future employment. In coping with these problems, Liu proposed the "two kinds of labor" and "two kinds of education" systems.

In May 1964, Liu issued a directive on regularizing the practice of temporary labor, thus giving rise to two kinds of labor. Even before this measure was taken, the enterprises had employed the contract worker (ho-t'ung kung) or temporary workers (lin-shih kung) by concluding contracts whenever they deemed necessary.[37] Liu proposed anew that the enterprises employ more temporary workers and eliminate the redundant regular workers. He contended that the temporary workers would gradually acquire skills and eventally become the regular workers. In pursuit of economic efficiency, Liu was willing to tolerate, at least for the time being, a stratified labor system that rewarded the regular workers as a privileged group rather than the temporary worker, as K'ang Sheng later charged in 1967.[38] The regular workers were protected by their union and the national health insurance while the temporary workers had none of these benefits. With the two kinds of labor, Liu also encouraged those unemployed temporary workers to go back to the countryside, where they could become worker-peasants.

In order for the regime to plan future employment, however, it had to devise its educational policy in accordance with the prospect of manpower needs. Hence, job placement was inseparable from education. Besides, from 1963 on, Mao demanded a major reform in the current educational system (discussed later). Responding to these circumstances Liu initiated "two-track" education in line with the two kinds of labor, thus reviving in May 1964, the work-study system he had proposed in May 1958. The over-all aim of this reform was to universalize the secondary schools within the means of the state funds and the individual family.[39] Liu envisioned that such work-study schools would gradually replace the current full-time schools. Since over half the middle-school graduates could not afford the full-time high schools, the state had to establish a new school for them. After graduating from the middle schools, the students had a choice of going either to the full-time high schools or the work-study high schools. In the countryside, the communes or brigades were to set up the "farming-study" schools so that the students could work on the farm half a day and study in class half a a day. In the cities, the work-study schools were to conclude contracts with nearby factories so that students could work there for four hours and study at the school for another four hours, that is, the "four-four" system. Since the students' work constituted half their school time, they were to earn some money for their labor as their grades progressed.

Liu contended that, in the long run, instituting these vocational schools would best meet China's man-power needs. Since the state could not place every graduate of the secondary schools, Liu made it clear that the graduates of the work-study schools had to work as workers and peasants or worker-peasants. With this system, then, the state could not only alleviate its financial burden but also train more workers, technicians, engineers, and administrators. Hence, this new system could "kill three birds with one stone," by effecting man power, production, and technology.[40]

In 1964, Liu issued a directive specifying these measures in the name of the Central Committee. He visited some seventeen provinces and municipalities, making over twenty reports, and envisioned setting up eventually a second Ministry of Education with its own agencies and bureaus for the vocational schools.[41] After the central directive was transmitted, various localities began to experiment with this new type of school and labor as a practice of Party policy.[42]

It was only during the Cultural Revolution that Mao's supporters accused Liu of having stolen Mao's 1958 policy of half-work and half-study. The difference between Liu's policy and Mao's centered on the question of reforming the full-time schools: Liu wanted to preserve both the current full-time schools and the work-study schools, though he expected that the ratio of the latter to the former would gradually increase; but Mao wanted to transform all full-time schools into half-work and half-study schools. In fact, Liu also recognized the danger of revisionism that would follow the seizure of power by the proletariat, a point Mao had often made. To prevent such revisionism, however, Liu believed that the work-study system as he defined it would be one effective measure, together with two other measures: the Four Cleanup campaign and the participation of cadres in manual labor.[43]

Liu's approach to problem solving, exemplified in these areas, was unmistakable. He sought the most efficient economic means to achieve the desired goals. To make efficient use of limited man power, resources, and capital, he advocated that they must be organized, centralized, and differentiated. The trust derived from this quest for efficiency. Liu's attempt to develop the available resources gradually, stressing the adequacy of procedures, led to a sequential development, with industrialization the first order of business. To Liu, the prime tasks of the socialist state were to solve the question of distribution, to organize social life, and to promote material well-being. The fulfillment of these tasks required a solid, industrialized economy. In building this economic base, he regarded material incentives as a crucial motivation.[44] In 1965, this policy found its expression in the local press. For example, when a woman worker in Peking asked the Party if she could wear flowery clothes, the Party's answer as reported in the *Peking Daily* was particularly revealing:

One may, according to one's needs, choose what to eat and what to wear when spending one's wages and other rational remunerations. This should not be interfered with. We must wage an arduous struggle, work hard, and practice economy in building socialism. But this does not mean that the people's living conditions should not be gradually improved. The Party and the government consistently stand for gradual improvement in people's living conditions on the basis of production development. That the people buy some new clothes and new articles with their wages on the basis of a reasonable arrangement for livelihood is a matter of doing what is right, and is a good sign of improvement in people's living conditions. As to the purchase of some expensive things, those who are financially well-off may certainly do so. We may not judge one's thought simply by what he wears and what he buys.[45]

It is worth noting here that Mao's wife Chiang Ch'ing once told Liu's wife Wang Kuang-mei *not* to wear a brooch when she accompanied her husband abroad. (But she did when she accompanied Liu in Indonesia.[46]) It is also interesting that, to the husband of the worker cited above who regarded buying such expensive items as a bourgeois habit, the article offered the following criticism:

Why do some comrades improperly interpret the bourgeois idea and improperly connect it with the trivialities of life? The reasons are complicated. Theoretically speaking, it has something to do with their insufficient knowledge of the socialist principle. Socialism will eliminate exploitation and classes instead of demanding that personal requirements and everyday life are equalized and made uniform. Stalin said: "To draw the conclusion that socialism calls for equalization, for the leveling of the requirements of the members of society, for the leveling of their tastes and of their personal and everyday life, and that according to the Marxist plan all should wear the same clothes and eat the same dishes in the same quantity . . . is to utter vulgarities and to slander Marxism."[47]

This policy of encouraging material incentives as a source of individual motivation acknowledged, at least for the time being, the existence of social inequality as a fact of life.

MAO'S POLICY INNOVATIONS IN EDUCATION AND HEALTH CARE

In contrast, Mao began to address himself to the question of social inequality in general and the gap between the cities and the countryside in particular. He was more concerned with preventing the rise of any privileged stratum in China, and to this end he asked in 1963 for lowering the salaries of high-level cadres.[48] One of the lessons that the CCP sought to draw from the experience of the CPSU spelled out this concern:

The system of high salaries for a small number of people should never be applied.

The gap between the income of the working personnel of the Party, the government, the enterprises and the people's communes, on the one hand, and the income
of the masses of the people, on the other, should be rationally and gradually narrowed and not widened.[49]

Mao's quest for equality was manifested in his calls for reform
mainly in the current system of education and health service. But the
Party Center's responses to Mao's calls fell short of his intentions, producing additional tensions between Mao and his associates.

Reforms in Education

As a result of the regularization and specialization attained during
1961-62, wrought by such documents as the Forty Articles on Primary
Education, the Fifty Articles on Secondary Education, and the Sixty
Articles on Higher Education, all schools by 1962 resumed their full-
time schedules.[50] To understand Mao's educational reforms, therefore,
it is necessary to know about the current state of the education that he
wanted to reform.[51] A seven-year-old could enroll at the six-year primary schools administered by the hsien (or the communes) and the
cities. After graduation, by passing the entrance examinations the
graduates could go to the three-year middle schools and after that, the
three-year high schools, both of which were run by the hsien and the
cities; finally, by passing the entrance examinations the high-school
graduates could go to the universities and colleges run by the Ministry
of Higher Education: the four-year liberal arts colleges, the five-year
science and engineering colleges, and the six-year medical colleges.

The entrance examination for the universities and colleges was a
uniform test throughout the country administered by the Ministry of
Higher Education. An applicant could only specify the academic spe-
ciality he wanted to study; he was allowed to indicate six choices in the
order of his preferences. The ministry then determined a university for
him strictly in accordance with the result of his test. Tremendous competition existed behind closed doors. Those who scored the highest
marks could go to the most prestigious institutions: Peking University,
an outstanding liberal arts university, or Tsinghua University, a top-
notch polytechnic university in Peking.[52]

The curricula at these schools were also arranged in such a way that
the students had to make good marks in tests. At the middle schools,
for example, fourteen subjects were taught: Chinese, mathematics,
foreign languages, politics, history, geography, physics, chemistry, production knowledge, athletics, music, painting, and labor. At the high
schools, all of these except music and painting were taught, while at
some high schools foreign languages could be substituted for production

knowledge.[53] The work loads were generally heavy. If a student failed in more than two subjects, he was required to repeat them; if he failed in one of the core subjects such as Chinese and mathematics, he also had to repeat them. At high schools and universities, if a student failed a course more than twice, he was expelled. In some colleges the graduates were required to write graduation essays.[54]

One informant revealed that in placing the college graduates, the academic record was the primary yardstick, followed by the political status. In Kwangtung, the government gave favorable consideration to the overseas Chinese students when their records turned out to be the same as other students. In any case, even if a graduate was assigned to an entirely different post than what he had aspired to, say, to a remote area in Inner Mongolia, he had no choice but to obey the state. Those who could not get a job or rejected work were sent either to the countryside or to areas of land reclamation; if they could afford it, they became vagabonds (*hei-jen hei-hu*) and faced the same fate when caught.[55]

This system naturally encouraged teachers to place inordinate emphasis upon academic achievement. Not only did they require their students to do voluminous reading, but more importantly, they singularly honored those who distinguished themselves academically. In 1965, Shanghai's *Wen-hui pao* reported on the middle-school teachers' prevailing attitude: "The main task of the students is to study. They will gain our favor if they study well."[56] Whenever a student got an A in any subject, for instance, he was praised as "a good student seldom found in the school." Accordingly, the teachers educated their students in their own images. A teacher confessed that he used to praise beautifully written lyric essays and that only after having participated in labor himself, could he cherish a simply written essay about physical labor.[57]

These teachers had acquired their appreciation of stylish writing from their professors in the colleges, who had encouraged them to read foreign classics instead of contemporary and revolutionary literature.[58] For instance, Professors Chien Po-tsan and Fung Yu-lan of Peking University lectured their students that the old feudal lords had made some concessions to the peasants. But these professors could hardly teach such a heresy without the acquiescence of the higher authorities.[59]

In June 1964, the Ministry of Education was divided again into the Ministry of Higher Education and the Ministry of Education, Yang Hsiu-feng becoming minister of higher education and secretary of the Party committee, and Chiang Nan-hsiang becoming vice-minister and deputy secretary. Ho Wei became minister of education. The old ministry had been revising teaching materials before this reshuffle, ever since 1962. In 1963, for example, the State Scientific Commission proposed a program creating academic degrees and titles; Teng Hsiao-p'ing promptly approved it but Mao prevented it from being enacted.[60]

Education was not entirely the teachers' responsibility, however, for the parents also shared some beliefs with the teachers. The *Peking Daily* reported that a mother had advised her child: "When you become an adult, don't be a waiter in a restaurant like your father. How mean it would be! Study hard and go to the high schools and college. Be an athlete, which is a road to fame, or a doctor so that your mother will benefit from you when I am ill."[61] Another report said that even if the children wanted to study Mao's works at home, their parents refused. When a mother was honored as "four-good housewife," she declined the title, saying: "Why should I ask for trouble?"[62] Evidently, the revolution had not penetrated the people's homes.

It was not easy for the children of the peasants or the lower income workers to climb up the educational ladder described above. First of all, they could hardly meet the financial requirements. In Canton areas, the average earning of a peasant per month was about twenty yuan whereas the starting salary of a regular worker was forty yuan. T'an Chen-lin once remarked that those who swept the ground in the city made thirty or forty yuan a month but the peasants could hardly earn two or three hundred yuan a year.[63] In Peking the parents paid the fee of twenty-five yuan including tuition and board each month to send their children to kindergarten. As for the primary school, the parents had to pay one or two yuan per term in Canton areas.[64] The tuition in the middle and high schools in Canton was one or two yuan per month for room and board. In some schools no tuition was charged, but even there the students had to buy most of their textbooks.

Although the universities did not require tuition, the students nonetheless had to pay for room and board. As the majority of the students did not get full scholarships, they relied on their parents for monthly remittances. Liu Shao-ch'i reportedly gave twenty yuan per month to his daughter who was a student at Tsinghua.[65] In Canton, the room and board for a university student cost about fifteen yuan. As the Maoists accused, this educational system was elite-oriented, and it was true that those whose monthly income was less than one hundred yuan could ill afford to send their children to the universities.[66] On top of this financial burden, the length of school years, the heavy work loads, and the rigorous examinations all worked against the poor.

It was this educational system that Mao set out to reform. In February 1964, he issued the Spring Festival Instruction on Education, in which he demanded a far-reaching reform in the current school system, teaching method, and examination, because all of these "trampled people underfoot."[67] He called for shortening the school year, for sixteen or twenty years was too long for a student to graduate from a university. Mao futher noted that neither Li Po nor Tu Fu, two eminent T'ang poets, had been a graduate of the Hanlin Academy; nor were Confucius, Benjamin Franklin, or James Watt university graduates. Mao complained that students in China spent such a long period in the schools that they were entirely divorced from labor and the masses, so much so that many of them did not know what cattle or rice paddies looked like. Therefore, he suggested five-year primary schools and four-year secondary schools. Before going to college, he maintained, the students should have a period of practical experience, perhaps for two years. In this way, he proposed that the school term be reformed to enable the students to take jobs at twenty-three or twenty-four.[68]

Mao also pointed out that too many subjects were being studied and too much academic work was being done. He suggested that half of them be cut. Due to poor lighting and heavy assignments, many students suffered from myopia. He referred to his favored program of all-out education with equal emphasis on recreation, swimming, and sports. "If one reads too many books," he said, "he would become a bookworm, a dogmatist, and a revisionist."[69]

Mao then called upon the teachers to make drastic changes in their teaching methods. He maintained that the students should be allowed to doze off in classes rather than be forced to listen to dreary lectures, and that if the teachers made "a lot of noise," the students should also be allowed to leave. He suggested that lecture notes be distributed at universities as he had done a long time before at the Canton Peasant Training Institute, instead of requiring that the students take notes.[70] He was more critical of faculty of literature and arts; he wanted to drive them out of the cities to the countryside.

Lastly, Mao advocated a complete overhaul of the examination system. It occurred to him that the current examinations were like attacking enemies by surprise, seeking only stereotyped answers. He proposed that several questions be made known to the students in advance so that they could select some and contribute their original ideas on them. He went so far as to support cunning by saying that the students should be allowed to whisper to each other and to copy the other's correct answer during examination.[71] One month later, in March 1964, Mao returned to these themes when he issued another directive on curricula. What was unusual about the directive was that he pointedly stated : "It should be read by P'eng Chen."[72]

The educational authorities sought specific ways and means then, to implement these instructions. Even before Mao's 1964 spring festival instruction, Chou En-lai in 1963 had already directed that all university graduates participate in productive labor for at least a year before being assigned to their jobs. In May 1964, Liu Shao-ch'i called a central work conference to discuss educational reforms, and presented the two kinds of education. Mao also acknowledged these efforts at reform in progress.[73] The Party policy for education reform was that the government first experiment with the secondary work-study schools while making thorough studies and preparations for reforming the full-time schools.[74] In his report at the NPC of December 1964, Chou En-lai confirmed this policy as follows:

In accordance with the instructions of Chairman Liu Shao-ch'i, we should, for a number of years, continue to carry out reforms in the existing full-time school system, seriously apply the policy that education must serve the politics of the proletariat and be combined with productive labor, and popularize elementary education in its various forms by relying on the masses to the fullest extent; at the same time, experimenal part-time work and part-time study schools should be set up.[75]

As far as Mao's specific demands were concerned, the initial reaction of the Propaganda Department and the Ministry of Higher Education was cautious. Lu Ting-yi, director of the Propaganda Department, warned against the "blind direction" response characteristic of the GLF. Yang Hsiu-feng advocated the virtue of well thought-out preparations before introducing any reform, saying, "Chairman Mao's spring festival speech must not be oversimplified and must not be interpreted in vulgar ways." In the name of moderation, Chiang Nan-hsiang precluded any change in the current university system, specialities, and teaching plans, for reform in the universities required comparable reform in the high schools; therefore, merely being "left in form" would not solve any problem.[76] Mao complained about the hesitancy of these responses to a visiting Nepalese educational mission in August 1964, saying that many people were opposed to his reform plan.[77]

In yet another directive issued in 1964, the "July 7 directive," Mao insisted that one-third of the curricula be cut and that teachers should join with students in working out reforms. Before this, in June, he had told Wang Hai-jung, his niece-in-law (who became an assistant foreign minister in 1972) that children of high-level cadres had become arrogant; he advised her to rely on herself instead of relying on her seniors or teachers. He questioned the value of pedagogics by asserting that truth lies in one's own hands. He called upon the teachers to become a pupil first before becoming a teacher. In September, when he talked with Mao Yüan-hsin, he stated that class struggle should be the main content of education and that grades must not be emphasized.[78]

As the Learn from the PLA and the Mao-study campaigns gathered momentum in 1965, their influence indeed began to be felt at the schools. But the Ministry of Higher Education warned the universities against excesses. Chiang Nan-hsiang, now the minister of higher education, decreed that since institutions of higher education had their special characteristics, not all experiences of the PLA could be applicable, nor could quotations from Mao be recited as if they were "incantations of the White Lotus Sect." In July, therefore, Chiang specifically directed that the PLA's formula of practice-theory-practice should not be mechanically adopted in teaching.[79]

These leaders did not oppose Mao's reforms outright, but attempted to implement them gradually and cautiously, after thorough investigation. In June 1965, Liu Shao-ch'i actually urged the Ministry of Higher Education to send down to the hsien level the university graduates in the arts, and Chiang Nan-hsiang prepared to enforce this plan. The Ministry of Education and the Ministry of Higher Education were preparing other programs to heed Mao's plea. But as such reforms were undertaken, Liu warned about the lower quality of education that might result from the shortening of school years and the complete abolition of required courses. Typical of this cautious approach was the remark Liu made at a meeting of the Politburo held in November 1965 and attended by members of the Central Committee and the State Council: "We should never give direction blindly while we are not sure ourselves."[80] At this meeting he asked the two ministries to make further preparations for another meeting to exhaust other possibilities.

Mao, however, was impatient with this foot-dragging pace. In December 1965, he deplored the current emphasis on philosophical study made by such scholars as Wu Han and Chien Po-tsan at a conference held at Hangchow. Refuting the thesis about a policy of concession toward the peasants, he contended that only the revolutionary made concessions while the reactionary revenged. He asked those who studied philosophy to go to farms and factories. The longer one went to schools and the more books he read, Mao reiterated, the more ignorant he became. Urging the people to learn dialectical philosophy, Mao was insistent that a revolution be made in higher education.[81]

Reform in Health Service

In 1964, Mao also called for a drastic change in the existing health service on the ground that it was primarily urban oriented. Most workers and Party-state cadres benefited from the health insurance system, which covered over 50 percent of fees. The administrative cadres, for example, met only the cost of registration and medicine. Yet the peasants still paid for medical care they received from the state-run hospitals.[82] Besides, most hospitals and medical personnel were concentrated in the cities. According to one report, over 60 percent of medical personnel served the urban population, which constituted some 15 percent of the entire population. From 1960 to 1963, health centers in the countryside decreased from 280,000 to 70,000 whereas joint clinics in the cities increased from 43,000 to 84,000 and private practitioners rose from 16,000 to 86,000![83]

In August 1964, Mao called upon the Ministry of Health to make a basic reorganization of the nation's health service. He advocated the abolition of the Health Insurance Bureau, which was modeled after the Soviet's, serving only those who were covered by the policy. Commenting on his own health, he disclosed that he had a gentleman's agreement with his doctor: If he did not send for him the doctor had done a good job; only if he sent for him could the doctor attend to his health. He listened only to half of what his doctor said, for one would become more sick if he entirely listened to the doctor. He contended that specialized doctors practicing under the health insurance program actually became unspecialized doctors, for they could not treat a variety of diseases. He pointed out that there were many doctors but few patients in Peking Hospital. Calling the hospital a "hospital of lords," he demanded that it be opened to all. At the same time, he asked the Ministry of Health to select some senior doctors from the cities and send them to the countryside.[84] In response to this directive, the Ministry of Health in January 1965 began to organize medical teams. These teams were supposed to go first to the key hsien at which the Socialist Education Movement was being carried out and then to other places on a rotation basis. As for medical education, the ministry selected 15 of the existing 52 medical colleges as experimental spots where teaching could be shortened and student enrollment increased by introducing the two-track system. The ministry still maintained, however, the existing 16 specialized medical schools. Of the 230 intermediate hygiene schools, the ministry selected 20 and planned to transform them into the three-year specialized schools. With the exception of 5 colleges founded in 1958, the ministry planned to transform the other 19 colleges of traditional Chinese medicine from six-year schools to three- to four-year schools the guiding principle for these reforms was to achieve less but finer results. And Mao gave approval to these plans.[85]

Liu Shao-ch'i also asked Ch'ien Hsin-chung, minister of health, to send the medical personnel to the countryside in groups: the first goal was to send one-third and then one-half. In Shanghai, about one-third of the doctors were sent down but in Peking twelve teams of over one hundred people were sent down.[86] Ch'ien set up several model hsien such as the T'ung hsien of Peking, Chü-jung of Kiangsu, and Hsiang-yin of Hunan. He himself spent a week in the T'ung hsien; two other vice-ministers and director of the political department squatted at the other hsien. P'eng Chen agreed with Ch'ien's method of spreading the medical teams from the cities to the hsien and then to the grass-roots level.[87]

Again, Mao was impatient with this gradual approach. In June 1965, he issued another directive criticizing the performance of the Ministry of Health. He pointed out that the ministry was still working for only 15 percent of the population and therefore, was in the process of becoming the "Ministry of Urban Health" or the "Health Ministry of the Urban Lords."[88] As for reform in medical education, he maintained that the students need not read so many books, nor was it necessary for the medical schools to enroll only the middle or high school graduates, for a three-year course for the primary school graduates was also necessary. Since the current health service was tailored to the needs of the cities, and most of the man power and resources available were devoted to the study of complicated and rare diseases, it was divorced from the mass. Mao even jibed the doctors for wearing masks, saying that they were afraid of being infected.[89]

After this June 1965 directive, Ch'ien Hsin-chung conceded that the Ministry of Health lacked a democratic work style and had alienated itself from the masses. But he denied that the ministry had ever committed any error of political orientation. When the ministry's Party committee drafted a report to the Center on its rectification plan, Ch'ien made the drafting group revise the report seven times until it omitted the error of orientation from the final draft. As for sending down the medical personnel to the countryside, in July 1965 Liu Shao-ch'i again ordered the minister and vice-ministers of health to take a leading part in such a movement; in September, he suggested that the doctors make more home visits.[90] Due to the shortage of doctors, however, the ministry was hard pressed to meet the rural need swiftly. Ch'ien opposed a rapid expansion in health services not only because of the lack of adequate medical resources but because it threatened existing health services, saying: "When the dust of the earth is fanned up, it provides people with more chances of inhaling viruses and spreads tuberculosis."[91] Lu Ting-yi also was opposed to the shortening of the training period in medical education, for he regarded three years as essential even to the rural medical personnel.[92]

The principle underlying Mao's reforms in education and health service was to achieve a maximum degree of equality. Since the reforms called for almost instant action, Mao's approach to problem solving again pointed to a comprehensive and simultaneous mobilization of resources. Except for reference to the mass line, however, Mao's proposals failed to specify how they were to be implemented, nor did they indicate a preferred sequence of development. But reforms could bear fruit only through processes. When it came to implementation, the Party and state organizations in operational charge of education and health service had to establish developmental priorities. However earnest this concern for technical and procedural imperatives, so long as it delayed Mao's reforms, it was seen as inaction and resistance. Mao continuously issued demands, while the Party Center groped for ways to accommodate him.

These policy conflicts between Mao and the Party's central *apparatchiki* culminated at a national conference on industry and communication held in March 1966. In a letter to this conference, Mao called upon central and other provincial units to study Hupeh's example in agricultural mechanization, which was based on the principle of self-reliance and decentralized manufacture. Characterizing the Soviet policy of completely state-financed and highly centralized mechanization as like emptying the pond to catch fish, he justified his policy as particularly necessary in order to prepare for war and natural disaster, and do everything for the people.[93] By this time, however, the intra-Party conflicts had already escalated into the Cultural Revolution. Hence, after this conference policy began to shift abruptly in favor of Mao's innovations in all issue areas.

POLICY AND POLITICS ON THE EVE
OF THE CULTURAL REVOLUTION

The policy conflicts within the CCP during 1962-66 illuminate long-standing differences among the first-generation revolutionary elite over many issues regarding China's revolution and development. In this period, the operational leaders of Party policy under Liu Shao-ch'i attempted to consolidate the adjustment policies of 1959-62, but Mao and his supporters challenged the status quo in order to reverse some of the existing policies. The differences revolved around a basic question: how should the regime allocate and plan its material and human resources? In grappling with this problem, Liu and Mao each prescribed different policies, thus revealing two diverging approaches to problem solving.

Policy: Quest for Development and Quest for Revolution

The guiding principle underlying Liu's policy innovations was the quest for development, defined as increasing production and income. For this purpose, Liu assigned a clear agenda of priorities to the allocation of scarce resources and talents. The procedural arrangement of this policy was a sequential development: the gradual state-financed agricultural mechanization to keep pace with industrialization; the step-by-step incorporation of enterprises into centralized trusts; the regularization of temporary labor; and the implementation of the two-track education system. Moreover, Liu sought to implement these programs through a series of incremental processes.

In seeking these policies, Liu stressed the role of the state in organizing social life and in raising productivity, for he believed that building a sound economic base was the prime task of a socialist state. This approach, however, left the inequality between the urban areas and the rural areas unabated, and brought about the trend toward centralization, differentiation, and stratification.

By comparison, the guiding principle of Mao's policies was the quest for revolution, defined as transforming social structure and human attitude. Through radical reforms, Mao set out to reverse the trend to social inequality, which he considered inimical to China's long-run interests. Accordingly, his innovations were concerned more with distribution and social service. He wanted to reform the rigid and specialized educational system, and abolish as well the urban-oriented health insurance system, calling for an all-round education and for the transfer of urban medical personnel to the rural areas. What was lacking in Mao's reforms was a system of priorities, for they required a comprehensive mobilization of resources and simultaneous development.

To Mao, the promotion of material incentives at the expense of an egalitarian goal was unacceptable. His reforms were all designed to prevent the rise of a privileged stratum. In carrying out such reforms, therefore, he preferred the impetus of local initiatives and diffuse mass movement.

Thus, Liu was more concerned with regulative issues whereas Mao with distributive and redistributive issues.[94] In comparative terms, it appears that more conflicts attended the issues of reform in education and health care than those in the economy. Clearly, Mao regarded education and health care as part of social service; hence, they were redistributive issues. As Oksenberg points out, in the 1950s Mao was more concerned with the allocation of resources necessary for production but in the 1960s he increasingly addressed himself to the redistributive issues of providing social service to the needy.[95] He paid particular attention to education and culture, having been deeply involved in the CCP's ideological polemic with Soviet revisionists during the 1960s, for education and culture would train the future successors to the Chinese Communists. Because ideological correctness was at issue (compromises were not possible in matters of principle) policy conflicts in this area were bound to intensify further.

Politics: Mao versus the Party Center

Distinctive as these contrasts are, the policy conflicts within the CCP cannot be attributed solely to the diverging outlooks of Mao and Liu. Rather, they can be better understood as the political and institutional interaction between Mao on the one side and the Party Center on the other; ultimately, such conflicts had to be resolved through power struggle. In fact, the different institutional positions within the Party apparatus held by Mao and his associates helped aggravate policy differences, for the cleavages over substantive policy were inseparable from those over its implementation. Although from 1963 on Mao endeavored to return to the first line of policy processes, his authority was still confined to defining broad lines or vetoing existing policy. Liu, on the other hand, was in charge of implementation and could reshape policy.

These differing outlooks and differing instruments for implementing policy undermined the synchronization between Mao's demands for radical reform and the Party Center's responses. To a certain extent, this was inevitable because those in operational charge of policy had to arrange sequences and make preparations to implement them. The tensions between Mao and his associates reflect some common problems of all modernizing societies: the quest for equality demands instant action that may reduce efficiency, whereas efficiency demands sequences that may compromise equality. The egalitarian strand of Maoist ideology made these tensions more intense in China. Hence, conflicts often become violent as revolutionary modernizers and managerial modernizers struggle for power in preindustrialized societies.[96]

These leadership conflicts over policy affected the entire sweep of political life in China. The state ownership of the means of production made all conflicts *political* because it precluded any possiblitiy for dissociation of wealth and power. This fact makes conflicts more intense and violent in a communist society than in a pluralist society.[97] These leadership conflicts also created some societal tensions as well, though they were mostly potential. For example, Liu's industrial trusts gave rise to some latent tensions between management and workers, and the central company and its local branches; the regularization of temporary labor increased tensions between regular and temporary workers; so too with tensions in the two-track schools between full-time and half-time students. On the other hand, Mao's educational health reforms may have benefited the half-time students and the peasants but may have harmed the full-time students and those regular workers who were protected by the national health insurance.

These were some of the common tensions inherent in any industrializing society. But the conflict of such latent interests between societal groups had no open outlet in a Communist society. Only when the leadership allowed these interests to assert themselves could they become manifest interests.[98] This, in fact, was precisely what happened in the Cultural Revolution of 1966-67, the result of long-accumulating conflicts within the Party leadership. When these conflicts reached a culmination they did come into the open, appearing first in the leadership and then spilling over into the society at large.[99] In China, they further deepened in the course of reforms in culture and finally escalated into the Cultural Revolution.

8
Policy Conflicts
in the Cultural Circle

Of the policy conflicts that surfaced in 1962-66, those over reforms in literature and arts, particularly in Peking opera, were directly related to the Cultural Revolution.[1] The conflicts in this realm occurred between Mao's supporters, especially Chiang Ch'ing, who set out to replace the traditional themes of Peking opera with more contemporary themes, and the Party Propaganda Department, which showed little enthusiasm for such reforms. The initial issue at conflict centered on whether cultural reforms were a political or a purely academic question. Mao's supporters regarded them as part of a political struggle but the Party authorities and the cultural community treated them as part of an academic debate. This difference became one of the conflicts that eventually precipitated the Cultural Revolution.

THE BACKGROUND, 1962-63

In order to understand why Mao raised a political question and why the Party propaganda leadership tried to evade Mao's reforms through an academic debate, certain background knowledge is required about this debate. Mao's reforms in this period must be traced back to the adjustment period, for the object of his reforms were those works produced by the intellectuals in 1960-62 that had vilified his policies in the guise of artistic form. For example, the liberalized atmosphere prevailing in 1960-62 made it possible for Wu Han to publish the play *Hai Jui Dismissed from Office*, for Teng T'o and company to write the "Three-

161

Family Village" column in the *Peking Daily*, for Yang Shu and others to write the "Long and Short Notes" (*Ch'ang-tuan-lu*) in the *People's Daily*, and for T'ien Han and Meng Ch'ao to write such plays using the ghost motif as *Hsieh Yao-han* and *Li Hui-niang*. All these works were devoted to satirizing certain aspects of the GLF in the guise of ancient themes that actually caricatured the contemporary society.

Li Hui-niang, for example, had been a concubine of Chia Szu-tao, a corrupt prime minister of the Southern Sung dynasty. Chia murdered her for fear that she might one day disclose his crimes. After her death, Li's ghost approached Chia and deplored his cruelty. In this fashion, the writers endeavored to produce works that were both entertaining and historically appealing.

Writers in 1960-62 probed for more effective forms of expression as well. In August 1962, for example, Shao Ch'üan-lin (vice-chairman of the Writers Association) convened the Dairen conference on creative writing, a forum where he propounded the thesis of portraying "middle characters" (*chung-chien jen-wu*). "Since the both ends [heroes and villains] are few while the middle are many," he asserted that writers should portray the complex situation of such middle characters. Contending that it was not enough to portray only those heroic characters who always dared to think and act, Shao pleaded for writers to reflect the complex reality of the masses; for by drawing attention to the middle characters, they would be describing the multitude itself.[2] This was part of his effort to expand and diversify the scope of literary themes, in line with the principles stipulated by the 1962 Eight Articles on Literature and Art.

Throughout this process of liberalization, the Party-state authorities and their constituent organizations came to form a coherent circle. The leading proponents of this movement were the leaders of the so-called literature of the 1930s. In the Party Propaganda Department, Deputy Director Chou Yang assumed an over-all leadership concurrent with Lin Mo-han, the department's chief of the Bureau for Culture and Arts and concurrently vice-minister of culture. In the Ministry of Culture, Minister Mao Tun and Vice-Ministers Hsia Yen and Ch'i Yen-ming took the lead, while among the practitioners, leadership fell to Yang Han-sheng (vice-chairman of the All-China Federation of Literary and Art Circle [ACFLAC]), Shao Ch'üan-lin, T'ien Han (vice-chairman of the ACFLAC and chairman of the Playwright Association), and Meng Ch'ao (director of the Playwright Association).

After Mao served notice on the anti-Party activities of writers and directly criticized Chou Yang at the Tenth Plenum in 1962, the political mood in the cultural circle also shifted. Chou Yang performed a self-criticism for not "having made full mental preparation," yet he maintained that any act of going to the other extreme must be avoided.[3] Also at this time, Mao's wife, Chiang Ch'ing, began her efforts to eliminate those plays using ancient themes, particularly the ghost plays. Yet Ch'i Yen-ming, for one, was opposed to this move. Ch'i attributed the prevalence of ghost plays to the paucity of themes, saying that ghosts were made to say what people could not say openly.[4] Chiang Ch'ing then pressed her case in the field of cinema by appealing directly to the director of propaganda and the minister of culture. However, they turned a deaf ear to her. Teng Hsiao-p'ing also neglected Chiang Ch'ing's efforts: When she met Tso Lin (Teng's wife) at a reception, she intimated to Tso Lin that Mao's cultural policy had not been implemented and that Teng could do something about it. Yet nothing came from Teng Hsiao-p'ing.[5]

As her efforts in Peking were fruitless, Chiang Ch'ing went to Shanghai. With the help of K'o Ch'ing-shih, mayor of Shanghai and first secretary of the East China Bureau, Chang Ch'un-ch'iao, secretary of the Shanghai Municipal Committee, and Yao Wen-yüan, a young staff member of *Chieh-fang jih-pao* (Liberation Daily), she started the drive to introduce contemporary themes into the Peking opera. From Shanghai Chiang set out to rally support for Mao *outside* the Party Center. Yet, she brought up neither *Hai Jui* nor "Three-Family Village" at this time despite being as well aware as Mao of these writings. But her aim was unmistakable, for she knew that such plays as *Hai Jui Dismissed from Office* and *Li Hui-niang* portrayed the behavior of emperors and court beauties in the name of uncovering tradition.[6]

In 1963, as Chiang Ch'ing was recuperating from an illness in Shanghai, she had the opportunity to conduct a systematic examination of current theatrical works. She was prepared at this time to criticize Wu Han's play on Hai Jui; but at P'eng Chen's suggestion, Mao restrained her in order to protect a number of historians. P'eng Chen had maintained that Chiang Ch'ing was casting aspersions on the whole circle of historians. Chiang Ch'ing then asked Mao whether or not she could reserve her own opinion for the time being; with his approval she was secretly preparing an article exposing the political culpability of Wu Han's *Hai Jui Dismissed from Office*.[7]

The Party Center's policy with regard to cultural reforms was to confine them within the category of academic and artistic discussions. Embittered by previous campaigns, the cultural circle strived to avoid another overheated political struggle, groping for unity and stability. The writings of such prominent historians as Wu Han, Lo Erh-kang, and Chou Ku-ch'eng spelled out this aim. From August 1963 on, however, some young critics, possibly under Chiang Ch'ing's direction, began to challenge the authority of these historians. But they could only do so within the framework of academic discussion.

These critics began their endeavor by challenging Wu Han's theory of moral inheritance.[8] A young writer named Hsü Ch'i-hsien wrote an article in the *Kuang-ming Daily* questioning Wu Han's contention that certain moral values of the ruling class in the feudal society such as benevolence (*jen*) and loyalty (*ch'ung*) were worthy of being inherited by the socialist society. He pointed out that such feudal morality directly clashes with socialist morality. In response to this, Wu Han defended his position that as far as morality was concerned, one class can inherit some of another class's values.[9] This debate continued in a scholarly manner until the end of 1963, but at no time did the articles discussing Wu Han's historical views bring out the question of *Hai Jui*.[10]

The Wu Han question surfaced again in August 1963, when Ch'i Pen-yü wrote an article challenging the standard Party interpretation of Li Hsiu-ch'eng advanced by Lo Erh-kang, the noted historian of the Taiping Rebellion and director of Taiping Heavenly Kingdom Museum in Nanking. According to Lo's interpretation, Li Shiu-ch'eng, a Taiping general, was a hero who merely pretended to surrender to a Manchu court general, Tseng Kuo-fan, subsequently writing an autobiography (*tzu-shu*) for Tseng only to disorient the Manchu troops and give the Taiping troops more time to strengthen their forces.[11] In fact, the play, *The Death of Li Hsiu-ch'eng* written by Yang Han-sheng in 1937 (and revised by him in 1956 and restaged in 1963) depicted Li Hsiu-ch'eng in this fashion. Ch'i Pen-yü, however, contended that Li's autobiography was a true renegade document that really slandered the Taiping for rebelling against the Manchu court.[12]

Chiang Ch'ing personally brought Ch'i's article to Mao's attention. After reading it, Mao—who apparently believed Li had genuinely harmed the Taiping cause—commented: "Black characters written on white paper furnish proof as unshakable as a mountain. Disloyalty in his declining years is an example not to be followed."[13] (This remark was revealed in 1967.) In 1963, however, in response to Ch'i Pen-yü's challenge, Chou Yang called an emergency meeting of the Propaganda Department, which served to reaffirm the view that Li Hsiu-ch'eng was a national hero, and not a renegade. The participants at the meeting, individuals such as Teng T'o, Wu Han, and Chien Po-tsan, concluded that Ch'i's article was not only politically damaging but also academically dubious. Subsequently, they decided to repudiate the article. Only Mao's direct intervention put a halt to this move.[14]

At stake in this clash between Ch'i Pen-yü and the Propaganda

Department was not so much verification of the historical facts as certain political implications of the two different interpretations, for the whole incident could be compared to the self-examination written by sixty-one Communist leaders to secure their release from Kuomintang jails in 1936. Apparently, an old and hotly debated issue was whether these confessions, written with the approval of Liu Shao-ch'i (then in charge of the CCP Northern Bureau in Kuomintang areas) had betrayed the CCP (as Ch'i Pen-yü charged in 1967).[15] Thus, the attack on Li Hsiu-ch'eng was perhaps a veiled attack on Liu Shao-ch'i and others associated with the 1936 incident. The attack also gave warning to those in the Propaganda establishment who had not carried out Mao's cultural policy, and particularly, the literary figures of the 1930s who had been defying Chiang Ch'ing's request for contemporary themes in Peking opera.

Following the controversy over Li Hsiu-ch'eng, in September 1963 Yao Wen-yüan challenged Chou Ku-ch'eng's aesthetic view that art reflects the spirit of all groups in society, even transcending class division. Chou, a professor at Futan University, held that the spirit of an era represents actually an amalgam of all ideologies. Yao refuted this by contending that Chou's view denied the existence of antagonistic class consciousness, for the spirit of the contemporary era was revolutionary. In November 1963, Chou replied that Yao's view was only an abstract generalization, for, in fact, nonrevolutionary spirit does exist in the contemporary era. As in the Wu Han case, this debate also subsided until it recurred in May 1964.[16]

REFORMS IN PEKING OPERA, 1963-64

Against this background, Chiang Ch'ing in Shanghai started the campaign for the reform of Peking opera. But the Propaganda Department continued to curtail her efforts by mobilizing counterargument from the authorities in each field. Witnessing this resistance, Mao directly intervened in the disputes between Shanghai and Peking by issuing several directives that demanded certain drastic reforms in Peking opera. But as the Party authorities still tried to enforce them according to their own methods, conflicts deepened between Shanghai and Peking.

In 1963, Mao issued two important directives for cultural reforms. In September, he made a statement in which he called upon the cultural circle to "develop the new from the old." Part of the statement read as follows:

Those in charge of literature and arts, ballads and the cinema should also pay close attention to the question of developing the new from the old. The stage is now dominated by emperors, kings, generals, prime ministers, household and servant girls. Any change in form should be accompanied by a change in content. In developing the new from the old, what should be emphasized? Feudalism or Socialism? Try to evolve new content from the old forms. If nothing is done, then nobody will have any interests in [opera and stage plays] 20 years later. The superstructure should always conform to the economic base.[17]

Yao Wen-yüan later revealed that when Mao made this statement, he also pointed out that the Ministry of Culture under the leadership of Ch'i Yen-ming, Hsia Yen, and Lin Mo-han was a ministry of "emperors and ministers, scholars and beauties."

Despite this warning, Chou Yang took the position that the Peking opera was an art form specially suited to depicting emperors and ministers. On the premise that much had been achieved in the reform movements, Chao cautioned against the "oversimplified method of using labels indiscriminately."[18] In November 1963, Mao reiterated his warning to the Ministry of Culture, saying: "If nothing is done, the Ministry of Culture should be changed into the Ministry of Emperors, Kings, Generals, Ministers, Scholars and Beauties, or the Ministry of Foreign Things and the Dead."[19] In December, when K'o Ch'ing-shih made a report on the reform plan in Shanghai, Mao issued the second directive pointing out that problems still abounded in all forms of arts, for "the dead" still dominated many artistic fields.[20]

In response to these demands, the Party found that it had to take certain steps, and consequently, Liu Shao-ch'i convened a Politburo meeting in January 1964. Reporting on the Propaganda Department's attitude to this meeting, Chou Yang recommended three principles: (1) On the whole, the achievements made thus far in literature and arts outweighed the mistakes and therefore, they had to be upheld; (2) the mistakes made by the Ministry of Culture were not necessarily one of line but a question of understanding; and (3) the Party had to promote creation and construction rather than destruction, for destruction was always easier than construction. Liu Shao-ch'i, Teng Hsiao-p'ing, and P'eng Chen all endorsed this report.[21]

On the method of approximating the socialist culture, however, Liu differed from Mao. Once again, he advocated a gradual reform of Peking opera that would make contemporary themes of primary importance while the ancient themes would be secondary. He proposed, futhermore, that at least 80 percent of the plays be concerned with contemporary themes. He was aware that "some people" might not be satisfied with this policy, but nonetheless, he stressed that criticisms in this area must be made for the sake of genuine reform, not for the sake of vilifying some people as if they were the enemy. In evaluating the quality of the current works, Liu's view was also at variance with

Mao's. Liu allegedly maintained that the artistic level of the New Democratic era was not so high as that of the feudal era, nor were contemporary works as good as some of the feudal era. As he saw it, this accounted for the continuing portrayal of emperors and ministers in many plays.[22] Lin Mo-han went farther than this by saying that Mao's criticism of the Ministry of Culture was so laughable that he could not transmit it![23]

The wide disparity of outlook over reform at the top level was soon reflected in its implementation. This was inevitable when Chiang Ch'ing's supporters in Shanghai suggested proposals for reforms that the Party leadership in Peking could not accept. As early as New Year of 1963, K'o Ch'ing-shih proposed to the literary and art workers in Shanghai that they write about the past thirteen years to reflect the reality of the Chinese revolution since 1949.[24] In response, the ACFLAC council convened an enlarged meeting in April-May 1963, and passed a resolution that the writers portray all kinds of contradictions and struggles of the era. At this meeting, Chou En-lai urged a strident anti-revisionist movement in the literary circle, pointing out that some harmful influences of the bourgeoisie had appeared on the cultural front.[25] Chou Yang, however, took a different position. He contended that no matter what themes the writers chose, they could all reflect the spirit of the era; hence, he advocated a division of labor in writing.[26]

It is important to note that Chiang Ch'ing chose to question the *form* of artistic expression rather than the substance at this juncture. She began to press her cause with an attack on the ghost play *Li Hui-niang* and Liao Mo-sha's theory that "ghosts are harmless."[27] The cultural circle promptly responded to this move, and in August 1963, the Ministry of Culture, the All-China Playwright Association, and the Cultural Bureau of Peking City jointly sponsored a forum of the playwrights to discuss reforms in plays. Participants at this forum recognized that some conservative trends existed in the current plays that failed to distinguish feudal and democratic elements.[28] Following this example, many papers such as *Hsi-chü pao* (Play and Drama News), the *Kuang-ming Daily*, and Shanghai's *Wen-hui pao* debated about such conservative plays, and criticized *Li Hui-niang* and the theory that ghosts are harmless. In an October report made at an enlarged meeting of the Department of Philosophy and Social Science of the Academy of Sciences, Chou Yang also called upon the academic circle to carry out a struggle against modern revisionism. But at the same time Chou warned against the oversimplified method of using labels indiscriminately.[29]

K'o Ch'ing-shih and Chiang Ch'ing were aware of this subtle resistance, and knew they had to demonstrate their case in Shanghai first to convince the Party leadership in Peking. From December 25, 1963, to January 22, 1964, K'o inaugurated the East China Contemporary Drama Festival in Shanghai. In a speech made at the festival, K'o sounded the keynote of Maoist thinking on the revolutionary revision of the Peking opera.[30] First of all, K'o called upon the writers and actors to do away with the vogue of taking up ancient themes about emperors, kings, ministers, generals, scholars, and beauties, and urged them to write on more contemporary themes about heroes and exemplary men imbued with socialist ideas. He proposed that traditional dramas be adapted in such a way as to enable the ancient mode to serve the present. Even though the Chinese economy had become socialist, the arts still remained that of New Democracy; and even though the artists ate socialist food and wore socialist clothes they still thought in terms of feudalism and capitalism. To change this mode of thinking, he asked them to portray workers, peasants, and soldiers.

K'o also called for more heroic and positive characters in literature and arts. Severely indicting the negative characters in general and the ghost plays in particular, he made the following statement:

There are certain people in our theatrical circles who pay lip-service to the line of art and literature serving the workers, peasants, and soldiers, but who do not follow this Party line in practice. For fifteen years, they did very little to reflect actual life and struggle under socialism; to tell the truth, one scarcely knows if they have done any thing at all. They are enthusiastic about plays and operas of the bourgeoisie and the feudal class, energetically propagate foreign and ancient ones, and put on plays and operas about "dead people" and ghosts on a big scale; they criticize and find fault with our socialist theatre and try to hold back its swift development. Certain people, Communist at that, turn a blind eye to such things; they are neither distressed by them, nor do they intervene, or put a stop to or oppose bad plays and operas publicizing feudalism or capitalism; in fact, they even find excuses for the latter, with such remarks as "there's no harm in ghosts," "there is a popular character to feudal ethics."[31]

Further, the Shanghai first secretary argued that literature and arts must not merely be things to amuse and entertain but must be weapons for carrying out the Chinese revolution by educating and inspiring the people. Therefore, he repudiated the naturalist trend of mirroring life as it was, for it made no distinction between right and wrong. He forcefully defended Mao's principle that political criteria must precede artistic criteria. Finally, K'o rejected the contention that the current artistic level was inferior to that of the 1930s, asserting that it had progressed to a higher level ever since Mao's 1942 *Talks on the Forum of Literature at Yenan.*

With backing from K'o Ch'ing-shih, Chiang Ch'ing then embarked upon a program of producing model plays (*yang-p'an-hsi*) with revolutionary themes. In November 1963, she selected one of the twelve scripts of the play *Hung teng-chi* (Red Lantern) being staged in Shanghai, a story about a family's struggle against the Japanese in 1939, and handed it to the Chinese Peking Opera House attached to the Ministry of Culture for adaptation into a Peking opera. Chiang Ch'ing asked the Peking Opera House to play up the positive role of Li Yü-ho, the hero of the story who resisted torture and atrocities by the Japanese gendarme. To depict Li as an epitome of the proletarian fighter, Chiang Ch'ing wanted to delete the parts that portrayed the agony of Li's daughter at her father's death, the gendarme's torture of Li, and a Chinese traitor's mental suffering. Chiang Ch'ing justified these changes on the ground that the crux of the play centered upon educating posterity to realize that political power of the proletariat was not easily won. But to the Ministry of Culture, such changes denied not only the substance of the story but the very characters of the Peking opera itself, and the ministry did not accept her ideas.[32]

More important than this was her second effort, which forced her into a direct confrontation with P'eng Chen. Chiang Ch'ing transmitted the script of a Shanghai play, *Lu-t'ang huo-chung* (Sparks amid the Reeds) to the highest ranking opera troupe attached to the Peking Municipal Committee. The play, an anti-Japanese war story, originally concerned eighteen wounded soldiers who were led by Kuo Chien-kuang, a political instructor of the New Fourth Army, and an old lady (an underground Communist agent) who ran a tea house in the Kiangsu village of Sachiapang, an area the army had vacated. Upon an order from the CCP underground organization, the lady cleverly avoided the two Japanese agents searching for the wounded soldiers and succeeded in hiding them in her village so that they could recuperate. When they fully recovered, she led them in an attack on the Japanese operating in the area. Chiang Ch'ing rewrote the whole story to feature the armed struggle and to relegate the underground activities to an insignificant subplot. She made Kuo Chien-kuang the glowing hero of the story, depicting an individual who, inspired by Mao's Thought, led his wounded colleagues, mobilized the peasants, and finally defeated the Japanese troops.[33]

P'eng Chen banned the staging of this adapted play because he believed that it was rewritten rather crudely and at random. He ordered Li Ch'i, director of the Propaganda Department of the Peking Party Committee, to respond to Chiang Ch'ing's request, but P'eng revised the letter three times before it was sent to her. The letter said that while the Peking Municipal Committee would allow the Peking Opera Troupe to experiment with her plot, it had to do so on a small scale. The Peking troupe also wanted to retain its own musical arrangements, saying that music was politically neutral: it could be used for plots involving emperors as well as the workers. When Chiang Ch'ing also attempted to make the opera into a symphony, Chou Yang ridiculed the idea, saying that twenty years must pass before the peasants could understand symphonic music.[34]

The conflict between Chiang Ch'ing and P'eng Chen over the play *Sparks amid the Reeds* was more than a mere disagreement over the artistic quality or the historical authenticity of the story. Apparently at issue was which orientation of the revolutionary experiences, that is, the armed struggle of the Soviet area or the underground activities of the white area before 1949, should be emphasized for the next generation. As in the controversy over Li Hsiu-ch'eng, this episode may have involved a Maoist challenge to the intellectuals in the white areas, and perhaps Liu Shao-ch'i's leadership.[35]

Chiang Ch'ing adopted a nonconventional method in producing her operas. First, the leadership set the theme; then the playwright wrote a script on the basis of actual experiences; if it was about a military action, the soldiers simulated the experience to supply the playwright with more lively materials. She called this method a three-way alliance (*san chieh-ho*) of the leadership, the playwright, and the masses.[36] Through this process, she produced such operas as *Chih-ts'ü wei-hu-shan* (Taking the Bandits' Stronghold), *Ch'i-shih pai-hu-tuan* (Raid on the White Tiger Regiment), and *Hai-k'ang* (On the Deck).

Besides the example of the Shanghai Municipal Committee, another larger organization followed Chiang Ch'ing's method: the PLA under Lin Piao. In April-May, 1964, the PLA held its literary and art festival in Peking. Stressing the role of art, Lin Piao called upon the participants of the festival to carry out these things simultaneously: viewing, writing, and alteration. This was an attempt to emulate Chiang Ch'ing's three-way alliance principle. Lin envisioned that the army's example in this field would become a national model, and the General Political Department made preparations to implement these instructions.[37]

But P'eng Chen, Chou Yang, and Lin Mo-han did not approve of such a method of producing Peking operas. They found that the model plays produced in such a way were uninteresting, comparable to "plain boiled water." The Propaganda Department faithfully complied with the Party policy that both traditional operas and the modern operas be staged under the principle of "walking on two legs."[38] Nothing can better illustrate this than Chou Yang's own remark about the role of his department: the Propaganda Department was to serve as a staff officer to the Central Committee, reflecting the situation below and executing Party policy.[39] It was under this policy that the department denied Chiang Ch'ing the necessary funds and access to the press.[40]

In 1967, Chiang Ch'ing reminisced about her frustration at this time:

It was that gang of people who feigned obedience! They were people who slandered others behind their backs and treated them rough. The Chairman wanted a certain play to be changed to give prominence to armed struggle, but they refused. For this reason the struggle had to drag on and on. Let us ask: "Without armed struggle could the Chinese revolution have succeeded?"[41]

She also said at another occasion:

The Chairman is still in good health and very much alive but some persons think that what the Chairman says can be ignored. When I was in Shanghai, the situation was rather delicate in the East China Bureau and the Shanghai Municipal Committee. They paid no heed to what Chairman Mao said, much less to what I said. But they regarded the words of certain persons simply as sayings in the Bible.[42]

This increasing conflict between Chiang Ch'ing's group and the Propaganda Department prompted the Party Center to take a more forceful measure than the existing one. The Party Secretariat then set up a top-level task force called the Five-Man Group, probably in May or June 1964, to coordinate activities in literary and artistic reforms. When P'eng Chen heard about Chiang Ch'ing's model plays in Shanghai, he allegedly said: "What model plays? I, head of the Five-Man Group, do not know about it."[43] The membership of this group, as revealed in 1967, consisted of P'eng Chen (as head of the group), Lu Ting-yi (director of the Propaganda Department), K'ang Sheng (secretary of the Secretariat), Yang Shang-k'un (director of the Secretariat office), and Wu Leng-hsi (editor of *People's Daily* and director of NCNA). Some additional staff supplemented this group: Liu Jen (second secretary of the Peking Municipal Committee), Cheng T'ien-hsiang (secretary of the Peking Secretariat), Hu Sheng (deputy editor of *Red Flag*), Yao Chen (deputy director of the Propaganda Department), Wang Li (deputy editor of *Red Flag*), and Fan Lo-yü (vice-rector of the Higher Party School).[44]

Before this Five-Man Group came up with a new Party policy, the conflict between Shanghai and Peking came to a head-on clash at the Peking Opera Festival on Contemporary Themes held between June 5 and July 31, 1964. On June 6, Mao asked why there were so many literature and art associations in Peking. These associations, he pointed out, were transplanted from the Soviet Union; yet their performance in the festival was the worst, lagging behind that of the army and even those from the localities. By issuing another directive that called for a drastic rectification of this festival, Mao, in fact, declared an ultimatum to the cultural circles. He also approved Chiang Ch'ing's efforts in Shanghai, thus once again vetoing the Party Center's policy. A *Red Flag* editorial then claimed that the reform of the Peking opera was not only a cultural revolution but also a social revolution.[45]

Actually, Mao and Chiang Ch'ing had planned this festival in September 1963.[46] All important leaders of the cultural bureaucracy such as Lu Ting-yi, Chou Yang, Mao Tun, Ch'i Yen-ming, and Liu Chih-chien were present; Chiang Ch'ing also participated. Yet of thirty-five plays submitted from eighteen provinces and municipalities, only four plays were produced by Chiang Ch'ing—Red Lantern, Sparks amid the Reeds, Taking the Bandits' Stronghold, and Raid on the White Tiger Regiment. With the exception of Lin Piao, all top leaders including Mao Tse-tung, Liu Shao-ch'i, and Chou En-lai saw some of the plays presented. Mao saw two: Sparks amid the Reeds and Taking the Bandits' Stronghold. On June 23, Chou En-lai, K'ang Sheng, Chiang Ch'ing, and Chang Ch'un-ch'iao made speeches, none of which was published at that time. Only the speech that P'eng Chen made on July 1 was released.[47]

Judging from Chiang Ch'ing's speech, which was made public for the first time in May 1967, a confrontation took place between Chiang Ch'ing and P'eng Chen at the festival. Chiang Ch'ing pointed out that of three thousand theatrical companies only some ninety were concerned with contemporary themes. In addition, Chou En-lai for the first time publicly denounced the Eight Articles on Literature and Art—the document that served as the charter permitting the limited freedoms in the arts. He reminded that Mao had issued a directive supporting contemporary themes in 1958. K'ang Sheng and Chang Ch'un-ch'iao also spoke in support of Chiang Ch'ing.[48]

P'eng Chen, however, noted that some differing opinions had existed within the Party as to how the reform in Peking opera should be carried out. While agreeing with the principle of promoting contemporary themes, he cautioned that many difficulties appeared in the form of reform. He stressed that, tactically, the Party should take into account the special problems inherent in writing, directing, acting, and singing, for the reform cannot be done at one stroke. As if addressing himself to Chiang Ch'ing, he stated:

Everyone should listen to all kinds of constructive criticisms and discuss them together. If there are criticisms they should be made face to face and not behind someone's back. This should become a habit. In the past among Peking opera circles it was a matter of "you form your group, I form mine"; bickering between this and that company, and between this and that guild was quite serious. This bad habit was a left-over from the old society. Has it all been swept away at one stroke? It is not likely. "You put on an opera and I pull away a prop behind. I put on an opera and you pull away one of my props from behind." That was how things were. Each held together his own group but they did not want to form the big group of the People's Republic of China, not to speak of the big group of proletarian internationalism.[49]

Despite this appeal to unity and cooperation, Mao supported Chiang Ch'ing's argument. On June 27, Mao commented on the report of the Propaganda Department concerning its plan for rectification in the ACFLAC as follows:

In the last fifteen years these associations, most of their publications (it is said that a few are good) and *by and large* the people in them (that is, not everybody) have not carried out the policies of the Party. They have acted as high and mighty bureaucrats, have not gone to the workers, peasants, and soldiers and have not reflected the socialist revolution and socialist construction. *In recent years*, they have slid right down to the brink of revisionism. Unless they remould themselves in real earnest, at some future date they are bound to become groups like the Hungarian Petofi Club.[50]

This June 27 Directive was notable in that Mao accused the intellectuals of having acted as high and mighty bureaucrats and having even slid to the brink of revisionism. It must be noted in this regard that approximately at this time (June 16) Mao also issued the directive calling upon the Party to train revolutionary successors. Without question, Mao became increasingly concerned about the influences of bureaucratization and revisionism upon the second generation. On July 23, after seeing the performance of *Sparks amid the Reeds*, Mao transmitted his instructions concerning the play through Chiang Ch'ing, in which he stressed armed struggle and the relationship between the army and the people. He also ordered the name of the play be changed to *Shachiapang* (the village depicted in the play).[51]

THE RECTIFICATION MOVEMENT AND THE CULTURAL REVOLUTION, 1964-66

In order to avoid being labeled bureaucrats, the Party Center had to step up its efforts to rectify deviations in the cultural circle. Thus, from August 1964 to September 1965 the cultural bureaucracy and its constituent associations did carry out such rectification. But in doing so, they sought to minimize the scope of rectification through various devices. Since Mao could no longer accept these attempts to accommodate his directions, the conflict gradually turned into a larger political struggle.

Immediately following Mao's June directive, Liu Shao-ch'i applied certain policy measures for the task of rectification. He first convened a conference of representatives from the various associations belonging to the ACFLAC and from the Ministry of Culture. At this conference, P'eng Chen, Lu Ting-yi, and Chou Yang called upon all the associations to carry out rectification. Chou Yang led the way by offering a self-criticism of his "bureaucratic" error. The Ministry of Culture also set up the four-man leading group, consisting of three vice-ministers—Ch'i Yen-ming, Ch'en Huang-mei, Hsü Kuang-hsiao—and Li Ch'i of the Peking committee.[52]

In carrying out this rectification, however, the cultural bureaucracy opted for an institutional approach, instead of the ad hoc mass movement that had been the previous format in this type of campaign. The Party Center laid down two guidelines: first, it was to be directed by the Party organizations; second, it was to be conducted in the form of academic and artistic discussions. The Propaganda Department and the Ministry of Culture assumed over-all leadership by specifying the initial targets. For example, the Propaganda Department singled out Hsia Yen, vice-minister, as one such target at the Ministry of Culture; the Ministry of Culture, in turn, chose Yang Han-sheng of the ACFLAC, Shao Ch'üan-lin of the Writers Association, and T'ien Han of the Playwrights Association. With this strategy, the leadership and the practitioners protected each other. Liu Pai-yü, secretary of the Writers Association Party Committee, for example, maintained that the writers' errors had affected their leadership whereas Chou Yang informed the accused of the charges made against them in advance. When literary journals offered their self-criticisms in the form of an "editor's note" or a "notice to the reader," Chou Yang and Lin No-han personally reviewed their wordings. Accordingly, such publications as Wen-i Pao (Literary Gazette), Hsi-chü Pao (Plays and Drama), and Min-chien wen-hsüeh (Folk Literature) joined in a common chorus in stating that they had erred mainly due to their lack of understanding; but on the whole, their achievements outweighed their defects. After these self-criticisms were voiced, in November 1964, the ACFLAC ceased to function.[53]

The Propaganda Department also made every effort to confine criticisms to artistic and academic discussion designed to ascertain the truth, and curbed personal attacks or political struggle. In criticizing Hsieh Yao-han, for example, Chou Yang intended to separate the author T'ien Han from his work. In directing academic debate (discussed below) as well, Chou Yang and Lin Mo-han called for differentiating the past from the present and political from academic issues, to prevent such excesses as lack of analysis, exaggeration, and simple labeling.[54]

These caveats indeed rendered the rectification a sham, as Yao Wen-yüan later charged. The Ministry of Culture was a case in point. As soon as the Propaganda Department's work team under Chou Chin and Su Ling-yang (Chou Yang's wife) left the ministry after having directed the rectification movement, the three vice-ministers—Hsia Yen, Hsü

Kuang-hsiao, and Ch'i Yen-ming—tried to alter the records of their own involvement in the 1960-62 policy adjustments. Later, when Chou Yang himself led a work team at the ministry, he reaffirmed the principle that criticism of any leaders be approved by the department in advance, and advised cadres at the ministry that they should not betray but rely on each other.[55]

While the Propaganda Department and the Ministry of Culture were groping for self-preservation, a few young critics, in August 1964, as in August 1963, suddenly challenged some prominent academic authorities and writers. By and large, they called into question the theories and concepts espoused by such writers as Yang Hsien-chen, Shao Ch'üan-lin, and Feng Ting. At the same time, they also revived the debate on Li Hsiu-ch'eng, and Chou Ku-ch'eng's aesthetic view. Although these critics couched their argument in academic terms, unlike 1963 they increasingly touched upon the political orientation of the writers despite the prohibition of such attempts in Party policy.

On July 17, 1964, two students of the Higher Party School revealed in an article of the *People's Daily* that Yang Hsien-chen, the school's rector, was the very mentor of the students who had propounded the theory of "two combine into one" in the *Kuang-ming Daily* of May 29, 1964. According to their charge, Yang maintained that in everything one divides into two opposites but the two opposites are also united in one. Hence, the position that two combine into one was a world view whereas the position that one divides into two was a methodology. Between July 1964 and the spring of 1965, many critics such as Lin Chieh, Kuan Feng, and Ai Ssu-ch'i each refuted Yang's philosophical view, charging that it advocated class reconciliation. One *Red Flag* article went so far as to say that Yang's theory catered to the demand of modern revisionism, serving as a theoretical weapon to resist the Socialist Education Movement in China. Yang's theory challenged Mao's theory of uninterrupted revolution so fundamentally that the Party Center apparently disposed of the case by removing Yang from his post.[56]

After the case of Yang Hsien-chen was opened, Ch'i Pen-yü in August 1964 revived the historical debate on Li Hsiu-ch'eng. As for this debate, the Party Center allowed some exchange of views between the contending parties. For example, after Ch'i restated his original charge that Li had been a betrayer of the Taiping, Lo Erh-kang made rebuttal based on historical verifications. As for Chou Ku-ch'eng's spirit of the era, Chou defended his contention that although the spirit of an era is reflected by different classes, at the same time a unified integral whole does exist in the era. But his critics charged that such an argument amounted to idealism, instead of dialectism, for it transcended class viewpoint. In the end, they pointed out that Chou's theory was based on subjectivism and individual creativity, which was reactionary because it denied class consciousness.[57] Clearly, these critics no longer raised academic issues but turned to the political implication of Chou's aesthetic view.

In the realm of literature and philosophy, the two other unorthodox theories were subject to rectification: the concept of middle characters espoused by Shao Ch'üan-lin and the theory of human nature proposed by Feng Ting, professor of philosophy at Peking University.[58] In the case of Shao, the Propaganda Department subjected him to criticism as an example of the revisionist trend in literature. Portraying middle characters who were neither revolutionary nor reactionary was so antithetical to Mao's doctrine of mass line that the cultural bureaucracy had no choice but to present it for criticism. In September 1964, the *Literary Gazette* initiated the criticism on Shao by publishing for the first time part of his speech made at the 1962 Dairen conference. The editorial department of the journal called Shao's view a bourgeois stand.[59] This signaled other literary associations to follow suit; and subsequently, editors of other literary journals published their own self-criticisms. Particularly at a time when the PLA was popularizing Lei Feng as a revolutionary hero who sacrificed himself to become a "rust-proof screw" of the revolutionary wheel, the ambiguous middle characters were indeed an anathema to Maoist ideology. Further, the contention that such characters comprised the majority of the masses denied the heart of Mao's populist beliefs. Yao Wen-yüan, for example, rejected Shao's contention that only a minority actively supported the revolution, insisting that the overwhelming majority of the masses were firmly for the revolution.[60]

As for philosophy, from September 1964, *Chung-kuo ch'ing-nien-pao* (Chinese Youth) carried articles repudiating Feng Ting's view on human nature and happiness. These criticisms centered on Feng's view that human nature is basically selfish and that therefore, according to the law of human nature, individuals strive to satisfy their own desires. From this view stemmed Feng's definition of happiness: happiness comes from satisfying individual desire and aspiration. Feng once remarked: "If an individual cannot live himself, how can he possibly serve the masses?"[61] He called this stand a commonplace truth.[62] This image of man's nature fundamentally clashed with that of Lei Feng. If, indeed, Chinese youth were to heed Professor Feng's teaching, instead of learning from Lei Feng, they would hold Lei in contempt. Accordingly, the critics charged that Feng's philosophy was antirevolutionary.[63]

Finally, the rectification movement spilled into the realm of films. This was a natural development because some of the existing films such as *Pei-kuo chiang-nan* (Northern Country and the South of the Yangtze River) written by Yang Han-sheng actually portrayed life in the image of middle characters.[64]

When Chiang Ch'ing attempted to introduce reforms in films comparable to those in Peking opera, the Propaganda Department allowed only two for criticism: *Pei-kuo chiang-nan* and *Tso-ts'un erh-yüeh* (Early Spring in February). When the department reported this to Mao in August 1964, Mao ordered them to bring out more films.[65] At the end of 1964, Chiang Ch'ing asked Lu Ting-yi and Chou Yang to open more films for criticism, but the Propaganda Department again allowed only two more: *Lin-chia fu-tzu* (Lin's Store) based on a novel by Mao Tun and edited by Hsia Yen, and *Pu-yeh ch'eng* (City Without Night) edited by K'o Ling. After this, Hsia Yen made a self-criticism, admitting that he had harbored a bourgeois philosophy.[66] But the Propaganda Department tried to carry out criticism in a directed fashion, emphasizing the special character of the cultural circle. When the campaign against these films gained momentum, P'eng Chen, in March 1965, ordered Chou Yang and Lin Mo-han *not* to question the political orientation of the two films. Subsequently, Teng Hsiao-p'ing called a Secretariat meeting to head off "overheating" in the rectification program. Contending that there had been excessive attacks on the writers, Teng observed: "Some people just want to be famous by criticizing others." As a result, NCNA received only two manuscripts in one day. After this meeting, the criticism of Hsia Yen and T'ien Han was halted for a while.[67]

By the end of 1964, it became clear that without changing the leadership of the cultural circle, the program of rectification could not meet with Mao's demands. In 1965, for instance, the Party Center reorganized the Ministry of Culture. But as long as the top leadership remained unchanged—particularly when P'eng Chen still supervised and Chou Yang still implemented Party policy—a mere change of personnel at the Ministry of Culture could not yield much result. Once this much was clear, Mao sought to change the entire Party leadership in Peking by initiating the Cultural Revolution.

In his report to the third NPC in December 1964, Chou En-lai stated that a great debate on a series of questions of principles had been under way within the Party.[68] And it soon became apparent that this debate was taking its toll. At the NPC, Mao Tun, the minister of culture and a "democratic" writer who also was chairman of the Writers Association, was removed and Lu Ting-yi assumed the ministership.

Subsequently, in April 1965, Lu dismissed three vice-ministers: Hsia Yen, Ch'i Yen-ming, and Ch'en Huang-mei. He then appointed Hsiao Wang-tung, then deputy Party secretary of the Nanking Military Region, as first vice-minister and secretary of the Ministry Party Committee; Shih Hsi-min, then secretary of the Shanghai Party Secretariat, as second vice-minister; at the same time, Lu appointed four new vice-ministers: Yen Chi-sheng, Chao Hsin-ch'u, Liu Pai-yü, and Li Ch'i.

Despite this reshuffling of the Ministry of Culture, no equivalent change took place at the Propaganda Department, which was responsible for directing the ministry's work. Therefore, in summing up the rectification program thus far, Chou Yang still maintained that writing about life during the three hard years of 1960-62 was of educational value, and that although mistakes were made in those years, they had been subsequently corrected. He defended the 1962 Eight Articles on Literature and Arts, saying that the document had been instrumental in curbing oversimplified critiques.[69]

As far as Chiang Ch'ing's model opera movement was concerned, only *Red Lantern*, among those she had produced, was staged in Peking, for the new Vice-Minister of Culture Hsiao Wang-tung did not heed her demands for banning all ancient operas. He made it clear that the Party Center supported the continuation of older operas because those operas had been well received by the masses. Under crossfire from Chiang Ch'ing and the Party Center Hsiao chose to comply with the Party command, saying: "There are too many family heads in the ministry, but I will listen only to one of them."[70] Tormented by this rejection, Chiang Ch'ing speeded up her preparation of the article unmasking the political culpability of Wu Han's *Hai Jui Dismissed from Office*. After K'o Ch'ing-shih died in April 1965 at Chengtu, she entrusted the writing of the article to Chang Ch'un-ch'iao and Yao Wen-yuan, for both of whom she said some security measures must be taken. She kept the secret for eight months during which the article was revised several times.[71]

On the other hand, P'eng Chen sensed that something was afoot and made certain efforts to accommodate Mao's demands. In July 1965, when Hsiao Wang-tung confessed his inexperience at his new job, P'eng told him that he had been chosen precisely because of his amateurism in literature. The new leadership of the Ministry of Culture under Hsiao finally drafted a document called An Outline Report to the Central Committee from the Ministry of Culture Party Committee on Some Problems in the Current Cultural Work, and on July 13, 1965, Hsiao presented this report to a meeting of the Five-Man Group. Those present at this meeting were P'eng Chen, K'ang Sheng, Lu Ting-yi,

Lin Feng, Chou Yang, Wu Leng-hsi, Chiang Nan-ksiang, Teng T'o, Lin Mo-han, Hsü Li-chün, Hsiao Wang-tung, Shih Hsi-min, Liu Pai-yu, and others. In this report, Hsiao proposed to send some opera troupes down to the countryside and to cut the traditional operas drastically. As for films, he recommended further investigations. Upon hearing all this, K'ang Sheng immediately objected to the report by pointing out that the current operas were not suitable to the countryside, and that the question of suspending the traditional operas had not yet been solved. But P'eng Chen, Lu Ting-yi, and Hsü Li-chün all commended Hsiao's report.[72]

The Party Center also approved the report. On September 9, 1965, Hsiao Wang-tung delivered the outline report to a meeting of the Politburo Standing Committee, attended by Liu Shao-ch'i, Teng Hsiao-p'ing, P'eng Chen, Lu Ting-yi, Po I-po, and Chou Yang. When Hsiao stressed the need to struggle against those who had paid only lip service to Mao's directive, Liu Shao-ch'i concurred. But Liu regarded the problem as one of understanding, and therefore, warned against hastiness in rectification. As for Hsia Yen and Ch'i Yen-ming, Liu suggested that they join the four-cleanup campaign. Lastly, Liu asked Hsiao to discuss the report at the National Conference of All Heads of Provincial Cultural Departments.[73] The next day, the Ministry of Culture convened the scheduled national conference, and Hsiao Wang-tung explained the outline report to this conference. Interestingly, Chou Yang invited Hsia Yen and Yang Han-sheng, two targets of the rectification program, to the presidium; he even consoled them, saying: "It is inevitable that sometimes criticism is too harsh or too slight."[74] At this meeting, P'eng Chen also made two important statements for which he was to be condemned: "Everyone including Chairman Mao is equal before the truth," and "there should be construction before destruction."[75]

These moves prompted Mao to confront the Party Center in the fall of 1965. Once he realized that the Party Center had no plan to criticize Wu Han and that P'eng Chen would not fulfill his wishes either, he then called the central work conference (i.e., "the meeting of the Politburo's Standing Committee") in September-October, 1965, attended by a number of leading members of the regional bureaus, at which Mao specifically asked P'eng Chen to criticize Wu Han. It was during this conference, too, that he declared the existence of a real danger of revisionism at the Central Committee, and asked what the local committees could do about it should it actually happen.[76] However, there was still no response from P'eng Chen even after this crucial meeting. As Mao recalled in 1967, revisionists held some departments in Peking so tightly that "no drop of water could penetrate them." He had no choice but to go to Shanghai. On November 10, 1965, Chiang Ch'ing's long desired condemnation of Wu Han's writings on Hai Jui was realized when Mao ordered *Wen-hui pao* to publish Yao Wen-yüan's article, "On the New Historical Play *Hai Jui Dismissed from Office*," which Mao had read three times before giving his approval. By calling Wu Han's play a "poisonous weed" that "satirized the present in the pretext of the old," Yao's article made it clear that literary reform was a political question.[77] And by hinting at revisionism at the Party Center, Mao turned the conflict into a major political struggle to be fought in the form of the Cultural Revolution.

THE POLITICS OF PEKING OPERA

Mao's cultural reforms in 1962-66 started as an artistic debate and then gradually turned into a major political conflict among the Party leadership. This transformation took place through a series of disputes between Mao's radical supporters in Shanghai and the Party Propaganda Department in Peking. Ostensibly, the issue at conflict was an artistic question, but the real issue was the political culpability of those playwrights who had vilified Mao's policies in the aftermath of the GLF. As soon as China's economy began to recover from the crisis of 1960-62, Mao waged a counterattack on those writers. But the more he did so, the more he ran into clashes with the Party leadership.

Thus, through the reform of Peking opera in particular, Mao came to conclude that the Party's propaganda bureaucracy had been sabotaging his cultural policies. As a result, when Chiang Ch'ing raised political questions, P'eng Chen and Chou Yang responded with academic debates. Having witnessed this, Mao accused the propaganda bureaucracy of having slid to the brink of revisionism just as he had accused "those persons in authority" of having taken the capitalist road in the SEM. To overthrow this Party establishment, he finally resorted to the Cultural Revolution; and then, the politics of Peking opera was absorbed into the politics of the Cultural Revolution.

What is significant about this evolution is that political disputes were couched in cultural debates. Thus, in the final analysis, all issues including academic and cultural ones became political in Communist politics; as such, they required a political resolution. Art and literature in particular created ideas and attitudes, that is, the superstructure, in China. For this reason, Mao expressed his keen concern for reforms in the area. As a result, more intense and sometimes violent conflicts were present in the policy processes in this area than in other areas. Mao perceived that there had emerged a widening gap between the socialist superstructure and the socialist economic base in China; to fill this gap with a new culture he called for the Cultural Revolution.

PART IV
*The Cultural Revolution
and Its Aftermath
1966-1976*

The Great Proletarian Cultural Revolution was absolutely necessary and extremely timely.

Mao Tse-tung, 1969

The Cultural Revolution had created a mess in political, economic, and social life.

Teng Hsiao-p'ing, 1975

> Loyal parents who sacrificed
>   so much for the nation
> Never feared the ultimate fate.
> Now that the country has become
>   red, who will be its guardian?
> Our mission unfinished may take
>   a thousand years.
> The struggle tires us, and our hair
>   is grey.
> You and I, old friends, can we just
>   watch our efforts be washed away?
>   *Mao Tse-tung, a poem to Chou En-lai, 1975*

9
The Making of the Cultural Revolution

The Great Proletarian Cultural Revolution (GPCR) in China evolved out of a long political process dating from the publication of Yao Wen-yüan's article on Wu Han's play *Hai Jui Dismissed from Office* in November 1965 to the convening of the Eleventh Plenum in August 1966. This period is significant for two reasons. First, the events unfolded in those ten months represented the culmination of all important cleavages within the Party resulting from the adjustment and consolidation measures it had carried out in 1959-65. Second, the events in this period also exposed the inner workings of the policy process through which Cultural Revolution policies were made, thus vividly showing the interaction between one charismatic leader, Mao, and the institutionalizing Party apparatus. Therefore, a study of this period presents a rare case of the Chinese policy process in action.

The central questions to explore are two: what triggered the Cultural Revolution and how the decisions concerning the revolution were made. The first question concerns the timing of the revolution and the second the policy process.

THE TIMING: LINKAGE OF DOMESTIC AND EXTERNAL POLITICS

One of the questions that has always intrigued students of revolution is: what event actually triggers the outbreak of a revolution or transforms a society's latent interests into manifest interests?[1] A crucial question for our purpose is the timing of the Cultural Revolution. Why did Mao raise the Wu Han issue *at the particular time of September-October 1965*, although Wu Han had written his play in 1960 and the play had been staged in 1961? Why did he raise the question of revisionism *within the Central Committee* at the same time? Perhaps Mao's innermost motives for doing these will never be known, but rarely are public policies made in a social vacuum. Mao's decisions may well have resulted from specific fears and hopes about his role in history.[2]

Hence the historical and political context in which Mao made his decisions must be analyzed to answer the questions. Specifically, the relationship between the Cultural Revolution in China and the external situation surrounding China in 1965-66 reveal a good case of what is called "linkage politics."[3] The culmination of the policy conflicts between Mao and the Party Center was linked in several ways to the Soviet offer to form a united action toward the Vietnam War in 1965. First, the CCP leadership had shared consensus on China's foreign policy under Mao's over-all direction but this consensus began to erode in 1964-65 when Mao raised the specter of domestic revisionism at the Party Center. Once Mao shifted his concern from Soviet revisionism to the possibility of such revisionism in China, Sino-Soviet relations became a crucial issue in domestic politics. Second, Soviet pressure for a united action came just when Mao decided to purge his domestic revisionists, apparently deepening his sense of imminent crisis for China. For Mao to accept the Soviet proposal under the circumstance would certainly strengthen the hands of his domestic opponents and thereby undermine his quest for a true Communist society in China. For this same reason his opponents also may have welcomed the Soviet proposal, hoping that it would perhaps moderate Mao's attempts to reverse the policies that they had painstakingly consolidated.

The Debate on Military and Foreign Policy, 1965-66

Various explanations have been offered about the relationship between the military and foreign policy debate within the CCP in 1965-66 and the Cultural Revolution. Zagoria and Ra'anan, for example, contended that the differences among some CCP top leaders over the Soviet offer for a united action in 1965 was a major issue of the debate preceding the Cultural Revolution.[4] In criticizing "Kremlinology" of Zagoria and Ra'anan, Yahuda argued that their studies had not sufficiently taken into consideration the historical and political context of the strategic debate, particularly the "complex process involving a series of interactions between domestic and international factors."[5] What is lacking in these studies is an analysis of the linkage between the strategic debate and Mao's fear of revisionism as he perceived it.

It is important to note that the strategic debate in 1965 heightened Mao's vigilance against Soviet revisionism. For the first time since the P'eng Teh-huai case in 1959 a major challenge to Mao's military and foreign policy arose in 1964-66. Lo Jui-ch'ing, the army's chief of staff, had evaded the military doctrines of Mao Tse-tung and Lin Piao by resisting the excessive emphasis placed on political work in the army. According to an unconfirmed source, Mao, from 1960 on, had asked Lo to transfer several army divisions from the hinterland to the coastal provinces, an action Lo had put off for years. Commenting on China's Third Five-Year Plan, Mao, in June 1964, asserted that agriculture and defense industries should be given first priority; for this purpose he recommended that each province develop its own defense industries. In another talk on June 16 he pointed out that provincial first secretaries and the political commissars had not carried out their duty. Hence he urged them to pay more attention to military affairs in general and the militia work in particular so that the nation should be adequately prepared for war, including a nuclear war. In making these suggestions he stressed the importance of political work in the army.[6]

In July 1964, Mao brought up these subjects when he criticized Lo for his inaction. Lo had also evaded Lin Piao's directives on strengthening the militia through the participation of PLA soldiers in the Socialist Education Movement, which was under way in the countryside. Although Hsiao Hua, acting director of the army's General Political Department, had transmitted Lin Piao's call for the intensification of political work through the "four first" campaign in 1964, Lo instead initiated large-scale military maneuvers to test military techniques. These exercises continued from January to October; Lo made thirteen trips across the country to make certain that regional units carried them out. On June 15 and 16, 1964, Mao also reviewed one of these exercises, the military contest between Peking and Chinan troops.[7]

Lo continued to defy Lin Piao's order for intensified political work in 1964. At the end of this year, Lin issued a directive on the political campaign, but Lo altered its contents eight times in ten days until it lost all the original meaning.[8] Lo put his views on the army's political work as follows:

If politics does not fare well, everything goes wrong. But if only politics is done well and everything else is not, the whole thing will collapse. I am afraid this kind of politics cannot be considered good politics. Rather, it is bogus politics. . . . One must correctly understand Commander Lin's directive. Unless politics is done well, the troops will run backward in war. If you cannot shoot accurately, the other side will advance on you. Where else would you run but backward.[9]

Lo shared Lu Ting-yi and Chou Yang's view that in the name of politics one should not vulgarize the study of Mao's works. He was equally critical of the army's cultural activities becoming devoid of any artistic taste, "otherwise mere reading of quotations from Mao's writings would suffice."[10]

A situation similar to that between Mao and the Party Secretariat seems to have existed then between Lin Piao and Lo's general staff. As a secretary of the Party Secretariat, Lo was obligated to convey the Party Center's directives to the military commands; but in doing so, he was accused of having distorted them. In April 1965, Lin Piao specifically ordered Lo to refer to the standing committee of the Military Affairs Committee whenever he appointed certain cadres, but Lo failed to do so. He often bypassed the MAC and the GPD by directly reporting to the Party Secretariat. He went so far as to suggest through Yeh Chün, Lin Piao's wife, that Lin should care less about military affairs but more about his own health. If Lin was really sick as was generally thought, this may have been a statement voiced out of Lo's genuine concern.[11] In any case, the conflict between Lin Piao and Lo had become acute by early 1965.

The bombing of North Vietnam by the United States must also be understood against this background. Even though Mao met Edgar Snow in January 1965, prior to the start of the bombing in February, his talk with Snow was very revealing. In response to Snow's questions, Mao said that U.S. forces would not be leaving at that time, but would probably fight for one or two more years. After that, "the United States troops would find it boring and might go home or somewhere else."[12] Mao thought that the Vietnamese could cope with their situation and that a Sino-American war could occur only if American troops came to China. Where his views on Khrushchev and the new leadership of the Soviet Union were concerned, he said that China would miss Khrushchev as a negative example and that despite the new leadership Sino-Soviet relations would not improve very much.[13] According to his perception of the Southeast Asian situation, Mao felt that U.S. involvement would remain limited; it was not necessary for China to forge a united action with the Soviet Union, for, in the long run, the ideological and military threat of the Soviet Union was far more serious than that of the United States.

Lo Jui-ch'ing, however, challenged Mao's view of the Vietnam situation and Sino-Soviet relations. Although the Maoist post hoc charge leveled against Lo contained only one reference to the Sino-Soviet dispute—he suggested that the Chinese side had created an artificial tension in the Sino-Soviet border clash of 1962[14]—his downfall was directly tied with his strategic view toward the American escalation of the Vietnam War and the subsequent Soviet proposal for a united action against the war. On May 10, 1965, Lo wrote a major article in commemoration of V-E Day that made two important points pertinent to the Vietnam War. First, he took the U.S. bombing of North Vietnam as a serious challenge to the Communist bloc in general and to China in particular, comparable to Hitler's offensive after the Munich agreement. To meet this challenge, he suggested what he called the "strategy of active defense," which he claimed Stalin had adopted against Hitler. This strategy was not to hold or capture territory but to concentrate superior forces to destroy the enemy's effectiveness in advance. Second, in order to carry out this strategy successfully, he advocated a united front with the Soviet Union. He contended that such a "united front with the Soviet Union and the world proletariat as its main force" under Stalin's leadership had brought victory in World War II.[15]

Apparently, some debate existed on these points within the army itself. Since Lo's strategy required a greater degree of professionalism, it clashed with Mao and Lin's military doctrine, which stressed political work—not just for enhancing military discipline but more importantly, for maintaining ideological vigilance against the corrosive influence of modern revisionism, that is, Soviet revisionism. On August 1, 1965, when the CCP celebrated the founding of the Red Army, Ho Lung, vice-chairman of the MAC, wrote an article that indicated the existence of strategic debate within the PLA. Ho pointed out that some soldiers regarded the "three democracies" and the mass-line method as unnecessary in modern times.[16] These soldiers may have supported the idea of united action with the Soviet Union.

It was to this debate that Lin Piao addressed himself in September 1965. In his article "Long Live the Victory of People's War! " written in commemoration of V-J Day, Lin refuted the argument advanced by Lo Jui-ch'ing. Recalling the Red Army's experiences in fighting the Japanese, Lin championed Mao's doctrine of guerrilla warfare. On the premise that the world situation was excellent for China, he expounded a strategy of political offensive, thus repudiating Lo's strategy of active defense. Lin extolled the people's war in which the rural areas of the world (Asia, Africa, and Latin America) were to encircle the cities of the world (North America and western Europe). He categorically rejected the idea of united action with the Soviet Union; instead, he proposed the united front of all rural areas of the world. He then asserted that Khrushchev revisionists had come to rescue U.S. imperialism when the latter was most panic-stricken, asserting that they had no faith in the masses or the oppressed people of the world. Instead of relying on the Soviet Union, Lin emphasized the principle of self-reliance as the basic line of Chinese foreign policy.[17]

Lin Piao's thesis could not end the debate, however, for some Party leaders did share Lo Jui-ch'ing's view and the unfolding of international events also appeared to weaken Lin's argument. The Indonesian Army's crackdown on the Communist Party in September 1965 was one example; but more important was China's failure to exclude the Soviet Union from the second Bandung conference to be held in Algeria. While the Chinese were suffering these diplomatic blows, the Communist Party of the Soviet Union under its new leadership made serious efforts at reconciliation with the CCP by inviting the latter to its forthcoming Twenty-Third Congress. And many Communist parties, especially the Japanese and the North Korean, welcomed the Soviet efforts. These moves, however, directly threatened the very legitimacy of Mao's ideological struggle against Soviet revisionism, and Mao had to come up with actions designed to counter these pressures.

Mao's Fear of Revisionism and the Cultural Revolution

Such external pressures heightened Mao's fear of revisionism, which originally had referred to Khrushchev's innovations in Soviet ideology and practice after the Twentieth Congress of the CPSU in 1956. Mao opposed this Soviet revisionism for fear that it would adversely influence Chinese communism as he defined it; thus, external and internal developments since 1956 reinforced his struggle. Particularly after the failure of the GLF, he became increasingly concerned about the danger of regression in the Chinese revolution as a result of internal setbacks and the external influence of Khrushchev revisionism.

In order to keep Soviet revisionism from infiltrating Chinese communism, Mao challenged Khrushchev by presenting his ideas about communism to the Soviet Party. When the CPSU, in September 1963, rejected the CCP's first twenty-five-item comprehensive proposal concerning the general line of the international Communist movement, the CCP plunged into polemics with the CPSU by publishing its celebrated Nine Comments, each dwelling on an important issue that divided the two parties. Thus, what started as an ideological dispute between the CCP and the CPSU has increasingly turned toward conflicts of divergent national experiences and interests. When this dispute escalated so far as to involve border talks between the two Communist nations in February 1964, the Soviet Union set forth four points: (1) cease public polemic, (2) send Russian technicians to China again, (3) hold Sino-Soviet border talks, and (4) increase trade. Commenting on these proposals, however, Mao said that the border talks only would start on February 25 and that a little business could be done with the Soviet Union, but not too much because Soviet products were "clumsy and expensive." For China's trade experiences with the Soviet Union, Mao charged that the Soviet Union had always held back what they had and that therefore, it was not as easy as working with the French bourgeoisie who, Mao said, had at least some business ethics.[18] Thus, by 1964 Mao had all but abandoned the hope of persuading the Soviet leadership to accept his views.

In June 1964 the CCP summed up its arguments in its last comment, which follows: (1) Stalin had erred in denying the existence of class struggle after the means of production had been socialized; (2) the CPSU had made errors to the extent that a man like Khrushchev could usurp the leadership of the CPSU and subsequently bring about a privileged stratum, which had come to dominate the entire Soviet society; (3) as Khrushchev revisionists substituted material incentives for the socialist principle of distribution, capitalism was being gradually restored in the Soviet Union; and (4) since the theory of "the state of the whole people" and of "the Party of the whole people" that the CPSU adopted in 1961 meant, in effect, no Communist state or Party, it denied the Leninist theory of the dictatorship of the proletariat. This brand of communism was a "goulash communism"; it was no longer interested in abolishing classes but actually perpetuated them in the name of a better life for every man.[19] These charges, then, presented a projection by Mao of the kind of things he did not want to see happen in China, which explains why the CCP made public all the documents from the CPSU in 1963-64 so that the Chinese cadres could use them as negative examples.

Because these lines were formulated by the CCP's Politburo, the Party leadership appeared to have taken a common stand upon the general principles of the Sino-Soviet polemics. But as the polemics progressed, some top leaders such as Liu Shao-ch'i, Teng Hsiao-p'ing, and P'eng Chen apparently had some reservations over the specific methods of carrying out the antirevisionism campaign. Liu actively took part in drafting the "two editorials" of 1956 and the "nine comments" addressed to the CPSU, the later vilification of him as China's Khrushchev notwithstanding.[20] Yet in 1962, Liu advocated seeking common ground while reserving differences with the Soviet Union. At a conference of the Academy of Science in 1963, he stated that the struggle against foreign revisionism was necessary to prevent Chinese revisionism. It was also known that Teng Hsiao-p'ing drafted the first version of the twenty-five-item proposal in 1963. But Mao found that it was unusable and reformulated it himself. In December 1964, when Chou En-lai made his report to the NPC, he disclosed for the first time that quite a few people in China had advocated what he designated "three reconciliations and one reduction" (san-ho i-shao). By this he meant reconciliations with imperialism, the reactionaries, and modern revisionism, and reduction of aid to the revolutionary struggle. In 1966, Liu identified Teng Hsiao-p'ing as one of those who had proposed such measures in 1962.[21] In March 1964, Mao himself stated that Wang Chia-hsiang also had supported it.[22] Despite these differences, however, so long as Mao did not interfere with their internal policies, these Party leaders apparently rallied behind Mao in support of China's foreign policy posture vis-à-vis the Soviet Union and other countries. As a result, Mao was left alone in his preoccupation with the struggle against the CPSU.

But when his polemics with the CPSU produced few results, Mao became obsessed with the danger of revisionism and shifted his concern to the CCP's internal problems. This led him to confront the Party leaders in many respects. To forestall the rise of revisionism in China, he urged the Party to carry out the Socialist Education Movement in the countryside and cultural reforms in the intellectual community. In both cases, however, the Party leaders such as Liu, Teng, and P'eng sabotaged his demands, though they all paid lip service to Mao. By the end of 1965, Mao could not help but perceive that all these trends were antithetical to his ideological and policy lines, emerging as manifestations of revisionism. Specifically, the erosion of ideological commitment, the policy drift toward material incentives at the expense of revolution, and such bureaucratic phenomena as hierarchy, specialization, and routinization were all seen as buds of revisionism.

Mao's fear of revisionism should be understood in this context, for by 1964 he apparently had come to perceive that no great difference existed between Soviet revisionism and Chinese revisionism. In fact, the CCP's ninth comment claimed that "Khrushchev's phony communism" actually taught the CCP a lesson, in that the Party ought to take appropriate measures to prevent such a peaceful evolution of revisionism in China. This comment also drew fifteen lessons from the Soviet experience, which, in effect, summarized Mao's domestic theories and policies. Headed by the doctrine of uninterrupted revolution, they included such familiar Maoist themes as: the mass line, the organization of the poor and lower-middle peasants, the SEM, the people's commune as the best suitable form of organization in the transition period, the cadres' participation in labor, egalitarian salary, and Party control of the armed forces and public security agencies.[23] It is clear that Mao's fear of Soviet revisionism and Chinese revisionism was joined in these measures.

It is in this light that the Soviet pressure for a united action with China can be properly explained. To do so, it is worth repeating a point

made earlier, that by the summer of 1965 the conflicts between Mao
and the Party apparatus had considerably worsened. Soviet pressure
coming at this juncture put Mao on the spot, for many of his internal
opponents not only defied his domestic policies but also challenged his
foreign policies by supporting the Soviet offer of a rapprochement.
Although Mao had already rejected the Soviet offer in July 1965, P'eng
Chen, Teng Hsiao-p'ing, and Liu Shao-ch'i—in addition to Lo Jui-ch'ing
—continued to support the Soviet overture. Perhaps they did so out of
their genuine concern for China's security in the face of the U.S. escalation of the war near the Chinese border or to defend their stakes in the
debates with Mao on other domestic issues. In any case, P'eng welcomed the Soviet proposal by calling for a broad international united
front against U.S. imperialism of all socialist countries at the rally cele-
brating the sixteenth anniversary of the Chinese Republic on October 1,
1965. P'eng also advocated sending a Chinese delegation to the Twenty-
Third Congress of the CPSU. In March 1966, just before he was purged,
P'eng reiterated his support for a united action at the welcoming rally
for Kenji Miyamoto, secretary general of the Japanese Communist
party, who came to Peking precisely to promote such an action. P'eng
and Kenji actually agreed upon a joint statement to that effect, but
Mao's disapproval kept it from being made public. According to Snow's
report, Liu also wanted to send a Chinese delegation to the Soviet
congress to reactivate the Sino-Soviet alliance.[24] But at an enlarged
meeting of the Politburo on March 20, 1966, Mao made it clear that the
CCP would not attend the Twenty-Third Congress of the CPSU. If the
CCP did not attend, he predicted, the most the Soviet Union could do
was to threaten China with troops; if this did not happen, the dispute
would just continue to be a battle on paper.[25]

These debates, it would seem, contributed to Mao's sense of a crisis
in the making, for he had long taken the stand: "If the revisionists did
not abuse us but fawned on us and applauded us, then we would not be
much different from them and would become revisionists,"[26] as Wang
Jen-chung (first secretary of the Hupeh Provincial Committee) pointed
out in April 1966. If, indeed, the CCP accepted the Soviet overture, it
followed that the Party itself would become revisionist. Particularly
when his internal opponents catered to Soviet pressure, Mao probably
perceived that Soviet revisionism and Chinese revisionism were coalesc-
ing. Accordingly, in response to this ominous threat, he resorted to the
Cultural Revolution.

In September-October 1965, he convened the central work conference to discuss these problems. It was at this conference that he asked
P'eng Chen to criticize Wu Han while admonishing the Party about the

imminent danger of revisionism within the Central Committee. With
still no positive response from P'eng, Mao then went to Shanghai and
initiated the Cultural Revolution by authorizing the publication of Yao
Wen-yüan's criticism of Wu Han on November 10.[27]

Thus, the turn of internal politics was directly linked with certain
external pressures in 1965-66. It was more than coincidental that the
article rejecting a united action with the Soviet Union appeared on
November 11, 1965, the day after Yao's article on Wu Han came out.
"Since there is a difference of fundamental line," the article asserted,
"the achievement of unity requires either that we discard Marxism-
Leninism and follow their revisionism, or that they renounce revisionism and return to the path of Marxism-Leninism."[28] The article took
note of the domestic view of supporting such a united action:

Some people ask, why is it that the Marxist-Leninists and the revolutionary people
cannot take united action with the new leaders of the CPSU, yet can unite with
personages from the upper strata in the nationalist countries, and strive for united
action with them in the anti-imperialist struggle, and can even exploit the contradictions among the imperialist countries in the struggle against the United States?[29]

The answer to this was that the Soviet idea of united action was not
based on principle but was a device for "splittism," for Khrushchev
revisionists interposed friend and enemy by taking a united action
with the United States, not against it.

This article therefore stressed striking a balance between strategy
and policy in formulating Chinese foreign policy. It also severely
attacked the 1965 Kosygin reforms in Soviet enterprises, accusing
them of restoring capitalism. Finally, the article revealed a new contention by Mao: "Comrade Mao Tse-tung has often said to comrades from
fraternal parties that if China's leadership is usurped by revisionists in
the future, the Marxist-Leninists of all countries should likewise reso-
lutely expose and fight them, and help the working class and the masses
of China to combat such revisionism."[30] To prevent this situation, Mao
had to show his own efforts first.

Mao indeed justified the Cultural Revolution with just such a
rationale. The Sino-Soviet disputes and the Cultural Revolution, then,
were part of his efforts to fight revisionism. And the intricate interplays
between domestic politics and external conditions in 1965-66 reinforced this trend, the external pressure in particular serving as a trigger.

THE POLICY PROCESS OF THE CULTURAL REVOLUTION, 1965-66

The policy process of the Cultural Revolution from September
1965 through August 1966 can be observed in several distinct stages.
These stages corresponded roughly to the sequential steps of policy

making: problem identification, policy formulation, policy legitimation, policy implementation, and policy evaluation.[31] Although these stages are mainly analytical distinctions, it is important to delineate the major pattern of conflicts developed in each stage to see how conflicts in one stage gave rise to those in another until the Eleventh Plenum formally endorsed the idea of the Cultural Revolution.

Identifying the Problem: The Wu Han Question, Political or Academic?

In identifying the problem of the Cultural Revolution, Mao and the Party Propaganda Department differed over the issue of how the Party should deal with the Wu Han question: was it to be a political or a purely academic issue? In a larger context, this issue touched upon two different goals and methods of the Cultural Revolution that Mao and the Party propaganda leadership envisioned. Hence, conflicts were inevitable between Mao's supporters and the Propaganda Department in defining the problem.

From the outset Mao had questioned the political nature of Wu Han's play on Hai Jui; but P'eng Chen, representing the Party Center, responded with an academic debate. At the Politburo meeting of September-October 1965, when Mao posed the question to P'eng Chen: "Can Wu Han be criticized?," he also asked the local Party committees what they could do if revisionism occurred at the Party Center. P'eng Chen chose to dodge this question, replying that only some of Wu Han's errors deserved criticism.[32] P'eng subsequently informed the Peking Municipal Party Committee of Mao's demand but said nothing to the Five-Man Group in charge of cultural reforms. This issue had already been raised over the reform of Peking opera in 1963-65, for it should be recalled that the Party Secretariat had set up this task force known as the Five-Man Group in 1964.[33] As he had done then, P'eng Chen again treated the Wu Han question as a purely academic issue, because, as he had told a September meeting of provincial cultural departments, everybody including Mao should be equal before the truth and construction should come before destruction.[34]

This difference over the Wu Han issue was the beginning of the conflict between Shanghai and Peking over the goal of the Cultural Revolution. Peking was under the tight control of P'eng Chen, so Mao had no choice but to go to Shanghai. There he authorized the publication of Yao's article after having read it three times; he wanted to show it to Chou En-lai and K'ang Sheng but Chiang Ch'ing opposed the idea and wanted it published as soon as possible. The article suggested that in his play Wu Han praised P'eng Teh-huai's attack on Mao at the 1959

Lushan conference by satirizing his dismissal by Mao in the guise of the Ming official Hai Jui whom the emperor Chia Ch'ing had dismissed despite his uprightness.

The publication of the article resulted in a series of conflicts between Shanghai and Peking, and between the army's propaganda instruments and the Party's. Yao's article, published without prior approval from the Center, was indeed in violation of normal Party discipline. Therefore, in the name of Party character (*tang-hsing* and *partiinost'* in Russia) P'eng Chen decided it should be suppressed. As a result, with the exception of Shanghai's *Chieh-fang jih-pao*, of which Yao was an editor, no other paper published the article. Only when the army's *Liberation Daily* reproduced it on November 29, 1965, then, did the *People's Daily* follow suit. Witnessing this development, Mao ordered that pamphlets of the article be printed in Shanghai. When the Shanghai Party Committee asked the Peking Party Committee to purchase these books, no reply was forthcoming. On the contrary, P'eng Chen several times censured the Shanghai committee for its breach of Party discipline by allowing such publication; he asked the Shanghai committee: "What has happened to your Party character?" Moreover, at a meeting initiated by Chou En-lai in Peking on November 28, Teng T'o (secretary of the Peking committee) reported that some powerful person must have been behind the Yao article; P'eng Chen argued that this was not important: what mattered was to uphold the truth.[35]

The Party's view as P'eng Chen formulated it was to treat Wu Han as an academic issue in the tradition of the Hundred Flowers campaign, thus excluding any political issue. But Mao's supporters challenged this. The difference became apparent in two diverging responses of the *People's Daily* and the *Liberation Daily*. The "editor's note" of the Party organ held that because diverse views existed on the question of Hai Jui, the Party would adopt the policy of Hundred Flowers Bloom. But the note of the army organ refuted this stand, declaring:

In 1961, comrade Wu Han wrote a Peking opera *Hai Jui Dismissed from Office.* This was a great poisonous weed. The author did everything in beautifying the feudal ruling class and in praising the theory of class harmony. He said that we do not need revolution. He distorted historical truths, using the method of satirizing the present in the guise of the old. The author purposefully created the image of Hai Jui to show that the people of our socialist era should "learn" from Hai Jui's so-called "returning land," his "pacifying of local tyrants," his "upright and unflattering spirit as a great statesman" and so on. Is it not clear what he wrote for?[36]

By contrast, the *People's Daily* evaded this question and reaffirmed the Party's view: "Our policy is to allow the freedom of criticism and countercriticism; as for the mistaken views we shall adopt the method of reason and persuasion, seeking truth from facts."[37]

The Shanghai-Peking tensions were further aggravated when all local papers except the *Kuangchow jih-pao* carried the *People's Daily* note. This meant that with the exception of Shanghai all local Party organizations were still under the control of the Party Center. In Peking, Yao Chen (deputy director of the Propaganda Department) had already conveyed to the Peking papers P'eng Chen's directive that they should not carry the Yao article. To counter this, on December 9, 1965, Mao's young supporter Ch'i Pen-yü published another article in *Hung-ch'i* attacking, by implication, Wu Han's historiography. In response, Teng T'o, using the pseudonym Hsiang Yang-sheng, wrote an article in the *Peking Daily* entitled "From *Hai Jui Dismissed from Office* to the Theory of Moral Inheritance," which defended Wu Han on the ground that his stand on moral inheritance was justified. On December 14, P'eng Chen himself said to Wu Han: "You should examine your thinking for wrong things and persist for right things."[38]

Faced with this resistance, Mao again had to confront P'eng Chen. Before a meeting of Ch'en Po-ta, K'ang Sheng, Ai Ssu-ch'i, and Kuan Feng at Hangchow on December 21, he praised Yao Wen-yüan for having created such a shock effect; he also commended Ch'i Pen-yü's article, which he said did not specify the person under attack. For the first time Mao revealed P'eng Teh-huai's attack on him at the 1959 Lushan conference: "In Yenan you cussed me for 40 days. Now you will not allow me to cuss you for 20 days."[39] Complaining about such intellectuals as Wu Han and Chien Po-tsan, who had advocated the theory of the concession policy made by the feudal lords, he said that these men should go to factories and farms. The next day P'eng Chen was present at the meeting. Mao then told P'eng Chen, K'ang Sheng, and Yang Ch'eng-wu (now the army's acting chief of staff) that the crux of Wu Han's play on Hai Jui was the dismissal from office. P'eng Chen, however, insisted that Wu Han had had no contact with P'eng Teh-huai. P'eng then requested a private talk with Mao on December 23; after this he insisted that Mao agreed with him in not raising a political question about Wu Han.[40] P'eng apparently thought that he could accommodate Mao's demands in his own way. The *Peking Daily* of December 24 published Wu Han's self-criticism, stating that the play on Hai Jui actually aimed at opposing "some people" who looked upon themselves as Hai Jui. On January 2, 1966, P'eng Chen convened a meeting of over thirty leaders from the cultural-educational systems. It was at this forum that Hu Sheng (deputy editor of *Hung-ch'i*) first conveyed Mao's view of Wu Han. Acting as Mao's spokesman, K'ang

Sheng then disclosed more of Mao's talk, thereby clashing with P'eng Chen; but other participants all agreed with P'eng Chen's attitude toward Wu Han.[41]

From this time on, Mao no longer trusted P'eng Chen. His young propagandists then challenged P'eng's authority by submitting several articles to him, exposing what Mao considered to be the crux of the Wu Han question. Then, Hsü Li-chün (deputy director of the Propaganda Department) banned the publication of such articles. Hsü called the editors of three newspapers and three magazines in Peking: *Jen-min jih-pao* (People's Daily), *Kuang-ming jih-pao* (Kuang-ming Daily), *Pei-ching jih-pao* (Peking Daily), *Hung-ch'i* (Red Flag), *Hsin chien-she* (New Construction), and *Ch'ien-hsien* (Frontline); he told them that with the exception of *Hung-ch'i* they all must get approval from the Propaganda Department when publishing articles. After this meeting, several pieces actually defended Wu Han's position on Hai Jui by verifying the historical facts.[42] It was through these academic debates that P'eng Chen endeavored to protect Wu Han and other authors of the "Three-Family Village" columns written in 1961-62.

Formulating Policy: The February Outline Report vs. The Summary of the Forum

Because of these diverging views between Mao and P'eng over the Wu Han question—Mao raising political questions and P'eng responding with academic debates—Mao and the Party Center came to formulate two different policies toward the GPCR. Although Mao's supporters were a minority, they justified their case in the name of Mao's correct ideology. P'eng Chen's associates, however, won the support of the Party Center and the intellectuals. Because of these differences, two diverging documents were drafted: the Party Center formulated the February Outline Report and Mao's supporters the Summary of the Forum.

The February Outline Report

This Outline Report evolved out of the Party Center's continuing efforts to implement those of Mao's cultural policies set forth since 1963. This report actually was based on the previous outline report prepared in July 1965 by the Ministry of Culture under Hsiao Wang-tung, which the Party Center transmitted in January 1966.[43] The transformation of the 1965 report into the February 1966 report provides an interesting case of the policy-making process at the top level.

The Five-Man Group under P'eng Chen drafted the February

Report through the normal Party process of policy making. P'eng Chen ordered Hsü Li-chün, on January 31, 1966, to prepare materials for formulating a comprehensive directive. On February 3, P'eng convened an enlarged conference of the Five-Man Group, attended by eleven leaders, where he distributed seven documents prepared by Hsü Li-chün and Yao Chen; among these were plans for criticizing Kuan Feng and Ch'i Pen-yü, Mao's two propagandists. Hsü reported that many scholars were tense over the Wu Han question, an observation with which Lu Ting-yi and Hu Sheng concurred. But K'ang Sheng again dissented, asserting that the struggle against Wu Han was a class struggle; he also defended Kuan Feng and Ch'i Pen-yü, pointing out that Wu Han's play on Hai Jui actually depicted the dismissal of P'eng Teh-huai. P'eng Chen refuted this, however, saying that some critiques used too much "gun-powder," which hindered free debate. To back up his case he had Cheng T'ien-hsiang (secretary of the Peking Party secretariat) testify that no connection had existed between Wu Han and P'eng Teh-huai, and further insisted that the political question should not be raised. P'eng then proposed to submit a memorandum about their discussion to the Politburo Standing Committee and entrusted its writing to Hsü Li-chün and Yao Chen.[44]

P'eng Chen personally supervised the preparation of this memorandum. The night of February 3, he summoned Hsü and Yao to his house and told them: "Commit a political mistake rather than a disciplinary mistake because in a political mistake we can still rely on the organization to defend ourselves." On February 4, Hsü and Yao went to T'ai-yu-t'ai to write the report, apparently without informing K'ang Sheng. In the evening they handed their draft to Wu Leng-hsi (editor of the *People's Daily*); after making certain revisions, Wu forwarded it to P'eng Chen.[45]

This report went through the standard authorization process as well. On February 5, Liu Shao-ch'i convened a meeting of the Politburo Standing Committee at his house, attended by Teng Hsiao-p'ing, P'eng Chen, Wu Leng-hsi, Hsiao Wang-tung, Hsü Li-chün, and Hu Sheng. P'eng Chen told the meeting that the Five-Man Group had not discussed the report because of the time pressure. Hsü presented an oral report on the draft; Liu and Teng then approved of its contents. According to one source, P'eng Chen did not bring up the essence of the Wu Han question as Mao saw it. Yet he won Liu's approval to present a similar report to Mao.[46]

As a final step, P'eng Chen sought Mao's authorization. He ordered Hsü Li-chün, Hu Sheng, Yao Chen, and Wu Leng-hsi to make more revisions. On February 7, he led the team of Hsü Li-chün, Hu Sheng, and Wu Leng-hsi to Wuhan whereupon they presented this report to Mao the next day. In the course of the presentation Mao twice asked P'eng Chen: "Is Wu Han anti-Party?" to which P'eng replied that Wu Han was still on the side of socialism. Mao opposed the rectification plan against Kuan Feng. Yet, after this meeting, P'eng again concluded that Mao approved the report. He asked Hsü and Hu to add a few final revisions and then to submit the document to the Party Center. On February 12, the Party Secretariat formally transmitted this report; thus the Outline Report on the Current Academic Discussion by the Five-Man Group in Charge of the Cultural Revolution, commonly known as the February Outline (*erh-yüeh t'i-kang*), came into existence.[47]

The contents of the February Outline revealed many provisions that contradicted Mao's policy. Although it upheld Mao's Thought, the outline stressed more than anything else academic and theoretical questions, which explained the document's emphasis upon a program of rectification against scholar tyrants (*hsüeh-fa*) and the "staunch Left" despite Mao's opposition to such a plan. Furthermore, the outline adopted an institutional approach to the methodology of the Cultural Revolution by stating that it be carried out under direction and with the approval of the leading bodies concerned. The February Outline also laid down several caveats for the Cultural Revolution by stating that: (1) the debate should be widely opened; (2) everyone is equal before the truth; (3) it is necessary to raise academic and professional standards; and (4) without construction there is no destruction.[48]

P'eng Chen immediately made preparations to ensure the implementation of these measures, but in the process he ran into conflict with Mao's supporters. Hsü Li-chün and Hu Sheng explained the outline to a meeting of some eighty leaders of the cultural and educational systems. Wu Leng-hsi instructed the *People's Daily* and *New China News Agency* to treat the Wu Han question strictly as an academic issue. P'eng, Hsü, and Hu also visited Szechwan to explain the document, which they called a great document, comparable to Mao's Twenty-Three Points on the Socialist Education Movement. P'eng also ordered the law faculty of Peking University to provide textual research about Hai Jui; the result of this research was delivered to Chiang Nan-hsiang (minister of higher education), Teng T'o, Fan Chin, and Sung Shih. Finally on March 2 P'eng sent Wu Han to Ch'ang-p'ing hsien to join a four-cleanup work team with the pseudonym of Li Ming-fa. But it could soon be seen that Mao's group was not content with these measures. On March 11, a member of the Shanghai Party Committee asked the Propaganda Department about the meaning of "academic tyrants"; Hsü Li-chün referred this inquiry to P'eng Chen: P'eng said that the term did not imply any particular person but meant "Ah Q" or whoever had a scar on his head.[49]

The Summary of the Forum: Mao's Policy

Since P'eng Chen had ignored the crux of Mao's policy in the February Outline, Chiang Ch'ing in Shanghai set out to prepare a counterdocument. Deprived of the Party's propaganda instruments, this group sought the support of Lin Piao and the People's Liberation Army leadership. The group eventually produced the Summary of the Forum on the Work in Literature and Art in the Armed Forces with Which Comrade Lin Piao Entrusted Comrade Chiang Ch'ing, commonly known as the Summary of the Forum (tso-t'an-hui ch'i-yao).[50]

This document was formulated outside the machinery of the Party Center. On February 1, 1966, Chiang Ch'ing asked Lin Piao in Peking to send responsible cadres of the army to Shanghai. In response, Lin selected some cadres and directed them to refer all army documents on culture to Chiang Ch'ing from that time on. From February 2 to February 20, Chiang Ch'ing conducted an army forum on literature and art, together with Hsiao Hua, director of the army's General Political Department, Yang Ch'eng-wu, and Liu Chih-chien, deputy director of the GPD. While this discussion was going on, the Liberation Daily published a series of editorials from February 3 on exhorting the people to put politics in command and to study Mao's Thought. The new document that the army forum finally prepared was revised by Mao three times, yet this document was not a formal Party directive until it was approved by the Center. On March 22, Lin Piao sent the revised draft to the standing committee of the Military Affairs Committee for further discussion before submitting it to the Center.[51] The existence of this summary, in fact, was first revealed in May 1967: "February 1966 was an unusual month, a month of intense struggle between the proletariat and the bourgeoisie in China. And it was at this time that two diametrically opposed documents appeared in our Party."[52]

The contents of the Summary of the Forum lent credence to this claim. Starting with the premise that a class struggle continues on the cultural front, the summary sought to fight revisionist ideas. Specifically, the document singled out such ideas as: Hu Feng's "truthful writing," Shao Chüan-lin's "middle characters," T'ien Han and Hsia Yen's contention that "themes are decisive factors," and Chou Ku-ch'eng's "merger of various trends as the spirit of the era."[53] The summary pointed out that the Great Socialist Cultural Revolution

(GSCR) was to forge a proletarian ideology while liquidating bourgeois ideology. For the first time the document stated openly: "We must destroy the blind faith in what is known as the literature and art of the 1930s (in the Kuomintang areas of China)"; thus the summary attacked the "literature of national defense," which was allegedly opposed to "a mass literature for the national revolutionary war." (The latter was conceived by Lu Hsün and had had Mao's approval in the 1930s.) And calling upon writers to make the past serve the present and foreign work serve China, the summary directed the spearhead of its struggle at Wu Han and his company.[54]

The summary also rebuked the February Outline in its reference to the method of the revolution, for it stressed the mass line, stating: "We favor 'rule by the many' and oppose 'rule by the voice of one man alone.'" The summary then called for revolutionary militant mass criticism to break the monopoly of criticism by a few so-called critics, for only when writers plunged into life and made firsthand investigations could they select the proper material for their art. Destruction actually precedes construction, the document claimed, and stressed the role of the army in the Cultural Revolution.[55]

Legitimizing Policy: From the GSCR to the GPCR

It should be clear by now that Mao legitimized the Summary of the Forum by defining the problem and policy of the GSCR in ideological terms. Any policy had to be ideologically sanctioned in China. For this, Mao enjoyed a unique authority because only he, as the Party's Supreme Leader, could rule on ideological correctness. Yet, in order to legitimize the GSCR as he defined it in the summary, Mao had to transform it into a much larger movement, the GPCR. Before doing this, however, he had to eliminate the forces behind the February Outline, for the outline also was duly approved by the regular institutions of the Party. To achieve his goal, therefore, he sought to formalize the purge of a leading opponent in the army first—Lo Jui-ch'ing, for Mao had been relying on the PLA leadership to counter the Party Propaganda Department. Then, by fully using the resources of the PLA, he aimed at the core of the Party's opposition forces: P'eng Chen, Lu Ting-yi, and Yang Shang-k'un. To reestablish his authority in this way, Mao had to overcome not just the resistance of the Propaganda Department but the whole Party apparatus. For this purpose he eventually transformed the GSCR into the GPCR. This process became formalized at the Hangchow conference in May 1966, where Mao disposed of the four leaders and issued the May 16 Circular launching the GPRC.

The Case of Lo Jui-ch'ing

Lo, who had been sabotaging Mao's and Lin Piao's orders for quite a time, became the first victim. Lo was last seen with General Lon Nol on November 26, 1965, when Mao received the Cambodian military mission in Shanghai.[56] On December 8, the Party convened a meeting in Shanghai to criticize Lo. Chou En-lai tried in vain to persuade him to examine his errors. At an army political work conference held from December 30, 1965, through January 18, 1966, Hsiao Hua attacked those who advocated that an equal emphasis should be given to both politics and the military, a clear allusion to Lo's defiance of Lin Piao's military doctrine, which stressed the study of Mao's Thought.[57]

Mao handled the Lo Jui-ch'ing case cautiously, working through normal Party procedure. In December 1965 the Party Center appointed a seven-man team to investigate Lo's errors. The known members of this team are Yeh Chien-ying, who headed it, Hsieh Fu-chih, Hsiao Hua, Yang Ch'eng-wu, Liu Chih-chien, and An Tzu-wen. The composition of this group was noteworthy: Yeh, the former chief of staff of the Red Army, was a respected military statesman who was soon to replace Lo as secretary of the Party Secretariat; Hsieh had been Lo's replacement as minister of public security but Lo's influence still haunted Hsieh because two of Lo's close associates, Yang Ch'i-ch'ing and Lin Yün, remained as vice-ministers; Yang Ch'eng-wu, Hsiao Hua, and Liu Chih-chien were all Lo's deputies; and An Tzu-wen was director of the Party Organization Department. Mao's choice of these men, except for An, may have been to take advantage of their latent grievances against Lo.[58]

From March 4 to April 8, 1966, this team conducted a face-to-face struggle against Lo, the meetings proceeding in two phases. The first phase lasted for thirteen days with representatives from the MAC, the Ministry of Public Security, the Ministry of Defense, the National Defense Scientific Commission, the Military Science Academy, and the military regions; Lo himself took part in these sessions. On March 12, Lo offered a self-examination but the investigators found it unacceptable; this compelled Lo to attempt suicide on March 18 by jumping from a building. This incident ushered in the second phase, which began on March 22 and which was conducted without Lo's participation.[59]

Apparently, Mao purged Lo after he took control of the Ministry of Public Security and after Liu Shao-ch'i left China for a South Asian trip. For example, Lo's two cronies at the ministry, Yang Ch'i-ch'ing and Lin Yün, were last seen on March 26, 1966, when they received an Albanian athletic team.[60] In the meantime, Mao coopted Hsieh Fu-chih into his rank. It was reported that when Hsieh came under attack from Red Guards in 1967, Chiang Ch'ing defended him by saying: "Originally,

Hsieh was Teng Hsiao-p'ing's disciple but he was the first one who exposed Teng Hsiao-p'ing."[61] On the other hand, Liu left China on March 26 for Pakistan, Afghanistan, and Burma. (This trip was decided upon in March 1965, after Pakistan President Ayub Khan visited China.) According to the *People's Daily* of March 27, Liu and his wife, Foreign Minister Ch'en Yi and his wife, and Vice-Minister of Public Security Wang Tung-hsing (who had been Mao's bodyguard) had left Peking a few days before; they were seen off at the airport by Chu Teh, Chou En-lai, P'eng Chen, K'ang Sheng, Li Hsien-nien, T'an Chen-lin, and Hsieh Fu-chih. Liu's team returned to Kunming on April 19, but by this time Lo's case had already been disposed of.

Circumstantial evidence indicates that Lo was arrested sometime after March 26, 1966. According to one source, P'eng Chen had An Tzu-wen defend Lo in the investigation; but Lin Piao smashed this scheme.[62] On April 8, the second phase of the investigation ended, and on April 12, the four core members—Yeh Chien-ying, Hsiao Hua, Yang Ch'eng-wu, and Liu Chih-chien—made a report to the Central Committee, which in this case was a report to Mao since Liu was still abroad. The charges leveled against Lo were as follows: (1) he had been hostile to Mao and his Thought; (2) he had defied Mao and Lin Piao's directives; (3) he had violated Party discipline by reporting directly to the Party Secretariat without first consulting Lin Piao; (4) he had been an opportunist individualist; and (5) he had attempted to usurp the army leadership by asking Lin Piao to step down, citing Lin's poor health. On April 30, the Party transmitted this report and dismissed Lo from all of his posts.[63]

The Case of P'eng Chen, Lu Ting-yi, and Yang Shang-k'un

With the purge of Lo Jui-ch'ing, Mao made major inroads into the army leadership, but the Party propaganda leadership still remained in the hands of his opponents. In attacking this group Mao's supporters primarily relied upon Mao's personal prestige and the army leadership. Lin Piao later confessed this strategy: "Our Cultural Revolution depends on two conditions: Mao's Thought and prestige, and the PLA's capacity."[64] Now that the army leadership came under his control, Lin then proceeded to use Mao's authority. In a letter to a conference of industrial and communication workers in March 1966, Lin stated: "Our country is a great socialist country of the proletarian dictatorship, with a population of 700 million. She needs a unified thought, a revolutionary thought, and that is the thought of Mao Tse-tung."[65]

Mao himself actively responded to this trend. On March 17, 1966, he convened an enlarged Standing Committee meeting of the Politburo.

He pointed out that the Party policy of absorbing the intellectuals had had both positive and negative results; one of the latter had been the manner in which such bourgeois intellectuals as Wu Han and Chien Po-tsan had controlled all cultural departments, thereby forming an opposition Party. In order to educate these people he encouraged the younger generation of writers to break some laws. Deploring the Propaganda Department for holding up the manuscripts of such young writers as Kuan Feng and Ch'i Pen-yü, Mao threatened that the department might become "a rural work department," the rural work department having ceased to function after 1958 when its director, Teng Tzu-hui, opposed Mao's GLF, calling it a reckless advance.[66]

On March 28, then, Mao launched a direct attack upon the February Outline. Before the group made up of Chiang Ch'ing, K'ang Sheng, and Chang Ch'un-ch'iao (secretary of the Shanghai Party Committee), he declared that the outline made no distinction between right and wrong, but instead suppressed the masses while shielding the bad people. He was particularly angry about the Party treatment of the Yao article. Recalling that the 1962 Tenth Plenum had adopted a decision on class struggle, he complained: "How could so many reactionary articles like Wu Han's be approved by the Propaganda Department?" In spite of this, the department blamed the Shanghai committee for having the Yao article published without its approval, which caused Mao to ask: "Did not the Central Committee's decision count at all?" He, therefore, continued to criticize the Propaganda Department: "The Propaganda Department is actually the demon king's palace. We must overthrow and liberate these little devils. . . . I always call upon local committees to rebel against and attack the Central Committee whenever the Center does bad things. More and more 'sun-wu-k'ung' [the legendary monkey king] must come out from all places to make a rampaging raid on the heavenly palace."[67] Finally, Mao demanded that P'eng Chen's Five-Man Group, the Propaganda Department, and the Peking Party Committee be disbanded.

Once Mao scorned the Propaganda Department, his supporters soon launched an all-out attack. K'ang Sheng informed P'eng Chen of Mao's criticism and asked him to apologize to the Shanghai Party Committee, and Chiang Ch'ing organized a group of young radicals in Shanghai. Beginning in April 1966, Yao Wen-yüan, Ch'i Pen-yü, Lin Chieh, Kuan Feng, and Wang Li carried out direct attacks on Wu Han's play on Hai Jui, claiming that Wu Han had attempted a reversal of the verdict on P'eng Teh-huai.[68] By criticizing Wu Han in this way, these critics were actually challenging P'eng Chen's authority.

P'eng Chen and his associates in Peking also responded. On April 1,

P'eng ordered Liu Jen and Wan Li of the Peking Party Committee to prepare a criticism of Teng T'o and his "Three-Family Village" columns. Liu Jen held an emergency meeting of the Peking committee, which set up the three-man team of Liu Jen, Wan Li (secretary of the Peking Party Committee), and Cheng T'ien-hsiang, and the four-man staff office of Li Ch'i (director of the Propaganda Department), Fan Chin (editor of *Ch'ien-hsien*), Chang Wen-sung (P'eng Chen's brother-in-law and director of Peking's education department), and Sung Shih. From April 2 on, P'eng Chen himself was preparing a self-examination with Wu Leng-hsi and Hu Sheng. On April 3, the Peking council went ahead with the election of its new council members as scheduled.[69] But behind the scenes P'eng was making every effort to placate Mao. The more he did so, however, the more he aggravated the situation; for he tried to extricate himself in such a cliquish manner that Mao began to suspect him more and more. On April 5, P'eng gathered leaders of the Propaganda Department and the Peking committee at his house. At this occasion, it was reported, P'eng shed tears, saying that he had not erred in agricultural cooperation and in opposition to revisionism but lagged behind only in the academic debate. He pleaded with his associates for help: "As the old saying goes, we depend on parents' protection at home but depend on friends' kind help outside. I am now looking forward to your help."[70] That evening Cheng T'ien-hsiang convened a meeting of the Peking secretariat to discuss the Teng T'o question; only then did Liu Jen and Wan Li start criticizing Teng T'o. When the secretariat submitted its report to P'eng Chen, recommending Teng's removal, P'eng changed the plan by inserting a provision to the effect that: "We plan to deal with him organizationally after criticizing him within the Party."[71] On April 8, the Peking committee finally filed this report with the North China Bureau and the Party Center.

These episodes demonstrate how tightly P'eng Chen controlled Peking, warranting Mao's accusation of it as "an independent kingdom." Aware that their own fate lay with P'eng's, his associates also tried to protect one another. From April 6 through April 12, some twenty cadres of the Peking Party Committee carried out well-rehearsed criticisms of Teng T'o under Liu Jen's supervision. On April 10, P'eng Chen presided over a meeting of the Standing Committee; he still insisted that Teng T'o was different from Wu Han because Teng had supported the Three Red Banners. When P'eng blamed himself for having affected his associates like Wu Han, Cheng T'ien-hsiang consoled him, saying: "We also have influenced you and are responsible."[72] It was at this meeting that P'eng first revealed Mao's criticism of the Peking committee. Yet he contended that in criticizing Peking, Mao was actually criticizing all other departments as well, for the problems Mao raised for Peking equally applied to the entire country.[73]

Against this background, Teng Hsiao-p'ing (general secretary of the Party Secretariat) convened the Secretariat meeting, which ran from April 9 through 12 and which Chou En-lai also attended. Here, K'ang Sheng again conveyed Mao's view of Peking, But P'eng Chen persisted in the policy of Hundred Flowers Bloom saying that he had never opposed Mao. Ch'en Po-ta then brought out many old errors by P'eng Chen, dating back to the 1930s. In the end the meeting decided to suspend the February Outline and the Five-Man Group, and to establish a new committee for directing the Cultural Revolution.[74]

This shift of Party policy began to be felt in the cultural circle. On April 10, 1966, at last, the Ministry of Culture transmitted Chiang Ch'ing's Summary of the Forum to its lower units. On April 14, Vice-Minister of Culture Shih Hsi-min made a report on the Cultural Revolution to the Thirtieth Enlarged Standing Committee of the National People's Congress, emphasizing the study of Mao's Thought. Yet K'ang Sheng immediately opposed the report; as a result, it was not published. It was at this meeting that Kuo Mo-jo, a close friend of Mao and chairman of the All-China Federation of Literary and Art Circles and president of the Chinese Academy of Sciences, made an open self-criticism in which he confessed: "Speaking in terms of today's standards, what I have written before must all be burned because it has no relevance whatsoever."[75]

Sensing this dramatic development, P'eng Chen made increasingly desperate efforts at self-survival. Unlike Kuo Mo-jo, however, P'eng's approach was to find an accommodation rather than to accept a total self-negation. On April 15, the Peking Party Committee drafted a self-criticism of Teng T'o; P'eng added a final touch and decided to publish it the next day so that it would coincide with the opening of the Hangchow conference, which was to determine his own fate. While P'eng was at Hangchow, his associates in Peking had the *New China News Agency*, Radio Peking, and the Post Office disseminate the *Peking Daily*'s article, "Criticism of 'Notes from a Three Family Village' and 'Night Chat at Yenshan.'" This article admitted for the first time that the real authors of these writings, signed as Wu-nan-hsing, were Wu Han, Teng T'o, and Liao Mo-sha. The article also acknowledged that such writings were indeed "poisonous weeds," satirizing the present in the guise of the old as Yao Wen-yüan charged.[76] While attending the Hangchow conference P'eng Chen, on his part, was in constant contact with Liu Jen in Peking: P'eng informing Liu of the conference and Liu reporting to P'eng on the situation in Peking.[77]

But Mao had already made the decision to purge P'eng no matter what P'eng might do. On April 20, Mao personally sent seven documents indicting P'eng to the Peking Party Committee. Upon receiving these, Liu Jen consulted Li Fu-ch'un, the only Politburo member remaining in Peking; Li advised Liu that P'eng had committed serious errors. Then, from April 22 to April 26, the Peking committee held the consecutive plenary session in secret. At this session Liu Jen expressed his puzzlement about Mao's documents: "What does he [Mao] want anyway?" While some forty members of the Peking committee were agonizing, they received some additional documents on P'eng Chen from Mao. Trapped in a real quandary—repudiating their own boss or evading Mao's demands—they had no recourse but to stick together. Liu Jen, Hsiang Tzu-ming, and Li Ch'i even tried to seek access to K'ang Sheng, who was attacking P'eng Chen at the Hangchow conference. And when P'eng returned to Peking on April 27, they sought his views first. By then, however, the Peking committee had become literally paralyzed, even before the work team headed by Huang Chih-kang arrived from the North China Bureau on May 11.[78]

P'eng Chen's fall signaled not only the collapse of the Peking committee but the complete reshuffling of the Propaganda Department. While P'eng was under attack at Hangchow, on April 18, 1966, the *Liberation Daily* editorialized on "Holding High the Great Red Banner of Mao Tse-tung's Thought and Actively Participating in the GSCR." The editorial stated almost verbatim Chiang Ch'ing's Summary of the Forum. By holding out Mao's Thought as the supreme guide, the editorial opened up a full-fledged attack on the Propaganda Department. On May 4, the army paper published another editorial, "Never Forget the Class Struggle," asserting that the anti-Party elements, though still unnamed, were "waving 'red flag' to oppose the Red Flag and donning the cloak of Marxism-Leninism and Mao's Thought to oppose them." In a reply to Lin Piao's letter on May 7, Mao himself issued the May 7 Directive calling upon soldiers, students, workers, and peasants to study simultaneously politics, the military, culture, and production.[79] (This became later the rationale for the May 7 cadre schools in 1968.)

Thus, Mao again resorted to the PLA as a countervailing force to the Propaganda Department. By attacking "Notes from a Three-Family Village," his supporters then challenged the department that had protected the authors of such columns. On May 8, the *Liberation Daily* and *Kuang-ming jih-pao* disclosed the origin of "Evening Chat at Yenshan" and "Notes from a Three-Family Village" in 1960-62. Two days later, Yao Wen-yüan wrote another article in Shanghai's *Wen-hui pao* that rejected the self-criticism of the *Peking Daily;* Ch'i Pen-yü also hit squarely at the heart of the problem in another article. Yao pointed out, for example, that in the guise of academic discussions the 1960-62 writings created public opinion to attempt a revisionist peaceful evolution in China; Ch'i asked who directed the *Peking Daily* to use such subterfuges of sham criticism, that is, "sacrificing the knight in order to save the queen" (*i-sheng ch'e-ma pao-chen ch'ang-shih*).[80] These articles made it clear that the Party propaganda leadership was primarily responsible for the current situation.

With these facts exposed, Mao purged the "four shops" of Lo Jui-ch'ing, P'eng Chen, Lu Ting-yi, and Yang Shang-k'un. After the former two were disposed of, the latter two received the same fate. On April 28, 1966, the Ministry of Public Security arrested Lu Ting-yi's wife Yen Wei-ping for her criticism of Lin Piao; at the Hangchow conference Lu Ting-yi was dismissed from office. As for Yang, he was apparently involved in P'eng Chen's maneuver to deny K'ang Sheng any information concerning the Secretariat operation. (Yang was accused later of having eavesdropped on Mao for P'eng.)[81] The formalization of these purges required a conference at the highest level and Mao called the Hangchow conference for just this purpose.

The May 16 Circular: The Onset of the GPCR

The Hangchow conference marked the onset of the GPCR. This was an enlarged meeting of the Politburo, attended by first secretaries of the regional Party bureaus, convened to discuss the fate of the four culprits. Apparently, the first phase of the conference lasted from April 16 to April 28, possibly without Liu Shao-ch'i's participation; then, it adjourned briefly to welcome an Albanian mission headed by Mehmet Shehu on May Day. The second phase appeared to have started on May 4; the *People's Daily* of May 11, 1966, reported Mao's first public appearance in four months. He received Shehu, together with Teng Hsiao-p'ing, Chou En-lai, and Lin Piao. At the Hangchow conference, Mao made a major speech to indict the Propaganda Department; he subsequently issued the May 16 Circular for the GPCR. On May 18, Lin Piao also made a speech in support of Mao. Judging from these speeches, sharp debates took place at this time over the question of the Cultural Revolution.

Mao and Lin justified the Cultural Revolution by accusing P'eng Chen's group of having attempted a coup. Mao suggested that "some comrades" were afraid of the masses and had become "spookish things." In order to do away with such practices he urged criticism and self-criticism.[82] Consequently, Lin Piao made a keynote speech, jumping the gun on other Politburo members. Referring to a counterrevolutionary coup d'état, Lin said:

In recent years, especially last year, Chairman Mao reminded us of the problem of preventing revisionism, inside and outside the Party, on every front, in every area and at high and low levels. I understand he refers chiefly to the leading organs. Chairman Mao, in recent months, has paid particular attention to the prevention of a counter-revolutionary coup d'etat and adopted many measures. After the Lo Jui-ch'ing problem, he talked about it. Now the P'eng Chen problem has been exposed, and he again summoned several persons and talked about dispatching the armed forces and the public security systems in order to prevent a counter-revolutionary coup d'etat and the occupation of our crucial points. This is the "article" Chairman Mao has been writing in recent months.[83]

Lin went on to state that there had been sixty-one coups in the world since 1960, averaging eleven per year even if the most recent ones in Ghana, Indonesia, and Syria were excluded. In China, the Party had been so preoccupied with construction that it paid little attention to this problem. Asserting that there were two prerequisites for a successful coup—"gun barrels and inkwells"—he attacked the four culprits: "Lo Jui-ch'ing was the one who controlled military power. P'eng Chen controlled the General Secretariat. The commander in chief of the cultural and ideological war front was Lu Ting-yi. Confidential affairs, intelligence, and liaison were in the hands of Yang Shang-k'un."[84] Of these four Lin found P'eng the most dangerous because he had organized the Peking Party Committee as a Party within the Party, one that could not be penetrated. This proved that the danger of revisionism was imminent at the top level, Lin asserted, and he therefore urged the Party to use Mao's Thought as a weapon to fight such revisionism, for Mao was a proletarian genius, even exceeding Marx and Lenin. Lin concluded with this exhortation: "Whoever is against him [Mao] shall be punished by the entire Party and the whole country. Whoever makes a secret report after his death as Khrushchev did shall be punished by the entire Party and the whole country."[85]

After these debates, the Hangchow conference eventually decided to dismiss the four leaders and replace them with new appointees. At this time, Mao distinguished Liu Shao-ch'i and Teng Hsiao-p'ing from P'eng Chen, for, as he later said, Liu and Teng conducted activities openly, whereas P'eng acted in secret. (Wang Kuang-mei, Mrs. Liu, also defended Liu in 1967 on this ground, saying that Liu had never conspired against Mao behind the scenes.)[86] The reshuffling of the Peking committee and the Propaganda Department was then announced in early June. Li Hsüeh-feng, first secretary of the North China Party Bureau, replaced P'eng Chen as first secretary of the Peking committee whereas Wu Teh, first secretary of the Kirin Provincial committee, replaced Liu Jen as second secretary. On May 25, this team had already reorganized the staff of the *Peking Daily* and the *Peking Evening News*, and had suspended *Ch'ien-hsien*. In the Propaganda Department, T'ao

Chu, first secretary of the Central South Bureau, replaced Lu Ting-yi. T'ao then appointed Chang P'ing-hua, first secretary of the Hunan Provincial Committee, and Yun Wen-t'ao, secretary of the Central South Bureau, as deputy directors. At the same time, T'ang P'ing-t'ao, deputy editor of the *Liberation Daily*, replaced Wu Leng-hsi as editor of the *People's Daily;* Hsiung Fu, deputy director of the Propaganda Department, took charge of the *New China News Agency*. In the Secretariat, Yeh Chien-ying replaced Lo Jui-ch'ing as secretary and Wang Tung-hsing replaced Yang Shang-k'un as director of the Secretariat office.[87] As Lin Piao's speech suggested, these changes may have taken place after troops occupied some key posts in Peking.[88]

After gaining control over the propaganda machinery, Mao rebuked the February Outline and issued the May 16 Circular at the Hangchow conference. The conference disbanded the Five-Man Group and organized a new Cultural Revolution Group (CRG) that was to operate directly under the Politburo Standing Committee. Ch'en Po-ta, Mao's long-time secretary, became chairman of the new group; K'ang Sheng and T'ao Chu became its advisers; among its vice-chairmen were Chiang Ch'ing, Wang Jen-chung (first secretary of the Central South Bureau), Liu Chih-chien, and Chang Ch'un-ch'iao; and its members included Chang P'ing-hua, Yao Wen-yüan, Ch'i Pen-yü, Kuan Feng, Lin Chieh, and Wang Li. [89] Thus, Mao's supporters dominated the CRG.

A year after the Hangchow conference, it was known that the Party Center had issued on May 16, 1966, a document called Circular of the Central Committee of the Chinese Communist Party, commonly known as the May 16 Circular (*wu i-liu t'ung-chih*). [90] Several facts cast some doubt on whether the Hangchow conference officially adopted this document. For one thing, Lin Piao mentioned that Mao had been writing an important article on May 18, 1966; if he meant this to be the circular, it could not have been issued on May 16. For another thing, the format of the document called "circular" was neither an outline report (*hui-pao t'i-kang*) nor a resolution (*ch'üeh-ting*) but a circular (*t'ung-chih*) that central leaders used to convey their instructions. Moreover, in July 1966, when Mao made a speech on the current situation, K'ang Sheng pointed to the accomplishments of the Cultural Revolution thus far as the reorganization of the Peking Party Committee and the Propaganda Department, and the abolition of the Five-Man Group; yet he failed to mention the May 16 Circular.[91] Nor was it mentioned in the communique and the Sixteen-Point Decision of the Eleventh Plenum in August 1966, despite the listing of such other directives as the Former Ten Points and the Twenty-Three Points, which Mao had formulated for the SEM.

Mao himself shed more light on this point in 1967. He recalled:

Comrade Yao Wen-yüan's article was simply the signal for the GPCR. Therefore, we specially formulated the May 16 Circular. Since the enemy was extremely sensitive, he had to respond to this signal, too, and we also had to react to him. At that time, however, most of the people disagreed with me, sometimes leaving me alone, and saying that my views had become outdated. The only thing I could do was to put forward my views at the Eleventh Plenum for discussion.[92]

This talk confirms that most participants of the Hangchow conference did not heed Mao's view. Finally, the circular itself seemed to contradict some of its own claims: At the outset it stated that P'eng Chen alone had formulated the February Outline but later on, the document referred to "they" to designate the authors of the outline. Moreover, in its conclusion the circular asked the local Party units to compare the February Outline and the May 16 Circular itself to see which was right.[93] These points lead to the conclusion that the circular was a personal directive issued by Mao.

The goal and method of the Cultural Revolution described in the circular also showed the clear imprint of Mao Tse-tung. The document charged that the February Outline had actually opposed the Cultural Revolution while "feigning compliance" (yang-feng yin-wei, literally, obeying in the light but sabotaging in the dark) and had avoided the key question of Wu Han's play on Hai Jui. The passages in boldface setting forth the goal of the revolution seemed to be Mao's. In the GPCR, the Party had to:

thoroughly expose the reactionary bourgeois stand of those so-called academic authorities who oppose the party and socialism, thoroughly criticize and repudiate reactionary bourgeois ideas in the sphere of academic work, education, journalism, literature and art and publishing, and seize the leadership in these cultural spheres. To achieve this, it is at the same time necessary to criticize and repudiate those representatives of the bourgeoisie who have sneaked into the Party, the government, the army, and all spheres of culture, and to clean them out or transfer some of them to other positions. Above all, we must not entrust these people with the work of leading the cultural revolution.[94]

Claiming that there existed within the Party a number of counter-revolutionary revisionists who would seize political power once conditions were ripe, the circular made an unmistakable warning to the top Party officials, including Liu and Teng: *"Some of them we have already seen through, others we have not. Some are still trusted by us and are being trained as our successors, persons like Khrushchev, for example, who are still nestling beside us."*[95] Hence, the GPCR had to overthrow "those Party people in authority (tang-ch'uan-p'ai) taking the capitalist road who support the bourgeois scholar tyrants," that is, the Party establishment.

As for the method of the revolution, the May 16 Circular sought to destroy the taboos of the February Outline. The circular first pointed out that many areas in China simply did nothing to begin the revolution because, in the name of "the approval of the leading bodies concerned," the February Outline had suppressed the proletarian Left while giving free rein to all kinds of "ghosts and monsters" (niu-kui ssu-shen). The stratagem of "opening wide" was to shield Wu Han; the slogan that Everyone Is Equal before the Truth was to protect the bourgeois intellectuals. In this way the outline "waved 'red flags' to oppose the Red Flag" as did the old-line Social Democrats and the modern revisionists. The circular, therefore, reaffirmed Mao's tenet that there is no construction without destruction. In carrying out the GPCR, the document stressed that the struggle centered around whether the Party would implement or resist Mao's policy of the mass line.[96]

In short, the GPCR was to be an unprecedented mass movement. Yet, except for exhortations to adhere to the mass line, nowhere in the May 16 Circular did Mao specify concrete methods such as the use of big-character posters and work teams, which he would later claim he opposed. This ambiguity led to further conflicts in the implementation of the Revolution.

Implementing the GPCR: From Work Teams to Red Guards

Implementing the GPCR aroused conflicts similar to those that occurred in the making of the revolution. This was inevitable because policy making and implementation were fused in the Chinese policy process. In fact, the implementation of the GPCR was still left to the Party apparatus. The initial experiences in Peking then set the basic pattern of these conflicts. The first case was the confrontation between the University Party Committee and the big-character poster raised by a dissident student group at Peking University; after the Party committee collapsed before the rebels, such a confrontation took place between the work team sent by the Party Center and the rising Red Guard groups seeking to overthrow the work team at Tsinghua University. As this pattern spread into other localities, the Cultural Revolution involved an increasing clash between the established authorities and the increasingly militant rebels.

The GPCR in Peking

Peking University (Peita) and Tsinghua University became two pace setters for implementing the Cultural Revolution in Peking, and the struggles at these two universities represented a microcosm of the conflicts throughout the country between the Party Center and the newly organized Cultural Revolution Group. And as was the case with the Hangchow conference, only Mao's intervention and the convening of another central work conference could bring the conflict to a resolution.

Peita: The Party Committee vs. the Big-Character Poster. As often happened in the past, Peita became, once again, the first battlefield. This was triggered by the conflict between the University Party Committee and the posting of a big-character poster (*ta-tzu pao*) at the instigation of the dissident group led by Professor Nieh Yüan-tzu. Actually, this was an extension of a previous dispute that had taken place over the method of the Socialist Education Movement in 1965. At that time, the Party committee suppressed a central work team that made an alliance with Nieh's group and tried to isolate the Party committee from the new "three-way alliance" of cadres, work team, and students. Now this group again challenged President Lu P'ing, possibly with Mao's support, by raising the poster.

This event resulted from the gulf that existed between the newly organized Peking Party Committee and Mao's supporters in the CRG. After the "Three-Family Village" came under attack, Sung Shih (deputy director of Peking city's university department) convened an emergency meeting of university presidents to give instructions on the Cultural Revolution. According to Sung's instructions, the students were not allowed to hold big rallies or to post big wall posters; instead, they were to hold only small discussion meetings and to post small posters. They were to conduct theoretical debates under the direction of the Party committees but at no time could they leave their classes. On May 14, 1966, Lu P'ing and P'eng Pei-yün, first and second secretaries of the Peking University Party Committee, transmitted these instructions to the Party committee, telling its members that they should not divulge the contents to non-Party members.[97]

The dissident group at Peita immediately challenged these conditions. On May 25, the group consisting of Nieh, an assistant professor, five assistants, and one student at the department of philosophy, posted a big-character poster questioning what Sung Shih, Lu P'ing, and P'eng Pei-yün were doing.[98] (Of the seven dissidents Nieh had written Mao during the SEM in 1965.) Apparently, such Maoists as K'ang Sheng, Kuan Feng, and Ch'i Pen-yü were directing these dissidents behind the scene. For example, later in July 1966, when Mao questioned K'ang Sheng concerning the identity of K'uai Ta-fu, another dissident leader at Tsinghua, K'ang Sheng replied: "One among the revolutionary masses." Liu Shao-ch'i, however, disputed this, saying: "I consider him a demon. I think you are behind him."[99] In any case, there is no doubt that Nieh was aware of Mao's May 16 Circular, for she pointed out that the Peking University Party Committee did not comply with Mao's directive, asking "Why are you so afraid of wall posters?" She contended that the committee was suppressing the masses by imposing all sorts of taboos.[100]

When the university authority indeed suppressed the poster, Mao intervened. Before this, however, Lu P'ing labeled Nieh's group counter-revolutionary, for they rebelled against the duly organized Party committee representing the Central Committee. At first, the majority of the students sided with Lu P'ing and raised posters denouncing Nieh's group because they perceived that Nieh's poster indeed was tantamount to being counterrevolutionary—at least they had been so taught. With the support of the majority, Lu P'ing succeeded in isolating Nieh's group. Realizing this, Mao telephoned K'ang Sheng during the evening of June 1, 1966, asking him to broadcast the poster, calling it "the declaration of the Peking Paris Commune in the 1960s."[101] The next day the *People's Daily* published the poster with a commentary, "Hailing a Big-Character Poster of Peking University," which held that whoever opposed Mao must be punished. By this time the Party organ had been placed under Ch'en Po-ta and T'ang P'ing-tao; from June 1 through June 5 the *People's Daily* ran six editorials, hailing Mao's Thought as the supreme guide.[102] Under this circumstance, Chou Yang and Lin Mo-han, two deputy directors of the Propaganda Department, were openly attacked.

After Mao's approval of the poster became known, the Peking University Party Committee ceased to function. The collapse of the Party committee meant the surrender of established authority in the face of an open student rebellion. Once Mao deprived the committee of its legitimacy, the students no longer obeyed it. As this experience spilled into other schools, Lu P'ing's example was repeated; for example, Chiang Nan-hsiang of Tsinghua, Wang Ya-ming of Nanking University, and Li Ta of Wuhan University all received a similar fate.

Tsinghua: The Work Team vs. the Red Guards. Tsinghua produced another typical experience after its Party committee fell. In this case, the main issue revolved around the use of a work team and the challenge to it made by a Red Guard group. The case of Tsinghua was unusual in that the conflict involved Wang Kuang-mei on the side of the work team and Chiang Ch'ing on the side of the Red Guards. Before explaining the case of Tsinghua, however, an account of the background for sending down work teams is in order. The publication of Nieh's poster baffled every sector of the Chinese population, particularly the students, who reacted as if they had encountered "a spring thunder." Once they confirmed that it had Mao's blessing, the news took the lid off the students in their struggle against the school authorities. Student groups then vied in raising posters against their Party committees and the school authorities simply collapsed one after another. It was against this background that the Politburo Standing Committee dispatched work teams to the schools to prevent the outbreak of mob rule.

In the "fifty days" following June 1, 1966, Liu directed the Cultural Revolution in Peking while Mao remained at Hangchow. Only after July 18 did Mao use his veto power on the implementation of the revolution under Liu. Since the Party committees no longer functioned at the campuses, many central departments, the Peking Party Committee, and the Young Communist League actually asked Liu to authorize the dispatch of work teams to investigate the situation and to restore a revolutionary order. Liu simply gave approval to these requests, for there was neither time to think otherwise nor any real alternative, as Teng Hsiao-p'ing later argued: "Without the work team, who could substitute for Party leadership?" Even some student factions themselves seeking the overthrow of the Party committees wanted the work team.[103] In spite of this, Chiang Ch'ing claimed later, in December 1966, that Mao had instructed the Party not to send down work teams hastily but that some comrades had not heeded his instructions.[104] This ex post facto charge actually confirmed that Mao had not specifically banned the work teams altogether. It was not, then, so much the use of the work team per se as what it did that Chiang Ch'ing opposed, for Chiang Ch'ing herself once said that some teams had taken correct measures.[105]

The work team was neither a novel concept nor a devious practice but a time-tested ad hoc instrument to which the CCP had resorted whenever necessary. Starting with the first team at Peita, the Party Center sent out over four hundred teams comprised of over ten thousand members; of these fifty-seven went to universities and colleges, and others went to the secondary schools and government agencies. Of the ten thousand men, about six thousand were recruited from the industrial and communication systems under the control of Po I-po, chairman of the State Economic Commission and an alternate Politburo member.[106] On June 3, 1966, before those work teams were released, the Center laid down the eight-point policy guidelines (chung-yang pa-t'iao) designed to conduct the Cultural Revolution within the framework of Party control. The eight points were: (1) to post no big-character posters on the street; (2) to distinguish between being inside the Party and being outside; (3) to hold rallies inside the schools but not on the street; (4) to ban parades or demonstrations on the street; (5) to guard against the leakage of state secrets; (6) to ban beating and insulting; (7) to remain at one's post; and (8) to prevent any encirclement of private residences.[107]

The implementation of these measures led the Standing Committee to clash with the CRG, for they blocked the kind of mass movement Mao envisioned. Although the CRG had hold of the Party's propaganda organs, it had to comply with the Standing Committee for policy matters. For example, Ch'en Po-ta wrote the *People's Daily* editorial of July 1, 1966, "Long Live the Thought of Mao Tse-tung," but Liu and Teng deleted a passage: "Comrade Mao enjoyed the highest prestige among our people and the people of the entire world."[108] Only on July 9 was Ch'en Po-ta identified as chairman of the CRG.[109] In addition, both the Peking Party Committee under Li Hsüeh-feng and the Propaganda Department under T'ao Chu complied with the Standing Committee; moreover, the whole regional and local Party apparatus still remained under the control of the Party Center, and the work teams also acted as the agents of this Party apparatus from above. To fight such formidable organizations, Mao had no other recourse but to seek some form of extra-Party force, and he mobilized the Red Guards from below for this purpose.

The work team-Red Guard conflicts at Tsinghua, then, were the sequel to the Party committee-big character poster confrontation at Peita. On June 4, following the example of Peita, a group of the YCL leaders such as Ho P'eng-fei and Liu T'ao raised a poster denouncing Chiang Nan-hsiang, president of Tsinghua. The University Party Committee at Tsinghua also ceased to function. On June 9, the Party Center sent down a work team headed by Yeh Lin, vice-chairman of the State Economic Commission; upon arrival the team forced all the old cadres to stand aside (*kao-pien chan*) and assumed itself the responsibility of the old Party committee.[110] (In 1967 the Maoists claimed that such a policy led to "suspecting everyone and hitting at many to protect a handful.")[111] On June 11, the work team gathered all cadres and told them that no poster would be raised and no meeting would be held without its approval. This action was taken because some students in Peking had already forced some of their cadres to parade on the street with dunce caps on. In light of this situation, the majority of the students again welcomed the work team's new directive. The team then began to single out a few old cadres and made them offer self-criticisms.

A "royalist" student group was formed to direct this struggle; interestingly enough, the leaders of this group consisted of high Party officials' offspring. Ho P'eng-fei (Ho Lung's son) became its chairman; among other leaders were Liu T'ao (Liu Shao-ch'i's daughter), Liu T'ao-fen (Liu Ning-yi's daughter), Li Li-feng (Li Ching-ch'üan's son), Ch'iao Chung-wei (Ch'iao Kuan-hua's son) and Wang Hsiao-p'ing (Wang Jen-chung's daughter).[112] The main task of this group was to help the work team and restore law and order.

In opposition to this, another protest group sprang up to challenge the work team. In fact, many of these groups arose at schools besides Tsinghua. Of fifty universities and institutes in Peking, nine schools already had these protest groups opposing the work teams. And even at this juncture these groups formed revolutionary ties (*ke-ming ch'uan-lien*) with each other; as a result, "things were indeed thrown into some disorder."[113] Although their numbers constituted a minority, these groups' opposition to the work teams became intense and sometimes violent. At Tsinghua the leader of this protest group was K'uai Ta-fu, a student at the department of chemical engineering. K'uai's group soon aimed to seize power from the work team because the team did not allow them to raise posters and to drag out the old cadres as they wished. Given the group's attack upon the work team instead of the old Party committee, Liu Shao-ch'i began to suspect that such a move had the backing of some important people.[114] On June 19, to get firsthand information, Liu sent his wife Wang Kuang-mei to Tsinghua; she read some of the posters that day. On June 21, she formally assumed her job as a member of the work team recommended by the Party Center. On June 23, she ordered the suppression of K'uai Ta-fu's poster urging the overthrow of Yeh Lin. The next day, she ruled that K'uai was a counter-revolutionary having connections with the old Party committee, for whoever opposed the work team was against the Central Committee and whoever seized power from the work team was seizing power from the Party.[115]

Once again, a central decision, coupled with Mao's approval, could resolve this struggle for legitimacy between the royalist group and the protest group at Tsinghua. Here again, the majority of the students first sided with Wang Kuang-mei and the royalist group. But K'uai's protest group did not relent in its struggle against the work teams, drawing its support from Mao's Thought. On June 27, when K'uai spoke at a struggle meeting, Wang Kuang-mei had Ho P'eng-fei rebut him. The work team then divided K'uai's group into four small units and kept them from communicating with each other. K'uai began a hunger strike and constantly wrote letters to Yeh Lin proclaiming that he was following the spirit of Mao's Thought. When a second struggle meeting was held on July 8, K'uai was not allowed to speak. In this way, the work team managed to keep the rebellious students under control; but this also provoked Mao's supporters to counterattack. K'ang Sheng protested to Liu Shao-ch'i that preventing K'uai from appealing to the Party Center was a denial of his constitutional rights. As a result, on July 15, the work team permitted K'uai to visit the Cultural Revolution Center of the Central Committee; at this time, a member of the work team and two students escorted K'uai at his request. After Mao returned to Peking on July 18, he immediately approved of the Red Guard struggle against the work teams. On July 22, while a central work conference was in session, Ch'en Po-ta, K'ang Sheng, Wang Li, and Kuan Feng came to Tsinghua and encouraged K'uai to keep up with his struggle; finally, on July 28, the work team was withdrawn from Tsinghua.

The formation of student groups at Peita and Tsinghua was the precursor to the formation of Red Guard groups. The name *Red Guard (Hung-wei ping)* was first used by Mao on August 1, 1966, in a letter acknowledging the two posters that the Red Guards of the middle school attached to Tsinghua had sent to him.[116] These students were already using the term in their poster, Long Live the Spirit of the Revolutionary Rebellion of the Proletariat, published on June 24, which stated among other things: "Revolution is just a rebellion and the soul of Mao's Thought is rebellion."[117] It was on August 18, 1966, that Mao championed this Red Guard spirit when he received their armband from Sung Pin-pin (Sung Jen-ch'iung's daughter), a student of the middle school attached to Peking Normal College.[118] But the case of Tsinghua had already set a basic pattern of the work team-Red Guard conflict. Initially, children of high Party officials, as pointed out above, organized their own Red Guard groups mainly on the basis of "blood stock," excluding those from poor revolutionary backgrounds. After the Eleventh Plenum, for example, Tsinghua's Ho P'eng-fei and Liu T'ao led the Supervisory Corps (Chiu-ch'a-tui), which later became the backbone of the Federated Alliance (Lien-tung) group. In opposition to this, K'uai Ta-fu led the Chingkang-shan Corps, which became the mainstay of Chiang Ch'ing's storm troops fighting the Party apparatus, together with Nieh Yüan-tzu's New Peking University (Hsin Peita) group.

The GPCR in Canton: Authority vs. Rebellion

The conflict between the Party committees and work teams on the one hand and the Red Guard groups on the other gradually became a struggle between authority and rebellion. The pattern of this struggle in Peking fanned out into other localities, as the Party Center disseminated its experiences in Peking throughout the country. For example, on June 18, 1966, when Lu P'ing was assaulted by a Red Guard group, Chang Ch'eng-hsien, head of the work team at Peita, denounced such an act as being counterrevolutionary. He subsequently made a report to the Center about his experiences at Peita, which was praised by Liu Shao-ch'i, Teng Hsiao-p'ing, Li Hsüeh-feng, and T'ao Chu, and promoted as a model for the entire country. Li first introduced the report to the North China Bureau; after this, it was transmitted into other regions.[119] The way in which other localities responded to the Peking situation provides a glimpse of Center-localities interactions in the Chinese political process.

The case of Canton is just such an example. In June 1966, T'ao Chu instructed the Central South Bureau to send work teams down to the schools and also asked Hsüeh Kuang-ch'ün, secretary-general of the bureau, to submit a report on the situation in the Canton area. On June 23, Hsüeh, together with Chin Ming and Hsüeh Huang-chün (both secretaries of the Secretariat), went to Wuhan to consult with Wang Jen-chung, who had assumed the position of first secretary of the Central South Bureau after T'ao Chu left. This team decided to single out 3 percent of the university students and 1 percent of the high-school students for Cultural Revolution struggles. As for the province of Kwangtung, T'ao Chu separately directed Chao Tzu-yang, first secretary of the Kwangtung Provincial Party Committee, to differentiate the true Left from the false Left by strengthening Party leadership, and to release about one-half of the four-cleanup work teams. A month later, on July 21, the Central South Bureau summed up its experiences in a document submitted to the Center.[120]

By this time, the Cultural Revolution had caused a suspension of all school activity in China. On June 6, 1966, two Peking high-school students wrote letters to Mao, asking for the abolition of the current school system. On June 13, the State Council decreed that all schools would be closed for half a year as part of a process of reforming the educational system and carrying out the Cultural Revolution. And on June 24, a group of students at the middle school attached to Tsinghua raised the poster declaring Rebellion Is Justified and sent it to Mao. As news of this spread, rebellion indeed became contagious throughout the country.[121]

Again, in Canton, school Party committees had ceased to function by June, a condition of stasis that was followed by the work team-Red Guard conflicts. This happened after certain links were forged between Peking students and Canton students. On June 24, for example, a student of South China Engineering Institute wrote an open "letter from Peking," which declared that students could suspect any official except Chairman Mao and the Central Committee.[122] Surprised by this act, Chao Tzu-yang immediately called a conference to denounce the letter as counterrevolutionary; he ordered Chang Yün, deputy secretary of the provincial committee, to strengthen up the work team at the institute.

Interviews with former students in Canton reveal a telling story about the confrontation of authority and rebellion in the schools.[123] For example, those teachers who were openly denounced by a few students as counterrevolutionaries strangely remained silent, much to the astonishment and disbelief of other students. In July 1966, however, the news that students in Peking were overthrowing work teams reached Canton through various channels, including "the little broadcast" (*hsiao kuang-pa*), an informal person-to-person mode of communication. The students in Canton also raised several unsigned posters asking for the withdrawal of work teams. At first the work teams labeled such posters anti-Party and had public security men patrol the schools. But as the students' perception of Party authority changed, they became more and more emboldened to rebel against the authorities.

Under the direction of the Kwangtung Party Committee, however, the work teams managed to contain student rebellion by pitting the royalist groups against the protest groups. Thus, as long as these teams could act in the name of the Party Center, they could enforce law and order at the local levels. And since both the work teams and the Red Guards claimed legitimacy, only the highest policy-making body could resolve the conflict. At the top level, the Standing Committee backed the work teams but the CRG supported the Red Guards. Hence, the authority versus rebellion confrontation between the work teams and the Red Guards was a function of the Party Center versus the CRG conflicts.

Evaluating Policy: The Sixteen-Point Decision of the Eleventh Plenum

As these conflicts continued throughout July and August 1966, Mao evaluated Cultural Revolution policies by supporting the activities of Red Guards. In July, he called a central work conference where he endorsed the Red Guard attack on the work teams despite strong opposition from central leaders; finally, in August he called the Eleventh Plenum, which approved Mao's version of the Cultural Revolution by adopting the Sixteen-Point Decision.

The July Central Work Conference: Withdrawal of Work Teams

By rallying the support of the army leadership from above and by mobilizing the Red Guards from below, Mao went out of his way to reassert his personal authority over the Party. On July 25, the *People's Daily* suddenly broke the news that Mao had swum in the Yangtze River on July 16—swimming over thirty miles in but an hour and five minutes at the age of 72! And by the time Mao returned to Peking— probably July 18—the city had come under the control of Lin Piao's troops, a fact ascertained by a Yugoslavian news story.[124] Sometime after July 19 then, Mao convened the central work conference, attended by regional and provincial secretaries, to discuss the question of work teams.

The purpose of the July work conference was to re-evaluate policy guidelines for the Cultural Revolution, for apparently the majority of the central and regional leaders were opposed to the Red Guard attacks on Party authority. Addressing these regional and CRG leaders on July 21, Mao asked, however, that they go down to the universities to learn from the students. He maintained that the revolution must be carried out by revolutionary students and teachers, not by the work teams, because the teams tended to obstruct the revolution by virtue of their simply sitting back and watching the students fight one another. As to many leaders' concern about the attendant chaos, Mao emphasized that strife itself was part of revolution; therefore, he called upon the leaders to become pupils first, by learning from the Red Guards and not just by sending down orders.[125] To eliminate the emergence of a bureaucratic work style, Mao called for a simplification of government organizations, justifying struggle first and then transformation, the "struggle" meaning destruction and the "transformation" meaning construction. Charging that Li Hsüeh-feng and Wu Teh were afraid of revolution, busy attending to only routine work, he issued a stern warning to such leaders: "If good people arrive and you do not come out to meet them, then I will meet them myself."[126] Thus, according to one source, Mao had already drafted the Sixteen-Point Decision at this meeting.[127]

The Cultural Revolution Group led the way in responding to Mao's call. From July 22 on, Ch'en Po-ta, K'ang Sheng, Chiang Ch'ing, and Ch'i Pen-yü all went to Peita to "learn from the masses as pupils of the masses." Subsequently, the Standing Committee members also followed this example: Liu went to the Peking Institute of Architectural Engineering, together with Ch'i Pen-yü, whom he invited as a representative of the CRG; Teng went to the People's University. Liu and Teng then admitted error in sending out work teams, although they contended that the Party Center had nonetheless made a collective decision. Teng, for example, stressed the notion that due to the lack of understanding the Party Center had not practiced the mass line. Stating that the old revolutionaries faced a new problem, Teng asked the CRG to take over.[128]

The central work conference eventually decided to suspend the work teams, and on July 28, 1966, the Party Center formally decreed that the teams be recalled. That night Liu Shao-ch'i suggested somewhat bitterly to Liu T'ao that at least the work teams had carried out their tasks in public, which could not be said for P'eng Chen. Liu also told his younger daughter Liu P'ing-p'ing (a student of the middle school attached to Normal College) that Ho Feng-fang (a leader of the Red Guards opposing the work team at the school) might seize power, given the support of a few central leaders for such a plan. But Liu also told his daughter that once the Cultural Revolution bogged down, the masses would certainly be able to discern true Left. With these words, Liu perhaps expressed his hope that the GPCR would fail as did the GLF, and that then an adjustment period would follow. In any case, he was quite unhappy with the decision to call back the work teams. Portraying her father's mood at this time, Liu T'ao wrote: "I had never seen my father so upset."[129] In his self-criticism of October 1966, Liu did hold himself responsible for the fifty days after June 1, 1966; yet he was not sure why he had made such errors. Only when Mao posted his first big-character poster on August 5, denouncing the fifty days as a period of "bourgeois dictatorship" which had imposed "a white terror," did Liu realize that he had made serious mistakes.[130] By attacking Liu's leadership in this manner, Mao made it clear at the Eleventh Plenum that his goal was to overthrow the Party leadership all together.

The Eleventh Plenum: The Sixteen-Point Decision

The Eleventh Plenum in August 1966 was called to transform the minutes of the July work conference into the Party line. It was the first plenum held since 1962; hence, it gave approval not only to Mao's concept of the GPCR but to all other policies Mao had sought since 1962. In achieving this feat, Mao again fully utilized the instruments of the PLA. On August 1, the thirty-ninth anniversary of the Red Army formation, the *People's Daily* editorialized that "The Whole Country Should Become a Great School of Mao's Thought," revealing Mao's unpublished May 7 directive that held out the army as the model for the nation to emulate.

In fighting the Party leadership, Mao again resorted to non-Party forces. Of 179 living Central Committee members, for example, about 80 seem to have participated in the plenum, judging from the roster of those who appeared at T'ien An Men on August 18, 1966. Besides, some "representatives of revolutionary teachers and students from institutions of higher learning in Peking," that is, the Red Guards, took part, together with representatives of regional leaders and the PLA commands. This extraordinary practice led most central leaders to say that the situation was beyond control.[131] However, not only did Mao justify such an irregular method, which clearly violated the Party constitution, but he also threw himself into the confusion by siding with the rebellion.

To break the stalemate between his supporters and his opponents at the plenum, Mao wrote a letter on August 1 to the first Red Guard group, approving their slogan: Rebellion Is Justified; on August 5, he wrote his own poster: Bombard the Headquarters, championing Nieh's poster of May 25 as China's first Marxist-Leninist poster and accusing "some comrades" of having acted in "a diametrically opposite way." In this poster, he blamed not merely the fifty days but brought back the whole deviation of the Party since 1962, saying that some comrades had committed Right deviation in 1962 and then had become Left in form but Right in essence in 1964. Mao later wrote another poster to refute the view that "we must see the development of the last stage of the movement." Insisting that China would become more proletarian at the last stage, he claimed that the first stage was thus more crucial.[132]

The tone of Mao's protest demonstrates how strongly the Party leaders resisted his idea of the Cultural Revolution. In 1967, Mao reminisced about this:

The only thing I could do was to call the Eleventh Plenum to put forth my views for discussion. It was only through the discussion that I could obtain agreement from *a little over half of them*. At that time, many people still did not understand me; neither Li Ching-ch'üan nor Liu Lan-tao understood. Comrade Ch'en Po-ta talked with them but they said: "Since we do not understand in Peking, we still will not understand after going back either!"[133]

Clearly, Mao's forces were a minority at this plenum, but as with the 1959 Lushan plenum, the fear of a Party split or even a civil war probably prompted those one-half of the Central Committee members to go along with Mao.

On August 8, as a result, the Eleventh Plenum finally adopted the Sixteen-Point Decision, unequivocally endorsing Mao's concept of the Cultural Revolution. Reminding the Party of Mao's Tenth Plenum dictum—that to overthrow a political power it is always necessary to create public opinion— the decision set forth the goal of the GPCR as follows:

Although the bourgeoisie has been overthrown, it is still trying to use the old ideas, culture, customs and habits of the exploiting classes to corrupt the masses, capture their minds, and endeavor to stage a come-back. The proletariat must do the exact opposite: it must meet head-on every challenge of the bourgeoisie in the ideological field and use the new ideas, culture, customs and habits of the proletariat to change the mental outlook of the whole of society. At present, our objective is to struggle against and overthrow those persons in authority who are taking the capitalist road, to criticize and repudiate the reactionary bourgeois academic "authorities" and the ideology of the bourgeoisie and all other exploiting classes, and to transform education, literature and art and all other parts of the superstructure not in correspondence

with the socialist economic base, so as to facilitate the consolidation and development of the socialist system.[134]

This was testimony to the widening gap between the Party's ideological commitment and its actual practice; therefore, the GPCR was to
make the superstructure congruent with the economic base. After the
bourgeoisie had been physically overthrown, a second revolution
within the revolution was necessary to prevent the comeback of the
bourgeoisie in the superstructure. Since this revolution was intended
not only to repudiate the academic authorities but also to overthrow
the Party establishment, its goals were twofold: it was to be an idelog-
ical as well as a power struggle.

As for the method of the revolution, too, the Sixteen-Point Decision
reaffirmed Mao's mass line principle. The decision stated: "The outcome of this great cultural revolution will be determined by whether or
not the Party leadership dares boldly to arouse the masses."[135] The
decision also envisioned a truly mass polity, as the masses would join
cultural revolution groups, committees, and congresses at all units; their
leaders were to be elected by a system of general elections like that of
the Paris Commune of 1871 so that the leaders and the masses could
engage in direct and constant dialogues of criticism—struggle—self-
criticism.

Subsequently, Mao took deliberate action himself to implement
these measures because he was not all sure that the Party would do so.
First of all, he chose Lin Piao as his official successor, replacing Liu
who had been his number two man since 1942. Lin, now designated as
Mao's sole "comrade-in-arms," accepted the new assignment with an
expression of total loyalty, pledging in his acceptance speech at the
plenum: "I shall do everything according to Chairman Mao's order."[136]
The Politburo was also reshuffled so that Mao and Lin could assume the
first line leadership, making Liu and Teng abdicate their responsibility.
When the new lineup of the enlarged Standing Committee became
known, composed of Mao Tse-tung, Lin Piao, Chou En-lai, T'ao Chu,
Ch'en Po-ta, Teng Hsiao-p'ing, K'ang Sheng, Liu Shao-ch'i, Chu Teh,
Li Fu-ch'un and Ch'en Yün, Liu, for example, had fallen from second
to eighth place in the hierarchy.

The Sixteen Points did provide some cautious caveats about the
excesses that might result from the Cultural Revolution. One example
was the emphasis placed upon the use of reason and persuasion as
opposed to coercion and force. Another was the provision that the
masses should struggle against only a handful of anti-Party cadres while
uniting with the majority of "good and comparatively good cadres."

There was also the warning that scientific and productive activities should not be disrupted, for the Cultural Revolution was to take hold of both revolution and production at the same time.

On August 12, the Eleventh Plenum adopted its official communique, a document even more emphatic in upholding Mao's ideological and policy lines. Calling Mao's Thought "the Marxism-Leninism of the era," the communique also revived Mao's cherished policy of simultaneously developing industry and agriculture, marking Mao's triumph in the continuing policy conflicts of 1963-66. In fact, the communique stated that the Eleventh Plenum fully approved all of Mao's directives that had been issued in the previous four years. Among these were the Former Ten Points of 1963 and the Twenty-Three Points of 1965 for the SEM, and nine other policy directives Mao had proposed since 1962.[137] Thus, with the Sixteen Points and the communique adopted, the Eleventh Plenum legitimized not only Mao's GPCR but also all the ideological and policy themes Mao had pursued since the Tenth Plenum.

THE POLITICS OF POLICY-MAKING

The process of making and implementing the GPCR revealed the many inner tensions and conflicts that had accumulated within the Chinese political elite. Upon analysis, two points emerge: in the long run the GPCR marked the culmination of diverse political trends set in motion since the GLF; in the short run it provided vivid glimpses into the policy processes involving interactions between one supreme leader's quest for mass mobilization and the Party's impetus toward bureaucratization.

The Historical Context

The events unfolded from November 1965 to August 1966 revealed the historical context within which the major political cleavages had appeared within the CCP elite prior to the Cultural Revolution. The failure of the GLF and the subsequent retreat from it in the years of 1959-62 had sounded the first notes of the discord of 1963-66 which, in turn, culminated in the Cultural Revolution. What Mao set out to accomplish in this revolution was a redirection of the over-all policy, institutional, and ideological trends set in motion in 1959-65. In attacking the Party's Propaganda Department, for example, Mao's supporters brought out those old articles written in 1960-62 that had ridiculed the GLF in the guise of academic themes. In exposing the political culpability of these writings, Mao's supporters also relied upon the PLA's resources. This, however, was an extension of the 1962-65 trend, for Mao had already held up the army over the Party as the model for the whole country. Thus, the Eleventh Plenum represented the culmination of two trends that had surfaced following the Tenth Plenum: Mao's quest for revolutionary regeneration and the Party's institutional responses.

Two Patterns of Policy Process:
Institutionalization vs. Mass Mobilization

The initial phase of the GPCR dramatized the clashes of two patterns of policy processes: institutionalization and mass mobilization. The conflict between Mao and the Party apparatus can be understood in this perspective. Having been alienated from the operational instruments of the policy process, Mao sought to formulate and implement policies above and outside the Party's regular organizations by appealing to his correct ideology and the mass line. But the Party tried to make and implement such policies through its institutional machinery. These clashes contained all elements of the normal political process.[138] There were differences over identifying the problem of the revolution, though expressed in ideological terms, centering on whether or not the revolution was a political struggle or a purely academic debate. Such differences also involved the alternative policies for carrying out the revolution: was it to be carried out as a mass movement, or as a Party-directed rectification? Mao sought a political struggle to be carried out through a mass movement but the Party Center treated the revolution as a cultural rectification to be conducted within the confines of Party control. It follows that conflicts were inevitable between these two sides; hence, politics had to determine the final outcome.

These conflicts intensified in all phases of the policy process—identifying the problem, formulating the policy, legitimizing it, implementing it, and evaluating its consequence. When they reached a peak, policy making became the naked struggle for power. And Mao made such power struggle an ideological crusade. Despite the enormous resilience of the institutionalized Party authority, Mao was able to justify rebellion against this authority, using his position as the final arbiter of conflicts in defining the correct ideology and thereby bestowing legitimacy to policy. Thus, the Eleventh Plenum sanctioned Mao's method for furthering the Cultural Revolution, for the central leaders, though a majority, conceded to Mao for fear that without him the Party itself would fall apart. Coming back to the first line of the top leadership, Mao waged a deliberate assault on the Party establishment. Under the slogan Rebellion Is Justified, he fully mobilized an extra-Party force, the Red Guards. Not only did he heap praise upon these youngsters but he actually made conscious efforts to forge a direct link with them. From the first rally of the Red Guards on August 18, where he championed their rebellious cause, to the eighth rally in December 1966, he reviewed over thirteen million of them. The Red Guards also actively responded to Mao's call by plunging into "the great exchange of revolutionary experiences." A form of radical mass polity indeed held sway at the height of this Red Guard movement. Yet the Sixteen Points excluded the army from the Red Guard attack. This enabled the army to emerge as the only viable organization in the struggle between the rebels and the establishment.

Huntington suggests that political stability in changing societies depends upon the ratio of mass participation to institutionalization.[139] The Great Proletarian Cultural Revolution indicates that the intensity and violence of these variables are more important than the ratio. As the intensity and violence of Mao's mobilization overtook the Party's institutional responses, such a mobilization generated a momentum of its own that, in turn, disrupted the Party-state institutions and processes and eventually brought about their disintegration. Party authority was predicated upon Mao's acceptance of its legitimacy. Once Mao withdrew such legitimacy, the Party committees were subject to rebellion. The mobilization and rebellion, thus sanctioned by Mao, were destined to leave a profound legacy in Chinese political life: the disintegration of institutionalized authority.

10
Conclusion:
The Dynamics
of Chinese Policy Processes

The Chinese policy process has shifted from time to time since 1949. Why and how did these shifts occur? Why did Mao initiate the Cultural Revolution by violating established patterns of policy formulation in 1965-66? What changes have the Cultural Revolution and its aftermath brought about in Chinese politics? What does the death of Mao portend for China's search for political order? To explore these questions requires that the events since 1949 be viewed from an analytical perspective.

The policy process in China displays certain forces that result from the efforts of the Chinese Communist Party and Mao Tse-tung in particular to solve difficult problems without sacrificing their revolutionary commitment. The making of policy in China reveals a complex process of conflicts and consensus building, however, that is basically similar to all political processes. Specifically, three themes can be elaborated about this broad observation. First, the policy process in 1958-66 tended to be institutionalized, with values and routines that effectively blunted both Mao's authority and his call for mass movements. Hence, Mao's decision to launch the Cultural Revolution in the way he did in 1965-66 was in response to the substantive and procedural conflicts generated by his attempts to redirect the post-Great Leap Forward policy process; it was neither an irrational nor a fanatical decision, but one necessary to his goal, and it can be explained within the historical context of a transformation-consolidation cycle. Second, the

229

Cultural Revolution and its aftermath in particular seem to have broken the previously established pattern of the transformation-consolidation cycle, and Mao's death in 1976 is likely to further support this trend. As a result, the post-1969 policy process has presented a blend of both transformation and consolidation, of mobilization and institutionalization, although the Cultural Revolution itself roughly corresponded to a transformation phase and its aftermath to a phase of consolidation. Finally, in the wake of the Cultural Revolution and particularly since Mao's death, the Chinese policy process has been uncertain in tenor, but the over-all direction seems to be swinging again toward an institutionalizing one under a reorganized Party.

POLICY PROCESSES FROM 1949 to 1966

What distinguishes the Communist political system from other systems is its ideological commitment to Marxism-Leninism as a guide for action. This point deserves emphasis, despite the view that in comparative perspective Communist politics and non-Communist politics have many aspects in common.[1] When the ideological commitment of a Communist system remains intense as defined by the Supreme Leader of the Party, as it did in the Chinese system, such commitment serves as one of the most important constraints on the policy process.

Ideology and the Transformation-Consolidation Cycle

According to Barnett, "Ideology defines certain general values and goals, ways of analyzing situations, and methods of approaching problems. It sets parameters to the range of acceptable policy choices."[2] This is so especially when revolutionary dynamism is high and the political system continues to legitimize its rule by its ideological commitment.

Policy, power, and ideology, then, are inseparable in Communist politics. As circumstances change, however, the Party has to adapt its policies, and Party leaders understandably advocate different policies even though they agree on the Party's ultimate goals. So long as these leaders share a reasonable consensus on policy matters they can surmount their differences, but when they fail to reach such a consensus, they are bound to conflict over three broad issues: the policies for solving the immediate problems of the Party, the processes of formulating and implementing the policies, and the means of rationalizing the policies and the processes. Hence, conflicts and cooperation are inevitable in choosing a correct policy, process, and ideology.

More specifically, the first issue at conflict centers on whether the Party should give the highest priority to perpetuating the revolution or to promoting economic development. The second issue centers on two modes of formulating and implementing policy: one emphasizes mass mobilization and the other institutionalization. Finally, since the Party leaders must justify their differences in ideological terms, the issue centers on whether the Party should stress its official ideology or its practical problems. Thus, the changing context of the Communist political system generates three distinct issues that heighten the tension in the policy process: revolution or development, mobilization or institutionalization, and ideology or practice.

First, the tensions between revolution and development arise from the Party's dual commitment to building socialism and to carrying out economic development, two goals that are not necessarily simultaneously achievable. Revolution calls for a solution of distribution problems, thus emphasizing equality. Development calls for a solution of production problems, emphasizing efficiency. Each requires a different strategy to be successful; the former seeks a comprehensive policy of simultaneous development to enhance equality, thereby servicing all sectors of the society, but the latter seeks an incremental policy of sequential development to enhance efficiency, thereby solving the imminent problems of the society.

Second, the possibility of conflict has been heightened by the choice of policy process modes—mobilization or institutionalization. The different perspectives of Mao and the Communist Party further increased such a possibility. He often sought a direct link with the masses to expand the arena of policy making by involving the masses; his preferred method of implementation was the recruiting through mass movements of activists who responded to his policy. The Party, on the other hand, defended its institutional unity and processes to preserve the existing area of policy making by stressing its authority; its preferred method of implementation was an orderly administration in which the professional bureaucrats played a vital role. Two conflicting Leninist principles exacerbate these tensions, for the principle that the highest Party authority defines the correct ideology is not totally compatible with the principle that the Party, as the vanguard of the proletariat, must maintain its unity at all costs. On one hand, Mao, the Supreme Leader, could ignore the majority view of the Party when he saw that ideological correctness was at issue. The Party, for its part, could not tolerate any splitting activity that might jeopardize its unity.[3] These conflicting principles rule out any institutional framework for settling differences. Therefore, when the Party leaders cannot reach consensus, their differences must be resolved through political struggles and crises. The intensity and violence of conflict increase as the stakes increase. Ultimately, a new winning coalition must emerge out of such power struggles.

Last, the conflict between ideology and practice arises from the gap between the Party's official doctrine and its changing reality. These gaps occur in other societies as well when values and structures, perceived expectations and actual capabilities, are not compatible.[4] But here again, the Leninist legacy that the highest Party authority defines the correct ideology heightens tensions. A Supreme Leader may brand as incorrect any action he personally disapproves. This creates inherent tendencies for polarization in Communist political discourse, for whenever he finds it necessary, the leader can reduce all alternative courses of action on important issues to two roads: socialism or capitalism. Mao indeed treated ten such issues in terms of what he called the "struggle between the two roads."

From this description we can derive two models of policy, power, and ideology, as shown in table 1. Huntington suggests that the evolution of a revolutionary one-party system into an established one-party system goes through three phases: transformation, consolidation, and adaptation.[5] In China the first two phases have alternately occurred thus far, and the last phase is yet to come. As a result, China has alternated between the transformation phase and the consolidation phase, and the contention between these two approaches eventually culminated in the Cultural Revolution.

TABLE 1

TWO MODELS OF POLICY, POWER AND IDEOLOGY

	Transformation	Consolidation
Policy	Revolution	Development
	Distribution	Production
	Comprehensive (simultaneous)	Incremental (sequential)
Power	Mobilization (the leader)	Institutionalization (the Party)
	Participation	Regulation
	Movement (activists)	Administration (professional)
Ideology	Ideology	Practice
	Change	Status quo
	Struggle	Compromise

Three points must be made about table 1. First, the comparison made here is a configurative phenomenon. It should be clearly understood that it is a comparison of degree rather than kind, that is, *more or less*, not *either or*. In fact, most distinctions in the social sciences involve this type of continuum—of an ordinal rather than nominal nature. Because the comparative variables above represent simplification, the actual difference in substance and subtleties should be empirically ascertained. Second, the Chinese leaders' perception of a given situation is no less important than the situation itself. Problems are not problems unless they are seen as such. It is just as important to understand how the Chinese themselves see the situation, as to ascertain empirically how it actually comes about. Third, the swing back and forth between the two phases does not represent a cycle in its precise meaning but rather a shift in emphasis, for each swing results from a different situation with problems that differ considerably from those of previous situations.

With these caveats, it is still possible to say that revolution, mobilization, and ideology are stressed most in the transformation phase. When the Supreme Leader stresses these with increasing intensity, the ideology he defines becomes almost a religion. Such an ideology is not merely the justification of the political system, but a substitute for consensus. In short, it becomes a self-fulfilling prophecy. But this prophecy must be subjected to reality testing when it must come to grip with reality.[6] Then begins the consolidation phase in which development, institutionalization, and practical problems are emphasized. With ideology no longer serving as a means of achieving consensus, information becomes the basis for reaching decisions, and the Party revises its original transformation programs on the basis of this information. As a result, the policy process in the transformation phase tends to be comprehensive and mobilizational, whereas that in the consolidation phase is incremental and bureaucratic.

These policy cycles occur frequently in other societies as well, but the context of Chinese politics has made such shifts more radical and often violent. There are additional variables that constrain the shift of the phases.[7] First, the intensity of the Party's ideological commitment sets the basic tone of Chinese political life. To a large extent, Mao determined this. His theory of wavelike development holds that in doing anything there has to be a period of high speed and a period of low speed; he actually tried to shake the political system from time to time. Second, the leaders' experiences and styles also constrain policy making. In comparative terms, the revolutionary modernizers who had led guerrilla wars before 1949 were more active in the transformation phase and the managerial modernizers who had experienced underground work before 1949 were more active in the consolidation phase. Typifying the differences between these two groups were the different approaches and styles of Mao Tse-tung and Liu Shao-ch'i.[8]

Third, certain environmental factors, internal and external, also constrain the shift of policy patterns. Among the internal factors are the age of revolution, the level of economic development, and physical and cultural conditions. While the first generation of revolutionaries was still in power, the intensity of revolutionary dynamism sustained itself. If a lower level of economic development persists, the Party is more likely to seek mobilization and transformation. Two important cultural concepts governed traditional Chinese thinking: the concept of rite (*li*) in Confucianism holds that men be educated and ruled internally according to the rites, whereas the concept of law (*fa*) holds that men be regulated and controlled externally according to the laws. Richard Solomon, for example, held that Mao's revolution aimed at the destruction of traditional authority relationships in Chinese political culture, in which subordinates always avoided conflicts and emotion in deference to their superiors. Mao stressed the need for struggle and campaign to undermine such a dependency relationship.[9] As for the external factors, Thornton has suggested that the Soviet Union, Japan, and the United States have affected the course of Chinese internal politics at several decisive moments in history.[10] Because Mao personally directed Sino-Soviet polemics in the 1960s, Sino-Soviet relations became an issue in China's internal politics. Since 1949 there have been several years in which external development affected internal politics decisively. These include the ramification of de-Stalinization and its impact in Hungary during 1956-57, Khrushchev's attack on the Great Leap Forward prior to the Lushan conference in 1959, the Soviet proposal to form a united action toward the Vietnam War in 1965, the Soviet invasion of Czechoslovakia in 1968, and the Sino-American rapprochement in 1971-72.

Lastly, as in other societies, politics ultimately determines the precise course of policies. Two levels of politics should be distinguished. One involves the elite: at this level politics means the struggle for power among contending personalities and factions. The other level involves broader societal cleavages such as occupational or generational groups and bureaucracies, including the military. Although it is difficult to ascertain group configuration, Riker's theory of coalition making offers useful insights into the Chinese political process.[11]

All of these factors are at work in the shift of policy cycles. In the long run the consequences of transformation become the causes of consolidation and vice versa. Each phase itself can be divided into two distinct periods. In the first period, policy makers usually share consensus based on either ideology or information, but in the second period conflicts gradually set in, indicating a possible shift of policy.

The Great Leap Forward and the
Cultural Revolution, Post-1959

In a simplified form, one can delineate six cycles in the Chinese policy process as evolved since 1949. These are shown in table 2.

TABLE 2

Six Cycles of Policy Development

Phase	Period	Major Decisions
1. *Transformation*	*1949-53*	Land reform; agricultural cooperativization; joint-private enterprise; state control of commerce; marriage reform; Three and Five Anti-Campaigns; suppression of counterrevolutionaries
2. *Consolidation*	*1953-55*	State constitution; First Five-Year Plan
3. *Transformation*	*1955-59*	Agricultural cooperativization (higher agricultural producers' cooperatives); Twelve-Year Agricultural Development Plan; Hundred Flowers Campaign; decentralization of economic management; Great Leap Forward
4. *Consolidation*	*1959-66*	Retreat from and adjustments in the Great Leap Forward; Socialist Education Movement; the army's emulation campaigns; reforms in the economy, education, health care, and culture; Sino-Soviet polemics
5. *Transformation*	*1966-69*	Great Proletarian Cultural Revolution
6. *Consolidation*	*1969-76*	Party and state rebuilding; Sino-American rapprochement; the campaign to criticize Lin Piao and Confucius; the campaign to study Lenin's Theory of the Dictatorship of the Proletariat; the campaign to criticize Teng Hsiao-p'ing; the death of Mao Tse-tung

Among these six cycles the Great Leap Forward and the Cultural Revolution are by far the two most important. This is why the period between the two events is critical for understanding the Cultural Revolution, for it provides a good empirical test of the transformation-consolidation cycle. The policy consensus and the Mao-Liu coalition that had emerged in 1949 lasted during the first two cycles in 1949-55, when China followed the Soviet model of revolution and development. But they slowly began to erode in the third cycle of 1955-59, when Mao sought agricultural collectivization before industrialization while the majority of the Party Center wanted to continue the current policy of industrialization before collectivization. The advent of de-Stalinization temporarily moderated Mao's drive, but after the Hundred Flowers Campaign aborted and after he failed to change Khrushchev's views in Moscow, Mao renewed his quest for a Chinese way to revolution and development, which culminated in the Great Leap Forward.

And then, the self-fulfilling prophecy of the GLF as Mao defined it called for a simultaneous development of "walking on two legs," for a polity in which the Party and the masses could directly interact, and for an ideology of uninterrupted revolution. The Lushan conference of 1959 in which P'eng Teh-huai openly challenged Mao's policies and leadership further widened the fissure occurring during 1955-56 in the old consensus and leadership coalition while the leadership was engaged in China's industrialization debate. When the Party went through the process of reality testing in 1959-62, it had to retreat and make decisive adjustments in the GLF. A new policy consensus based on information and a new coalition of first-line leaders under Liu Shao-ch'i and Teng Hsiao-p'ing emerged after Mao stepped down to the second line of policy making to concern himself more with broad policy and ideological problems. What resulted, however, widely diverged from the GLF as the Party adopted the strategy of sequential development, concentrating its efforts on agriculture under the new economic policy of Agriculture as the Foundation and Industry as the Leading Factor, and resuming highly centralized and specialized structures for formulating and implementing policy under the Liu-Teng collective leadership. They justified these measures in the name of Adjusting and Consolidating, a slogan that served as an operational ideology by making compromises between the Party's ultimate ends and its immediate problems. When Mao called for a renewed class struggle at the Tenth Plenum in 1962, addressing himself to some corrosive effects of the adjustments, he could not change the Party's policies and leadership. The divergence between the Party's ideological rhetoric and its actual practice emerging in 1962 foreshadowed continuing conflicts in the subsequent years, necessitating eventually the Cultural Revolution.

During the second period of this consolidation phase in 1962-66, therefore, the policies and the institutional processes harnessed in 1959-62 came under increasing challenge when Mao again called for new policies and mass campaigns. But Liu and his associates sought to moderate Mao's efforts by devising policies to reinforce the 1959-62 policies. This was revealed in their support for state-financed agricultural mechanization, highly centralized industrial trusts, a two-track school system, and the regularization of temporary labor—all of which were designed to promote industrialization as the best means to consolidate a socialist economic base. But Mao attempted to reverse this trend by introducing reforms in education, health care, and culture so as to benefit the countryside and to promote self-reliance and egalitarianism. As a result, while Mao demanded a simultaneous development, the Party responded with a sequential development.

These conflicts over substantive policies were manifested also in the process of formulating and implementing them. Mao initiated the Socialist Education Movement after the Tenth Plenum to encourage mass mobilization and participation among the cadres and the peasants. But unlike the campaigns of the 1950s, the mass campaigns of the 1960s turned ineffective with diminishing returns as they emerged from the organizational processes developed by the Party. For example, when Mao's First Ten Points for the SEM drafted in May 1963 went through these processes, it was found that the Party's organizational units "factored" the broad ideological goals into more operationally manageable subgoals. Thus, when the Party Secretariat revised Mao's original document in September 1963 and Liu amended again the Secretariat's revised document in September 1964, the result was that they altered the long-range goals Mao had set to short-range goals of organizational rectification. Accordingly, the Party organizations implemented the SEM through their network of committees and work teams, paying little more than lip service to mass mobilization. This factoring process apparently pervaded even the lowest level of cadres.[12]

It was clear then that even Mao's directives had to go through the Party's institutional procedures to be implemented. Realizing that the entire Party bureaucracy and particularly its top leadership had been sabotaging his policies, Mao formed the conception of the "Party establishment taking the capitalist road" and decided to restructure it and purge Liu when he issued the Twenty-Three Points for the SEM in January 1965. In contrast to the Party, however, the army under Lin Piao followed Mao's policy of training revolutionary successors by carrying out ideological emulations. This was why Mao turned to the army as the national model.

These conflicts inevitably became associated with ideological struggles. Alarmed with the trend toward inequality and bureaucratization, which he regarded as manifestation of revisionism, Mao called for the SEM in the countryside and educational and cultural reforms in the cities. But the Party treated these as a means to correct mistakes or to uphold academic truth. Even after Mao specifically admonished the Party's top leadership at the crucial Politburo meeting in September 1965 about the danger of revisionism, P'eng Chen and his associates still opted for accommodating Mao's demands. The more intensely Mao committed himself to his ideological beliefs, the more sharply he resented interference and the greater his urge was to eliminate the source of such interference. The pressure from the Soviet Union to forge a united action toward the Vietnam War in 1965-66 further deepened his anxiety about revisionism. Yet his repeated attempts to reorient the entire policy process had been frustrated as he recalled in February 1967:

In the past we waged struggles in rural areas, in factories, in the cultural field, and we carried out the socialist education movement. But all this failed to solve the problem because we did not find a form, a method, to arouse the broad masses to expose our dark aspect openly, in an all-round way and from below.[13]

This was so because the incremental policies, the bureaucratic processes, and the practical compromises used by the Party effectively restricted Mao's calls for comprehensive policies, mass movements, and ideological struggles. Mao realized that the Party had, in effect, become a self-perpetuating bureaucracy, suppressing mass initiative and avoiding open struggles according to what Western organizational theorists call standard operational procedures of routine rules and secrecy.[14] In all probability, therefore, the policy process of 1959-66 approximated an institutionalizing polity under the Party.

To overcome this institutional resistance and to find a method to arouse the masses, Mao had to violate the rules and procedures of the established process. By making the decision in 1965-66 to enlist Lin Piao's support and to mobilize the Red Guards against the Party leadership and bureaucracy, which the Eleventh Plenum in August 1966 finally endorsed, he at last found the form to achieve his goal: the Cultural Revolution. In this perspective, the Red Guard phase of the Cultural Revolution was not irrational but necessary for him to renew his ideological commitment. When he took this extraordinary measure, the accumulating clashes evolved in the policy process from 1959 broke out into the open.

AFTERMATH OF THE CULTURAL REVOLUTION, 1969-76

Historically, the Cultural Revolution of 1966-69 presented another transformation phase. But its aftermath in 1969-76, although comparable to another consolidation phase, appears to have broken the transformation-consolidation cycle by unleashing events that make it difficult for the Party to restore earlier policy consensus and processes. The political development after the Cultural Revolution and the death of Mao in 1976 seem to rule out any drastic cycle. As a result, the post-1969 policy process has produced an uneasy blend of both transformation and consolidation impulses. Mao's attempt during the Cultural Revolution to enforce his concept of the correct policy, authority structure, and ideological posture had unanticipated consequences: the Lin Piao incident and its aftermath in 1971-73; the Tenth Party Congress in 1973; the campaign to criticize Lin and Confucius in 1973-74; and the second rise and fall of Teng Hsiao-p'ing in 1974-76.

Transformation: 1966-69

There were two distinct phases of the Cultural Revolution. In the first year, from August 1966 to July 1967, Mao and his supporters tried to fill the apparent gaps between the Party's rhetoric and its practice by changing the existing policies and power structure. When this move toward radicalization brought China to the brink of a civil war in July 1967, Mao began to temper his original programs. In the second phase, from August 1967 to April 1969, moderate forces gained momentum to curtail intense and violent factional struggles. The external pressures emanating from the Soviet intervention in Czechoslovakia and the so-called Brezhnev Doctrine finally brought the Cultural Revolution to an abrupt halt.

The First Phase

This phase saw the rapid development of Red Guard movements inspired by Mao's exhortation that Rebellion Is Justified. Initially, Mao's supporters in Shanghai launched the Cultural Revolution by attacking Wu Han's play *Hai Jui Dismissed from Office*, asserting that it praised P'eng Teh-huai's challenge of Mao's GLF policies in the guise of a historical allegory. By exposing this play, these critics formed the public opinion that they claimed precedes actual power seizure. They also attacked the current educational system by mobilizing dissident students against the school authorities. To encourage reforms in education, which he felt to be revisionist, Mao ordered the closing of schools so that the students could participate in the Red Guard movements. China's health-care system also came under attack. The May 7, 1966, directive, which was not published until August 2, and the sixteen-point decision of the Eleventh Plenum reaffirmed the policy, power, and ideological themes Mao had consistently pursued.

On policy matters, the strategy of simultaneously grasping revolution and stimulating production was restated, as were the slogans, In Agriculture Learn from Tachai and In Industry Learn from Tach'ing. Mao's May 7 directive, for example, encompassed some of these principles:

While the main task of the workers is in industry, they should also study military affairs, politics, and culture. . . .

While the main task of the peasants in the communes is agriculture (including forestry, animal husbandry, side occupations, and fishery), they should at the same time study military affairs, politics, and culture. . . .

This holds good for students too. While their main task is to study, they should, in addition to their studies, learn other things, that is, industrial work, farming, and military affairs. They should also criticize the bourgeoisie. The school term should be shortened, education should be revolutionized, and the domination of our schools by bourgeois intellectuals should not be allowed to continue.[15]

In response to this directive, some enterprises and communes actually restored larger units of production, suspended such material incentives as wage increases and bonuses, and carried out mass criticisms, despite resistance by some of the workers and the peasants. To avoid disrupting the economy, Mao's supporters directed the criticisms at the policies that Liu Shao-ch'i had consolidated in 1959-66. Except for the suspension of material incentives, therefore, the impact of the Cultural Revolution on the economy was not so serious as that of the GLF. Its impact on education, health care, and culture, however, was quite revolutionary.

Since Mao aimed to overthrow the Party establishment, the most devastating impact of the revolution was on the power structure, as Mao's supporters sought to replace the institutionalized Party with unprecedented mass movement.[16] Mao first built a leadership coalition with Lin Piao and his associates in the army from above and then mobilized a non-Party force, the Red Guards, from below against Liu and the bureaucracy. At the top, Mao made himself the sole source of authority; his directives were issued jointly by the Cultural Revolution Group, the Central Committee, and the Military Affairs Committee. Instead of persuading Liu and his associates to support his policies as he had done in the GLF, he set out to eliminate them.

The Red Guards brought the central Party apparatus to heel in the January Storm of 1967. Then the focus of the revolution shifted to the provincial level. Some of the old leaders apparently offered concerted resistance in February under Tan Chen-lin's leadership. The mass movement gradually accentuated internal struggles among the Red Guards themselves. To cope with such factional struggles and the resistance of old power holders, Mao reluctantly brought the army into the fray. He had to abandon the original plan of organizing Paris commune-type structures by accepting a provisional type of revolutionary committee in which representatives of the army, the revolutionary cadres, and the masses participated in the three-way alliance. Although six of these committees were formed by radical leaders before July 1967, Mao could maintain only loose contact with diverse groups of the Red Guards and the rebels, who were pursuing disparate paths in the name of Mao's Thought. As a result, the institutional distinction between the Party's internal and external communications disappeared.[17] Only Mao's cult and the army's organizational instruments could maintain a semblance of order. Thus, the first year of the Cultural Revolution saw a truly mass polity in which Mao and the masses interacted through mass movements.

Mao legitimized these policy and institutional changes by justifying destruction before construction. Even though the economic base had been socialist, he contended, the superstructure still remained bourgeois. To make the superstructure congruent with the socialist economic base, a revolution was necessary to remold both the power structure and human mentality. With the red books of Mao's quotations serving as the guide for dialectical struggle and thought reform, over twenty million Red Guards roamed the country to exchange revolutionary experiences, forming fighting groups against the old ideas, culture, customs, and habits. Meanwhile, the Maoist propagandists depicted Liu as China's Khrushchev, accusing him of having denied the existence of class struggle in a socialist society.

The Wuhan Incident and the Second Phase, 1967-69

The intensity and violence of the Red Guard movement brought China to the brink of internal war when the commander of the Wuhan military region, Ch'en Tsai-tao, kidnapped two representatives of the Central Cultural Revolution Group. This incident provoked the most radical group, the May 16 Corps, to attack the army, seeking its overthrow, but this actually enhanced the army's involvement in Chinese politics. Thus, the Wuhan incident became a watershed of the Cultural Revolution.

During 1967-69, the radical features of the first phase had to be moderated in the face of the consequences of the Red Guard movements. Mao's supporters began to curtail excessive egalitarianism in their policy pronouncements, took certain measures to prevent factional struggles by strengthening the army's authority, and sought to focus ideological discussions on revisionism and selfishness. Finally, the advent of Soviet pressure on Chinese borders in 1969 compelled Mao to end the Cultural Revolution.

On policy issues, Mao's innovations assumed pragmatic forms. The merging of production brigades into larger units was no longer suggested. In the cities, the exhortations for temporary workers to take over enterprises subsided, and instead, in March 1968, Mao singled out the Shanghai Machine Tool Company as a national model, encompassing the three-way alliance of technicians, cadres, and workers, and the principle of combining industry and agriculture. According to this model, factory managers were to share authority with workers in decision-making processes. In July 1968 he also suggested that the primary and secondary schools, and the colleges of natural sciences be reopened. His educational policy was best expressed in his July 21, 1968, directive:

It is still necessary to have universities; here I refer mainly to colleges of sciences and engineering. However, it is essential to shorten the length of schooling, revolutionize education, put proletarian politics in command and take the road of the Shanghai Machine Tools Company in training technicians from among the workers. Students should be selected from among workers and peasants with practical experiences, and they should return to production after a few years' study.[18]

Despite this directive, only the primary and some secondary schools began to resume classes in 1969. Mao praised the training of youngsters as "barefoot doctors" to serve the people in rural areas; he also endorsed the establishment of medical cooperatives among the peasants. For culture, only eight revolutionary operas produced under Chiang Ch'ing's direction were shown throughout the country. Although experimentation continued, the emphasis gradually shifted from revolution to production.

It was also in this second phase that the army emerged as the authority that linked the elite and the masses. The power struggle also moved from the Red Guard-Party confrontation to the Red Guard-army confrontation. Continuing factionalism among the Red Guards precipitated the ultraleftist May 16 Corps into dragging out a handful of capitalist roaders from the army, an attack that prompted regional military leaders to defend the integrity of the army. Mao's September 5, 1967, directive enhanced the army's power by sanctioning the use of force in pacifying local conflicts. It was at this time that Chou En-lai contributed his mediating skills in preventing China from slipping into anarchy. Despite these efforts, armed struggles continued. Mao finally had to purge the May 16 Corps in March 1968. Lin Piao fired Yang Ch'eng-wu, then acting chief of staff, who challenged Lin's authority by writing an article praising Mao's Thought. Commenting on the behavior of some Red Guards in July 1968, Mao expressed his desperation: "Some behaved like rascals. Their purpose is nothing but to make little money and to play with women." He then warned them: "If you cannot handle the problem, we may resort to military control and ask Lin Piao to take command."[19] Indeed, he ordered the army under Lin Piao to send the Red Guards to the countryside so that they could resettle and learn labor from the peasants. At the same time, he asked that the soldier-worker propaganda teams be sent into schools to pacify feuding factions.

As a result of the army's involvement in politics, the military assumed the core leadership, occupying 70 percent of the membership of the revolutionary committees completed in August 1968. Among the five Field Armies still stationed in their original bases, Lin Piao's Fourth Army rose in power.[20] The purged cadres were sent to the May 7 cadre schools for thought reform. The military was now charged with the task of rebuilding the Party after the Twelfth Plenum in October 1968 expelled Liu, calling him "traitor, renegade, and scab." The new leadership began to restore the distinction between internal and external communication. By convening the Ninth Party Congress in April 1969, they attempted to formalize their power. Since the military took over 50 percent of the newly chosen Central Committee members, it is fair to say that a praetorian regime resulted from the Cultural Revolution.

Mao's supporters defended this military rule, saying that the army was founded by Mao and commanded by his comrade-in-arms, Lin Piao. For the sake of unity Mao called for a great alliance against revisionism, lumping all deviant policies in the category. The criticism focused on six doctrines that Liu had allegedly propounded: class struggle dies out; Party members become the docile tools of the Party; the masses are backward; people join the Party to climb up the hierarchy; inner Party peace should be maintained; and private and public interests merge. By portraying Liu in these black and white terms, Mao's supporters sought to stimulate mass movements and to form a new revolutionary consensus. Liu served as the symbol of all the wrongs Mao had tried to correct.[21] But the external threat posed by the Soviet invasion of Czechoslovakia and Soviet pressure on China's borders compelled Mao to bring the Cultural Revolution to an end and to hold the long-delayed Ninth Party Congress.

Convened in April 1969, the Ninth Party Congress legitimized three trends emerging from the Cultural Revolution. First, it approved of the new policies stressing the countryside, service to the people, hard work, self-reliance, and egalitarianism, especially in the areas of education, health care, and culture. More important than the substance, however, the revolution had allowed debates not only on policy implementation and implementors but also on policies and policy makers themselves. Even though the new leadership guided such debates within the framework of two-road struggle, the legacy of open debate was destined to have far-reaching implication in the future, for it opened a Pandora's box that transformed the latent interests of social groups into manifest interests.

Second, the Cultural Revolution replaced an institutionalizing polity under the Party with a praetorian regime under the military. It purged two-thirds of the old leaders, most of whom were associated with Liu Shao-ch'i and P'eng Chen, thereby ending the post-1949 leadership coalition. In their place, Mao formed another coalition with Lin Piao as his designated successor and with relatively younger leaders. At the provincial level, factional struggle enabled the military to assert its regional power. Yet by providing that local units could appeal

directly to the chairman of the Party without going though the interlocking bureaucracy, and also by sanctioning the spirit of Going against
the Tide in the Party Constitution, Mao sought to institutionalize mass
mobilization and class struggle.

Third, the revolution renewed the Party's commitment to Mao's
Thought as its guide and to the continuation of class struggle under the
dictatorship of the proletariat.

The Aftermath, 1969-76: Blend of
Transformation and Consolidation

The aftermath of the Cultural Revolution in 1969-76 was comparable to the aftermath of the GLF in 1959-66, but unlike the latter,
revealed a blend of both transformation and consolidation, suggesting
uncertainty in the relationship of policy, power, and ideology. The
reason for this may be that the legacies of the Cultural Revolution were
basically different from and more enduring than those of the GLF. The
GLF was a mass movement designed to transform physcial nature by
mobilizing all the available resources under the Party's direction. Its consequences disrupted China's economic order, but the Party under the
leadership of Liu and Teng was able to somehow weather the crisis by
introducing decisive adjustments and consolidation measures in 1959-
62, measures that Mao acceded to. By contrast, the Cultural Revolution
was a mass movement designed to transform organizational and human
nature by mobilizing non-Party forces against the Party bureaucracy
itself; the revolution disrupted China's political order but Mao's legitimizing of rebellion made it difficult for the new leadership to effect a
decisive consolidation program, although Teng did try in 1974-75.

There were also two distinct phases in the post-Cultural Revolution
period. The first extended from the Ninth Party Congress in April 1969
to the Tenth Party Congress in August 1973; the second from the
Tenth Party Congress to the death of Mao in September 1976. In the
first phase the new leadership controlled by the military made a concerted effort to rebuild the Party and state structures but ended in Lin's
alleged coup attempt against Mao. In the second phase, Mao and his
supporters tried to eradicate Lin's influence by restoring some old
policies and leaders. Chou En-lai was instrumental in rehabilitating Teng
so that the latter could bridge the gulf between the military and the
Party leaders in the task of consolidation. This, in turn, created further
tensions between what was called "the old things" and the "newly born
things" that resulted in the campaign to criticize Lin and Confucius in
1973-74, the campaign to study Lenin's theory of proletarian dictatorship in 1975, and the second purge of Teng in 1976. The death of Mao

in September 1976 casts further doubt on the future of China's political order.

The Lin Piao Incident, 1969-73

In 1969-73, the new leadership had to consolidate what they had gained. The emphasis swung back to production, institutionalization, and practical problems. As policy innovations began to take concrete forms in this phase, there was no longer any mention of temporary workers' control of enterprises. The reforms in education, for example, produced a new school system: five-year primary schools, three- or four-year secondary schools, three-year liberal art colleges, and four-year polytechnical or medical colleges. The production brigades took over many of the primary schools while the communes took over the secondary schools, running them on a self-sufficient basis. The new curricula were tailored to practical training and the study of Mao's Thought. Beginning in 1970, college enrollment began but only those applicants who had had two years of practical experience in enterprises or communes were recommended by their localities. New operas and musical repertoires were added to the existing eight models. The barefoot doctors were trained more systematically for six months at commune clinics. To meet the Soviet threat, Mao urged the people to prepare for natural disasters and war. Thus, the Party Center sought to devise policies to consolidate production and national defense.

The leadership was preoccupied with the task of rebuilding the Party hierarchy but this effort actually increased the political status of the army. When the provincial Party committees were completed between December 1970 and August 1971, for example, the military took over 60 percent of the leading posts against the 16 percent they held in 1966; such commanders as Ch'en Hsi-lien, Hsü Shih-yu, and Li Teh-sheng rose in power at the expense of ultraleftist civilian leaders.[22] As a result, conflicts were inevitable between the attempt to restore Party authority and the army's entrenched power.

Lin Piao, in earning Mao's trust by helping his supporters during the early Cultural Revolution, caused considerable resentment among regional military leaders when the ultraleftist elements attacked their command. Now that these elements came under attack, the regional military leaders took advantage of the changed situation to reassert their power. As a result, most of the radical chairmen of the revolutionary committees formed in 1967 lost power to the military in 1970-71. Somewhat alienated from both the radicals and the regional leaders, Lin apparently tried to consolidate his power base at the Center by recruiting Ch'en Po-ta to his side. But to make his position firm, he had to outrank Chou En-lai. He may have tried to achieve this by aspiring to the state chairmanship when the leadership was drafting a new state constitution. Despite Mao's opposition to such a move, Ch'en proposed the establishment of the post at the Second Plenum in August 1970. Mao then took measures to undercut Lin and his associates, thus abandoning the leadership coalition when its principal member asked for too large a side payment. At this, Lin allegedly attempted an armed coup against Mao without success. Mao then sought to curtail the role of the army, which was becoming a self-perpetuating organization like the old Party. In a larger context, this incident was a by-product of the clashes between institutionalism and praetorianism.

This incident ended the ideological campaign to criticize ultra-leftists. In September 1971 Mao issued a directive calling upon the Party to observe the Three Must Nots—revisionism, split, and conspiracy—but to be above board; he also asked all Party members to sing the *International*, insisting that class struggle would continue even after communism was realized. The problem posed by the Lin Piao incident was acute because Lin was purged so soon after having been chosen as Mao's successor. In 1971-73, therefore, the Party sought to eradicate Lin's influence in Chinese political life by consolidating its discipline, culminating with the convening of the Tenth Party Congress in August 1973.

After the Lin Piao incident, the Party restored some of the old policies, which intensified existing cleavages as the newly born interests protested. The Party Center specifically banned any practice by local cadres going beyond policy guidelines. In 1971-72 regular teaching started at Peking and Tsinghua universities. Old regulations and personnel were coming back under the pretext of adjustment and consolidation; as a result the number of administrative personnel increased and the workers once again were busy responding to demands from higher levels. For agriculture, the Party issued a new central directive on communes in December 1971 requiring the production teams to distribute their income according to the work their members carried out; the teams were also asked to consult their members in Learning from Tachai, banning any attempt to "transplant Tachai."[23]

Education became once again a controversial issue. From early 1973 on the applicants to colleges, for example, had to take written examinations and interviews with the recruiting officers after they had been recommended by their localities. This set off a series of challenges by those who failed the tests. Since the educational reform and the policy of sending students down to the countryside had already generated powerful constituencies and interests, those who failed naturally challenged the legitimacy of the new measure by invoking the spirit of rebellion.

Foreign policy was another area of adjustment. The 1972 turnabout in Sino-American relations must have been decided by the Politburo. Mao and Chou favored this course of action to counter China's primary enemy, the Soviet Union, which had amassed sixty-four or sixty-seven divisions (40 percent of its entire ground forces) and fifteen thousand tanks (one-third of its total number) on Chinese borders.[24] In addition, the Chinese leaders perceived that such a move could force the United States to recognize their claims to Taiwan.

The Party sought to re-establish its control over society by reorganizing most of the previous state and mass organizations. To staff these units, the Party had to rehabilitate many of the old power holders to positions of responsibility. In a somewhat reduced size, the State Council resumed its normal work with increased specialization. The State Planning Commission recommenced under a new director, Yu Ch'iu-lu, an old power holder. The Young Communist League, the Women's Federation, and the Trade Union, all had completed their reorganization by the spring of 1973. The Party tightened up its channels of communication, prohibiting any unauthorized ones, and stressed the importance of unified and collective leadership. A number of old leaders reappeared: Teng Hsiao-p'ing, Tan Chen-lin, Li Ch'ing-ch'üan and even Ch'en Tsai-tao. The May 7 cadre schools also became routinized as they adopted a rotation system. While these changes took place, Lin and his followers were accused of being "Liu-type swindlers." The army was now asked to rectify its work style by fighting complacency and arrogance. Around the end of 1972 Lin Piao was relabeled "ultrarightist."

The criticism of Lin likewise gradually encompassed those who had opposed the Cultural Revolution. Since Lin once likened Mao to Emperor Ch'in Shih-huang, who buried Confucian scholars, Professor Yang Jung-kuo of Sun Yat-sen University opened in July 1972 criticisms on Confucius for his defense of feudal institutions. A year later Yang resumed his critique, this time focusing his attack on Confucius's aprioristic idealism, perhaps alluding to Lin's promotion of Mao as a genius. Soon after, the campaign to criticize Confucius was well under way against those who "opposed the present by invoking the old," who termed the result of the Cultural Revolution a "mess."[25]

The Party convened its Tenth Congress in August 1973 to formalize the political changes precipitated by the Lin Piao incident. First, the congress defended the Cultural Revolution as absolutely necessary and timely, quoting Mao's words. Second, the new Party constitution

adopted by the congress endorsed two diverging trends of institutionalization and mass mobilization. On the one hand, it reaffirmed the
principle of Party discipline and democratic centralism. But at the same
time, it also provided the spirit of Going against the Tide, saying that it
was absolutely impermissible to suppress criticism or to retaliate. The
congress also did away with a designated successor and instituted a
collective leadership by choosing five vice-chairmen of the Party and
eight members of the Politburo Standing Committee. In selecting these
leaders, the new constitution adopted another formula of the three-way
alliance: the old, the middle-aged, and the young. By this arrangement, such young radicals as Wang Hung-wen became one of the
vice-chairmen as well as such middle-aged leaders as Hua Kuo-feng, a
Politburo member, mostly at the expense of military leaders associated
with Lin Piao. Lastly, the congress reaffirmed Mao's Thought as the
Party's dogma and pledged that more cultural revolutions be carried out
in the future.

The Criticism of Lin and Confucius and the
Rise and Fall of Teng Hsiao-p'ing, 1973-76

In the second phase of the post-Cultural Revolution period, the two
diverging trends emerging from the Tenth Party Congress found themselves in growing conflict. The trend of reradicalization was expressed
in the campaign to criticize Lin and Confucius as unfolded in 1973-74;
and that of policy consolidation in the second rise of Teng and his
leadership in 1974-76. The conflicts between these two forces came to
the open in the T'ien An Men Square riot in April 1976.

The campaign to criticize Lin and Confucius first started as an
academic debate on Confucianism and Legalism couched in historio-
graphical discussions. The first issue of a new Shanghai journal, *Hsüeh-
hsi yü p'i-p'an* (Study and Criticism) launched in September 1973,
attacked Confucianism for defending the old order against the new. At
the same time, the Party's effort to bring the army under its control
was shown by the transfer of eight regional military commanders in
December 1973. The North China Art Festival held in Peking in January 1974, however, attacked a Shansi opera, *San-shang t'ao-feng* (Three
Visits to Peach Peak), as a poisonous weed, for it actually aimed to
reverse the verdict on Liu Shao-ch'i and his wife Wang Kuang-mei. The
People's Daily of February 2, then, editorialized on the campaign to
criticize Lin *and* Confucius, announcing that Mao had personally led it.
Subsequently, the rhetoric focused on Confucius's dictum: Restrain
Oneself and Restore the Rites (*ke-chi fu-li*). As in the Cultural Revolution, the campaign called for making the past serve the present,

implying that some people had used the past to criticize the present state of affairs. Apparently, such leaders from Shanghai as Chang Ch'un-ch'iao, Yao Wen-yüan, and Wang Hung-wen initiated this new campaign to protect the "newly born things."[26] Once it started, Mao may have endorsed it to justify the correctness of the Cultural Revolution.

Also as with the Cultural Revolution, the campaign embodied conflicting themes. Some writers emphasized Party character, others emphasized rebellion, even though the official position said that these two were not contradictory. In June 1974, however, wall posters denouncing officials appeared in Peking and other cities. Violence erupted at schools and enterprises; the worker-propaganda teams were sent back to these places. As a result, the campaign began to take its toll, disrupting production and communications. And like the Cultural Revolution, this campaign also generated a momentum of its own. Some criticisms appear to have been directed at Chou En-lai, for they attacked the efforts by some leaders to seek common goals on major issues while reserving differences.

It was against this background that Mao issued two important instructions in the summer of 1974: one urged the consolidation of the economy and the other called for unity and stability.[27] The latter read, in part: "It is time to settle down. The entire Party and army should unite."[28] Knowing that he had cancer, Chou named Teng in 1973 as acting premier with the task of consolidating the economy and of restoring unity while he went into a hospital. And Mao must have approved of this since a later report said that Chairman Mao had saved Teng and given him a chance to resume work.   Teng, for his part, had already made several self-criticisms, one in 1968 and another in 1972, pledging that he would never reverse the verdicts.[29] But once he was put in a position of responsibility he resurrected some of the old policies and cadres. With Chou's support, he set out to undertake decisive policy reviews and readjustments as he had done in 1959-62; in so doing, he encouraged experienced and qualified cadres to assist him with his work, saying that he was not afraid of being overthrown for the second time. His efforts were bound to affect the status of the new leaders, and their counterattack took the form of the campaign against Lin and Confucius.

Even though expressed in the guise of ancient events, the major themes of the campaign were unmistakable. First, they were in defense of newly born policies: the enrollment of workers, peasants, and soldiers in colleges; the sending down of medical personnel, including the barefoot doctors, to the countryside; the resettling of educated youth in the countryside; and the popularization of revolutionary operas.[30]

Second, by attacking such Confucian concepts as the Mandate of Heaven and the goodness of human nature, and by upholding such Legalist concepts as the conquest of heaven and the evilness of human nature, the campaign also sought to defend new power arrangements that had evolved: revolutionary committees; the state of Party committees; the three-way alliance of the old, the middle-aged, and the young; and the May 7 cadre schools.[31]

Finally, by attacking the Mencius concept of the Golden Mean and endorsing the concept of continuing class warfare, the campaign sought to defend Mao's call for class struggle and such practices as the study of Marxism-Leninism-Mao Tsetung Thought, the training of Marxist theoretical workers, and the study classes for training worker-peasant-soldier cadres that Chiang Ch'ing initiated in her favored Hsiao-chin-chuang brigade in Hopei. In short, the campaign was directed at those who maintained that the newly born things were inferior to the old things.

By the end of 1974, two conflicting trends had clearly emerged. The actual state of policy development tended to support a consolidation program, but the rhetoric of political discourse inclined toward transformation. Under this facade of the surfacing trends, however, there ensued intense conflicts within the Party. According to a secret speech by Wang Hung-wen made in January 1974, some old cadres still did not understand the Cultural Revolution, saying that in earlier days they had battled north and south but the Cultural Revolution was really a mess; therefore, they went so far as to suggest that young cadres should be sent back to their original posts. Wang defended the young cadres promoted during the Cultural Revolution and even proposed that young leaders over thirty be named commanders of military regions.[32]

Despite press attacks by such people as Yang Jung-kuo, Ch'u Lan, Liang Hsiao, and Ch'ih Heng, Chou and Teng made plans for the Fourth National People's Congress to be held between January 13 and 17, 1975. One important issue that might have developed within the leadership while they were drafting a new state constitution was the extent to which the constitution would guarantee "bourgeois rights," that is, the rights to private ownership and differential wages. Chang Ch'un-ch'iao and Yao Wen-yüan apparently sought to severely restrict these. Chang had clashed with Teng in 1958 precisely over this issue (see pages 32-33). In so doing, they again obtained Mao's support, for they later revealed that Mao had emphasized the need for restricting bourgeois rights in his instructions on theoretical problems issued at the end of 1974. Mao had actually warned Teng when he said: "If Lin-like people assume power, they would easily restore capitalism."[33] Nevertheless, the Party's Second Plenum convened between January 8 and 10, 1975, approved the new constitution, which clearly provided for the private plots and other rights to private ownership and the principle of distributing income according to work. The plenum also elected Teng as vice-chairman of the Party.

A most significant point about this congress was Chou En-lai's call for the completion of China's economic modernization by the end of the century:

We might envisage the development of our national economy in two stages beginning from the Third Five-Year Plan: The first stage is to build an independent and relatively comprehensive industrial and economic system in fifteen years, that is, before 1980; the second stage is to accomplish the comprehensive modernization of agriculture, industry, national defense, and science and technology before the end of the century, so that our national economy will be advancing in the front ranks of the world.[34]

Couched in the name of Mao's instructions, this was the most concrete statement that any Chinese leader had made concerning a time table for completing the four modernizations.

In normalizing the state bureaucracy, too, one finds Chou's attempts to insure an enduring coalition after he died. To place the army under the Party's control, the constitution provided that the Party's chairman was to command it; it also stated that the standing committee of the NPC, which Chu Teh would chair, was to function as the head of state. A coalition of leaders with diverse experiences formed the cabinet. Teng was designated as Chou's successor as the first vice-premier; he was later known to assume additional duties as vice-chairman of the Military Affairs Committee and the army's chief of staff; Chang Ch'un-ch'iao became the second ranking vice-premier and he was also known later as director of the army's political department; Yeh Chien-ying became a vice-premier and minister of defense, and Hua Kuo-feng a vice-premier and minister of public security. Among the ministers were such rehabilitated leaders as Chou Jung-hsin as minister of education and Wan Li as minister of railroads. On the other hand, the constitution incorporated some of the Cultural Revolution themes by providing that the masses had the right to rebel and strike. But the revolutionary committees were made permanent state organs.

Mao and his supporters were not fully satisfied with the outcome of the congress. Their worries again centered on the fate of the newly born things and were intensified when Teng undertook a systematic policy review by assigning a "theorist" for this purpose as early as January 6, 1975. No sooner was the NPC over than the *People's Daily* of February 9 revealed Mao's third important instruction on studying

Lenin's theory of proletarian dictatorship and on restricting bourgeois rights. Part of this instruction read:

China is a socialist country. Before liberation she was much the same as capitalism. Even now she practices an eight-grade wage system, distributing to each according to his work and exchange by means of money, which are scarcely different from those in the old society. What is different is that the system of ownership has changed. . . . These can only be restricted under the dictatorship of the proletariat.[35]

Soon after, Yao Wen-yüan, in a major article, quoted another sentence Mao had used to attack P'eng Teh-huai: "At present, the main danger lies in empiricism," charging that some people used expertise to carry out their counterrevolutionary acts; he condemned the hankering for material incentives, saying that Lin Piao and company attached particular importance to using wages to lure young workers; he asked these workers to reject the material inducements of the bourgeoisie that appeared in various forms, supported by "the idea of bourgeois rights." Chang Ch'un-ch'iao also warned in a similar article against the "bourgeois wind" that he alleged was blowing among high Party cadres; he cited one of Mao's statements made at the First Plenum in 1969 that much of the factory leadership was not in the hands of genuine Marxists. Yet he did not want to blow a "Communist wind" again. These arguments were clearly directed at Teng and his efforts, as reflected in a post hoc charge that Teng was "resentful and panic-stricken when he heard that bourgeois right was being criticized."[36]

Teng was no less forceful in defending his views against these veiled attacks. While agreeing to the necessity of restricting bourgeois rights, he maintained that such restriction also called for a material base. The main situation facing China, as he told a meeting on March 5, was economic construction; hence, the nation had to focus all of its energy on the four modernizations Chou had envisioned.[37] The key to the achievement of these goals he saw as comprehensive readjustments in all areas of public policy.

Judging from the accusations made later by his critics, Teng obviously believed that the Cultural Revolution had created a mess, especially in the areas of science and technology, higher education, and industrial development. Therefore, he sought to reverse the excesses caused by the revolution by a series of central directives in each policy area. The first of these was the Outline Report on the Work of the Academy of Sciences, drafted under the leadership of Hu Yao-pang.[38] He proposed that the purged scientists and scholars be reassigned to their original posts, saying that it was better to use them than to subject them to labor. Since too much politics and ideology hampered research and development, dictatorship in the scientific community was counterproductive. He said on another occasion: "The Academy of Sciences is an academy of sciences, not an academy of production or of education. It is neither an academy of cabbage nor one of beans but one concerned with sciences, and specifically natural sciences."[39]

Related to his concern with the Academy of Sciences, Teng also saw higher education as being in shambles. The emphasis on equality, practical labor, and political education hampered the quality, the academic study, and the professional aspects of education. Worker-peasant-soldier students were "rough country bumpkins" knowing little about education, for they did not study. Nor did the professors study; if they did, they did so in secret as if it were a crime. As a result, the quality of university students was below that of former high school students. Teng even raised the question of what would happen if China suddenly found herself at war with an enemy. He was also critical of the July 21 workers' colleges and the May 7 peasant colleges set up by factories and communes that had proliferated to fifteen thousand units accommodating 780,000 students by the end of 1975. In response to this concern, two professors of Tsinghua University wrote a letter in July 1975 to Mao pointing out that the new students graduated without being able to read a book and that the professors were unable to teach because students had no requisite level of intellectual capacity.[40] In July-September, Chou Jung-hsin apparently tried to resume academic study as the first priority of instruction and to restore the professors' authority in university governance. Teng's efforts in these areas remind us of his previous roles in drafting the Fourteen Articles on Science and the Sixty Articles on Universities in 1961 (see pages 63-64).

The second document Teng helped draft was the thirty-thousand-word Some Problems in Accelerating Industrial Development, also known as the Twenty Articles, which developed from six major and thirty minor revisions between August 17 and October 25, 1975.[41] Because industrial management was in chaos, quality was lower and accidents many. This situation required a strict regulation without which no discipline could be enforced. To restore a central direction, the document proposed that key enterprises serving the whole nation and requiring a nationwide coordination be turned over to the higher authorities to establish a centralized leadership. Since reliance on the workers, peasants, and soldiers was a relative thing, it proposed a set of new rules governing both management and workers so that factory directors and professionally trained personnel could assume leadership. This shift of policy may have caused some labor unrest like that in Hangchow in July 1975, which necessitated the mobilization of ten thousand troops.[42] The document recognized the importance of material incentives to motivate labor productivity, as long as distribution was carried out according to one's work and ability. Finally, it approved the import of foreign technology and equipment provided that it could be financed by long-term contracts so that China could pay for them by exporting her minerals. To achieve a technological transformation it was necessary to have access to the most up-to-date Western technology and to increase employment. Again, these points remind us of the Seventy Articles on Industry, which Teng had helped draft in 1961. Yet the Twenty Articles justified its rationale by quoting no less than sixty-six times from Mao![43]

The problem of coherent policy implementation after the Cultural Revolution was more serious than that after the GLF. A most serious problem was to resume a unified and centralized direction and control in the face of persisting factionalism and regionalism. To cope with this, Teng embarked upon a basic readjustment (cheng-tun) in Party organizations. This move again precipitated a confrontation between the new cadres and the old ones, and he was accused later of letting "the slave owners who had already fallen in disgrace come back and regain power." Teng contended, however, that promotion should be made step by step and not by jumping or by helicopter.[44] Urging the old cadres not to be afraid of a second downfall, he actually rehabilitated some of them to important positions. As a result, such military leaders as Yang Ch'eng-wu, Hsiao Hua, and even Lo Jui-ch'ing, and provincial leaders such as Chiang Wei-ch'ing and Chia Chi-yun had their verdicts reversed.

To provide a coherent guideline for these policy and institutional changes, Teng drafted a third document, On the General Program for All Work of the Party and the Country. This document, prepared between July and October as a general plan for the next twenty-five years, called for readjustments in nine policy areas: industry, agriculture, communication and transportation, science and technology, culture and education, public health, literature and art, the army, and the Party.[45] The General Program contained a series of statements by Teng. One of these was said to have defended the theory of productive forces by quoting one of Mao's statements: "The criterion of good or bad is whether productive forces are released." It was also alleged that this program reflected Teng's true intentions on "taking the three instructions as the key." That is, Teng directed the Party to take all of Mao's three instructions—strengthening the economy, enhancing unity and stability, and promoting class struggle—as the key to its work, for they were mutually complementary. Mao's spokesmen later charged, however, that in so doing Teng relegated the all-important class struggle to a secondary place.[46]

For Teng's part, however, he may have thought—genuinely—that his directive also accorded with Mao's instructions, for he was put to transform Mao's broadly and often contradictorily defined instructions into operationally manageable goals as he had done in 1963-64 for the SEM. His preoccupation with problem solving placed him in a position similar to that which Liu Shao-ch'i had occupied when he was trying to translate Mao's instructions for the SEM into organizational measures in 1964. What differentiated Teng from Liu and Chou, however, may have been the way he had gone about business; he was probably less diplomatic and more straightforward, a style that may have antagonized Mao's supporters. In any case, he pushed his program forcefully in July-September 1975; Liang Hsiao later charged that Teng issued four fabricated documents including statements purportedly made by Mao and Chou.[47] As a result, an intense policy and power struggle ensued between Teng and his challengers in the late half of 1975.

We now know that Mao did not approve of the way Teng conducted his post. On August 14, 1975, Mao, commenting on one of his favorite ancient novels *Water Margin*, made an indirect warning to Teng:[48]

The merit of the book *Water Margin* lies precisely in the portrayal of capitulation. It serves as teaching material by negative example to help all the people recognize capitulationists. . . . *Water Margin* is against corrupt officials only, but not against the emperor. It excludes Chao Kai from the 108 people. Sung Chiang pushes capitulationism, practices revisionism, changes Chao's Chu Yi Hall to Chung Yi Hall, and accepts the offer of amnesty and enlistment.[49]

The *People's Daily* editorial of September 4, revealing Mao's statement formally, opened the campaign against *Water Margin*. According to the critique, one of the heroes in the novel, Sung Chiang, climbed the Liang Mountains with the rebels but betrayed their cause by capitulating to the emperor, thus allowing the restoration of feudalism, that is, the old things. After Chao Kai, another hero, died, this capitulationist Sung Chiang not merely excluded Chao from the 108 heroes but changed the name of the rebel headquarters from Chu Yi Hall (meaning uprising center) to Chung Yi Hall (meaning loyalty center).[50] This argument implied Mao's fear that Teng, like Sung, might reverse his policies by capitulating to revisionism after Mao died.

Teng himself, however, professed the belief that the campaign had nothing to do with him when Hu Yao-pang interpreted it as an attack on him. Instead, Teng asked Hu to write articles counterattacking the attackers. On October 6 he planned a new journal for that purpose.[51] It should be noted in this regard that Teng's attitude toward the revolutionary model operas in particular may have touched the nerves of Chiang Ch'ing. By 1975 the eight model operas had increased to eighteen. Yet, as Ch'u Lan claimed, Teng had seen none of them; more-over, he was so upset with a new film *Ch'un miao* (Spring Sprout), depicting a gallant class struggle waged by a young barefoot doctor that he walked out, saying that it was really ultraleftist. To him these model operas presented only "one flower blooming," which actually tied the hands of writers, for in real life not everything was a class struggle. While the attack on Confucius was still going on, Teng did not hesitate to quote from Confucius when he met Helmut Schmidt: "The hege-monist often masquerades as an angel of peace to fool public opinion. But as one ancient saying goes, we must hear one's words but judge him by his deeds."[52] The campaign against *Water Margin* did not produce positive reactions from the provinces.

By contrast, another nationwide campaign on the Tachai brigade did produce a flurry of activities, both at the central and provincial levels. From September 15 through October 19 a national conference on agriculture was held in Hsiyang hsien, Shansi, with thirteen Politburo members including Teng, Hua Kuo-feng, and Chiang Ch'ing, twenty-five ministers, and sixteen provincial leaders attending. Hua made the summing-up speech calling for the establishment of Tachai-type hsiens throughout the country and for the mechanization of agriculture. Significantly, Hua also called upon the hsien Party committees to undertake a basic readjustment in their organizations.[53] After this conference was over, many provinces also held a series of follow-up meetings to study the messages of the national conference. It was about this time that Teng had completed his three directives.

Once again, Mao intervened in the policy process when the conflicts between Teng and his challengers became acute. Mao reportedly issued several instructions in October 1975 to students at Tsinghua University so that they could repudiate "counterrevolutionary educational poli-cies."[54] Apparently, Teng's opponents again sought to mobilize support from among the students for their cause. The students at Tsinghua began debate meetings on November 3 to criticize the two professors who had written to Mao.[55] Even while Teng was meeting with President Ford in Peking, these students suspended classes and carried out struggle meetings by putting up wallposters; they attacked the attempt to reverse educational policies. These activities soon spilled over to Peking University even though none was reported at that time. But the *People's Daily* of November 22 renewed the defense of the newly born things, claiming that to oppose the newly born things meant really to oppose Mao.

It was apparent that the Party's propaganda apparatus was some-how beyond Teng's control. In December the press began to report about Hsiao-chin-chuang brigade and the revolutionary model operas after a hiatus of silence. It is also important to note that the Chinese press had never fully reported Mao's two instructions on the economy and unity even though it did the one on class struggle; nor did it report Teng's directive on taking the three Mao instructions as the key. This indicates perhaps that Mao also was not in full control of the Party apparatus. Teng himself was acutely aware of this anomolous situation, allegedly saying: "Many things become acceptable as soon as Chairman Mao's words are quoted." He complained about the advent of so many campaigns, for once a campaign started, the old workers and cadres usually got hit, and as a result, more important daily chores were set aside.[56]

While Teng was struggling to salvage his consolidation program, Mao was clinging to his commitment to transformation. Yet by this time he appeared to have realized the limit of his own life, vividly expressing his anxieties in a poem he wrote for his ailing comrade Chou En-lai:

> Loyal parents who sacrificed so
>   much for the nation
> Never feared the ultimate fate.
> Now that the country has become
>   red, who will be its guardian?
> Our mission unfinished may take
>   a thousand years.
> The struggle tires us and our hair
>   is grey.
> You and I, old friends, can we just
>   watch our efforts be washed away?[57]

By the end of 1975, Teng's critics had been able to cultivate Mao's support or use his name for their cause. The 1976 New Year editorial of the *People's Daily* published one of Mao's statements that was seemingly directed at Teng's work: "Stability and unity do not mean writing off class struggle; class struggle is the key and everything else hinges on it." Citing another sentence by Mao, "New things always have experienced difficulties and setbacks as they grow," the editorial championed the achievements of the Cultural Revolution in various policy areas. Clearly, the struggle between Teng and his opponents had reached a breaking point.

The death of Chou En-lai on January 8 brought the intensifying conflicts into the open. Chou's death ended the career of a dedicated revolutionary, a competent administrator, and a skillful mediator who did much to save China from degenerating into anarchy during the Cultural Revolution and yet who did not lose Mao's confidence. But he died before his chosen deputy Teng developed an effective leadership.

Ironically, Teng's last official duty was to eulogize the passing of his erstwhile boss on January 15, 1976. He then disappeared from public life for a second time.

Once Chou's death removed the restraints, the attack on Teng became more explicit. Commenting on *Water Margin*, for example, one article issued an ominous warning: "We are telling you that if the capitulationists gain power, millions of heads will roll."[58] The *People's Daily* of February 6 stated that "an unrepentant capitalist roader" within the Party still refused to mend his ways by using the four modernizations as a big club to kill the socialist newly born things. The next day, contrary to all expectations, Hua Kuo-feng was identified as acting premier. Hua appeared to be a dark horse whose choice was the result of compromises between warring factions within the Politburo.

The appointment of Hua did not settle the matter, however, for strong support for Teng still existed. As revealed later, some cadres actually wrote letters to the Central Committee asking for Teng's appointment as premier. Others apparently tried to come up with compromises on policy and power stakes, arguing that neglecting politics and neglecting science are both wrong. Teng's opponents termed such compromises as revisionism.[59] The *People's Daily* editorial of March 10 further exposed this Right deviationist's crime by saying that he continued his black-white cat analogy under the pretext of taking the three Mao instructions as the key; by so doing, this still unnamed man sought to reverse the correct verdicts. But Mao could not tolerate such a move, for "reversing verdicts will not win the people." Yet, this editorial strictly banned any exchange of revolutionary experiences or the formation of fighting groups in carrying out the struggle against the culprit. Soon after, the press reported Mao's verdict on Teng: "This person does not grasp class struggle; he has never referred to this as the key. . . . He said he would never reverse the verdict. It cannot be counted on."[60]

Surprisingly, these attacks on Teng precipitated a violent reaction from his supporters, an open riot at T'ien An Men Square in Peking. The result was the formal purge of Teng. On April 5, 1976, the traditional Chingming Festival to mourn the deceased, when people gathered at the monument to the martyrs of the Revolution to commemorate Chou En-lai, they found the wreaths that had been placed for Chou removed. About ten thousand people then surged across to the steps of the Great Hall of the People to present a petition but they were refused. The demonstrators grew to about one hundred thousand people; some of them openly said that Teng's assumption of the Central Committee earned great satisfaction from the people throughout the country and others hoisted placards with a poem: "Devils howl as we pour our grief. We weep but the wolves laugh. We spill our blood in the memory of the hero. . . . Gone for good is Ch'in Shih Huang's feudal society."[61] Since these emotional orgies were explicitly directed at Mao, the riot was an unprecedented event in recent political history. Only when the army and militia were mobilized did the demonstrators disperse.

Shocked by this incident, the Politburo upon Mao's instruction abruptly dismissed Teng from all of his posts on April 7. The announcement charged that Teng was behind the incident and declared that "the Teng Hsiao-p'ing problem" had become one of antagonistic contradictions. At the same time, the Politburo appointed Hua as premier and the only first vice-chairman of the Party, thus indicating his official designation as the successor to Mao. Hua's rise to power marked the advent of a change in generations in the Chinese leadership. For the first time, a relatively unknown leader of the second generation was catapulted to top leadership over many experienced older leaders.

Now that Teng was categorized as a class enemy even though he was allowed to remain a Party member, the press attacked him by name. Between April 8 and 15 over five million people marched to support the Politburo decisions and to pledge their allegiance to Hua. The campaign against Teng still spoke of capitalist roaders in the leading positions of the Party. Teng failed in his consolidation program because he could neither get Mao's approval nor build his own authority. His task was made more difficult because some of the new policies, although unsuccessful, had not failed so grossly as had the GLF and as a result had developed their own vested interests over a period of time. On the other hand, the campaign directed at him also had been unable to generate another cultural revolution even with Mao's support; it was Mao's last hurrah.

The struggle against Teng seemed to have been heightened by Mao's declining health, and Mao's death threw the Chinese policy process into further uncertainty. Mao had not seen any foreign dignitaries since he met Ali Bhutto on May 27, 1976. While he was seriously ill on July 1, his spokesmen reissued his statement made for the SEM in 1964 to attack the bureaucratization of the Party: "Management is also a class struggle."[62] This was to counter the attempt to restore bureaucratic processes by emphasizing the importance of industrial management. The death of Chu Teh on July 6 ended the career of another of the older and distinguished leaders.

The earthquakes that shook Tientsin-Tangshan-Peking regions on July 28 and their aftershocks compelled the divided leadership to rally around Hua, enabling him to build his prestige by concentrating on the relief works. But on September 9, 1976, while the relief work continued, Mao died, bringing his era to an end. In mourning his death, the leadership pledged themselves to continue the cause Mao left unfinished. In his eulogy, Hua asked the Chinese people to unite by turning their grief into strength. Yet while the grief of the people was still fresh, Ch'ih Heng called upon them to continue the struggle against the capitalist roaders in the Party.[63] The leadership decided to embalm Mao's body, thus breaking the convention of cremation followed for breaking the convention of cremation followed for other heroes.

THE POLICY PROCESS WITHOUT MAO

Mao's death means the removal of the biggest inhibition on Chinese political life. The loss of his unique position and style will have a profound immediate impact on Chinese political development; his legacy to China will probably be those aspects of his Thought that are congruent with Chinese traditional heritages or useful in contemporary needs. As the leadership addresses itself to the aftermath of the Cultural Revolution and other problems arising from recent changes, it will have to strengthen the Party's institutional processes. First of all, uncertainty in several policy areas calls for some form of readjustment. For the past number of years institutes of research and higher education have been experimenting with various ways to promote egalitarian, practical, and political education. But China may have to go beyond the use of existing knowledges and resources in order to meet the requirements of her economic development and national defense. Any endeavor to improve performance necessitates some organizational measures under the Center's direction.

The succession problem is at least momentarily solved with the appointment of Hua Kuo-feng as Chairman of the Party and of the Military Affairs Committee. Since five of the nine-member Politburo Standing Committee, Tung Pi-wu, K'ang Sheng, Chou En-lai, Chu Teh, and Mao Tse-tung, died in 1975-76, the leadership must necessarily devolve on the next generation. The repudiation of Chiang Ch'ing and the radical Left from Shanghai—Chang Ch'un-ch'iao, Wang Hung-wen, and Yao Wen-yüan—shortly after Mao's death suggests that a moderate coalition will provide the Party authority to allay the erosion of public order and discipline created by natural disasters and the death of these top leaders.

The most likely mechanism to cope with the uncertainty, disorder, and divisiveness and to reconcile conflicts will be some form of codified rules and procedures. Factional conflicts have plagued post-Cultural Revolution politics in various forms. There have been conflicts between the old and the young, between civilians and the military, between regions and occupational groups, between college students and rural youth, activists and professionals, and so on. If these conflicts are not resolved peacefully, the military may again take over. Thus, one viable alternative to an anarchic mass polity or to another praetorian regime is an institutionalized polity under the Party. As shown by table 3, Chinese politics now is heading toward such a polity after a long zigzagging process.

TABLE 3

POLITICAL REGIMES IN CHINA SINCE 1959

Period	Type	Leadership	Level of Institutionalization	Level of Mass Participation
1959-66	Institutionalizing	Party	high	low
1966-67	Movement	Supreme Leader	low	high
1967-71	Praetorian	Military	medium	medium
1971-76	Institutionalizing	Mixture of Party, Supreme Leader, and military	high	medium

The changes subsequent to the Cultural Revolution and the death of Mao will tend to make Chinese policy processes more complex and pluralistic. Actually, the Chinese political system has never been totalitarian in the strict sense of the word, for there have been debates at the Center and constant feedback between policy makers and policy administrators. But the Cultural Revolution and its aftermath have further expanded the arena of central policy making by drawing societal forces and some form of public opinion into the policy-making process. As a result, the pattern of conflicts has shifted from that revolving around Mao to one having multiple actors. At the cost of some distortion, this shift can be summarized as follows: (1) from the conflicts between Mao and the elite to those among the elite themselves; (2) from those between Mao and the bureaucracy to those among several bureaucracies such as the Party, the army, the state, and the mass organizations; (3) from those between Mao and groups to those among the groups themselves; and (4) from those between Mao and professionals to those among the professionals themselves. It follows that the quality of politics will probably be substantially different; it will likely be more factional, bureaucratic, group-directed, and functional, reflecting organizational and social interests. This will involve a complex process of conflict and cooperation, bargaining and compromises; from it will probably emerge a ruling coalition and a policy consensus.

The pattern of policy processes also depends on the nature of issues. In the short run, the issues at conflict will be in the areas of science, education, culture, industrial management, and Sino-Soviet relations. In the long run, however, the coalition players will argue over more specific issues such as organization and management, the allocation of resources, and diplomatic-strategic doctrines. Depending on the issues, different coalitions may be formed. In any case, the players will pay more attention to regulative and managerial issues than redistributive and ideological ones.

What makes Chinese politics still volatile is the lack of consensus on basic issues. Chinese policy processes without Mao thus illustrate the difficulties that the Party is facing in solving problems without sacrificing its revolutionary commitment. Once the succession is resolved,[64] however, the institutionalization of policy processes will probably gain further momentum and the Chinese political system will enter a postmobilization stage. But even then, China will continue her efforts to bridge the gap between ideas and reality in her own way.

11
Epilogue:
Reflections on Mao Tse-tung

China's search for political order continues, despite the death of Mao in 1976. His efforts to regenerate mass movements by such campaigns as those to criticize Liu, Lin, Confucius, and Teng have not yet resulted in another dramatic phase of transformation. Now that he is gone, does this mean the end of the transformation and consolidation cycles? What part did he play in the Chinese policy process?

Mao has embodied Chinese history and politics since the 1930s, acting as a central and independent variable and thereby directly affecting the shifts of policy, power, and ideological configuration. In this capacity, Mao had several roles, and each in turn decisively changed the direction of Chinese history and politics.

In somewhat simplified terms, one can delineate five major roles and various subroles over Mao's long career. First, he emerged as the *Symbol of the Chinese Revolution and Nation* when he declared at T'ien An Men Square on October 1, 1949: "The Chinese people have stood up." This historical moment represented the culmination of a century in which the old Chinese society had been disintegrating and the old empire had been humiliated by foreign powers. Like many of his contemporaries, ever since the 1910s Mao had been at odds with Chinese society as well as with the foreign influences. He regarded these struggles as the basis from which he formed his ideas about human problems. He started his career as a rebel first against his own father and then against society. He was one of the founders of the Chinese

Communist Party in 1921. Soon dissatisfied with the Party's policies as directed by the Comintern in 1921-27, he went to Chingkang-shan where he and Chu Teh built the Red Army on a peasant foundation. It was during this Kiangsi period of 1927-35 that he formed his coherent ideas about the peasant revolution as a strategist and a tactician of guerrilla warfare. When Japan invaded north China, he combined this social revolution against Chinese society with the national revolution against the foreign enemy by calling for the united front with the Kuomintang during the Yenan period of 1935-49. Likewise as a revolutionary and a nationalist, he had developed a vision for China by applying Marxism-Leninism to China's reality as he understood it. His ideas led the revolution eventually to success and his leadership gave rise to the new identity of the People's Republic of China in 1949. Since this time he has filled the role of an emperor by integrating diverse elements into one nation under his symbol. In this role the cult of his personality, first developed in 1942, served as a unifying force.

Second, Mao was the *Supreme Leader* of the Party, the army, and the state. As such, he continually balanced and manipulated both the other top leaders and institutions within the Party. He assumed the Party's leadership at the Tsunyi conference in 1935 by allying with the military leaders against the International Faction. At the Seventh Party Congress in 1945 he made a broad coalition with the white-area leaders headed by Liu Shao-ch'i to exclude the International Faction from the ruling coalition. As well as founding the Red Army in 1927, he was chairman of the Party's Military Affairs Committee from 1935. He also became chairman of the Republic in 1949, and even after he yielded this post to Liu in 1959 he continued to function as the de facto head of the state and its chief diplomat. In 1959 he hurled back a major challenge by P'eng Teh-huai to his leadership for the GLF. He also purged Liu and his associates during the Cultural Revolution by making a temporary coalition with Lin Piao and his lieutenants. When his own designated successor Lin aspired to too much power, Mao did not hesitate to purge him in 1971 and tried to rebuild the Party even at the cost of calling back Teng Hsiao-p'ing. When the latter attempted to undo what the Cultural Revolution had achieved, Mao also purged Teng. In each of these struggles he chose to mobilize the masses against his political enemies, thereby developing strong ties with the people. More often than not, he operated outside the rules and procedures established by the Party, the army, and the state. Accordingly, he displayed many of the characteristics of führer-type leaders. As the Chinese used to call him, he was indeed the helmsman on whom the Chinese ship depended. In this capacity Mao exercised a supreme authority by issuing directives, resolving policy disputes, and defining the correct ideology.

Third, Mao was an *Innovator and Agitator*. He sought to change natural resources, social inertia, and human nature by seeking to conquer them or shake up their development from time to time. As an innovator, he believed that both society and human beings develop an inertia that allows a drift toward inequality and hierarchy unless there is a conscious attempt to transform them through uninterrupted class struggles. This commitment to transformation and struggle impelled him to concern himself primarily with the broad issues of revolution, equality, mass mobilization, and ideology.

This role was most conspicuous in the transformation phase of the policy cycles. He initiated or supported all of the major policies adopted during the transformation phases in 1949-76. Especially since 1955, he had taken direct charge of the transformation programs with singleminded determination, even over the opposition of the Party's majority. Without Mao there would have been neither the Great Leap Forward nor the Cultural Revolution. His principal motivation in launching these mass movements was the possibility of regression in China's revolution and development as he defined them. In this perspective, his domestic policies and his foreign policies (particularly with regard to the Soviet Union) were closely intertwined. To him, not only had Soviet revisionism not helped China's security after the Quemoy incident in 1958, but more seriously it had tried to subvert and even kill Chinese communism. To forestall this almost obsessed his thinking. In the Great Leap Forward he renewed the Party's commitment to transform the economic base and productive relations, to stress mass enthusiasm and self-reliance, and to narrow the gap between the cities and the countryside through a multifunctional approach like the people's commune. In the Cultural Revolution he sought to transform the superstructure—the power structure, education, culture, and human attitudes, again emphasizing egalitarianism and self-criticism. Until his final moment he did not relent in his struggle against the reassertion of bourgeois rights. His role was to expedite transformation and those leftist policies associated with it, for rarely did he restrain these except for the ultraleftist phase of the Cultural Revolution in 1968-71. The Chinese aptly called him "the Reddest Sun." After the Cultural Revolution he actually attempted to institutionalize the practice of dialectical struggle by writing into the Party and the state constitutions the spirit of rebellion.

Fourth, Mao was the *Final Arbiter* of policies. While he was in direct charge of the policy process, usually during the initial period of the transformation phase, he himself was the locus of power and decision. When he was not in direct charge, usually in the later part of the transformation and mostly in the consolidation phase, he stepped down to the second line of leadership and concerned himself more with broad ideological and policy problems as he did in 1960-65, and to an extent, in 1969-76. His role here was a centrist, resolving conflicting claims to policy and power. He played this role when policy adjustments went so far as to seriously undermine the socialist road by allowing the re-emergence of old social, organizational, and human inertias. In so doing, he exercised a veto power on existing policies, thus restraining rightist tendencies. His veto often became one of the most important constraints on policy making as was demonstrated by his disapproval of the trend toward *san-tzu i-pao* in the 1960s and, more recently, of Teng's attempt to readjust policies in the academic community and production enterprises.

Mao's role as the final arbiter was also made inevitable by the organization of the Party structure and his position in it. Mao often issued vaguely defined instructions and entrusted their implementation to such others as Liu, Lin, and Teng, who had to reinterpret the instructions and to devise operational measures for their implementation, often with scarce resources. Their efforts, therefore, could easily diverge from the original goals Mao had set forth. When Mao became aware of the differences, however, he vetoed their policies and initiated another period of push. Thus, Mao himself was not accountable for the implementation of his own policies. By reigning over the policy process, Mao, in effect, reshaped it even by overruling the Party's majority and consensus.

Fifth, Mao was the *Definer of Ideology*. By defining the correct ideology, Mao was able to either grant legitimacy to a policy or brand it as deviationist, for he ultimately defined the contour of the so-called struggle between the two roads. It was this extraordinary authority that enabled him to reign above the Party. When he invoked this authority, his challengers were invariably put on the defensive while his supporters could have almost a free rein in policy debates simply by quoting from Mao. Since all policy and processes had to be justified in terms of Mao's Thought, Mao's words served as policy statements. At the peak of a campaign, Mao Tse-tung Thought thus served not merely as a guide for action but as a source of quasi-religious inspiration. Hence, the Chinese people were to learn his words by heart, calling him the Great Teacher. Mao's rule in this sense was indeed the "reign of virtue," for his leadership was basically educational and oriented toward affect. Such a style was aimed at creating "a new person" imbued with Maoist virtues with the result that his pupils treated him like a divinity, as Henry Kissinger remarked after his death.[1] It was this position in Chinese society that made his mass campaigns, which were designed to change human behavior, as successful as they were.

These roles as defined are analytical distinctions; in reality, they overlapped and were not so easily distinguished. In substantive content, we can discern five major themes in all of Mao's actions: (1) egalitarianism, (2) self-reliance, (3) the mass line, (4) class struggle, and (5) thought reform. His roles and these themes combined provided the core of Mao Tse-tung Thought, which has left important legacies, both positive and negative.

How can we evaluate, then, Mao's achievements and the impact they left on Chinese politics? Although one cannot attribute everything to Mao because the actual work was always done by his lieutenants and the people, his record in history seems secure, and one can identify several accomplishments in which he had played the crucial role.

First of all, Mao's leadership was indispensable in the establishment of the unified nation with a new sense of identity. Second, equally crucial, was the founding of the centralized authority structure over a territory huge in physical size and population, although the sustaining of this authority after the Cultural Revolution has been somewhat in doubt. Third, perhaps Mao's single most important achievement would be the basic transformation of Chinese society, particularly after the agricultural cooperativization and communization in 1955-58. This firmly placed China on a socialist course that would not permit China to change her color, as Mao insisted she must not; as a result, for the first time in history the Chinese peasants became full citizens, actively participating and sharing in the benefit and cost of national development with a measure of security and dignity. Compared to many other developing countries, this is no insignificant achievement, as testified by Dr. Joe D. Wray, who has a wide experience in the Third World. He was:

astounded by the complete absence of the chronic debilitating, spirit-sapping poverty that one comes to expect on a vast scale in countries with population densities and income levels not unlike those of the PRC. . . . China's achievements in raising the basic standard of living of the overwhelming majority of poorer people are nothing less than spectacular when compared with the conditions in similar countries of the world.[2]

Last, Mao's contribution to China's economic development may be most controversial, but here again, he did make a substantial contribution in adopting a rural-oriented development strategy and laying down an industrial base that produced atomic bombs, earth satellites, and exportable oil. His foreign policy, too, enabled China to regain her rightful place in the world: his policy towards the Soviet Union has kept China from becoming another Soviet satellite and his American policy has prevented China from unnecessary confrontation with the United States. As a result, China has been able to juxtapose herself between the two super powers and yet become the champion of the Third World.

It is obvious, however, that Mao did not achieve all he had hoped for. The human cost and incidental consequences of his policies must be duly noted. Unquestionably, the use of coercion and repression alienated many people from his professed ideals. As one campaign followed another, their capricious results caused havoc in people's daily lives. The Great Leap Forward disrupted the economy, resulting in a major setback in Chinese development; the Cultural Revolution led to chaos in the political order and uncertainty in many policy areas. Despite these turmoils, he left neither a designated successor nor a process for an orderly succession; instead, the consequences of the Cultural Revolution intensified conflicts within the elite as well as in society at large.

But Mao's impact was not so much in the actual outcome as the way China's revolution and development have been carried out. His ideas were crucial in mobilizing existing knowledge and resources to a maximum use and for practical purposes, and more importantly, in distributing equitably what was available. Because of his policies the average Chinese has come to live without abject poverty, inequality, or excessive bureaucracy, earning his living according to his work and his ability.

What distinguishes Mao from other major historical figures, therefore, is not so much the tangible as the symbolic impact of his ideas and policies. His will, vision, and personality kept his revolution alive; his erratic and risk-taking style kept his observers off balance and continuously curious. He was perhaps the single most important individual affecting the lives of Chinese on the mainland. Every Chinese surely heard and repeated his words, for his works permeated Chinese life and even conditioned the mode of their language and their thought.

One of the reasons why visitors to China have been impressed is the seriousness of purpose Mao had inculcated in the mind of Chinese people. If we regard equality as the most important aspiration of the world's people in the twentieth century, China stands as its symbol as America stood for liberty in the nineteenth. However Utopian it may sound to Western minds, the bulk of Mao's Thought is likely to remain, animating those who are still struggling for equality and justice. Some of his Utopian policies failed, but such failures dramatized the kinds of dilemmas that all nations face in solving human problems. Some of his policies were contradictory in themselves; their implementation also created unanticipated consequences; as such, the balance of their benefit and their costs in terms of human well-being was not always clear. What one can reasonably say about Mao's efforts is that when comprehensive policies and incremental policies, mass mobilization and institutional processes, and ideological fervor and practical problems did not synchronize with each other, extreme political change was inevitable. Such change did not necessarily solve the dilemmas: what the change does signify is that Mao had tried to solve them. As a result, China became a place for experimenting with the most drastic large-scale public policies ever attempted.

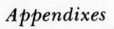

Appendixes

Appendix 1
A Comparison of the Rural People's
Commune, 1958 and Post-1962

One of the themes I have pursued in this book is that a self-fulfilling prophecy emerges in a transformation phase and then undergoes a process of reality-testing in the subsequent consolidation phase. A comparative study of the people's commune that evolved in 1958 and that emerged in 1962 after the adjustment period provides the best empirical test of the reality-testing process, for such a comparison will shed light on how the adjustments made in 1959-62 have affected the commune. This appendix, therefore, is included to illustrate in detail how the 1958 commune, defined as an ideal type of Communist organization, has been tempered by the harsh reality of China. In many aspects, the changes that have taken place in the commune provide a microcosm of the interaction between Maoist ideology and the changing conditions of Chinese reality. It is also significant that the basic features of the post-1962 commune remained largely unchanged despite the Socialist Education Movement and the Cultural Revolution.[1]

THE COMMUNES IN 1958
To compare the 1958 commune and post-1962 commune, we must start with a brief analysis of the commune in 1958, for it epitomized Maoist ideology and practice.

Size and Ownership: One, Big, and Two, Public

The salient feature was its big size and collective ownership as symbolized in the slogan, One, Big, and Two, Public (*i-ta erh-kung*), the former referring to its size and the latter to the two forms of public ownership, collective ownership and the ownership by the entire people. This was designed for an effective transition to communism; the Peitaiho Resolution stated that "people's communes are the best form of organization for the attainment of socialism and gradual transition to communism" and that "they will develop into the basic social units in Communist society."[2] As for size, several administrative villages (*hsiang*) were amalgamated into one commune; by the end of 1958, some 750,000 APCs were merged into 26,578 communes, with an average size of 5,000 households.[3] As for ownership, the commune owned the land and other important means of production.

Structural and Functional Integration: Three
Combined into One and Five Functions into One Body

A second key feature of the commune was its claim to "combine three into one" (*san-ko ho-i*), signifying its merger of political, societal (the former cooperatives), and economic institutions. As the *hsiang* (the lowest unit of government) and the cooperatives were merged into one commune, the new organization embraced the local government and other socioeconomic organizations. In addition, the militia also was incorporated into this structure, providing a combination of production labor and the military service (*lao-wu ho-i*). Later on, it incorporated all other economic organizations as well (such as the supply and market cooperatives [*kung-hsiao ho-tso-she*], the credit cooperatives [*hsin-yung ho-tso-she*], and the handicraft cooperatives), the mass organizations (such as the YCL and the Women's Federation), and even schools. This was designed to make maximum use of labor productivity and to minimize bureaucracy, so that the commune could be more amenable to the three unifications of policy, plan, and finance.[4] But the Wuhan Resolution specifically prohibited the merger of the Party and the commune.

In relation to these mergers, the 1958 commune also made an attempt at a functional integration by combining "five strata into one body" (*wu-wei i-t'i*) and "five functions into one body" (*wu-yeh i-t'i*). The Peitaiho Resolution succinctly stated:

In the present circumstances the establishment of People's Communes with all-round management of agriculture, forestry, animal husbandry, side-line occupations, and fishery, where industry (the worker), agriculture (the peasant), commerce (the trader), culture and education (the student), and the military affairs (the militia) merge into one is the fundamental policy to guide the peasants to accelerate socialist construction, complete the building of socialism ahead of time, and carry out the gradual transition to communism.[5]

Toward this goal, all separate structures dealing with the five functions were absorbed into the commune. The underlying assumption was that structural integration would lead to functional integration.

For one organization to undertake five different jobs simultaneously and to integrate them into one task was in accordance with the idea of simultaneous development and uninterrupted revolution. It was considered as the best device to eliminate the three disparities between the towns and the countryside, the workers and the peasants, and mental labor and manual labor, the last source of inequality of human beings.[6] Here, the half-study and half-work system found a proper role. This recurring emphasis on multifunctionalism in Mao's Thought was not only designed to promote egalitarianism but also to create a homogeneous, all-round man, both "red and expert," who could become a worker in a factory, a peasant on the farm, and a soldier if holding a gun.[7]

Management by Mass Mobilization:
Four Transformations

The commune supposedly facilitated mass mobilization through "three transformations" (*san-hua*) or "four transformations." The three denoted organizational militarization, militarization of action, and collectivization of life; the four included these three plus democratization of management. The commune was indeed organized along military lines; commune members, called labor troops, combined combat and production responsibilities. Militarization of action meant that everyone was to be a soldier in the communes as all commune members were burdened with the dual tasks of fighting the human enemy as well as nature. Labor competition and military training went hand in hand.[8]

Life in the commune involved a highly collectivized routine. Not only was all land (including private plots) collectivized, but the Peitaiho Resolution suggested:

Community dining rooms, kindergartens, nurseries, sewing groups, barber shops, public baths, happy homes for the aged, agricultural middle schools, "red and expert" schools are leading the peasants toward a happier collective life and further fostering ideas of collectivism among the peasant masses.

This referred to the "seven-guarantee" (*ch'i pao*) system promoted by Wu Chih-p'u in Honan whereby the commune was to guarantee the seven necessities of life: meals in the public mess halls, clothing through sewing groups, nurseries, kindergartens, "happiness houses" for the aged, dispensaries, and maternity centers. All able-bodied men and women were to work in the collective and to be paid according to their work; the regime recommended a fifty-fifty ratio between free supply and wages. As the commune took charge of commerce, the rural market also ceased to function. The Party called these "buds of communism."[9]

Democratization of management meant that all commune members, whether of the cadre or peasant, were to participate in any decisions governing management, either by attending meetings or by displaying wall posters. The cadres had to participate in productive labor and the commune members in management.[10] These four slogans represented Mao's efforts at institutionalizing mass mobilization and participation; the Party contended that they liberated production forces.

Leadership: Politics Takes Command

The commune professed to practice "politics in command." The Wuhan Resolution stated:

In running a people's commune well, the fundamental question is to strengthen the leading role of the Party. It is only by strengthening the Party's leading role that the "principle of politics in command" can be realized, that socialist and communist ideological education among the cadres and commune members and the struggle against all kinds of erroneous tendencies can be conducted in a thoroughgoing way, and that the Party's line and policies can be implemented correctly.[11]

Another aspect of the Party leadership was the Party's demand for its cadres to be red and expert. While the local Party committees propagandized the superiority of the commune, they assumed command of commune work, including its economic administration.[12]

THE COMMUNES AFTER 1962

The commune after 1962, however, revealed entirely different features in all these aspects.

Size and Ownership: One, Smallness, and One, Public

By 1962, large communes and public ownership no longer won unabated praise after the Party reorganized the command structure under the slogan of Readjusting and Consolidating. The size of the average commune after 1962 was about one-third that of 1958. The tripling of their numbers attests to this: the twenty-four thousand communes extant in 1958 had been increased to seventy-four thousand in 1963; on the average, the commune in 1958 comprised five thousand households, but only about sixteen hundred households in 1962. More importantly, by 1966 the number of production teams performing the bulk of the former commune's functions reached about five million.[13] Besides, no clear-cut divisions of commune, brigades, and teams existed in 1958; by 1962 these became distinct. The brigade comprised about two hundred households, which in most cases was equivalent to the former lower APCs. These figures are only over-all averages, however, and the size and the number vary with different local conditions.

TABLE 4

COMPARISON OF SIZE AND SCALE

	1958	After 1962
Ownership	Collective ownership + ownership by the entire people	3-level ownership
Tiers of Commune	2 tiers: Commune / Production Brigade	Commune / 3 tiers: Production Brigade / Production Team
Number of Brigades (average number of households)	24,000 (5,000)	74,000 (1,600)
Number of Brigades (average number of households)	500,000 (300)	700,000 (100-200)
Number of Teams (average number of households)	(40)	5,000,000 (20-30)

SOURCE: The number of communes is from *Ta-kung pao* (Hong Kong), November 8, 1963, p. 1; the number of brigades is from *Jen-min jih-pao* (Peking), August 29, 1963; and the number of teams is from *Ta-kung pao* (Peking), March 11, 1966.

While talk of uninterrupted revolution subsided, the Wuhan Resolution of 1958 abandoned the concept of state ownership, the "ownership by the whole people"; subsequently, the Lushan Resolution of 1959 upheld the idea of three-level ownership by the commune, brigades, and teams. No sooner had the production team become the basic accounting unit in 1962 than it came to own virtually all important means of production including land, farm tools, and draft animals.[14] Without approval of the hsien people's council, no other unit could use the land owned by the teams. The term *ownership*, however, meant essentially that the commune or brigade could no longer draw on the means of production from the teams. The teams collectively owned the forests and meadow lands and could, by contract, let their members use them.

In size as well as in ownership, then, the commune retreated to the state of the lower APCs. According to some local cadres' explanations, the team was the best unit for coordinating production and distribution, for every team got what it produced, efficiently organizing its labor and easily adjusting to the local conditions.[15] Once the size had been decided upon, it was to remain unchanged for a long period.

These changes indicated the leadership's recognition that without a comparable improvement in mechanization, a change in the relations of production could hardly liberate productivity. If China's agricultural techniques and level of industrialization remained unchanged while the Chinese regime's ideological commitment to collectivism continued, the size and ownership of the team in the post-1962 commune could serve as an optimum scale of agricultural organization.[16] This, however, was a far cry from the original assumption that the commune would lead to communism by releasing the people's productive forces.

Structural and Functional Differentiation: Three
Divided into Three and Five Divided into Five

With the division of the commune into three distinct levels and with the emergence of the team as the basic economic unit, the structural integration of the original commune ceased. In addition, the political, economic, and social organizations that had been incorporated into the commune of 1958 became differentiated again. While the commune and brigade levels continued to be essentially political organizations, the team became the productive unit. Moreover, all other economic organizations such as the supply and market cooperatives, the credit cooperatives, and the handicraft cooperatives split away from the commune structure, while other mass organizations, such as the schools and the militia units, also followed suit. Mao's experiment in search of community and a less rigid division of labor proved somewhat unrealistic. Merely integrating political, social, and economic organizations into one—in effect, seeking to merge three diverse sectors of society into one institution—did not lead to functional integration.[17]

A similar fate awaited the attempt to integrate five functions—agriculture, industry, commerce, education, and military affairs—into one organization. After the backyard iron furnaces were abandoned in 1959, the Party de-emphasized the development of industry by the commune.[18] Under the new economic policy of Agriculture as the Foundation and Industry as the Leading Factor, the Party gradually shifted its emphasis from the simultaneous development of industry and agriculture to the agriculture-first policy. The primary function the Party assigned to the commune after 1960 was agricultural production; in fact, production became the main job of the team, after the tasks of the three different levels in the commune were differentiated. And the commune level became the basic level of local government. It was a significant achievement that governmental authority penetrated to this level, in comparison to previous regimes whose authority, in most cases, did not extend beyond the hsien level. By 1962, the most important function of the commune management committee had become that of implementing the policies and laws of the Party and the central government.

Unlike the hsien government, the commune was not to formulate its own production plan, except for making proposals to the production teams, nor was it allowed to levy any local tax.[19] The hsien level still was the most important unit representing the central government. Administratively, the communes became an assistant to the hsien for implementing central policies. In assisting the hsien, the commune had to insure that its teams would meet the agricultural tax as well as grain sales quotas. The commune did not directly collect the tax and grain, but simply helped the hsien's tax and grain offices function at the commune level.[20] The commune and the brigades were specifically precluded from levying any grain (including the public reserve and welfare grains) from the teams. Since the state facilitated a unified plan for tax collection and the supply of commodities, it annually set the amount of the tax and the unified procurement the teams were to deliver, though the commune could modify the plan. The hsien sent the commune a detailed annual production plan, specifying the tax and the procurement targets that were based on the records of previous years.

As to managment of the teams, the commune management committee put forward proposals through the brigades to the production teams and coordinated the plans drafted by the teams. The committee inspected the labor and financial conditions of the teams and suggested advanced techniques mainly through demonstration plots, but in neither of these cases was it to coerce them. It could organize some concerted projects among the teams but this had to be done for mutual benefit under the principle of exchanging equal values; no labor or productive resources could be transferred from one place to another without proper compensation. Thus, in relation to both its upper and to its lower echelons, the first priority of the commune administration was to promote production so that it could meet the state plan on the one hand and the living requirements of the team members on the other.

The second major job of the commune management committee was to handle the administration of civil affairs such as population registration, marriage, law enforcement, education, and finance. Certain specialized sections and responsible chiefs fulfilled these functions; but most were agents of the hsien government; for example, the hsien controlled the public security branch and the armed forces department.

Lastly, the commune was burdened with the task of carrying out any propaganda and mass campaigns initiated by the hsien Party committee. (Since this is essentially the Party's activities, it will be discussed in that section.)[21]

The brigade management committee functioned as a small commune management committee officiating between the communes and the teams. The brigade supplemented the commune in the field of public security and propaganda. As an organization assisting the commune public security branch, the brigade had its own public security committee; as for disseminating the directives from above, most brigades had the "wire broadcast" stations. The brigade was more involved than the commune in helping the teams to improve production and management. It could sponsor some joint projects of irrigation, of forestation, and enterprises with the teams. In contrast to the commune cadres who were full-time state cadres, the brigade cadres were half-time functionaries who drew half of their income from the managerial task and the other half from their production labor.[22]

The brigade obtained its financial support from the teams, within 1 percent of a team's total output. The brigade arranged for cooperative projects among its teams, drawing an elaborate contract, which specified the benefits and compensations to be exchanged among teams. Under no circumstances, however, could the brigade draw man power and resources from the teams to the extent that it adversely affected agricultural production.[23] As the basic unit of the CCP, the general branch or branch, the brigade, assumed political leadership over the teams.

The production team management committee essentially assumed the economic function of agricultural production. It handled virtually all functions deriving from this: ownership, labor assignment, accounting, distribution, and social welfare. Team cadres were not exempt from labor, though they obtained their work points for the administrative work they did. Legally, the portion of "compensatory work points" could not exceed 1 percent of the team's total work points, although it frequently did.[24]

Thus, the commune and the brigade were primarily involved in administration and the team in agricultural production. One organization had proved unable to carry out the five functions at the same time. For example, the steel-smelting campaign mobilized so much of the labor force that agriculture suffered, for the means of achievement assigned to one goal could not be available for other goals. The commune could effectively pursue the five different goals by attending to them either in sequence or through differentiated means, not through simultaneous and undifferentiated means. The undertaking of five distinct functions by the multipurpose commune led to the neglect of its primary purpose and often to waste of time, resources, and energy, as P'eng Teh-huai pointed out in 1959 and as many subsequent investigations confirmed in 1960-61.[25]

The changes that have occurred in the commune and its affiliated structures since 1958 can also be observed in the operations of six functional systems: (1) industry and communication, (2) trade and finance, (3) culture and education, (4) military, (5) politics and law, and (6) agriculture and forestry. Since the team played such a major role in agriculture, the section on team management in that system will be discussed in detail below. This section, therefore, describes the five areas other than agriculture.

Industry and Communication

The commune level could still undertake industrial activities, but it could do so only with the consent of the teams by concluding a contract with them. The worker-peasant system widely publicized in 1964 was a case in point. Because the communes could no longer draw upon team labor or resources, commune or brigade level enterprises were mostly small and medium size; they were run either independently of the teams or by some form of contract with them. These small local industries have received wide publicity in the press, but they differed from the commune-sponsored small industry of 1958 precisely in that their management did not affect agriculture but was intended to support it.[26] Furthermore, such enterprises kept autonomous accounts and were responsible for their own gains and losses.

Where implements such as tractors were concerned, there were two forms of maintenance. First were the tractors kept by the state tractor stations and rented by the commune for a stipulated amount. Second were tractors owned by communes or brigades themselves. By 1964 about 88 percent of all tractors were maintained by 2263 stations scattered in some thirteen hundred hsiens. Reports from Liaoning indicated that the commune Party committees played a major role in tractor use; they worked closely with the tractor stations.[27]

Finance and Trade

Finance and trade in the 1958 communes were handled in three departments under the management committee: the finance department, the supply and market department, and the credit department. By virture of a January 1959 State Council decree, the government further decentralized financial administration under the slogan Two

Transfers, Three Unifications, and One Guarantee. Two transfers meant the transferring of personnel and property to the commune; all personnel of state commercial agencies and banks were transferred to the communes while funds, whether fixed or flowing, were also sent down to the communes. The three unifications meant the unified plan, policy, and management of finance and trade by the communes. Since the free markets and state commercial shops had been closed, the government attempted to employ these measures to facilitate the exchange of goods and funds within the commune. Finally, by one guarantee, the state guaranteed the commune that it could collect the agricultural tax and transfer whatever commodities it had at its disposal.[28] These measures, designed to insure the financial self-sufficiency of the commune, were never fully implemented for various reasons. For one thing, they were liable to create fragmented enclave economies in different communes. If that occurred, it would have been extremely difficult for the central government to expedite the exchange of goods and funds in accordance with the real demands and supplies on the national scale.

By 1962, all three of those departments concerning finance and trade had returned to their original organizational form. Since the commune no longer had a finance department, the hsien tax office was reactivated to collect agricultural taxes. The teams delivered the grain or other agricultural taxes to the hsien granaries located in the commune. In matters of banking, besides the People's Bank, the government established the Agricultural Bank in 1963 for supporting agriculture. In many places, the People's Bank shared its offices and cadres with the Agricultural Bank, displaying two signboards on the same door. The Agricultural Bank could grant two kinds of loans to the team: the long-term loan extending over two years charging almost no interest and the short-term loan, due within a year, charging an interest rate of 0.048 percent.[29] Whether it was short-term or long-term, rarely did the average team get such a loan.

Under the leadership of these two banks, the credit cooperatives that had been absorbed into the commune were restored in brigades to enhance mutual help among the peasants. (In some places, commune credit cooperatives existed as well.)[30] Since these cooperatives were self-help organizations, there was no national agency administering them. The peasants contributed the fund for their operating capital; in 1964, they handled roughly 60 percent of the peasants' deposits and loans. Their main function was to help those peasants experiencing financial difficulties by extending short-term loans. In most cases, one or two cadres handled the work of these cooperatives, and though they were not exempted from labor, they also worked as agents for the People's Bank and the Agricultural Bank.

Where commerce was concerned the state played the major role through its unified procurement and sales (*t'ung-kou*) programs. The government classified all commodities into three categories: the first included twenty-eight kinds of vital goods such as grain, edible oil, and cotton, which the state procured at a fixed price (*p'ai-chia*) and which were barred from trade on the free market. Production teams had to meet delivery quotas on these goods for which they were paid the fixed price. Output above the required quota that the team wished to sell also had to be sold to the state. Thus the state had a monopoly on these goods. The second category included some three hundred kinds of goods, mostly economic crops such as tobacco, peanuts, and jute, that were also procured by the state at a fixed price; hence, teams had to meet quotas on these goods as well. However, once state targets had been met, the teams could sell excess output on the free markets. The third category included all goods that teams did not have to deliver to the state; these could be freely exchanged.

The first and second categories were obviously subject to the unified state plan. Legally, the state concluded procurement contracts with the production teams for the delivery of those goods; the contracts were the important devices for facilitating the planned economy. In general, the fixed price was one-half or one-third of the market price. Up until the Cultural Revolution, the teams that went above their targets in sales to the state were rewarded with extra ration coupons for such commodities as grain, fabric, meat, and fertilizer. (These and other commodities were purchased only at the state-run shops with both coupons and money.)

The hsien commercial department directly collected categories one and two items through the supply and market cooperatives. The supply and market cooperatives were organized into a nationwide network, under the All-China Supply and Market Cooperatives general headquarters. The cooperatives had a commune office, branches in brigades and market places, and agents at the team level. On behalf of the state, they concluded the procurement contracts (*p'ai-kou ho-t'ung*) with the teams.[31] The peasants also participated in this cooperative by having a certain number of shares; they were keenly concerned with its work because it was the only agency supplying them with daily necessities and purchasing their surplus second-category products. Unlike the credit cooperatives, the supply and market cooperatives required a staff of full-time quasi-state functionaries. It was the central junction for goods flowing between the urban areas and the rural areas.

Closely related to these cooperatives were the commodities exchange conferences (*wu-chih chiao-liu hui*) frequently held between the communes themselves and among the hsien. Various administrative units organized these conferences. Not only did these conferences serve as the instrument of exchange but they also conducted fairs or exhibitions, which the PLA's Rear Service and government procurement agencies also attended to conclude various forms of procurement and supply contracts (*kung-hsiao ho-t'ung*). Another form of these conferences took place among the teams themselves or the team and other state organs for the exchange of the above-quota second- and third-category commodities at the market price.

Since the third-category goods were excluded from the state plan, they were sold on the free market. Traditionally, the rural markets (called *kan-chih* in the North, *ch'en-hsü* in Kwangtung) were held periodically.[32] With the rise of communes in 1958, the Communist authorities tried to abolish these markets, first by administrative measures and later on by allowing them to convene only once or twice a month. They replaced these markets with the commodity-exchange conference, but never succeeded in eliminating them simply because when the goods were in short supply, the black market flourished. In the beginning of 1960, the government instituted commodity shops (*huo-chan*), a variant of state-run brokers, to curb the black markets but failed again. When it became clear that the commune could not ban the exchange of goods by decree and prevent them from flowing into the black market, the government reopened the free market. The commune market management committees administered the free markets, investigating their conditions and setting the official price quotations on commodities. Peasants sold their products from their private plots and side-line occupations at the markets. Besides the third-category commodities, teams also sold their surplus second-category commodities after having met the state plan.

As suggested earlier, black market activities frequently arose within the free market despite the government's prohibitions. Although the government made continuous efforts to curb them, it never tried to eliminate them completely. In fact, the black markets performed an indispensable role: consumers could purchase there what they could not obtain either at state stores or at the free market. It is true, however, that the commune market management committees, the commune public security branches, and a mass organization called United Industry and Commerce Committee (*kung-chang-yeh lien-ho wei-yuan hui*) kept constant check on the black markets.

Clearly, the organizations concerned with the rural finance and trade became separated from the commune structure. After Ch'en Yün and Li Hsien-nien's unified plan for finance and trade was adopted in 1962, local financial organizations were incorporated again into the national system.[33] Under the principle of vertical leadership (*t'iao-t'iao ling-tao*) and horizontal leadership (*k'uai-k'uai ling-tao*), these units had to obey their immediate Party committees; at the same time, they also had to be guided by upper echelon Party organizations.[34] If disputes arose over breach of contracts or obligations among local units, the local Party committees acted as mediators to settle the conflict.

Culture and Education

The commune in 1958 sought to combine production and education, as the agricultural middle schools run by the commune or the brigade kept this principle alive. The commune also organized half-study and half-work schools that emphasized agricultural techniques and management. Tuition at these schools was low, since students worked on the school farms. The curricula included topics other than agriculture; those topics such as political subjects were studied during the winter or in regular two- or three-year courses. Graduates usually remained at their team level and became technicians, cashiers, and accountants.[35]

By 1962, all other schools, however, reverted to full-time schools, run by the hsien. Thus a two-track school system emerged: one for study and work, and the other for full-time study. The primary schools, mostly operating at the brigade level, were directly run by the hsien education department and the commune exerted little control over them. The teachers got their monthly salaries from the department, but in some places, one brigade or several brigades ran a primary school at their own expense. After graduation, the pupils either went to the hsien-run middle schools (usually located at the county seat), attended the agriculturally oriented commune-run schools, or became full-time workers at teams. Besides these regular educational organizations, the brigade conducted adult education primarily to increase literacy among the peasants.

To promote advanced techniques in agriculture, the state from 1963 on set up demonstration plots (*yang-p'an t'ien*) in the communes; in 1965, over ten thousand agronomists were working there.[36] The teams then supposedly emulated successful experiments achieved by these plots. As for other cultural activities, the hsien cultural department circulated films periodically, but some brigades maintained "people's auditoriums" where they showed films and staged plays.

Hospitals under the control of the hsien health department operated mostly at the commune seat. Because there were few regular-trained doctors, these clinics were manned by short-term trained doctors, or the Chinese traditional doctors (*chung-i*). Some brigades even ran health centers where a few nurses looked after minor cases. But whether hospitals or health centers, the peasants had to pay fees, though at nominal charges.

The Military

The hsien government had the military service department (*ping-i pu*) and the armed forces department (*wu-chang-pu*), but the commune only had the latter's branch. The armed forces department oversaw the commune militia, working closely with the commune Party committee. Organizationally, the militia usually had a separate command, independent of the regular commune administration: the regiment commanded at the commune level, the battalion or company commanded at the brigade level, and the platoon commanded at the team level, all of which were under the dual leadership of the Party and their superior organizations.[37] The platoon (*ying*) was subdivided into two separate militia organizations: the backbone militia consisting of males between sixteen and thirty, and females between sixteen and twenty-five, and the ordinary militia. Only the backbone militia received active military training and its chain of command stretched to the mobilization department of the provincial and regional military commands, leading ultimately to the army's chief of staff.[38]

The Party Cadres and Mass Organizations

As the foregoing analysis shows, the commune was organizationally incapable of integrating the five different functions, but there was one overarching organization that succeeded in this. That was the Party apparatus at each level of the commune, which controlled all other organizations. There were the Party committees at the commune level, the Party general branch or branch at the brigade level, and the small group (or Party cell) at the team level. The internal organization of the Party committee varied from one commune to another, depending on its size. In general, the commune Party committee had several functional departments dealing with political-legal affairs, organization, rural work, youth affairs, study, and propaganda, and for each of these departments a specific secretary was assigned. The brigade branch also charged its secretaries with similar responsibilities. One additional function of the branch was its direct leadership over the militia. While the commune committee met at least once a week, the branch committee met at least once every two weeks, and the team small group (or cell) met once a month.[39]

The first and foremost power of the Party committees was their decision-making prerogative. They discussed and decided almost everything before transmitting instructions to be implemented by specific organizations. The first secretary of the committee acted as the first among equals. The non-Party cadres of the management committees or of other government organizations like the supply and market cooperatives were invited to the discussions. For example, the commune director or brigade chief and their deputies attended ex officio the Party committees, whereas the Party secretaries also attended the management committees in the same capacity. In fact, the Party secretaries frequently wore two hats, serving concurrently as the commune directors or deputy-directors or the brigade chiefs or vice-chiefs. The lower the level, the greater the overlapping, for an insufficient number of qualified cadres was available to fill all the positions at each level. As a result, the peasants often called Party cadres below the commune level "omnipotent cadres" (wan-neng kan-pu). The number of Party cadres and members was proportionately small, perhaps not exceeding 2.5 percent of the population, but they were ubiquitous.[40]

The second task of the Party was the control of all other organizations. Not only did the Party committees perform this function through their overlapping membership, but they usually controlled personnel assignments in those organizations. It was generally accepted that the political-legal department or organization department of the commune Party committee and their responsible secretaries determined the appointment of all leading cadres of administrative agencies and mass organizations, whether they were elected or appointed. In 1963, there were about 1.5 million cadres of the communes and about 20 million cadres of the brigades and teams that comprised the bulk of leading cadres (ling-tao kan-pu).[41] The brigade and team cadres were called basic-level cadres (chi-ts'eng kan-pu); those working at administrative posts and who drew salaries from the State Treasury were known as administrative cadres (hsing-cheng kan-pu) or state cadres (kuo-chia kan-pu); and those who did not receive salaries were referred to as the general cadres (i-pan kan-pu).

These cadres were recruited from various sources. One study has cited eight categories: (1) old cadres who had joined the Communist guerrilla movement, (2) land reform cadres, (3) collectivization cadres and post-1955 peasant recruits, (4) army veterans, (5) young middle-school graduates, (6) cadres sent down from higher levels, (7) influential individuals from the old regime, and (8) retired cadres.[42] Among the commune cadres some were from other regions, particularly among the Party cadres, but the brigade and team cadres were mostly made up of native-born members, for any cadres from another region were likely to be unfamiliar with the local situation and, in many cases, unable to speak the local dialect.

These cadres were responsible for implementing the directives from above and representing local affairs to the higher echelons. They were the key to successful policy implementation. As the servant of the peoples, all of them had to take part in labor: the commune cadres had to work in the collective farm for at least 60 days a year; the brigade cadres had to work 120 days; and the team cadres were not exempted from labor at all. To assure that they implement Party policies, the Party required them to observe the "three grand disciplines and eight attentions."[43] The three disciplines required all cadres: (1) to implement Party and government policies and actively participate in socialist construction, (2) to observe democratic centralism, and (3) to reflect the actual reality. The eight attentions meant that cadres were: (1) to concern themselves with the masses' lives, (2) to take part in collective labor, (3) to treat the people with an attitude of equality, (4) to consult the masses and to treat them fairly, (5) to become part of the masses and never to acquire privileges, (6) to speak only after investigation, (7) to handle work in accordance with the real situation, and (8) to arouse the class consciousness of the proletariat.

In addition to meeting these standards, the cadres had to do everything to increase production and to fulfill the state plan. At the hsien level, cadres in the CCP's rural work department probably played the pivotal role in promoting agricultural production. At the commune and brigade levels, however, the first secretary assumed personal leadership of productive work, while all other Party cadres shared this responsibility. Since the hsien Party committee was preoccupied with production, members of the commune Party committees had to respond to all kinds of requests forwarded by the hsien units concerning the state of production. In 1965, when a nationwide discussion on hsien Party organization was carried out in the press, some commune Party cadres complained about the current situation, saying that the intense pressure from the hsien for greater production left little time to spend for political work.[44]

Despite the emphasis on production, the Party organizations at the commune did not neglect political work. The Party carried out propaganda and supervised the schools and various mass campaigns. Especially after the Socialist Education Movement was launched in 1963, the commune Party intensified its mass persuasion and mobilization activities.[45] The study secretary or the mass work secretary saw to it that this campaign reached into the production teams. For these activities, the local Party organizations needed the help of various mass organizations.

The training ground for the Party was the Young Communist League, which youth between eighteen and twenty-five could join. The

Party secretary in charge of the youth work at the commune and brigade level supervised the activities of the league. Below the YCL was the Young Pioneers' Corps, consisting of youngsters between seven and eighteen; the YCL supervised this corps. The Party also oversaw the women's representative congresses at the commune and brigade levels.

Amid the Socialist Education Movement in 1964, the Party began to organize the poor and lower-middle peasants at the commune; but it was only after Mao's Twenty-Three Points was transmitted in January 1965 that the poor and lower-middle peasants associations began to take shape on the provincial level. This association was supposed to become an assistant to the Party in the countryside by supervising the management committees at each level of the commune. The original intention was for the association committees to parallel the management committees.

Clearly, then, all the other organizations were to operate within the political framework of the Party, with the Party controlling them. The original idea of merging all organizations within the commune structure was not realized as the organizations became differentiated and complex; nonetheless, all of them were placed under an over-all control of the Party. By and large, there was a reversal in the allocation of power, through a recentralization of governmental power to the hsien, and a relegating of socioeconomic functions to the brigades and team levels.

Routine Management of the Production Team

The commune in 1958 sought the four transformations in management, intended to facilitate mass mobilization (organizational militarization, militarization of action, collectivization of life, and democratization of management). By 1962, however, all these four aspects either declined or entirely disappeared, and in their place, the small team enjoyed a management autonomy without resorting to military techniques.

Production

As far as productive activities were concerned, the team had replaced the commune as the basic unit. The team organized production and labor, and distributed the income that accrued from the production. In 1958, the commune likened producing crops to fighting battles. But the team's production management after 1962 was entirely different. After receiving the production target set by the hsien, the team worked out its own plan in accordance with local conditions (*yi-in-ti chih-i*). In some areas, the teams made seasonal plans and in other areas, annual plans. (Where the production brigade was the basic ac-counting unit, it naturally made the plan.) The team decided how to use land, man power, draft animals, and farm tools; it also determined when to plow and plant, and selected seeds and fertilizer. The team congress, however, passed the final plan. After approval, the team sent the plan to the brigade and the commune for additional suggestions. In setting the plan, the team management committee took into account the old and experienced peasants' opinions.[46]

As long as it met the state target, the team could draw up plans for production increase, provided that they were feasible and did not damage the natural resources. Under the policy of Grain as the Main Thing and Developing Multiple Undertakings, the team could freely develop its collective side-line jobs. It could open wasteland and exploit any resources within its boundary unless the undertakings adversely affected existing resources.[47]

Labor

In 1958, the commune divided its labor force into the full labor force and the half-labor force, the former being those who were young peasants and the latter those who were older. But this practice was suspended after 1962. In line with the socialist principle of to each according to his work and from each according to his ability, all able-bodied men or women had to work and were rewarded on the basis of their labor. All the peasants including children of eleven or twelve who contributed labor to the collective became team members.

There were two kinds of membership, however: regular and proba-tionary members. The latter included the four elements, that is, the landlords, the rich peasants, the counterrevolutionaries, and other bad elements who were allowed to participate in the collective labor and to receive income for their work just as the regular members; the only difference was that they were allowed neither to vote in the election of team leaders, nor to be elected as cadres. There was an additional obli-gation for them: they had to carry out one or two days of educational labor as stipulated by the team; they were also under constant surveil-lance by the commune public security branch and the brigade public security committee, both of which they had to report to whenever requested. As far as the regular collective labor was concerned, except for three or four days off for males and five or six days off for females per month, all members regardless of age or class status had to work on the collective farm.

The team recognized roughly two approaches in parceling out the collective work among its members: it called for assigned work (*p'ai-*

kung) for larger tasks and fixed work (*pao-kung*) for smaller tasks. The team generally followed the principle of assigning larger undertakings to its members on a rotating basis and of fixing smaller tasks to a group of four or five members with permanent responsibility (*ta-p'ai-kung hsiao-pao-kung*). Where the first approach was concerned, the team chief, in consultation with some experienced senior peasants, divided the team members into several production groups and assigned them to specific tasks. He then put the list of members' names and their work assignments on the team's bulletin board. The team had to assign suitable individuals to different jobs not only to raise labor productivity but also to satisfy his members' wish for equity. To do this, he often solicited poor peasants' views at team congresses. In general, the team used this method of assignment for grain production.[48]

The system of fixing work originated with the three-guarantee-and-one-reward or four-fix systems by which brigades assigned responsibility for work to the teams. After 1962, however, these arrangements were made between the team and its small groups. Thus, the team was allowed to assign a strip of land or a piece of work either to several small groups or to individuals in such a manner that those groups or individuals would be held responsible for the work assigned to them. If they surpassed their goal, they were entitled to receive some kind of bonus (usually in the form of extra work points).

The team adopted this system on a seasonal and temporary or permanent basis, depending on the kind of work it did. It should be noted that the Sixty Articles on Agriculture allowed this practice. What the regime tried to prevent was to assign output quotas to individual households (*pao-ch'an tao-hu*) or to divide land among them (*fen-t'ien tao-hu*), reviving in effect private farming. When the Maoists accused Liu Shao-ch'i and others of having advocated the revisionist responsibility system in 1961-62, they were referring to this *pao* system, the last item of *san-tzu i-pao* in addition to the private plots, the free market, and independent accounting by small enterprises. During the hard times of 1961-62, most communes relied upon this system of assigning production quotas or land to individual households to overcome the agricultural crisis. Even the poor peasants wanted this system, the official Party's claim to the contrary notwithstanding.[49] Only after the SEM penetrated into the countryside did these practices begin to ebb.

Even during the SEM, the practice of assigning quotas or land to small groups continued. Particularly in promoting multiple undertakings and collective side-line occupations, the team relied on this method to increase incentives. The team had to be careful to employ uniform standards in allotting land, draft animals, labor forces, and tools. And in evaluating the results, the team rigorously inspected them to make sure that small groups and individuals did not claim unearned bonuses.[50]

As for remuneration under this system, the group received a certain number of work points, which it subdivided among its members. In most cases, these small groups were set for years, although they may have been formed voluntarily. The team allowed its members to form these groups on the basis of personal ties and residential contiguity. Housewives worked near their homes to take care of their families. Those who shared a common skill, for example, in such a subsidiary undertaking as hog raising, were permitted to form their own group.[51]

In addition to the collective work, the team required its members to set aside one or two days every three months for its obligatory work in basic construction. These projects were undertaken by the commune or brigade. In general, this amounted to about 3 percent of a member's average annual working days; if it required more than that, the team paid wages from its reserve fund. The work on small-scale construction projects (such as repair of roads and dikes) yielded work points just as other farm work did.

Evaluating daily work performances involved complex procedures. In spite of regional and communal variations, all used the work point system. Variations occurred, however, in methods and standards of calculating the work points. Before 1962 when most communes had observed variants of time-rate system, the brigades awarded work points to the number of days worked in a month. Even after the team became the basic accounting unit, many teams regarded one day's work as ten work points and then set the number of basic working days per month; if a member exceeded it he got more points and if he failed to reach it, he lost some.[52]

Since it was very difficult to take into account individuals' differential labor productivity with this system, to avoid equalitarianism the teams experimented a great deal. After 1962 two forms were widely adopted; later on, a third system—the Tachai brigade model—gradually received wide publicity.

One of the two methods was the labor base-point (*lao-tung ti-pen*) system. In the Niwan commune, Kwangtung, the teams classified their members into three labor grades. For a day's work they allotted ten work points to the first grade, eight points to the second grade, and seven to the third grade.[53] Essentially a time-rate evaluation, this system nonetheless allowed the teams to take account of differential labor productivity. Its weakness, however, was the difficulty the teams faced in classifying each peasant into one of three grades. The teams did reclassify them periodically, but it was difficult to evaluate fully the actual labor performance of each member. For one thing, team members may have varied enormously in their capabilities, depending on the specific job at hand.

The more widely used method than this was the labor norm (*lao-tung-ting-e*) system. The team rated every possible piece of work in the light of its nature, the skill required, and the hardship involved.[54] Ingenuity and experience were required for the team to rationally evaluate each task—more so than in industry—because most agricultural jobs did not yield clear-cut piece rates. Those tasks for which it was difficult to establish performance norms received work points determined by the team in an ad hoc fashion. For work during the busy farming season, the team usually set higher work points than in the off season. The strength of this quota system was its taking into account each individual's ability, thereby providing incentives to exploit one's talents. Hence, the maximum development of rational labor norms increased labor productivity. The cadres and the old peasants, if they desired, also could use their experience about the quality of soil and the nature of the work.[55] But the system also had its defects. It was difficult, if not impossible, to set the proper norms for so many tasks and to assess the quality of completed work.

Neither of the two methods insured adequate quality control. Both invariably led the peasants to concentrate upon how many work points they earned, leading to "work points in command." Households with several able-bodied peasants prospered while those with few laboring members grew poorer, thus helping perpetuate class differences.

To cope with these problems the Tachai brigade came up with the model work point (*piao-ping kung-fen*) and the self-report and public evaluation (*tzu-pao kung-i*) systems in 1963.[56] As Ch'en Yung-kuei, secretary of the Tachai brigade Party branch, explained, the brigade's work-point recorder registered each member's work and the number of days he had worked every month. At the end of the month, the brigade singled out as a model a peasant who had not only worked well but who also exhibited the best political attitude, and decided how many work points he should get for a day. Using this pace-setter as a guide, each brigade member then evaluated and reported what he thought he deserved. Then, all the members publicly discussed each other and finally decided upon their work points case by case. (This method was widely publicized in March 1966, when the exhortations for more political work and the study of Mao's Thought gained momentum.) Clearly, this system did provide incentives for political activists. The rationale was for income to be allotted by the community not only on the basis of merit but also on the basis of service rendered to the entire community. While this wage system might reduce the peasants' concern for work points and prevent wide wage differentials, it could gloss over the differences of individual productivity; and because of the difficulty of measuring each member's political contribution, it could also reduce work incentives.[57]

Teams other than the Tachai brigade also awarded work points to their members for their participation in the political meetings called by the brigade or the commune. Interviews reveal that the peasants were very reluctant to attend such meetings without getting work points; even if work points were given, if they had a choice between working or attending such meetings, they would choose to work, for they tended to dislike struggle or criticism meetings, which made them feel ill-at-ease. Yet precisely to de-emphasize material incentives, the Party asked all the communes to learn from the Tachai brigade.

Whichever method the team might adopt, the team's recorder (chi pen-yuan) noted each member's work points in books made public every month. He also noted a member's work points in a work-point handbook (kung-fen chieh) kept by the peasants. Where disparities existed between the recorder's books and each member's handbook, the team chief would investigate the matter. If the team adopted the labor-norm system, the leaders of each production group established the work points earned by each member and reported them to the recorder. The team also awarded work points for the collection of fertilizer, but for the sake of convenience, the recorder kept a separate account for these fertilizer work points. The actual value of a work point, however, was determined at the end of the year when the share of distributable income for team members was computed. Since this varied with teams, the value of a work point also differed from team to team.

Distribution and Accounting

The commune of 1958 intended to pay the bulk of its members' income in the form of guaranteed supplies, with supplementary income in the form of wages. When the commune still ran the public mess halls, it really collectivized every facet of human life by the seven-guarantee system. But by October 1959, Li Hsien-nien stressed the socialist principle of distribution that each should get according to his work and ability. And in 1960, most of the seven guarantees were denounced as being errors of "Communist styles."[58]

By 1962, such extensive collectivism ceased to exist, and in its place, the team emerged as the autonomous unit of distribution and accounting.[59] Since the final computation of distributable income awaited the end of each fiscal year or at least the autumn harvest, the team made advance distribution of food grain (*kou-liang*) generally twice a year: after the summer and autumn harvest or whenever requested. All of these outlays were recorded as advance debit by the accountant (*k'uai-chi*).

The team distributed its income according to the principle that the interests of the state, the collective, and the individuals were to be considered in a proper ratio. The first care was always its duty to the state and to the collective's accumulation fund before distributing grain and available funds to its own members. State policy called for the team to consider the state first and then the collective, and the collective first, then the individual.

First of all, the team set aside grain to meet the agricultural tax (*nung-yeh shui* or *kung-liang*) and the unified procurement quotas (*t'ung-kou liang* or *kou-liang*). Although the tax currently has been set at 15.5 percent of the average output in a year, in Kwangtung it has been fixed at roughly 10 percent of the 1961 output.[60] As for the grain procurement, the quantity that the team had to sell to the state at the fixed price was generally about the same amount as the tax. But the actual figures varied with localities. For example, in 1966, a team in the Yangtan commune near Peking paid 6.5 percent of its total output in taxes, whereas the Mei-chin-mingyeh brigade of the Hsi-hu commune, Hangchow, paid 7 percent in 1965. Approximately, the amount of grain that the team contributed to the state ranged from 20 percent to 40 percent of its total income if the tax and procurement were combined and the estimated value lost in the procurement due to the difference between the fixed price and the market price was taken into consideration.[61] If a team was unable to meet state requirements due to natural disasters, it could petition the hsien government for an exemption.

The agricultural tax comprised about 7 percent of the entire government revenue.[62] But grain from the tax and the procurement program made up one major source of grain supply to the urban population. And many agricultural crops—either raw or processed—made up exports. The state, of course, encouraged the teams to sell more grain to the state. The income for the grain sale went into the team's treasury, but it was customarily deposited in the People's Bank. When the team delivered the grain tax or the procurement grain to the hsien granary, a receipt was made in triplicate: one for the granary itself, one for the team, and one for the bank. As for the cash from grain sales, the team usually used it for production expenses rather than distributing it to the members.

Secondly, after meeting obligations to the state, for the interest of the collective, the team deducted production expenses, reserve grain (*chu-pei liang*), the public accumulation fund, (*kung-chi-chin*), and the welfare fund (*kung-yi-chin*).[63] In theory, the remaining part of the team's income was distributable. But the Party demanded that the team set a proper ratio between its accumulation and distribution, encouraging neither little accumulation and much distribution nor much accumulation and little distribution. The largest item in the collective category was for such production expenses as seeds, fertilizers, insecticides, tractors, farm implements, and draft animals. The ratio of these expenses ranged from 20 to 30 percent of the total income, depending on the situation.

Next came the reserve grain, constituting 1 or 2 percent of the total *distributable* grain, but its precise amount was adjusted, depending on the size of each harvest.[64] Comparable to this, there had been mobilization grain (*chi-tung liang*) kept by the administrative units at and above the brigade level before 1962; but after that year, they could no longer levy any grain from the teams. The team used the reserve grain for assisting needy households, especially those five-guaranteed households (*wu-pao hu*), that is, the disabled, the childless, old widowers, widows, and orphans; and it also provided some subsidies and loans in emergency cases. After the SEM, the Party urged teams to get approval of the poor and lower-middle peasants in determining the amount of the reserve grain to be distributed so that it could be used for the poor.[65]

The team also decided how much to allocate to the public accumulation fund within the set range of 3 to 5 percent of the total distributable income. This fund financed the wages for basic construction, the contribution to the brigade, and the subsidiary work points (*fu-chen*) to be given to its cadres for their managerial work. The welfare fund, not exceeding 2 or 3 percent of the total distributable income, helped the sick, took care of accidents, and provided for sports and entertainment.[66] Together with the reserve grain, this fund was also used to provide those who had no means of support with five guarantees—food, clothes, shelter, other necessities, and funerals. But after 1959, with the renewed vitality of family life and the stress on work points, the team provided only minimal social insurance and welfare to its members. Each family provided for its own children, ill, aged, and disabled. Since the team's assistance was limited, households with few laborers and many dependents suffered most. The team could petition the upper echelons (including the brigade, the commune, and the hsien) for assistance to the needy, yet rarely did it get any subsidies, and when it did, the amount fell short of the need. Moreover, when the Party called for self-reliance of teams and condemned requesting state help, the team was reluctant to seek such help.

Finally, after deductions for the tax and procurement sale, and the collective funds (reserve grain, accumulation, and welfare fund), the remainder was available for distribution, the size of which varied among teams. On the average, it ranged from 30 to 60 percent of the total income.[67] Before 1962, most teams divided their distributable grain into two parts: the basic food-grain (*chi-pen kou-liang*) and the work point-food grain (*kung-fen kou-liang*). The Revised Sixty Articles on Agriculture also recommended this method. According to this method, the team first provided the basic food-grain to all people in the team, to meet basic food needs regardless of whether they worked or not. The remaining grain was then distributed to laborers on the basis of work points earned. The ratio of the former to the latter was left to the team to determine, but seven to three was most common.[68]

After 1962, however, most teams suspended the basic food-grain and began to distribute all the grain solely on the basis of work points while subsidizing indigents by drawing from the public accumulation grain reserve and the welfare funds. For grain, therefore, the peasants had to rely upon the work points that they obtained from working on the collective farm. To meet the team members' need for cash, the team also distributed any income available from its subsidiary production or other special crops to its members. As most teams took up monoculture —grain production—as the source of their income, the grain cultivation alone could hardly meet its members' thirst for cash. To obtain cash, therefore, most peasants had to resort to their private plots or family side-line occupations.

How did a team carry out its accounting? At the end of the year, the team actually computed the value of each work point and accordingly figured out its members' net income. The team determined the value of one work point by dividing its entire distributable income by the total sum of work points earned by its working members. And when each member multiplied the value of one work point by the total number of work points he had earned, he got the share of his own income.

$$\text{Peasant A's Annual Income} = \frac{\text{The Total Distributable Income of an Accounting Unit}}{\text{The Total Number of the Work Points Gained by the Members}} \times \text{The Number of Work Points Gained by Peasant A}$$

In general, the team paid these wages by 50 percent in kind and 50 percent in cash.[69] It seems generally accepted in China that a peasant needs at least 1 catty (*chin*) of grain a day for his basic food. Depending on the actual situation of each team, however, the average peasant rarely received more than 360 catties of grain and around one or two hundred yuan of cash a year. The precise ratio of distribution between the state, the collective, and the individuals also varied from team to team; one example is given in table 5.

TABLE 5

SECOND TEAM OF BAQUING BRIGADE
INCOME AND DISTRIBUTION, 1964

Grain Income (in yuan)	Expenditure	Amount (in yuan)	Percentage of Expenditure
33,950	Production	13,124	38.6
	Agricultural tax	2,207	6.5
	Reserve fund	1,697	5.0
	Welfare fund	330	1.0
	Reserve grain	1,488	4.4
	Distribution to members	15,104	44.5
33,950	TOTAL	33,950	100.0

SOURCE: *Peking Review*, no. 13 (March 25, 1966), p. 16.

For efficient management, the team had to keep careful and fair accounts. It was incredibly complex to set up work norms and to calculate the work points that so concerned team members. For this reason, all expenditures were carefully regulated; any important purchases had to be discussed by the team congress. On the other hand, the accountants and cashiers (*ch'u-na yuan*) could veto any expenditures that regulations prohibited.[70] Besides these two cadres in charge of finance, the custodian (*pao-kuan yuan*) took care of the team's grain, tools, and other materials. Also, the team chief or his deputy supervised the financial and custodial work, though he could not directly control cash and goods. Neither could the brigade or the commune meddle in the team's finance except for soliciting reports. As a device to prevent embezzlement, the accountant and the cashier each kept two identical books for cash and goods; only when the accounts in both books were found identical was an outlay made.

Despite all precautionary measures, if the team chief and the financial cadres collaborated, no adequate safeguards prevented them from taking advantage of their posts. Furthermore, there were few incentives for being cadres, for the cadres were neither treated differently nor guaranteed job security. On the contrary, being cadres meant financial sacrifices and troubles. As a result, such instances of corruption among the cadres as exchange of gifts, building private houses, and taking public funds were widespread.[71] How seriously the peasants were concerned about financial matters was shown by the request in 1965 by many team members for the abolition of the existing double-entry accounting because it was too complicated to understand, so much so that one accountant spent half a day to locate a single error.[72]

Responding to these demands, in October 1965, the Ministry of Agriculture, the Ministry of Finance, and the People's Bank cosponsored a national conference on commune financial work. This conference reaffirmed the principles of democratic management in financial affairs and called upon the poor and lower-middle peasants to supervise team finance. The conference made three important suggestions: (1) the single-entry system separately registering credits and debits, cash and goods, would be simpler than the double-entry system (it did not recommend, however, the outright abolition of the double-entry system); (2) coordination between the accountants, the cashier, and the custodian must be improved; and (3) all accounts should be periodically made public. After this meeting, most teams kept separate books for distribution of goods, cash, property, and work points. Of these, the teams made public (on its public bulletin board) every day the four accounts directly concerned with its members: (1) the receipt and outlay of goods, (2) the receipt and outlay of cash, (3) work points, and (4) fertilizer work points.[73] Also added to these was a more rigorous method of supervision over those accounts by making it obligatory that all accounts had to be approved by the small group of the poor and lower-middle peasants. In some teams, any expenditure over five yuan required the team congress's approval.[74]

These measures suggest that management at the team level indeed was democratic. For not only did the team members have their say over financial matters, but they also participated in making any decision that directly affected their own lives.

The Private Sector: The Individuals and Families

It is important to ascertain how the individual and his family fared in such team management. They had several legitimate rights in the team. They were entitled to the private ownership of such necessities as houses, furniture, clothing, bicycles, and sewing machines; they freely disposed of their bank deposits and credits, all of which were not to be confiscated by any persons or authorities. In addition, they owned their own farm tools, equipment, and other small-scale production materials. Insofar as these private properties were concerned, the term *own* truly made sense, for they could lawfully sell or rent them out. If private houses were confiscated for reasons of public construction, the owners had to be paid appropriate compensation, and at the same time, other residences provided.[75]

Besides private property, the team also granted another series of rights to its members. First, it assigned the private plots (*tzu-liu ti*) to them, generally within the limit of 5 to 7 percent of the entire arable land; once this was set, the ratio was not to be changed for a long time. In reality, many teams exceeded this ratio, reaching over 8 percent in some places.[76] Similarly, the team might allot bare mountains to its members so that they could cultivate there. With approval of the commune and the brigade, it also could allow its members to cultivate wastelands within the limit of 5 to 10 percent of the whole team area unless such cultivation affected natural resources. The team adjusted the size of the private plots allotted to its members, but in most cases they remained constant.

By making best use of their private properties and plots, the individuals thus could develop various forms of private side-line occupations. Families were allowed to raise any domestic animals except draft animals and to engage in handicrafts such as knitting, sewing, and embroidering. They were free to undertake such activities as fishing and raising silkworms and honeybees. Fruit trees existing around the private houses belonged to the families. These private properties and plots, together with the family side-line jobs, all provided individuals and their families with legitimate outlets for seeking their private interests. As the team could hardly meet their demands for diverse goods and particularly their demands for cash, these private undertakings became an integral part of the team system. With these allowances, the family system that was disrupted in 1958 returned to the pre-Leap pattern. All of this was possible because the Party's rural policy permitted such practices. In fact, the Party encouraged family side-line occupations as a supplementary part of the socialist economy.[77] The teams were asked to render every available assistance to them.

Another indispensable institution contributing to private interests was the free market. Ever since it was reopened in 1960, the free market attracted products from the private plots and the family side-line occupations. With the exception of category one and a portion of category two items, the remainder could be traded on the market. Neither the collective nor the state could confiscate such products or levy taxes on them. State agencies such as the supply and market cooperatives and handicraft cooperatives were to assist the peasants' side-line development by providing them with funds and markets. The portion of income the peasant families made from these private undertakings ranged from 20 to 30 percent of their total earning.[78] The peasants themselves aptly described this fact when they used to say: "Depend on the collective for food and on oneself for cash."

Hence, peasant income came from two sources—the team and private undertakings—and so did their income differentiation. The most important source of income, covering some 80 or 70 percent of the total, came from their labor on the collective farm as calculated in work points. Where the income from the private undertakings as well was concerned, the size of the labor force made quite a difference because most teams allotted private plots on the basis of the number of the labor force each family contributed to the team. The number of laborers and their productivity, then, were the two key determinants of income differentials. Accordingly, those families who had more laborers and higher productivity (i.e., more working adults) earned higher income than those who had fewer laborers and lower productivity (i.e., more old men and children but few working adults).

Some other factors also caused income differentials. Families with larger homesteads could cultivate more. Some possessed more farm implements to cultivate their plots, and others had special skills or managerial acumen in a particular kind of side-line occupation such as hog raising. Indeed, it often turned out that the former landlords and the rich peasants happened to have not only more of those large homesteads and other productive materials, but they and their offspring also had more talents and were healthier than others. Since these people had lived better in the past, they also had more relatives in the cities who might remit some money to them. Aside from this, in Kwangtung and Fukien, peasants who received money from overseas Chinese relatives lived a far better life.

In other words, sources of class differentiation existed even after capital (land in this case) had been expropriated. In fact, the official class division remained unchanged even after the Land Reform Law of 1951. Yet after the landlords and the rich peasants were deprived of their land, the middle peasants benefited most from collective farming: they became economically better off simply because they had larger, healthier families. This was why Mao, in 1955, redivided the middle peasants into two groups: the well-to-do middle peasants (*fu-yü chung-nung*) and the common middle peasants, giving rise to the poor and lower-middle peasants classification that he regarded as the backbone of revolution.[79] Despite frequent mobilization of these poor and lower-middle peasants in political campaigns, their life had not changed essentially, insofar as their economic conditions were concerned.

Because, in part, former landlords and rich peasants were still subjected to forced labor for a few days a month, they could not earn better income even if they had more laborers. But the well-to-do peasants still led the best life, economically speaking, as long as income was solely determined by labor. Next came the former landlords and the rich peasants, who ironically lived better, at least in material terms, that the poor and lower-middle peasants because of their residual benefits. The labels "landlords" and "rich peasants" had long since lost their *economic* denotation while retaining their political significance. Since the chances for the comeback of these class enemies were slim, class enemies to the peasants meant not only the physical presence of those classes but also the rise of a new class, the well-to-do peasants, who might well become like the old enemy. When Mao exhorted the peasants: "Never forget class struggle!" perhaps he was asking them never to forget their old sufferings so that the peasants could remain alert against the rise of a new class enemy. The poor peasants did benefit from the collective economy in that they were paid according to their labor; in this sense, their exploitation ceased. Not only for ideological reasons but also for practical purposes, however, the Party regarded the poor and lower-middle peasants as its class base in the countryside because they constituted over 60 percent of the rural population.

Clearly, the above description of production arrangements, labor organization, the distribution system, the accounting procedures, and family enterprises reveal that team management was not a simple matter of mass mobilization. Instead, for production, after 1962, the commune depended upon the team, which had developed a set of complex and institutionalized procedures.

Leadership: From Politics in Command
to Economics in Command

In 1958, under the slogan of Politics in Command, the commune Party committee assumed all functions including economic administration and management. Since such political mobilization disrupted economic administration, the Party soon curbed excessive mobilization to restore the economic order. The adjustments undertaken by the Party in the communes led to decentralization of authority, structural and functional differentiation, and team autonomy. Those changes resulted from the Party's preoccupation with agricultural production. As Li Ching-ch'üan, who had been so active in the communization of 1958, allegedly said in 1961: "Production should come first and politics second. Give prominence to politics? No, we should give prominence to fertilizer because it can solve problems."[80]

The exclusive attention to production in the communes was amply documented in 1965 during the Hsien Committee's Revolutionization campaign. As one commune Party secretary complained, the hsien Party committee demanded so many production statistics that the commune leaders had to spend all their time supplying such information.[81] In the wake of the 1959-62 adjustments, the primary concern of communes had to be production. But this eventually clashed with the desire of putting politics in command. In 1965 when the Kwangtung Provincial Committee convened a conference for the cadres above the brigade level to discuss the relationship between politics and production, the session participants spent all their time discrediting such arguments as: "politics cannot produce rice; production cannot be delayed overnight but politics may wait till next year; and production shows results in quantity but political work cannot be measured by a yardstick."[82] (Despite the Cultural Revolution, then, the commune described here has remained intact; furthermore in 1972 the regime renewed its commitment to it.)[83]

THE COMMUNE AS A MICROCOSM OF CHINESE COMMUNISM

The communes after 1962 had abandoned all the innovative features of the communes in 1958. The changes represented a microcosm of Chinese communism, for they concretely reflected the effects of the retreat from and adjustment to the GLF during 1959-62. Seen in this light, three points can be made.

First, the divergence between the Party's official stand on the commune and its actual policy implementation became apparent. For despite the Party's faith in the commune reaffirmed at the Tenth Plenum in 1962, the original form of the commune had disappeared. Therefore, local cadres became accustomed to interpreting loosely the Party's ideological pronouncements, adapting directives to their specific conditions. Second, the communes and teams assigned primacy to agriculture and gave secondary attention to other sectors. As priorities were set in this sequential order, first one thing and then another, the multifunctional structures of the 1958 commune became redifferentiated. Third, the team's routine administration and management procedures generated a momentum of their own through the operation of complex organizations instead of ad hoc arrangements.

These changes can be attributable to the Party's production policy in 1959-62. In 1958 Mao had sought to structure the commune in such a way as to provide a maximum practice of equality through a comprehensive mobilization of resources. But this policy had been found unworkable, at which point the Party sought to raise efficiency and productivity in the communes. To do so, the Party accepted an incremental utilization of resources as an alternative strategy. But these measures inevitably undermined Mao's political goals for the country-side.

To cope with the adverse consequences of such measures in the commune, Mao called for class struggle in 1962. Thus, the communes after 1962 began to reveal two contrasting qualities: a routine management continued at the local level while Mao stepped up ideological indoctrination at the Center. These inconsistencies reflected the diverging leadership orientations within the Party that gradually turned into open conflicts between Mao and the Party Center in 1963-65.

Appendix 2
Glossary of Chinese Terms and Phrases

Cheng-feng 整風 [Party rectification]. An abbreviation of *cheng-tun tang-ti tso-feng* (整頓黨的作風).

Ch'ien-hsien 前綫 [Frontline]. The theroetical journal of the Peking Municipal Party Committee before the Cultural Revolution.

Chung-yung 中庸. Mencius's concept of the Golden Mean; it means seeking a middle way in human affairs.

Fa 法 [the law]. The Legalist concept of law, meaning the external control of human behavior through force and regulation.

Fan mao-chin 反冒進 [reckless advance]. Teng Tzu-hui's characterization of Mao's agricultural collectivization policies in 1955-56.

Fan-mien ciao-yuan 反面教員 [teacher by negative example]. A Maoist concept that one can also learn from bad examples.

Hai Jui pa-kuan 海瑞罷官 [Hai Jui Dismissed from Office]. A play written by Wu Han in 1960, portraying an upright Ming official, Hai Jui, who was dismissed by the emperor, thus depicting P'eng Teh-huai's dismissal by Mao in 1959.

Hsi-t'ung 系統 [systems]. The functional line of specialization cross-cutting Party, state, and mass organizations.

Hsia-fang 下放 [transfer downward]. The practice of sending cadres down to the basic level for investigating and participating in labor.

Hsiang 鄉 [the township]. The basic level of administration before communization in 1958.

Hsiao kuang-po 小廣播 [little broadcast]. An unofficial means of communication, which is transmitted from person to person.

Hsien 縣 [the county]. The administrative level above the commune.

Hsin-sheng shih-wu 新生争物 [the newly born things]. Referring to innovations of the Cultural Revolution.

Hsing-tso shih-yu 形左實右 [Left in form but Right in essence]. Sabotaging Mao's directives while paying lip service to them.

Hsüeh-hsi yü p'i-p'an 學習與批判 [Study and Criticism]. The new theoretical journal of the Shanghai municipal Party committee started in October 1973.

Hung-ch'i 紅旗 [Red Flag]. Theoretical journal of the CCP Central Committee.

Hung wei-ping 紅衛兵 [Red Guards]. The organization of the youngsters who served as the vanguard of the Cultural Revolution.

I-ku feng-chin 以古諷今 [satirizing the present by means of the old]. Criticizing the current state of affairs in the guise of ancient events.

Jen-min jih-pao 人民日報 [The People's Daily]. The press organ of the CCP.

Jen-min kung-she 人民公社 [people's commune]. The basic level of administration in the countryside.

Ke-chi fu-li 克己復禮 [Restraining Oneself and Restoring the Rite]. The Confucian practice of exercising self-restraint by observing the rites as elaborated in the Confucian classics.

Kuang-ming jih-pao 光明日報 [The Bright Daily]. The Peking paper specializing in intellectual discussions.

Li 禮 [the rites]. The Confucian concept of internal control of human behavior. By following the rites, one is expected to act properly.

Mao-tun 矛盾 [contradiction]. In Maoist concept, conflicts in interests and ideas.

Mou 畝. Measure of land area; 6.6 *mou* equals one acre.

Ming-ling chu-yi 命令主義 [commandism]. The "subjective" error of ordering people around without consulting with them.

Nan-fang jih-pao 南方日報 [The Southern Daily]. The press organ of the Kwangtung provincial Party committee.

Niu-kui ssu-shen 牛鬼蛇神 [ghosts and monsters]. A derogatory reference to those who have criticized Mao's policies in the guise of academic or artistic discussions.

Pao-chia 保甲. A traditional form of village political organization for security; 100 households were organized into one *chia* with ten *chia* forming one *pao*.

Pao-kung 包工 [fixing output quota or work]. A sort of contract by which a productive unit entrusts work to individuals or a group of individuals so that they can be held responsible.

Pen-wei chu-yi 本位主義 [departmentalism]. An "empirical" error of forming factions and cliques.

P'i-lin p'i-kung 批林批孔 [criticism of Lin Piao and Confucius]. It started officially in February 1974.

San-chia ch'un ch'a-chi 三家村札記 [Notes from a Three-Family Village]. The title of the newspaper column that Wu Han, Teng T'o, and Liao Mo-sha wrote in 1961-64, criticizing Mao's policies.

San chieh-ho 三結合 [three-way alliance]. Refers to the combination of the military, cadres, and the masses in forming Revolutionary Committes; it also refers to the combination of the old, the middle-aged, and the young in placing leaders since 1973.

San-ho yi-shao 三合一少 [three reconciliations and one reduction]. Reconciliation with the Soviet Union, the United States, and other reactionaries, and reduction of aid to revolutionary movements; this refers to the Maoist charge that Liu Shao-ch'i had advocated such revisionist foreign policy in the 1960s.

San-shang t'ao-feng 三上桃峯 [Three Visits to Peach Peak]. A Shansi play singled out in January 1974 as a "poisonous weed," allegedly depicting the records of Liu Shao-chi's wife Wang Kuang-mei in the Socialist Education Movement in the early 1960s.

San-tzu yi-pao 三自一包 [the extension of the private plot, free market, and private enterprises, and the fixing of output quota to the household]. Revisionist economic policy in the 1960s.

Ssu-ch'ing 四清 [four cleanup]. Initially it referred to cleaning up in account books, warehouse, property, and work points in the commune; it was transformed later into the Socialist Education Movement.

Ta-tzu pao 大字報 [big character posters]. Wall posters protesting against certain policies or reporting about a given situation.

Tang-ch'uan p'ai 當權派 [those who are in authority]. The Establishment.

Tang-hsing 黨性 [Party character]. *Partiinost* in Russian; the concept that every Party member should observe certain Party rules.

Yang-feng yin-wei 陽奉陰違 [feigning compliance]. Literally, it means "obeying in the light but sabotaging in the dark."

Appendix 3
Who's Who

Chang Ch'un-ch'iao 張春橋, a secretary of the Shanghai Municipal
Party Committee until 1966. He helped Yao Wen-yüan publish the
article criticizing Wu Han's play on Hai Jui, which marked the
beginning of the Cultural Revolution. He became chairman of the
Shanghai Revolutionary Committee in 1967, was elected to the
Politburo in 1969, became first secretary of the Shanghai Party
Committee in 1971, and was elected to the Politburo Standing
Committee in 1973. In 1975 he became second deputy premier and
director of the army's political department. He was purged after
Mao's death in 1976.

Chang P'ing-hua 張平化 (1903-), first secretary of the Hunan
Party Committee and an alternate member of the Central Committee since 1958. In 1966, he became a deputy director of the Propaganda Department under T'ao Chu; he became chairman of the
Hunan Provincial Revolutionary Committee in 1967 but lost in
1970 during the antiultraleftist campaign.

Chang Wen-t'ien [Lu Fu] 張聞天 (1898-), one of the Twenty-
Eight Bolsheviks. He became general secretary of the Party in
1935-36, was vice-minister of foreign affairs from 1949, elected as
an alternate member of the Politburo in 1956, criticized Mao's
policies in 1959, as did P'eng Teh-huai. He was purged after the
Lushan conference of 1959.

Ch'en Hsi-lien 陳錫聯 (1913-), a veteran of the Long March. He
served in Liu Po-ch'eng's Second Field Army, was commander
of the Shenyang Military Region in 1959-73, elected to the Polit-

308

buro in 1969 and 1973. In January 1974 he became commander of the Peking Military Region.

Ch'en Po-ta 陳伯達 (1904-), editor of *Hung-ch'i* since 1958. He was head of the Cultural Revolution Group in 1966, elected to the Politburo Standing Committee in 1969, and allegedly joined Lin Piao's forces against Mao by proposing a state chairmanship at the Second Plenum in August 1970. He was purged in 1971.

Ch'en Yi 陳毅 (1901-1972), one of China's ten marshals. He commanded the New Fourth Army in 1941, which later became the Third Field Army, and was minister of foreign affairs in 1958-72. During the Cultural Revolution he was criticized by Red Guards for the liberal cultural policy he defended in 1962.

Ch'en Yün 陳雲 (1901-), a top economic expert. He served as director of the Party's Organization Department before 1949, managed China's economy in 1949-58 as a member of the Politburo Standing Committee. He opposed Mao's Great Leap Forward in 1958. In 1962, he briefly came back to the Party's policy-making arena but since then has not been active. He was elected a member of the Central Committee in 1969 and 1973.

Ch'en Yung-kuei 陳永貴 , first secretary and director of the famous Tachai brigade in Shanshi. Since 1963 he has been popularized as a hero for implementing Mao's policies. He was elected to the Central Committee in 1969 and to the Politburo in 1973.

Ch'i Pen-yü 戚本禹 , a young radical who challenged the Propaganda Department and Liu Shao-ch'i in 1966-67 on behalf of Chiang Ch'ing. He became a member of the Cultural Revolution Group in 1966. He was associated with the "ultraleftist" May 16 corps in 1968 and subsequently purged.

Chiang Ch'ing 江青 , Mao's wife since the 1940s. She was an actress in Shanghai during the 1930s. While in Shanghai in 1963-65, she masterminded the attack on Wu Han that set off the Cultural Revolution. As first deputy head of the Cultural Revolution Group, she was leading Red Guard groups during the Cultural Revolution. After the campaign to criticize Lin Piao and Confucius started in February 1974, her public activities became increasingly prominent; she is believed before Mao's death to have been in charge of education and culture. She was purged after Mao's death in 1976.

Chiang Nan-hsiang 蔣南翔 (1915-), minister of higher education and president of Tsinghua University until 1966. He was an alternate member of the Central Committee until 1966 and played a crucial role in adjusting educational policies in 1961-62. He was purged in 1966 after he was attacked by Red Guards.

Ch'iao Kuan-hua 喬冠華 (1914-), minister of foreign affairs. He was a journalist in the 1930s and served as secretary to Chou En-lai when he negotiated with the Kuomintang during the 1940s. After 1949, he frequently accompanied Chou on foreign trips. He became minister of foreign affairs in 1974.

Chou En-lai 周恩來 (1898-1976), premier and member of the Politburo Standing Committee. He became a member of the Politburo in 1927 and managed until his death in 1976 to survive all intra-Party struggles. During the 1930s and 1940s he was political commissar of the Red Army and the chief Communist negotiator with the Kuomintang and the U.S. From 1949 on, he was China's chief diplomat, well-known and respected by Westerners. During the Cultural Revolution he was deeply involved in mediating feuds among struggling factions. He was elected to the Politburo Standing Committee in 1969 and became the second ranking vice-chairman of the Party, delivering the political report to the Tenth Party Congress in 1973. At the peak of the anti-Lin and Confucius campaign he seemed to have been attacked. In the summer of 1974 he suffered a heart attack, enabling Teng Hsiao-p'ing to assume the bulk of his duties as premier. He was reappointed as premier in 1975.

Chu Teh 朱德 (1886-1976), a founder with Mao of the Red Army in 1927. He was commander of the Red Army in 1930-54 and chairman of the standing committee of the National People's Congress in 1959-66 and 1975-76. During the Cultural Revolution he was briefly attacked by Red Guards. In 1969 he was elected only as a member of the Politburo, but in 1973 he was re-elected as a member of the Politburo Standing Committee.

Fung Yu-lan 馮友蘭 , professor of philosophy at Peking University, educated at Columbia and Princeton Universities. In 1965 he was criticized for his view that the landlords in the feudal age had made certain concessions to the peasants. After the Cultural Revolution he resumed his scholarship, criticizing Confucian philosophy.

Ho Lung 賀龍 (1896-), one of China's ten marshals. He commanded in the Red Army in 1927-49 and was vice-premier and a member of the Politburo in 1955-66. During the Cultural Revolution he was attacked by Red Guards and purged.

Hsieh Fu-chih 謝富治 (1898-1972), political commissar under Liu Po-ch'eng. He succeeded Lo Jui-ch'ing as minister of public security in 1959 and was elected as a vice-premier in 1965. During the Cultural Revolution he was a supporter of Chiang Ch'ing; he became chairman of the Peking Municipal Revolutionary Committee and in 1969 was elected to the Politburo.

Hsü Shih-yu 許世友 (1909-), one of China's ten generals who served in the Red Army with Chang Kuo-tao in 1936. He also served under Hsü Hsiang-ch'ien and Liu Po-ch'eng. He was commander of the Nanking Military Region in 1955-73 and was elected to the Politburo in 1969 and 1973. In January 1974 he became commander of the Canton Military Region.

Hua Kuo-feng 華國鋒 , chairman of the Party and the Military Affairs Committee. Little is known about his background. He was born in Shansi and was a Party secretary in Mao's home district, Siangtan, Hunan, and vice-governor of Hunan in 1958-65. He was elected to the Central Committee in 1969, became first secretary of the Hunan Provincial Party Committee in 1970, was elected to the Politburo in 1973, and became a vice-premier and minister of public security in 1975. After Chou En-lai's death he was identified as acting premier in February 1975 and after the April 1976 riot in Peking was appointed premier and the first vice-chairman of the Central Committee. After Mao's death, he became chairman of the Party and the MAC.

Huang Yung-sheng 黃永勝 (ca. 1905-), Lin Piao's close associate and the army's chief of staff until he was purged with Lin Piao in 1971. He served in Lin Piao's 115th Division during the 1930s, was commander of the Canton Military Region in 1962-68, replaced Yang Ch'eng-wu as chief of staff in 1968, and was elected to the Politburo in 1969.

Jao Shu-shih 饒漱石 (1901-), political commissar of the New Fourth Army in 1939-42 and of the Third Field Army thereafter. He became director of the Organization Department in 1949 and was appointed as a member of the State Planning Commission in 1952. He was involved in Kao Kang's power struggle with Liu Shao-ch'i and Chou En-lai in 1953-54 and was purged.

K'ang Sheng 康生 (1899-1975), in charge of the Party's security work from the 1930s, having been trained in the Soviet Union as an intelligence expert. In the 1950s and 1960s he was China's liaison man with foreign Communist parties. During the Cultural Revolution he was active as Mao's trusted representative in the Secretariat and the Cultural Revolution Group. He became a member of the Politburo Standing Committee in 1969 and one of its vice-chairmen in 1973.

Kao Kang 高崗 (1902-1954), chairman of the Northeast People's Government in 1949-52 and of the State Planning Commission in 1952. He was involved in a power struggle with Liu and Chou in 1953-54 and committed suicide in 1954.

K'o Ch'ing-shih 柯慶施 (1902-1965), member of the North China

Bureau with Liu Shao-chi in the 1930s. He was mayor of Shanghai, a member of the Politburo in 1958-65, and first secretary of the Shanghai Party Committee in 1964-65. He was one of the first supporters of Mao's GLF in 1958 and the first to attack P'eng Chen's cultural policy in 1963-65.

Kuo Mo-jo 郭沫若 (1892-). Trained as a medical doctor in Japan during the 1920s, he gradually turned writer and Communist. He lectured at Mao's Peasant Movement Institute in 1926; he became thereafter one of Mao's trusted friends. He has been president of the All-China Federation of Literary and Art Circle and of the Academy of Sciences since 1949. In April 1966 he signaled the coming of the Cultural Revolution by suddenly making an open self-denial of his previous writings. After the Cultural Revolution he resumed his work, criticizing Confucius.

Li Ching-ch'üan 李井泉 (1906-). He served in the First Field Army during the 1940s. In 1958 he became a member of the Politburo and in 1965 first secretary of the Southwest Bureau. During the Cultural Revolution he was attacked as the chief power-holder in the Southwest. In 1973 he was rehabilitated and elected to the Tenth Central Committee.

Li Fu-ch'un 李富春 (1899-1975), a top economic administrator. He was vice-chairman of the Finance and Economic Committee of the government in 1949-52 and chairman of the State Planning Commission in 1954-73. In 1966 he was identified as a member of the Politburo Standing Committee and was elected to the Central Committee in 1969 and 1973.

Li Hsien-nien 李先念 (1907-), a leading financial specialist. He served in the New Fourth Army, was a member of the Politburo and the Secretariat in 1956-66, and became minister of finance and vice-premier in 1965. Although he was criticized during the Cultural Revolution, he has been active as vice-premier. He was elected to the Politburo in 1973 and became the third deputy premier in 1975.

Li Hsüeh-feng 李雪峯 (1906-1972), an organizational specialist. He served in the Central South Bureau in 1949-54, was a member of the Secretariat in 1956-66, and was first secretary of the North China Bureau in 1963-66. In the early Cultural Revolution, he replaced P'eng Chen as first secretary of the Peking Party Committee. He allegedly joined Lin Piao's force in a coup attempt against Mao in 1971.

Li Teh-sheng 李德生 (1916-), a rising star from the Cultural Revolution. He was born in Hupeh, served under Liu Po-ch'eng in the

1940s, and was commander of the Twelfth Army in 1959-67. In 1967 he was one of the first commanders who used force to support leftists in the Nanking region; he was sent to Anhui to support the Red Guards and became chairman of the Anhui Provincial Revolutionary Committee. In 1969 he was elected as an alternative member of the Politburo; in 1970 he was appointed director of the army's general political department; in 1973 he was elected as vice-chairman of the Party and a member of the Politburo Standing Committee. In 1974 he replaced Ch'en Hsi-lien as commander of the Shenyang Military Region.

Lin Piao 林彪 (1907-1972), a brilliant general who became Mao's successor after the Cultural Revolution. From the time he led the Communists' First Front Army in the Long March, he was one of Mao's trusted aids. He commanded the Fourth Field Army during the 1940s in Manchuria, was a member of the Politburo in 1956-66, and in 1959 replaced P'eng Teh-huai as minister of national defense and began an intensive indoctrination of the army by championing Mao's Thought. During the Cultural Revolution, he provided Mao with the support he needed; in 1969 he became Mao's official successor. In 1971, however, he allegedly attempted a coup against Mao without success and died in Mongolia while fleeing to the Soviet Union.

Liu Shao-ch'i 劉少奇 (1900-1972), chairman of the People's Republic of China in 1959-66 and model leader in the white areas before 1949. From 1942 he was the Party's second ranking leader. After the GLF collapsed, he exercised decisive leadership in restoring the economy at the apex of the Party bureaucracy. He was purged during the Cultural Revolution as the "top power-holder taking capitalist road."

Lo Jui-ch'ing 羅瑞卿 (1907-), a vice-premier and the army's chief of staff in 1959-65, replacing Huang K'o-ch'eng. He served in the Long March; he was minister of public security in 1949-65. He was one of the first to be purged in the Cultural Revolution in 1965.

Lu Ting-yi 陸定一 (1901-), director of the Propaganda Department from 1949. He was purged in 1966.

Mao Tse-tung 毛澤東 (1893-1976), a founding member of the CCP in 1921. He also founded the Red Army in 1927 with Chu Teh. He became chairman of the People's Republic of China in 1949 but yielded this post to Liu Shao-ch'i in 1959. From 1935, he led the CCP. He was the Supreme Leader of the Party, the army, and the state, symbolizing China, initiating innovative policies, resolving policy disputes, and defining the correct ideology until he died on

September 9, 1976. He was the only Communist leader whose body was to be embalmed.

Nieh Yüan-tzu 聶元梓 , an assistant professor of philosophy at Peking University, she raised the first big character poster in May 1966. During the Cultural Revolution she was the leader of the New Peking Revolutionary Committee in 1967 and an alternate member of the Central Committee in 1969, but was dropped from the Tenth Central Committee in 1973.

P'eng Chen 彭真 (1902-), mayor of Peking. He was a member of the Politburo and the Secretariat until he was purged in 1966. He was in charge of the Party's cultural affairs as the second ranking member of the Secretariat after Teng Hsiao-p'ing.

P'eng Teh-huai 彭德懷 (1898-), commander of the Eighth Route Army during the 1930s against Nationalist and Japanese troops. He was minister of defense from 1954 to 1959, when he was purged for attacking Mao's GLF.

Po I-po 薄一波 (1907-), chairman of the State Economic Commission. He was vice-premier and alternate member of the Politburo in 1956-66. During the Cultural Revolution he dispatched work teams to schools. He was criticized for this and purged.

Sung Jen-ch'iung 宋任窮 (1904-), first secretary of the Northeast Bureau in 1961-66. He served as political commissar in Kiangsi and Yenan and was minister of machine building in 1956-65. During the Cultural Revolution he was purged as the top power-holder in the Northeast, but he was rehabilitated and elected to the Tenth Central Committee in 1973.

T'an Chen-lin 譚震林 (1902-), a veteran Communist who took part in Mao's Autumn Harvest Uprising in 1927. He was a vice-premier, director of the State Council's Agriculture and Forestry Office, and a member of the Politburo until 1967. At that time he apparently attempted to defend some of his old comrades and was accused of being the ringleader of the "February Black Reversal." He was rehabilitated in 1973 and elected to the Tenth Central Committee.

T'ao Chu 陶鑄 (1905-), first secretary of the Central South Bureau until 1966. He replaced Lu Ting-yi as director of the Propaganda Department in 1966, but he fell in 1967 after trying to defend the old Party apparatus.

Teng Hsiao-p'ing 鄧小平 (1904-), general secretary of the Secretariat and member of the Politburo Standing Committee in 1956-66. He served in Kiangsi and Yenan as an organizational specialist. During the Cultural Revolution he was purged as the "second top capitalist roader" within the Party. But in 1973 he was rehabilitated and led the Chinese delegation to the special session of the United Nations. In the same year he was elected to the Tenth Central Committee; in 1974 he was identified as a member of the Politburo. He later assumed the bulk of Chou En-lai's duties as vice-premier and in 1975 became the first deputy premier and the army's chief of staff. However, in April 1976 he was dismissed from all of his positions.

Teng T'o 鄧拓 (ca. 1911-), editor of the *People's Daily* in 1952-59. He was secretary of the Peking Party Committee until he was purged in 1966 as one of the three authors of "Notes from the Three-Family Village," which satirized Mao's policies in the guise of ancient themes.

Teng Tzu-hui 鄧子恢 (1895-1973), an economic specialist. He served in the New Fourth Army. In 1949-53, he was in charge of land reforms and agricultural cooperativization in the Central South region, and in 1953 became director of the Party's Rural Work Department. In 1955-56, he attacked Mao's policy for agricultural cooperativization as "reckless advance." He subsequently disappeared from public view until 1969, when he reappeared as a member of the Central Committee.

Tung Pi-wu 董必武 (1886-1975), a founding member of the CCP with Mao. He was chairman of the government's Political and Legal Affairs Committee in 1949-54 and elected as vice-chairman of the People's Republic of China in 1959. After Liu's fall in 1966 he was acting chairman of the Republic and in 1973 was elected to the Politburo Standing Committee.

Wang Hung-wen 王洪文 , another rising star from the Cultural Revolution who became the Party's third ranking vice-chairman in his thirties at the 1973 Tenth Party Congress. Little is known about his background. He was a worker in a cotton mill in Shanghai; in January-February 1967 he was one of the leaders of the rebel headquarters that seized power from the old Shanghai Party apparatus; he subsequently became a "leading member" of the Revolutionary Committee. In 1969 he was elected to the Ninth Central Committee and in 1971 became the third ranking secretary of the Shanghai Party Committee after Chang Ch'un-ch'iao and Yao Wen-yüan. In April 1973 he became director of the Shanghai Federation of Trade Unions, in August the Party's third ranking leader. Wang may have been part of a deliberate effort by Mao to train a successor but was purged after Mao's death in 1976.

Wang Kuang-mei 王光美 , Liu Shao-ch'i's wife since the 1940s. In

1964 she led a work team to carry out the Socialist Education Movement at the T'aoyüan brigade in Shansi; in 1966 she led another work team to carry out the Cultural Revolution at Tsinghua University. For both of these tasks, she was severely criticized during the Cultural Revolution.

Wang Tung-hsing 汪東興 , vice-minister of public security and known as Mao's bodyguard. In 1966 he replaced Yang Shang-k'un as director of the Central Committee Office. He was elected to the Politburo in 1973. He helped Hua in the purge of Chiang Ch'ing in 1976.

Wu Han 吳晗 (1909-), vice-mayor of Peking and historian until he was purged in 1966. He wrote the play *Hai Jui Dismissed from Office*, which satirized the dismissal of P'eng Teh-huai by Mao in the guise of an upright official dismissed by an emperor in the Ming dynasty.

Wu Teh 吳德 (ca. 1910-), an alternate member of the Central Committee and first secretary of the Kirin Provincial Party Committee in 1956-66. In 1966 he replaced Liu Jen as second secretary of the Peking Party Committee. In 1967 he became vice-chairman of the Peking Revolutionary Committee and after Hsieh's death in 1972 became its chairman. In 1972 he was identified as director of the State Council's Culture and Education Group. In 1973 he was elected to the Politburo and in 1975 became a deputy premier.

Yang Ch'eng-wu 楊成武 (ca. 1912-), acting chief of staff of the PLA after Lo was purged in 1965. He served in the Long March and in Lin Piao's 115th Division during the 1930s. During the Cultural Revolution he helped Chiang Ch'ing's cause. In March 1968 he was purged, probably because he challenged Lin Piao's authority. In 1974 he was rehabilitated as a deputy chief of staff.

Yang Shang-k'un 楊尚昆 (1905-), director of the Central Committee Office in 1945-66 until he was purged during the Cultural Revolution.

Yao Wen-yüan 姚文元 , a staff writer of Shanghai's *Chieh-fang jih-pao* until 1966. In November 1965 he wrote the famous article "On the New Historical Play *Hai Jui Dismissed from Office*," which exposed Wu Han's intention, thus opening the curtain on the Cultural Revolution. He was active as Chiang Ch'ing's spokesman. He was elected as first vice-chairman of Shanghai's Revolutionary Committee in 1967, and to the Politburo in 1969 and 1973. He was purged after Mao's death in 1976.

Yeh Chien-ying 葉劍英 (1898-), one of China's ten marshals. He

taught at Whampoa Military Academy, served in Chang Fa-k'ui's troops in 1927, became chief of staff of Chu Teh's First Front Army in 1933, worked with Chou En-lai in the Communist liaison mission at Chunking during the 1940s, was director of the Armed Forces Supervision Department in 1954-65, and replaced Lo Jui-ch'ing in 1966 as a member of the Secretariat. During the Cultural Revolution he was involved in mediating conflicts among military units. In 1969 he was elected as a member of the Politburo, and in 1973 as a vice-chairman of the Party and member of the Politburo Standing Committee. In 1975 he became deputy premier and minister of national defense.

Yü Ch'iu-li 余秋里 (1914-), an economic specialist. He was minister of petroleum in 1958-66 and elected a vice-chairman of the State Planning Commission in 1965. During the Cultural Revolution he was attacked by Red Guards. In 1973 he was rehabilitated as a member of the Central Committee; he was also identified as chairman of the State Planning Commission. In 1975 he became a deputy premier.

Notes

CHAPTER 1
INTRODUCTION

1. Roger Hilsman, *To Move a Nation*, chap. 1; Amitai Etzioni, *The Active Society*, p. 317.

2. Austin Ranney, "The Study of Policy Content: A Framework for Choice," in *Political Science and Public Policy*, ed. A. Ranney, p. 3.

3. According to Huntington, the evolution of a revolutionary one-party system into an established one-party system goes through three phases: transformation, consolidation, and adaptation. See "Social and Institutional Dynamics of One-party Systems," in *Authoritarian Politics in Modern Society*, ed. Samuel Huntington and Clement Moore, p. 24.

4. Enid Curtis Bok Schoettle, "The State of the Art in Policy Studies, " in *The Study of Policy Formation*, ed. Raymond A. Bauer and Kenneth J. Gergen (New York: Free Press, 1968), pp. 168-79.

5. Robert Merton, *Social Theory and Social Structure*, pp. 475-90.

6. For this model, see Etzioni, *Active Society*, pp. 260-62.

7. For this model, see David Braybrook and Charles Lindblom, *A Strategy of Decision*, pp. 85-86.

8. For this methodological perspective, see Joseph Ben-David, "How to Organize Research in the Social Sciences," *Daedalus*, Spring 1973, pp. 39-52; Marc J. Roberts, "On the Nature and Condition of Social Science," ibid., Summer 1974, pp. 47-64; Chalmers Johnson, "Political Science and East Asian Area Studies," *World Politics*, no. 4 (July 1974), pp. 560-75.

9. Arthur L. Kalleberg, "Concept Formation in Normative and Empirical Studies: Toward Reconciliation in Political Theory," *American Political Science Review*, no. 1 (March 1969), pp. 33-34.

319

10. See Hong Yung Lee, "Utility and Limitation of the Red Guard Publications as Source Materials: Bibliographical Survey," *Journal of Asian Studies* 34, no. 3 (May 1975): 779-94.

CHAPTER 2
FROM CONSENSUS TO DEBATE

1. *Ten Great Years.*

2. Lucian Bianco, *Origins of the Chinese Revolution, 1915-1949*, pp. 54-82.

3. Chalmers Johnson, *Peasant Nationalism and Communist Power.*

4. Barrington Moore, Jr., *Social Origin of Dictatorship and Democracy*, pp. 224-27; Jacques Guillermaz, *A History of the Chinese Communist Party, 1921-1949.*

5. Stuart R. Schram, Introduction, in his *Authority, Participation and Cultural Change in China*, pp. 3-27.

6. *Mao Tse-tung Ssu-hsiang wan-sui* [Long live Mao Tse-tung thought], trans. in *Joint Publication Research Service* (hereafter cited as JPRS), no. 61269-2 (February 20, 1974), p. 206.

7. Mao Tse-tung, *Selected Works*, 2: 215, 202.

8. For studies on these, see Mark Selden, *The Yenan Way in Revolutionary China*, and Illpyong J. Kim, *The Politics of Chinese Communism.*

9. According to Riker, all coalition makers seek this to minimize sidepayments. See William Riker, *The Theory of Political Coalitions*, pp. 231-42.

10. Mao, *Selected Works*, 3: 50; Liu Shao-ch'i, *On Intra-Party Struggle*, p. 50; also see Harry Harding, Jr., "Maoist Theories of Policy-making and Organization," in *The Cultural Revolution in China*, ed. Thomas W. Robinson, pp. 123-31.

11. *Chieh-fang jih-pao*, July 21, 1943.

12. "Liu Shao-ch'i's Report on Questions of Union Work at the Northeast Workers Representative Conference," May 1949, in a Red Guard pamphlet.

13. See Mao, *Selected Works*, 2: 339-84; 3: 255-320; 4: 411-24.

14. According to Riker, a grand coalition does not last. See his *Theory of Political Coalitions*, pp. 231-42.

15. Mao, *Selected Works*, 4: 374.

16. John Wong, *Land Reform in the People's Republic of China*, p. 64.

17. *Agrarian Reform Law of the People's Republic of China*, p. 1.

18. *Mao Tse-tung Ssu-hsiang wan-sui*, JPRS, no. 61269-2, p. 255. Since there are two Chinese volumes, one dated 1967 and the other 1969, the first volume is hereafter called *Mao, 1967*, JPRS, no. 61269-1 and the second volume *Mao, 1969*, JPRS, no. 61269-2.

19. For a comparative study on this, see Thomas P. Bernstein, "Leadership and Mobilization in the Collectivization of Agriculture in China and Russia: A Comparison" (Ph.D. diss., Columbia University, 1970).

20. Franz Schurmann, *Ideology and Organization in Communist China*, p. 454.

21. *Mao, 1969*, JPRS, no. 61269-2, p. 252.

22. Jürgen Domes, *The Internal Politics of China, 1949-1972*, p. 42.

23. *Mao, 1967*, JPRS, no. 61269-1, pp. 16, 40.

24. Ibid., p. 34.

25. Cited in Edward Rice, *Mao's Way*, p. 126.

26. *Mao, 1967*, JPRS, no. 61269-1, p. 80.

27. *Constitution of the People's Republic of China*, p. 3.

28. For the Soviet case, see Alexander Erlich, *The Soviet Industrialization Debate, 1924-1928*.

29. *Agrarian Reform Law*, p. 88.

30. *Collected Works of Liu Shao-ch'i, 1945-1957*, p. 291.

31. *Jen-min jih-pao*, November 23, 1967 (hereafter cited as JMJP); ibid., February 4, 1968; *Chung-kuo ch'ing-nien-pao*, July 15, 1964; *Current Background* (Hong Kong: U.S. Consulate-General), no. 339 (1955), pp. 9-10 (hereafter cited as CB); *Ta-kung pao* (Peking), November 8, 1955.

32. JMJP, November 23, 1967.

33. Mao, *Selected Readings from the Works of Mao Tse-tung*, pp. 316-39.

34. JMJP, November 8, 1955; ibid., November 13, 1955.

35. *Mao, 1967*, JPRS, no. 61269-1, p. 82.

36. *Socialist Upsurge in China's Countryside*, pp. 7-10.

37. *New China News Agency* (Peking), January 25, 1956 (hereafter cited as NCNA); for a revised version, see CB, no. 781 (1966); for a detailed study, see Parris H. Chang, *Power and Policy in China*.

38. CB, no. 892 (1969), p. 21.

39. *Mao, 1967*, JPRS, no. 61269-1, pp. 32-33.

40. CB, no. 892, p. 34; *Hung-ch'i*, no. 1 (June 1, 1958), pp. 3-4.

41. JPRS, no. 49826 (February 12, 1970), p. 51.

42. *New China Advances to Socialism*, pp. 130-31.

43. Russian Institute, Columbia University, *The Anti-Stalin Campaign and International Communism*, pp. 28-29.

44. "On the Historical Experiences of the Dictatorship of the Proletariat," JMJP, April 5, 1956.

45. "Let a Hundred Flowers Bloom, a Hundred Schools of Thought Contend," in *Communist China, 1955-1959*, pp. 158-60.

46. *Eighth National Congress of the Communist Party of China*, 1: 56, 102, 124, 200.

47. Ibid., pp. 116-17.

48. Ibid., pp. 7-8.

49. *Mao, 1967*, JPRS, no. 61269-1, p. 56.

50. "Leninism or Social-Imperialism," *Peking Review*, no. 17 (April 24, 1970), p. 6.

51. "More on the Historical Experiences of the Dictatorship of the Proletariat," JMJP, December 29, 1956.

52. *Mao, 1967*, JPRS, no. 61269-1, p. 47.

53. *Selected Readings from the Works of Mao Tse-tung*, pp. 350-87; he made a similar speech in March, "Speech at the Chinese Communist Party's National Conference on Propaganda Work," ibid., pp. 388-402.

54. Sidney Gruson (Dispatch from Warsaw), *New York Times*, June 13, 1957.

55. *Mao, 1967*, JPRS, no. 61269-1, pp. 63, 71, 82.

56. Richard Solomon, *Mao's Revolution and the Chinese Political Culture*, pp. 304-9.

57. "Liu's Speech at a Party Cadre Conference of Shanghai City," April 27, 1957, in a Red Guard pamphlet.

58. JMJP, May 13, 1957; ibid., June 2, 1957; ibid., July 14, 1957; ibid., July 15, 1957; also see Dennis J. Doolin, *Communist China*, pp. 21-30.

59. *Carry Out the Great Revolution on the Journalistic Front*, p. 24.

60. JMJP, July 1, 1957; *Communist China, 1955-1959*, p. 304.

61. *Selected Reading from the Works of Mao*, p. 378.

62. JMJP, October 10, 1957; ibid., October 19, 1957; *Mao, 1967*, JPRS, no. 61269-1, pp. 74-75.

63. Cited in Joseph Peterson, *The Great Leap—China*, p. 327; also see *Khrushchev Remembers* (Boston: Little, Brown, 1970), p. 471.

64. Roderick MacFarquhar, *The Origins of the Cultural Revolution.*

65. Frederick C. Teiwes, "The Purge of Provincial Leaders, 1957-1958," *China Quarterly*, no. 27 (July-September 1966), p. 17; JMJP, January 25, 1958.

66. *Mao, 1967*, JPRS, no. 61269-1, pp. 78-84.

67. CB, no. 892, pp. 1-14.

68. *Mao, 1967*, JPRS, no. 61269-1, p. 141.

69. Ibid., p. 101.

70. "Chairman Mao's Speech at the Ch'engtu Conference," March 22, 1958, JPRS, no. 49826 (February 12, 1970), p. 47.

71. JMJP, September 1, 1959, editorial; *Selections from Chinese Mainland Magazines*, no. 600 (1968), p. 3 (hereafter cited as SCMM); ibid., no. 610, p. 10; *Chinese Law and Government*, no. 4 (Winter 1968/1969), p. 17.

72. *Mao, 1967*, JPRS, no. 61269-1, pp. 91, 122.

73. Ibid., pp. 101-18.

74. *Second Session of the Eighth National Congress of the Communist Party of China*, p. 49.

75. JMJP, May 26, 1958; *Second Session*, pp. 39-40.

76. Stanley Karnow, *Mao and China*, pp. 97-109.

77. JMJP, April 2, 1958; ibid., April 4, 1958; ibid., September 2, 1959; Peking *Ta-kung pao*, March 11, 1958; *Hung-ch'i*, no. 5 (March 1, 1961), pp. 10-11; ibid., no. 4 (July 16, 1958), p. 5.

78. "People's Communes (1): Establishment and Development," *Peking Review*, no. 34 (August 23, 1974), p. 16.

79. "Peitaiho Resolution," in *Communist China, 1955-1959*, pp. 488-502.

80. *Mao, 1967*, JPRS, no. 61269-1, pp. 136-38.

81. *Hung-ch'i*, no. 10 (October 16, 1958), pp. 1-2.

82. *Mao, 1967*, JPRS, no. 61269-1, pp. 191-225; *Mao, 1969*, JPRS, no. 61269-2, pp. 247-313; for a comment on these works, see Richard Levy, "New Light on Mao: His Views on the Soviet Union's Political Economy," *China Quarterly*, no. 61 (March 1975), pp. 95-117.

83. JMJP, January 14, 1958, editorial.

84. *Mao, 1969*, JPRS, no. 61269-2, pp. 256, 259.

85. For "comprehensive rationality," see Etzioni, *Active Society*, pp. 260-62; for "incrementalism," see David Braybrooke and Charles Lindblom, *A Strategy of Decision*, pp. 85-96; for Liu's justification, see *Second Session*, p. 45.

86. For this polity, see William Kornhauser, *The Politics of Mass Society;* also see Robert Tucker, "Toward a Comparative Politics of Movement Regimes," *American Political Science Review*, no. 2 (June 1961), pp. 281-89.

87. *Mao, 1967*, JPRS, no. 61269-1, p. 110; *Mao, 1969*, JPRS, no. 61269-2, pp. 306-7.

88. For this theme, see David Apter, *The Politics of Modernization*, p. 40.

89. "Examples of Dialectics," in *Mao, 1967*, JPRS, no. 61269-1, pp. 201-5.

90. Max Weber, *The Protestant Ethic and the Spirit of Capitalism*, pp. 117-18.

91. Benjamin Schwartz, "The Reign of Virtue: Some Broad Perspectives on Leaders and Party in the Cultural Revolution," *China Quarterly*, no. 35 (June-September 1968), pp. 14-15.

92. *Mao, 1969*, JPRS, no. 61269-2, p. 276.

CHAPTER 3
RETREAT FROM THE GREAT LEAP FORWARD

1. For an integrated analysis of the policy process in 1959-62, see Byung-joon Ahn, "Adjustments in the Great Leap Forward and Their Ideological Legacy, 1959-62," in *Ideology and Politics in Contemporary China*, ed. Chalmers Johnson, pp. 257-300.

2. Wang Kuo-fan, "Uninterrupted Revolution for Communes," *Kuang-ming jih-pao*, October 30, 1958 (hereafter cited as KMJP); *Sansi jih-pao*, September 5, 1958; Chen Po-ta, "Under the Banner of Comrade Mao Tse-tung," *Hung-ch'i*, no. 4 (July 16, 1958), p. 5; *Kung-jen jih-pao*, October 10-19, 1958 (hereafter cited as KJJP); "Tentative and Abridged Charter of the Weihsing Commune" (draft), JMJP, September 4, 1958.

3. "Long Live People's Commune!" JMJP, August 29, 1959, editorial.

4. "On Several Questions of People's Communes," *Hung-ch'i*, no. 13 (December 1, 1958), p. 26.

5. "Words of Antirevolutionary and Revisionist Wu Leng-hsi," *Kung-jen p'ing-lun*, June, 1968.

6. Commentator, "Refuting Skeptics in the Mass Movement on Industrial Front," *Hung-ch'i*, no. 12 (November 11, 1958); T'an Chen-lin, "Strive to Achieve Self-Sufficiency of Cloth and Food in Two or Three Years," ibid., no. 6 (August 16, 1958); Ting Wang, ed., *Teng T'o hsüan-chih* in *Chung-kung wen-hua ta-ke-ming tzu-liao hui-pien*, 2: 162.

7. *The Case of P'eng Teh-huai*, p. 120. The first Chengchow conference was held from November 3 through 10, 1958. See NCNA, December 17, 1958.

8. The provincial leaders' conference was held from November 21 through 27; and the Sixth Plenum was held from November 28 through December 10, 1958. See JMJP, December 18, 1958; for the resolution, see "Resolution on Some Questions Concerning the People's Communes," December 10, 1958 (hereafter, "Wuhan Resolution"), in *Communist China, 1955-1959*, pp. 494-95.

9. "Talks with Directors of Various Cooperative Areas," *Mao, 1967*, JPRS, no. 61269-1, p. 134.

10. "Wuhan Resolution," p. 494.

11. T'ao Chu, "Investigation Report of the Humeng Commune," JMJP, February 25, 1959.

12. Mao, "Speech at the Central Politburo's Chengchow Conference," February 1959, in *Chinese Law and Government*, no. 4 (Winter 1968/1969), pp. 22-24; "Speech at the Second Chengchow Conference," March 1959, in ibid., p. 45.

13. Ibid., p. 23.

14. "Comment on a Letter," July 26, 1959, ibid., p. 49; *Kung-tso t'ung-hsün*, no. 15 (April 5, 1961), p. 3.

15. *Mao, 1967*, JPRS, no. 61269-1, pp. 157-68.

16. K'o Ching-shih, "On the Whole Country as a Chessboard," *Hung-ch'i*, no. 4 (February 16, 1959); T'ao Chu, "The Whole Country as a Chessboard; the Whole Province as a Chessboard," *Nan-fang jih-pao*, March 21, 1959 (hereafter cited as NFJP); Ch'en Yün, "Some Important Problems in the Current Capital Construction Work," *Hung-ch'i*, no. 5 (March 1, 1959).

17. JMJP, January 10, 1959; *Fukien jih-pao*, January 27, 1959; JMJP, January 10, 1959.

18. *Szechwan jih-pao*, January 24, 1959; NFJP, January 19, 1959; JMJP, March 9, 1959; ibid., March 18, 1959; ibid., May 5, 1959.

19. "People's Communes Must Establish Sound Responsibility Production System," JMJP, February 17, 1959, editorial; Lin I-chou, "Fixing Output Must Be Implemented," *Hung-ch'i*, no. 24 (December 16, 1959), pp. 1-2; NFJP, January 19, 1959, p. 1.

20. *Szechwan jih-pao*, January 10, 1959; ibid., February 17, 1959; NFJP, January 6, 1959; ibid., January 22, 1959; *Yunnan jih-pao*, January 22, 1959; ibid., January 23, 1959; Fang Yüan, "Distribution According to Labor and Exchange of Same Value," *Hung-ch'i*, no. 7 (April 1959), pp. 19-20.

21. *Kung-jen p'ing-lun*, June 1968.

22. JMJP, April 8, 1959. This was held from April 2 through 5.

23. *Chinese Law and Government*, no. 4, p. 81.

24. *Mao, 1969*, JPRS, 61269-2, pp. 238-42; NFJP, May 6, 1959; JMJP, April 28, 1959; ibid., July 24, 1959.

25. *Szechwan jih-pao*, April 12, 1959; NFJP, April 4, 1959; *Chung-kuo ch'ing-nien pao*, July 8, 1959.

26. *Szechwan jih-pao*, January 15, 1959; *Liaoning jih-pao*, January 24, 1959.

27. Mao, "Speech at a Work Conference of the Central Committee," October 25, 1966, CB, no. 891 (1969), p. 75; *Yomiuri shimbun* (Tokyo), January 7, 1967, Mr. Seki's report from Peking.

28. *Mao, 1967*, JPRS, no. 61269-1, p. 148.

29. *Pravda*, January 28, 1959; JMJP, September 6, 1963, editorial.

30. *Chinese Law and Government*, no. 4, p. 92.

31. *Mao, 1967*, JPRS, no. 61269-1, pp. 182-84.

32. Ibid., pp. 15-21; *The Case of P'eng Teh-huai*, p. 38.

33. "P'eng Teh-huai's Testimony," in *The Case of P'eng Teh-huai*, p. 120.

34. Ibid., pp. 204, 180; also see David A. Charles, "The Dismissal of Marshal P'eng Teh-huai," *China Quarterly*, no. 8 (October-December 1961), p. 65. It is interesting to note that Red Guard sources have confirmed all facts included in Charles's article.

35. *The Case of P'eng Teh-huai*, p. 3.

36. Ibid.

37. Ibid., p. 4.

38. Ibid., pp. 304, 10, 11, 8.

39. Ibid., p. 6.

40. Ibid., p. 40; see "Resolution of Eighth Plenary Session of the Ninth Central Committee of Chinese Communist Party concerning the Anti-Party Clique Headed by P'eng Teh-huai" (excerpt), August 16, 1959, JMJP, August 16, 1967.

41. *The Case of P'eng Teh-huai*, p. 5. Interesting in this regard was that P'eng's visit to the commune of Mao's native village in 1958 to find out the truth about production increase, and his discovery that the increase was not as high as reported.

NOTES, CHAP. 3   325

Chou Hsiao-chou, first secretary of Hunan, told him that about a 14 percent increase had been accomplished but with large loans from the state. When P'eng asked Mao about this, Mao replied that he had not discussed it while he was there. Yet P'eng insinuated that Mao had indeed discussed this matter, implying Mao's dishonesty. See ibid., p. 1.

42. Ibid., pp. 36-37.

43. "Criticism of P'eng Teh-huai's 'Letter of Opinion' of July 14, 1959," *Chinese Law and Government*, no. 4, p. 26; also see J. P. Simmond, "P'eng Teh-huai: A Chronological Re-examination," *China Quarterly*, no. 37 (January-March 1969), p. 134.

44. Mao, "Speech at the Lushan Conference," *Chinese Law and Government*, no. 4, p. 35.

45. Ibid., pp. 36-41.

46. Ibid., pp. 38, 29.

47. Ibid., p. 40.

48. "Speech at the Eighth Plenary Session," August 2, 1959, *Chinese Law and Government*, no. 4, p. 60.

49. For Liu and Teng, see *The Case of P'eng Teh-huai*, p. 205; for Ch'en and Li, see *Ts'ai-mao hung-ch'i*, February 15, 1967; for Chow and Lin, see *The Case of P'eng Teh-huai*, pp. 20, 125; also see "Vice Chairman Lin's Talk about P'eng Teh-huai" (excerpts), October 12, 1959, *Ke-ming tsao-fan pao*, November 25, 1967; for Ch'en Po-ta, see *The Case of P'eng Teh-huai*, pp. 107-18; for K'ang, see "Communist Party Members Must Be Marxist-Leninist, Not Fellow Travelers of the Party," *Hung-ch'i*, no. 19 (October 1, 1959).

50. "A Letter to Production Team Leaders," November 29, 1959; CB, no. 891 (1969), pp. 34-35. According to another source, Mao wrote a similar letter in April. See *Mao, 1967*, JPRS, no. 61269-1, pp. 170-72.

51. *The Case of P'eng Teh-huai*, pp. 41, 297-305.

52. *Kung-jen p'ing-lun*, June 1968.

53. CB, no. 892 (1969), p. 38.

54. *The Case of P'eng Teh-huai*, pp. 41-42.

55. "Unlimited Future of the Public Mess Halls," JMJP, September 22, 1959, editorial; *Szechwan jih-pao*, September 19, 1959, editorial; *Kiangsi jih-pao*, October 29, 1959.

56. JMJP, September 4, 1959, p. 3; NCNA, October 16, 1959; JMJP, December 28, 1959.

57. JMJP, November 2, 1959; ibid., February 20, 1960; ibid., March 10, 1960; *Chieh-fang jih-pao* (Shanghai), July 12, 1959; JMJP, October 18, 1959.

58. "Constitution of Anshan Iron and Steel Company Sports Revolution and Production," *Peking Review*, no. 16 (April 17, 1970), pp. 3-5; also see *Mao, 1967*, JPRS, no. 61269-1, p. 230.

59. *Jen-min Shou-ts'e 1960*, pp. 3-5.

60. "Long Live Leninism," JMJP, April 22, 1960; ibid., August 16, 1967.

61. JMJP, July 4, 1960; ibid., November 20, 1960; *Chieh-fang jih-pao*, July 8, 1960, p. 2; *Ch'ing-tao jih-pao*, October 18, 1960; *Chekiang jih-pao*, October 15, 1960, p. 2.

62. *Kung-tso t'ung-hsün*, no. 6 (January 27, 1961), pp. 12-14; ibid., no. 13 (March 20, 1961), pp. 1-15.

63. Liao Lu-yen, "The Whole Party and the Whole People Take Up Agriculture in

a Big Way," *Hung-ch'i*, no. 17 (September 1, 1960), p. 1; *Jen-min Shou-ts'e, 1960*, pp. 175-76.

64. *Mao, 1967*, JPRS, no. 61269-1, p. 231; CB, no. 884 (1969), p. 18; *Hung-ch'i*, no. 17 (September 1, 1960), pp. 2-3.

65. *Mao, 1967*, JPRS, no. 61269-1, p. 232.

66. "Letter concerning the Urgent Directive from the Central Committee of the CCP concerning the Problems of the Present Policy toward the Rural People's Commune," *Kung-tso t'ung-hsün*, no. 6, pp. 6-7; the full text is available in Japanese. See Ajia kenkyūjō, *Jimmin kōsha sōran*, p. 573; also see *Union Research Service* 28, no. 12: 200-201 (hereafter cited as URS).

67. "Fully Display the Combating Role of Production Team," JMJP, November 25, 1960, editorial; ibid., December 21, 1960, editorial; NFJP, December 1, 1960, p. 2; Chin Ming, "How the Finance of People's Communes Can Serve Distribution," *Hung-ch'i*, no. 22 (November 11, 1960); JMJP, November 29, 1960; ibid., December 1, 1960; ibid., December 18, 1960; ibid., October 9, 1960; *Kung-tso t'ung-hsün*, no. 16 (April 19, 1961), p. 20.

68. Ajia kenkyūjō, *Jimmin kōsha sōran*, p. 573.

CHAPTER 4
ADJUSTMENTS AND THEIR LEGACIES

1. "Comrade Yang Chiu-ju and Others' Report," *Kung-tso t'ung-hsün*, no. 17 (April 25, 1961), p. 3

2. Ibid., p. 4.

3. Ibid., p. 6.

4. Ibid., p. 4.

5. Ibid., no. 1 (January 1, 1961), pp. 7-8.

6. "Selected Edition on Liu Shao-ch'i's Counterrevolutionary Crimes," in SCMM, no. 652 (1969), p. 4, and no. 653 (1969), p. 1; for its full text, see "Liu's Instruction of Receiving the Standing Committee of the Federation of Construction, Industry and Commerce" in a Red Guard pamphlet (n.p., n.d.) that included four other speeches and directives made by Liu, pp. 71-74. For Maoist charge, see JMJP, October 26, 1967, p. 2.

7. *Peking Review*, no. 4 (January 27, 1961), pp. 7-9.

8. *Kung-tso t'ung-hsün*, no. 1, pp. 1-6.

9. Ibid., no. 3 (January 7, 1961), p. 1. This passage was later incorporated into the 1969 Party constitution, but after the Lin Piao incident in 1971, it was deleted from the 1973 Party constitution. For further details, see the concluding chapter of this book.

10. CB, no. 894 (1969), p. 24.

11. *Kung-tso t'ung-hsün*, no. 3, pp. 1-9. The *three-eight work style* refers to firmly holding the correct political direction, preserving a hard and plain work style, and being flexible in mobile warfare, coupled with unity, intensiveness, seriousness, and alertness.

12. Ibid., no. 1, p. 11; CB, no. 894, p. 24.

13. *Kung-tso t'ung-hsün*, no. 8 (February 6, 1961), pp. 11-19; ibid., no. 15 (April 5, 1961), pp. 1-8; ibid., no. 4 (January 11, 1961), pp. 1-10.

14. Ibid., no. 23 (June 13, 1961), p. 8.

15. JMJP, January 23, 1964, p. 2.

16. *Kung-tso t'ung-hsün*, no. 23, p. 1; ibid., no. 13 (March 20, 1961), p. 21; ibid., no. 14 (March 29, 1961), p. 1.

17. Ibid., no. 12 (March 10, 1961), pp. 9-15; ibid., no. 6, pp. 1-11; JPRS, no. 50477 (May 7, 1970), p. 70.

18. *Kung-tso t'ung-hsün*, no. 1, pp. 5-6; *Mao, 1969*, JPRS, no. 61269-2, p. 430.

19. SCMM, no. 635 (1968), p. 21; *Peking Review*, no. 4 (January 27, 1961), p. 6.

20. Wang Wang, "Striving for High Speed Is the Soul of the General Line," *Hsüeh-hsi*, no. 139 (July 3, 1958); *Peking Review*, no. 4 (January 17, 1961), pp. 5-6; JMJP, November 26, 1960; NFJP, December 22, 1960.

21. "Speech at the Ninth Plenum of the Eighth CCP Central Committee," *Mao, 1969*, JPRS, no. 61269-2, pp. 237-45.

22. Ting Wang, ed., *Chung-kung wen-hua ta-ke-ming tzu-liao hui-pien*, 1 (1967): 486, 491; *Kung-tso t'ung-hsün*, no. 15 (April 5, 1961), p. 3.

23. *Fei-wei nung-ts'un jen-min kung-she t'iao-li ts'ao-an*. See articles 34, 37, and 40.

24. *Kung-tso t'ung-hsün*, no. 15, p. 1.

25. Ting Wang, ed., *Chung-kung*, 1 (1967): 491.

26. *Kung-tso t'ung-hsün*, no. 15, p. 1.

27. "Along the Socialist or the Capitalist Road?" JMJP, August 15, 1967; JPRS, no. 50792 (June 23, 1970), p. 45; Ting Wang, ed., *Chung-kung*, 2 (1969): 550; SCMM, no. 640 (1969), p. 19.

28. *Kung-tso t'ung-hsün*, no. 17 (April 28, 1961), p. 4; "The Struggle between the Two Roads in China's Countryside," JMJP, November 23, 1967.

29. Interview Protocols, no. 2 (November 1969), and no. 53 (March 1970). Interviewees were middle-level cadres in Canton. These refugee interviews were conducted in Hong Kong from September 1969 through July 1970.

30. SCMM, no. 652, p. 4; "The Struggle between the Two Roads in China's Countryside," JMJP, November 23, 1967.

31. "Facts about Liu Chien-hsün," a pamphlet published by central committee headquarters of Revolutionary Rebels of Organs of the CCP Honan Provincial Committee, March 12, 1967.

32. JMJP, August 28, 1967; *Kweichow jih-pao*, June 4, 1967; *Wen-hui pao* (Shanghai), April 18, 1967; *Radio Kiangsi*, August 19, 1967.

33. C. S. Chen, ed., *Rural People's Communes in Lien-chiang*, trans. Charles P. Ridley, pp. 105-6 (hereafter cited as Chen, *Lien-chiang Documents*).

34. JMJP, January 1, 1962, editorial; *Hung-ch'i*, no. 23 (December 1, 1961), pp. 36-37.

35. "Liu Shao-ch'i and Teng Hsiao-p'ing's Black Winds of Individual Farming in Honan," *Wei-tung* (Tientsin), no. 21 (May 12, 1967).

36. *Kung-fei nung-ts'un jen-min kung-she t'iao-li (hsiu-cheng ch'ao-an)* (Taipei: Nationalist Chinese Government, 1965) (hereafter cited as *1962 Regulations*). Also see "Resolution on the Further Strengthening of the Collective Economy of the People's Communes and Expanding Agricultural Production," in Chen, *Lien-chiang Documents*, pp. 81-89.

37. *Tsu-kuo*, April 1970, p. 43; *Kirin jih-pao*, July 29, 1967; *Chieh fang jih-pao*, June 4, 1967; *Yu-t'ien chan-pao* (Peking), June 28, 1967; *Nihon keizai shimbun*, April 19, 1967, morning edition; CB, no. 878 (1969), p. 10.

38. *Kung-fei kung-yeh cheng-ts'e ch'i-shih t'iao chu-yao nei-yung;* for Yu Ch'iu-li,

see *Hsien-feng* [Dangerous peak] , April 10, 1967, p. 5.

39. "Antirevolutionary and Revisionist Black Line in Finance and Trade As Seen from the Hsi-lou Conference," *Pei-ching kung-she*, May 26, 1967; for the Tenth Plenum's decision, see John W. Lewis, ed., *The City in Communist China*, p. 159.

40. SCMM, no. 646 (1969), p. 2.

41. Ibid., pp. 4-5, 10.

42. JPRS, no. 49826 (February 16, 1970), p. 16.

43. *Wen-hsüeh chan-pao* (Peking), June 30, 1967; Yao Wen-yüan, "Criticizing Counterrevolutionary Double-Dealer Chou Yang," *Hung-ch'i*, no. 1 (January 1, 1967), p. 29.

44. *Wen-hsüeh chan-pao*, June 30, 1967.

45. "Ten Articles on Literature and Arts," *Wen-hsüeh chan-pao*, June 30, 1967, pp. 5-6, 8.

46. SCMM, no. 635 (1968), pp. 26-27; see also Ch'en's self-criticism in *Hung-wei pao* (Peking), February 8, 1967; "T'ao Chu Is a Royal Knave of the Bourgeoisie," *Hung-wei pao* (Canton) ke-ming tsao-fan ping-t'uan ch'uan-tan [Handbill of the *Hung-wei pao* revolutionary rebel corps] , January 16, 1967.

47. "Do New Service for the People," *Tung-fang hung* (Peking), June 3, 1967; *Chingkang-shan* (Peking), May 23, 1967.

48. *Chiao-hsüeh p'i-p'an*, a pamphlet by the Cultural Revolution Committee of Peking University, no. 2 (1967).

49. Ibid.

50. Ibid.; "Chronology of the Two-Road Struggle on the Educational Front in the Past 17 Years," *Chinese Education*, no. 1 (Spring 1968), pp. 3-58.

51. *Chiao-hsüeh p'i-p'an*, no. 2; *Ajia keizai jumpō*, no. 7114 (1968), p. 4; *Chieh-fang jih-pao*, August 4, 1966.

52. *Chiao-hsüeh p'i-p'an*, no. 2 (1967).

53. Ibid.

54. Sao La-chi, "Liu Shao-ch'i's 'Sixty Points on Higher Education,'" *Chingkang-shan*, June 14, 1967, trans. in JPRS, no. 42887 (October 9, 1967), pp. 21, 25.

55. *Hsin Nung-ta* (Peking), May 10, 1967; "A Letter to Kiangsi Communist Labor University," 1961, CB, no. 891, pp. 30-31.

56. JPRS, no. 42887, p. 27.

57. JMJP, November 9, 1967, p. 4; JMJP, August 11, 1967, p. 4.

58. *Carry the Great Revolution on the Journalistic Front Through to the End*, p. 34.

59. *Peking Review*, no. 4 (January 27, 1961), pp. 6-7.

60. *Chingkang-shan* (Peking), April 18, 1967; "Teng Hsiao-p'ing's Hundred Cases against the Thought of Mao Tse-tung," ibid., March 9, 1967; *Pa-i-san hung-wei-ping* (Tientsin), April 17, 1967.

61. SCMM, no. 652 (1969), pp. 24-25.

62. "Democratic Centralism," January 1962, JPRS, no. 50792 (June 23, 1970), p. 52.

63. *Pa-i-san hung-wei-ping*, April 17, 1967.

64. Ibid.; *Chingkang-shan*, February 1, 1967; *The Case of P'eng Teh-huai*, pp. 137, 217; *Hung-an chan-pao* [Red rock combat news] , April 15, 1967; JMJP, August 16, 1967.

65. JPRS, no. 50792, p. 45.

66. Ibid., p. 42.

67. What follows is based on these sources: "Before and after the Ch'ang-kuan lou Affair," *Tung-fang hung* (Peking), April 20, 1967; *Pei-ching jih-pao*, August 7, 1967; *T'i-yü chan-pao* (Peking), May 18, 1967; *Hung-she tsao-fan tse* (Canton), May 13, 1967.

68. *Tung-fang hung* (Peking), April 20, 1967.

69. Ibid.

70. Dennis Doolin, "The Revival of the 100 Flowers Campaign and the Chinese Intellectuals: 1961," *China Quarterly*, no. 8 (October-December 1961), pp. 34-41; also see Merle Goldman, "The Unique 'Blooming and Contending' of 1961-1962," ibid., no. 37 (January-March 1969), pp. 54-83.

71. "Two Diametrical Documents," *Hung-ch'i*, no. 9 (May 27, 1967), editorial.

72. "Hai Jui Dismissed from Office," *Wen-hui pao* (Shanghai), December 7, 1965, pp. 4-6.

73. Wu Han, "Preface to *Hai Jui Dismissed from Office*," *Wen-hui pao* (Shanghai), December 7, 1965; also see his "On Hai Jui," in *Wu Han yü "Hai Jui pa-kuan" shih-chien* [Wu Han and the incident of *Hai Jui Dismissed from Office*], in *Chung-kung*, ed. Ting Wang, 4 (1969): 155-73.

74. Yao Wen-yüan, "On the 'Three-Family Village,' " *The Great Socialist Cultural Revolution in China* (1), p. 34; Lin Chieh et al., "Teng T'o's *Evening Chat at Yenshan* Is an Anti-Socialist Black Talk," *Chieh-fang chun-pao*, May 8, 1966; *Wen-hui pao* (Shanghai), May 14, 1966.

75. P'ao Wei-wen et al., "Look at the Really Reactionary Face of the 'Three-Family Village,' " *Wen-hui pao*, May 14, 1966.

76. JMJP, June 3, 1966. Levenson noted: "When Ch'ing scholar Chang Hsüeh-ch'eng criticized the Sung scholar Ou Yang Hsiu for niggling about choice of words, he called it 'three-house village scholarship' (a rough equivalent of 'provincial')." See Joseph R. Levenson, "The Province, the Nation, and the World: The Problem of Chinese Identity," in *Approaches to Modern Chinese History*, ed. Albert Feuerwerker et al., p. 282.

77. *Teng T'o hsüan-chih* [Selected works of Teng T'o], in *Chung-kung*, ed. Ting Wang, 2: 57; KMJP, May 17, 1966.

78. "Two Foreign Fables," *Pei-ching wan-pao*, November 26, 1961, in *Chung-kung*, ed. Ting Wang, 2: 166, and trans. in *The Great Socialist Cultural Revolution in China* (2), p. 21; emphasis in original.

79. "Three-Seven Mountain Medicine and Field Medicine," February 1962, in JMJP, May 26, 1966.

80. "Theory of Treasuring Labor Force," *Teng T'o hsüan-chih*, p. 41.

81. *Ching-chi yen-chiu*, no. 5 (May 20, 1966), p. 63.

82. *Teng T'o hsüan-chih*, pp. 56-58.

83. "Send Down Land," November 5, 1961, in *Ching-chi yen-chiu*, no. 5 (May 20, 1966), p. 63.

84. Yao, "On the 'Three-Family Village,' " p. 40; *Teng T'o hsüan-chih*, pp. 62-63; *Yang-ch'eng wan-pao*, May 30, 1966.

85. *Teng T'o hsüan-chih*, pp. 6-7, originally in *Pei-ching wan-pao*, March 26, 1961.

86. Chien Po-tsan, "Some Questions Found in Present-Day Historical Research," *Wen-hui pao* (Shanghai), March 28, 1966. Originally, Chien delivered this speech at an academic conference sponsored by the Nanking Society of History on May 4, 1962. For Fung Yu-lan, see "Black Commanders Liu and Teng Are Big-Time

Operators of Veteran Counterrevolutionary Fung Yu-lan," *Wen-hua ke-ming t'ung-hsün* (Peking), no. 11 (May 1967).

87. "Great Empty Talk," *Ch'ien-hsien*, no. 21 (November 10, 1961).

88. "The Way of Treating a Friend," *Pei-ching wan-pao*, April 6, 1961.

89. *Teng T'o hsüan-chih*, p. 25; Yao, "On the 'Three-Family Village,' "p. 42.

90. JMJP, May 26, 1966, p. 2.

91. Yao, "On the 'Three-Family Village,' " p. 49.

92. Ibid., p. 44; originally, "The Case of Chen Chiang and Wang Ken," *Pei-ching wan-pao*, June 22, 1961.

93. *Teng T'o hsüan-chih*, p. 144.

94. *Ch'ien-hsien*, no. 14 (July 1962), cited in *Chieh-fang chun-pao*, May 8, 1966.

95. JMJP, May 25, 1966, p. 2. It was written in 1961.

96. *Wen-hua ke-ming t'ung-hsün* (Peking), no. 11 (May 1967); CB, no. 842 (1967), p. 51.

97. *Teng T'o hsüan-chih*, p. 196.

98. SCMM, no. 652 (1969), p. 24; "Drag Out Liu Shao-ch'i and Show Him to the Masses," *Chingkang-shan*, April 18, 1967. According to an interview account, during 1960-62 peasants, particularly in Anhui, starved and some of them became beggars roving the country. See Miriam and Ivan London, "The Other China, Hunger: Part I," *Worldview* 19, no. 5 (1976): 4-11.

99. KMJP, August 8, 1967; URS, 48: 83.

100. *Chingkang-shan*, February 1, 1967; ibid., February 8, 1967; CB, no. 848 (1968), p. 22.

101. *Chingkang-shan*, April 18, 1967; SCMM, no. 652, p. 26.

102. JMJP, August 15, 1967; SCMM, no. 652, p. 27.

103. SCMM, no. 652, p. 22; JMJP, November 23, 1967.

104. "Democratic Centralism," January 1962, JPRS, no. 50792, p. 50.

105. URS, 48: 83.

106. JMJP, November 23, 1967; *Hsin Pei-ta* (Peking), January 20, 1967. According to the latter source, Teng asked Hu Yao-pang, chairman of the YCL, to delete his remark from the record soon after returning to his office.

107. SCMM, no. 652, pp. 24-25.

108. Ibid., no. 651, p. 19.

109. CB, no. 884 (1969), p. 19; *Chung-kung*, ed. Ting Wang, 1 (1967): 287.

110. JPRS, no. 50792, pp. 43, 51-52, 57.

111. SCMM, no. 652, pp. 28-29.

112. *Pei-ching kung-she*, May 26, 1967; "Down with Counterrevolutionary and Revisionist Ch'en Yün," *Tung-fang hung* (Peking), January 27, 1967; for Liu's role, see his "Self-Criticism," in *Collected Works of Liu Shao-ch'i, 1957-1967*, p. 361.

113. "Ch'en Yün Is the Vanguard in Restoring Capitalism," *Ts'ai-mao hung-ch'i* (Peking), February 23, 1967; ibid., February 8, 1967; "Another Top Capitalist Roader," JMJP, December 3, 1967.

114. For the circumstantial background of this revision, see Howard L. Boorman, "How to Be a Good Communist: The Political Ethics of Liu Shao-ch'i," *Asian Survey*, no. 8 (August 1963), pp. 372-83.

115. Liu Shao-ch'i, *How to Be a Good Communist*, pp. 81-82.

116. Ibid., pp. 89, 27; also see Liu, *On Intra-Party Struggle*, p. 50.

117. JMJP, June 5, 1967; for Liu's reply, see "Confession," in *Collected Works of Liu Shao-ch'i, 1957-1967*, p. 366.

118. "Self-Criticism," p. 361. The translation has been slightly changed in the light of a Chinese text available at Columbia University.

119. Mao, "Speech at the Tenth Plenary Session," *Chinese Law and Government*, no. 4, p. 86.

120. "Summary of Revisionist Li Hsien-nien's Anti-Mao Remarks in Finance and Trade," *Pei-ching kung-she*, May 26, 1967.

121. "Theoretical Weapon for Carrying Out Revolution under the Proletarian Dictatorship," *Peking Review*, no. 26 (June 24, 1967), p. 28.

122. Ibid.; also see the Communique of the Tenth Plenum in *Peking Review*, no. 39 (September 28, 1962), p. 6.

123. "Speech at the Tenth Plenary Session," p. 89.

124. Ibid., p. 91.

125. Ibid.; *Peking Review*, no. 39 (September 28, 1962), p. 7.

126. "Speech at the Tenth Plenary Session," pp. 92-93.

127. *Peking Review*, no. 39 (September 28, 1962), p. 6.

128. "Speech at the Tenth Plenary Session," p. 85; "Resolution on the Further Strengthening of Collective Economy," secs. I, II, V, and VII, in Chen, *Lien-chiang Documents*, pp. 81-83.

129. *1962 Regulations*, Article 20.

130. "Resolution on the Further Strengthening of the Collective Economy," sec. XII; *Peking Review*, no. 39 (September 28, 1962), p. 5; The Research Office of the Japanese Cabinet Secretariat, *Chūka jimmin Kyōwakoku soshikibetsu jimmeihyō* [Who's who in the People's Republic of China arranged according to organizations], p. 205 (Tokyo, 1967). The addition of K'ang Sheng took on special significance during the Cultural Revolution, for he was the only Maoist member in the Secretariat at that time; in 1967 Lu Ting-yi and Lo Jui-ch'ing were accused of having been handpicked by Liu Shao-ch'i and Teng Hsiao-p'ing.

131. Wang Jen-chung, "Bring Politics to the Fore, Put the Thought of Mao Tse-tung in Command of Everything," *Hung-ch'i*, no. 5 (April 5, 1966), trans. in SCMM, no. 523 (1966), p. 5; for Mao's remark, see "Bombard the Headquarters—My First Big-Character Poster," August 5, 1966, CB, no. 891 (1969), p. 63.

132. Samuel P. Huntington, *Political Order in Changing Societies*, pp. 12-13.

133. "Thoroughly Overthrow Liu Shao-ch'i's Traitor Group," *Chingkang-shan*, February 9, 1967. Of seven secretaries of the Secretariat, P'eng Chen took charge of the legal-political affairs while acting as deputy general-secretary; Wang Chia-hsiang headed foreign affairs, T'an Chen-lin agriculture, Li Fu-ch'un planning, Li Hsien-nien finance and trade, Lu Ting-yi propaganda, Lo Jui-ch'ing military affairs, and K'ang Sheng international Communist movement; of three alternate secretaries, Liu Lan-t'so took charge of control work, Yang Shang-k'un the Secretariat's operation, and Hu Ch'iao-mu the *People's Daily* and NCNA.

134. Parris H. Chang, "Research Notes on the Changing Loci of Decision in the Chinese Communist Party," *China Quarterly*, no. 44 (October-December 1970), pp. 170-71.

135. For Liu's responsibility, see "Self-Criticism," p. 361; for Mao's see "Speech at the Work Conference of the Central Committee," October 25, 1966, CB, no. 891, p. 75.

136. For the role of ideology, see Giovanni Sartori, "Politics, Ideology, and Belief System," *American Political Science Review*, no. 2 (June 1969), p. 402; for China, see Richard Solomon, "From Commitment to Cant: The Evolving Functions

of Ideology in the Revolutionary Process," *Ideology and Politics in Contemporary China*, ed. Chalmers Johnson, pp. 47-77.

CHAPTER 5
SOCIALIST EDUCATION MOVEMENT

1. Chen, *Lien-chiang Documents*, pp. 149-99.
2. NFJP, October 10, 1962, p. 3; Chen, *Lien-chiang Documents*, p. 94.
3. Chen, *Lien-chiang Documents*, pp. 94, 100.
4. Ibid., p. 140.
5. JMJP, August 29, 1967.
6. Chen, *Lien-chiang Documents*, pp. 140, 105-6.
7. Ibid., pp. 231, 234-39.
8. Ibid., p. 142.
9. Richard Baum and Frederick C. Teiwes, *Ssu-Ch'ing: Socialist Education Movement of 1962-1966*, Appendix B, pp. 61, 70.
10. "Ch'en Po-ta's Speech on the October 25 Central Work Conference," SCMM, no. 651 (1969), p. 6.
11. Baum and Teiwes, *Ssu-Ch'ing*, Appendix B, p. 63.
12. Lin Piao, "Report to the Ninth National Congress of Communist Party of China," *Peking Review*, no. 18 (April 30, 1969), p. 20.
13. See "Instructions on the Commune Education Movement" (May 1963) and "Speech at the Hangchow Conference" (May 1963) in *Mao, 1969*, JPRS, no. 61269-2, pp. 314-24.
14. Baum and Tiewes, *Ssu-Ch'ing*, Appendix B, p. 58; ibid., secs. I, II, III, IV.
15. Ibid., p. 20.
16. Ibid., secs. V, VI, VIII, IX, X.
17. NFJP, May 1, 1963, p.2; ibid., May 8, 1963, p. 2; ibid., May 9, 1963, p. 2; ibid., July 3, 1963, p. 2; ibid., July 4, 1963, p. 2; ibid., July 5, 1963, p. 2; *Kiangsi jih-pao*, June 19, 1963; *Anhui jih-pao*, August 6, 1963.
18. NFJP, July 28, 1963, p. 2; Baum and Tiewes, *Ssu-Ch'ing*, p, 75.
19. "Some Concrete Policy Formulations of the Central Committee of the CCP in the Rural Socialist Education Movement" (draft), September 1963 (Baum and Tiewes, *Ssu-Ch'ing*, Appendix C).
20. In the translated version, all dates were put as 1964 for 1963. See Liu, "Self-Criticism," *Collected Works of Liu Shao-ch'i, 1957-1967*, p. 362; also see "Three Trials of Pickpocket Wang Kuang-mei," CB, no. 848, p. 15.
21. For a different interpretation of the SEM in general and this document in particular, see Richard Dennis Baum, "Revolution and Reaction in Rural China: The Struggle between Two Roads during the Socialist Education Movement (1962-1966) and the Great Proletarian Cultural Revolution (1966-1968)" (Ph.D. diss., University of California, Berkeley, 1970); also see his *Prelude to Revolution, Mao, the Party, and the Peasant Question, 1962-1966*.
22. Baum and Tiewes, *Ssu-Ch'ing*, Appendix C, sec. I.
23. Ibid., sec. I; JMJP, November 23, 1967, editorial; also see *The Struggle between the Two Roads in China's Countryside*, p. 3.
24. Baum and Tiewes, *Ssu-Ch'ing*, pp. 79-80.
25. Ibid., secs. IV, V, IX, X.

26. Ibid., sec. VI.

27. Ibid., secs. VII, VIII.

28. JMJP, November 23, 1967, editorial.

29. Baum and Tiewes, *Ssu-Ch'ing*, Appendix C, p. 77.

30. Liu, "Self-Criticism," p. 362.

31. This and the following account are based on interviews with refugees in Hong Kong conducted in 1969-70. Because the informants' experiences are limited to Kwangtung, this account cannot be representative of the entire movement but can serve as an illustration. Interview Protocols no. 16 (December 1969); interviewee was a middle-level cadre in the Kwangtung provincial government.

32. Interview Protocols no. 12.

33. Ibid.

34 *Kiangsi jih-pao*, July 5, 1963; *Hunan jih-pao*, December 4, 1963.

35. JMJP, July 4, 1963, p. 5; ibid., August 27, 1963, p. 2; see also ibid., November 29, 1963, editorial; NFJP, February 20, 1964, p. 2; ibid., April 9, 1964, p. 2: *Yang-ch'eng wan-pao* (Canton), April 29, 1964, p. 2.

36. What follows is mostly based on interviews in Hong Kong.

37. "Eight Great Crimes of Chao Tzu-yang," *Hsiao-ping* [Little soldier], (Canton), February 25, 1967.

38. Interview Protocols no. 13 (December 1969); a letter clarifying this episode (October 30, 1970). Interviewee was a section chief in the Kwangtung provincial government.

39. Ibid.

40. Interview Protocols no. 13.

41. JMJP, November 23, 1967, editorial. For lack of a better translation, the cited passage is taken from Peking's official version. Literally, it means "passing through a place." See *The Struggle between the Two Roads in China's Countryside*, p. 20.

42. *Mao, 1969*, JPRS, no. 61269-2, pp. 337-52.

43. Baum and Tiewes, *Ssu-Ch'ing*, p. 120.

44. Ibid., Appendix D, sec. II.

45. NFJP, May 9, 1963, p. 2; ibid., May 25, 1963, p. 2; *Anhui jih-pao*, August 6, 1963; *Kweichow jih-pao*, August 6, 1963.

46. JMJP, November 14, 1964, p. 2; ibid., November 15, 1964, p. 2; ibid., November 20, 1964, p. 2; NFJP, November 9, 1964, p. 1; *Kweichow jih-pao*, November 25, 1964; JMJP, December 14, 1964, p. 5; *Kiangsu jih-pao*, December 21, 1964, p. 2; JMJP, September 20, 1965, p. 8; only in January and February 1966 were the first meetings of provincial associations held in Hunan, Anhui, Peking, and Kiangsi. See *Radio Hunan*, January 7, 1966; *Radio Anhui*; January 13, 1966; for Peking, see *NCNA Wire Service* (Hong Kong), February 12, 1966, p. 13; *Radio Kiangsi*, February 14, 1966.

47. CB, no. 848 (1968), p. 15. It should be made clear here that the following account of the T'aoyüan experience will serve only to illustrate the differences between Mao and Liu in their approach to the SEM, for it is based on the data provided by the Maoists' post facto revelations.

48. "Exposed by the Scheme for Restoring Capitalism," *Chieh-fang chun-pao*, September 6, 1967, editorial, in JMJP, September 6, 1967; "Wang Kuang-mei's T'aoyüan Experience Is a Poisonous Weed Opposing the Thought of Mao Tse-tung," *Tsan-fan yu-li*, February 12, 1967.

49. JMJP, September 6, 1967.

50. Ibid.; *Hsin-min wan-pao* (Shanghai), December 25, 1964, p. 1.

51. Liu, "Self-Criticism," p. 362; *Radio Kwangtung*, October 26, 1967.

52. SCMM, no. 652, p. 34; *Wen-hui pao* (Shanghai), April 28, 1969, p. 5.

53. JMJP, November 23, 1967; SCMM, no. 652, p. 36; "Previous Ten Points and the Twenty-Three Points Are the Sharpest Ideological Weapon in Criticizing Liu and Wang's Reactionary Line Which Is Left in Appearance but Actually Right," *Tsao-fan yu-li* (Peking), February 12, 1967.

54. CB, no. 891 (1969), p. 63. For a theoretical rendering of the difference between Mao and Liu in their approach to identifying policy problems, see Harry Harding, *Maoist Theories of Policy-Making and Organization*.

55. SCMM, no. 652, p. 37; *Tsao-fan yu-li*, February 12, 1967.

56. *Pa-I-san hung-wei ping* (Red Guard paper, Tientsin, August 13), May 13, 1967, p. 6; emphasis in original.

57. Ibid.; emphasis added.

58. Charles E. Lindblom, *The Policy-Making Process*, p. 26.

59. See *Hsin Pei-ta*, January 20, 1967, p. 4; SCMM, no. 639 (1969), p. 20; *Pei-ching k'e-chi hung-ch'i* [Peking scientific red flag], March 18, 1967; *Pei-ching kung-she*, May 26, 1967.

60. *Pa-I-san hung-wei ping*, May 13, 1967, p. 7; *Yang-ch'eng wan-pao*, July 15, 1965, p. 1.

61. "Drag Out Liu Shao-ch'i and Show Him to the Masses," *Chingkang-shan*, April 11, 1967; *Hung-wei-ping pao*, March 4, 1967; SCMM, no. 652, p. 32.

62. "Some Concrete Policy Formulations of the Central Committee of the CCP in the Rural Socialist Education Movement" (revised draft), September 10, 1964, in Baum and Tiewes, *Ssu-Ch'ing*, Appendix E. For criticism on this, see JMJP, November 23, 1967, editorial.

63. Baum and Tiewes, *Ssu-Ch'ing*, Appendix E, sec. I.

64. Ibid., p. 112.

65. Ibid., p. 105.

66. Ibid.

67. Ibid., p. 111.

68. Ibid., sec. VI.

69. Interview Protocols no. 13 (December 1969). Interviewee was a middle-level cadre in the Kwangtung provincial government.

70. *Kwangchow jih-pao hung-ch'i*, July 11, 1967, p. 1; *San-shih chan-pao* [Third headquarters news] (Canton), June 15, 1967, p. 2; JMJP, December 16, 1964, p. 2; *Kweichow jih-pao*, November 25, 1964; *Ta-kung pao* (Peking), December 24, 1964, p. 2.

71. *Peking Review*, no. 49 (December 1, 1967), pp. 22-27; *Hung-ch'i*, no. 5 (March 10, 1967), pp. 49-50; also see Baum, "Revolution and Reaction in Rural China," pp. 150-72.

72. SCMM, no. 639 (1969), p. 20; *Radio Kwangtung*, October 26, 1967.

73. SCMM, no. 590 (1967), pp. 8-16.

74. *Main Documents of the First Session of the Third National People's Congress of the People's Republic of China*, p. 28.

75. Baum and Tiewes, *Ssu-Ch'ing*, Appendix F.

76. *Tung-fang hung*, May 7, 1967, pp. 7-8.

77. "A Summary of the Discussion of the National Work Conference Convened by the Politburo of the Central Committee," January 14, 1965, in Baum and

Tiewes, *Ssu-Ch'ing*, pp. 118-26.

78. See "Highlights of the Forum on Central Committee Work" (December 20, 1964), "Interjections at a Central Work Conference" (December 27, 1964), "Speech at the Central Work Conference" (December 28, 1964), and "Talk on the Four Clean-Ups Movement" (January 3, 1965) in *Mao, 1969*, JPRS, no. 61269-2, pp. 408-32, 437-44. The quote appears on p. 441.

79. "Comment of Comrade Ch'en Cheng-jen's Report on Stay at a Selected Spot," CB, January 29, 1965, no. 891, p. 49.

80. "Speech at a Work Conference of the Central Committee,"·October 25, 1966, ibid., p. 75. I have slightly changed the translation.

81. "Premier Chou Talks about Why We Must Concentrate Fire Power on Criticizing the Top Capitalist-Roader within the Party," *Hung chan-pao* (Canton), November 29, 1967; for Snow's report, see *New Republic*, April 10, 1971, p. 19.

82. Baum and Tiewes, *Ssu-Ch'ing*, Appendix F, sec. I.

83. Ibid.

84. See *Peking Review*, no. 18 (April 30, 1969), p. 20. This passage appears on p. 120 of Baum and Tiewes, *Ssu-Ch'ing*, but the translation here followed Peking's official version in the *Peking Review* cited. For Mao's statement, see *Peking Review*, no. 22 (May 26, 1967), p. 44; emphasis added.

85. "Decision of the Central Committee of the Chinese Communist Party concerning the Great Proletarian Cultural Revolution," JMJP, August 8, 1966.

86. Baum and Tiewes, *Ssu-Ch'ing*, p. 120.

87. Ibid., Appendix F, secs. V, VI, VIII.

88. Ibid., sec. IX.

89. Interview Protocols nos. 11 and 16 (December 1969). Interviewee was a middle-level cadre in the Kwangtung provincial government. Also see *Tung-fang hung*, May 7, 1967.

90. *Tung-fang hung*, May 7, 1967, p. 8; *Pei-ching k'e-chi hung-ch'i*, March 18, 1967; *Radio Kwangtung*, October 26, 1967; for Lin, see CB, no. 894 (1969), p. 21.

91. "Liberate Many and Hit a Handful," *Hsin-pei-ta kung-she* [New Peking University commune], May 9, 1967; also see Victor Nee and Don Layman, "The Cultural Revolution at Peking University," *Monthly Review*, July-August 1969, pp. 42-43. Among the dissidents was Nieh Yüan-tzu who, together with six other students, was to hoist the first big-character poster condemning Lu P'ing on May 25, 1966, which, when suppressed, Mao ordered broadcast, thus involving the conflict in the Cultural Revolution.

92. NFJP, March 12, 1965, p. 2; also see Ezra F. Vogel, *Canton under Communism*, pp. 42-43.

93. NFJP, February 16, 1965; *Wen-hui pao* (Shanghai), March 12, 1966; *Chekiang jih-pao*, September 7, 1966; JMJP, March 13, 1966; ibid., January 13, 1966; ibid., February 14, 1966; ibid., February 18, 1966.

94. NFJP, July 7, 1965, p. 1; JMJP, July 25, 1965; KMJP, August 9, 1965.

95. *Circular of the Central Committee of the Chinese Communist Party, May 16, 1966*, p. 3.

96. JMJP, December 26, 1965, p. 3.

97. Ibid., October 12, 1965, p. 3.

98. Ibid.

99. Ibid., October 26, 1965, p. 3.

100. Ibid., October 13, 1965, p. 1; ibid., November 1, 1965, p. 2; ibid., November 15, 1965, p. 2.

101. Ibid., November 25, 1965, p. 2.

102. Ibid., October 29, 1965, p. 2.

103. Ibid., November 5, 1965, p. 2.

104. Ibid., November 19, 1965, p. 2; ibid., December 17, 1965, p. 2.

105. Ibid., November 26, 1965, p. 3.

106. Ibid., October 18, 1965, p. 2.

107. Ibid., December 20, 1965, p. 2; Kuan Feng, "Everything for Revolution," KMJP, October 1, 1965; KMJP, December 27, 1965.

108. JMJP, February 7, 1966.

109. Ibid., February 11, 1966; ibid., February 12, 1966; *Yang-ch'eng wan-pao*, February 25, 1966, p. 2.

110. *Hung-ch'i*, no. 4 (March 24, 1966), pp. 31-34.

111. *Hung-wei-ping pao*, January 22, 1967.

112. CB, no. 834 (1967), p. 26; *Pei-ching kung-she*, May 27, 1967; *Hung-ch'i*, April 4, 1967.

113. For this rule, see Carl Friedrich, *Man and His Government,* pp. 169-215.

114. For this theme, see Benjamin I. Schwartz, "A Personal View of Some Thoughts of Mao Tse-tung," in *Ideology and Politics in Contemporary China,* ed. Chalmers Johnson, pp. 352-72.

CHAPTER 6
ARMY'S EMULATION CAMPAIGNS

1. For Lin's over-all role after 1960, see Ellis Joffe, "The Chinese Army under Lin Piao: Prelude to Political Intervention," in *China: Management of a Revolutionary Society*, ed. John Lindbeck, pp. 343-76.

2. *Issues and Studies*, no. 11 (August 1969), pp. 87-101.

3. Mao Tse-tung, "On Correcting Mistaken Ideas in the Party," *Selected Works of Mao Tse-tung*, 1: 105-14.

4. For an excerpt from this document see *Fei-ching yen-chiu*, no. 4 (April 1967), pp. 71-73.

5. Ibid., p. 71.

6. Interview Protocols no. 21 (January 1970). Interviewee was a former officer in the public security forces. See also John Gittings, *The Role of the Chinese Army*, pp. 242-62, and diagram, p. 272.

7. *Kung-tso t'ung-hsün*, no. 8 (February 6, 1961), pp. 11-19.

8. Lin Piao, "Speech Given at an All-Army Conference on Guidance and Education," May 1961, JPRS, no. 50477, pp. 23, 62.

9. Interview Protocols nos. 24 and 30 (January 1970). Interviewee was the same as in no. 21.

10. See, for example, Edgar Snow, "The Army and the Party," *New Republic*, May 22, 1971, p. 12.

11. Interview Protocols no. 23 (January 1970), same interviewee; also see Michel Oksenberg, "Local Leaders in Rural China, 1962-1965: Individual Attributes, Bureaucratic Positions, and Political Recruitment," in *Chinese Communist Politics in Action*, ed. A. Doak Barnett, pp. 164-65.

12. The four goods are: good political ideology, good "three-eight" style, good military training, and good management of living (KMJP, January 23, 1964, p. 2).

13. Wu Yun-kuang, "Three Periods of Political Works in the Chinese Communist

Army," *Fei-ching yen-chiu*, no. 4 (April 1967), pp. 29-33; also see Gittings, *Role of the Chinese Army*, pp. 109-10.

14. Interview Protocols no. 30 (January 1970). Interviewee was the same as in no. 21.

15. JMJP, May 8, 1963; KMJP, January 22, 1964, p. 2.

16. JMJP, February 2, 1963; KMJP, January 27, 1964, p. 2.

17. This was published in JMJP, March 5, 1963, p. 1.

18. Ch'en Kuang-sheng, *Lei Feng, Chairman Mao's Good Fighter*, p. 7.

19. *Chung-kuo ch'ing-nien pao*, February 5, 1963.

20. JMJP, May 11, 1964, p. 3.

21. "Important Method of Raising Cadres' and Masses' Class Consciousness," *Ta-kung pao* (Peking), October 8, 1963, editorial.

22. KMJP, January 22, 1964, p. 2.

23. *Hsin-min wan-pao* (Shanghai), August 10, 1963, p. 4; NFJP, December 13, 1963, p. 2; *Chung-kuo ch'ing-nien pao*, December 26, 1963, p. 4.

24. SCMM, no. 639 (1969), p. 15.

25. Mao, "Instruction of the Central Committee on the Strengthening of Learning from Each Other and Overcoming Conservatism and Complacency" (excerpts), December 13, 1963, CB, no. 892 (1969), pp. 15-19.

26. Hsiao Hua, "Several Problems on the Current Construction of Political Work within the Army," KMJP, January 22, 1964, p. 2.

27. "Broadly Develop, Compare, Learn, Catch Up With, and Help Activities to Obtain Five Good Enterprises and Five Good Workers," JMJP, February 2, 1964.

28. CB, no. 891 (1969), p. 48; also see *Mao, 1969*, JPRS, no. 61269-2, p. 329.

29. SCMM, no. 639 (1969), p. 15.

30. JPRS, no. 50477 (May 7, 1970), pp. 90-96.

31. *Hung-ch'i* Commentator, "Ideological Work, Its Decisive Role," *Hung-ch'i*, no. 5 (March 17, 1964), as trans. in *Peking Review*, no. 17 (April 24, 1964), p. 13.

32. Ibid., p. 14.

33. See Ch'en Po-ta, "Under the Banner of Comrade Mao Tse-tung," *Hung-ch'i*, no. 4 (July 16, 1958), p. 5.

34. Commentator, "Political Work Is the Lifeline of All Works," *Hung-ch'i*, no. 6 (March 31, 1964), p. 41.

35. For some of these views, see chapter 5, particularly the section on the debate at the seven-thousand-cadre conference in January 1962; also see SCMM, no. 652 (1969), p. 22, and *Hsin Pei-ta*, January 20, 1967.

36. Commentator, "'Start from Practice' in Carrying Out Ideological Work," *Hung-ch'i*, nos. 7-8 (April 20, 1964).

37. Commentator, "Man's Role Is Decisive," ibid., no. 10 (May 23, 1964).

38. What constituted *five good* varied with the localities. In Hopei, for example, the *five-good communes* referred to the good grasp of politics and ideology, "three-eight" style, three democracies, scientific experiment, and fulfillment of duty; a *five-good commune member* had a good record in the collective economy, politics, fulfillment of duty, democratic management, and unity and mutual help; see *Radio Hupei*, March 16, 1964. Similarly, the *five-good enterprises* referred to the good grasp of political work, fulfillment of plans, management, management of living and work style; a *five-good worker* had a good record in politics and ideology, fulfillment of duty, observance of discipline, customary study, and unity and mutual help; see JMJP, February 2 and March 18, 1964; for the *five-good youth*, see *Chung-kuo ch'ing-nien pao*, March 5, 1964; for the *five-good women*, see KJJP,

March 8, 1964.

39. *Ta-kung pao* (Peking), February 24, 1964; ibid., April 4, 1964; also see JMJP, February 20, 1964; Po I-po, "Steeling of Furnace in Class Struggle," JMJP, May 5, 1964; KMJP, April 4, 1964, p. 4.

40. SCMM, no. 639, p. 15; "Tach'ing Spirit and Tach'ing People," JMJP, April 20, 1964.

41. *Chekiang jih-pao*, September 20, 1965; JMJP, December 28, 1964, p. 5; ibid., October 1, 1964, editorial.

42. Ch'en Chan-ch'ao, "We Must Teach Reading Materials by Negative Examples," *Hung-ch'i*, nos. 17-18 (September 23, 1964), pp. 37-38.

43. An Tzu-wen, "Training Successors for the Revolution Is the Party's Strategic Task," *Hung-ch'i*, nos. 17-18 (September 23, 1964), trans. in *Training Successors for the Revolution Is the Party's Strategic Task*, pp. 12-13; for Mao's instruction see "Talk on Putting Military Affairs Work into Full Effect and Cultivating Successors to the Revolution," June 16, 1964, in *Mao, 1969*, JPRS, no. 61269-2, pp. 356-60.

44. *Mao Tse-tung chu-tso hsüan-tu, chia*, was published by Jen-min ch'u-p'an-she and *Mao Tse-tung chu-tso hsüan-tu, yi*, by Ch'ing-nien ch'u-pan-she.

45. Yao Wen-yüan, "The Revolutionary Younger Generation Is Growing," *Hung-ch'i*, no. 6 (March 31, 1964).

46. Hsiao Hua, "How the Political Instructors of Our Army Study Mao's Work," JMJP, May 23, 1964.

47. "Ten Crimes of T'an Chen-lin," *Chingkang-shan*, March 15, 1967.

48. CB, no. 834 (1967), p. 24.

49. Ibid., no. 891 (1969), p. 70.

50. "Facts about Liu Chien-hsün's Crimes," a pamphlet published by the general command headquarters of the Revolutionary Rebels of the CCP Honan Provincial Committee, March 27, 1967.

51. "Record of Teng Hsiao-p'ing's Reactionary Utterances," *How Vicious They Are!* published by Liaison Post for Criticizing Liu, Teng, and T'ao, Red Flag Commune of Peking Railway Institute, Red Guard Congress, April 1967; JMJP, January 22, 1967; "National Conference on Political Theory Class Is 'Iron-Clad Proof of Liu-Teng's Opposition to the Thought of Mao Tse-tung,'" *Tou-pi-kai*, no. 1 (May 15, 1967).

52. *Hsin-wen chan-pao*, May 14, 1967; also see *Carry the Great Revolution on the Journalistic Front Through to the End*, pp. 42-43; *Tung-fang hung* (Mining Institute), May 7, 1967, p. 6.

53. *Wen-hui pao* (Shanghai), June 29, 1965; also see Alexandra Close, "Old Model Army," *Far Eastern Economic Review*, June 17, 1965, pp. 548-50.

54. *Chingkang-shan*, April 18, 1967; also see *Circular of the Central Committee of the Chinese Communist Party, May 16, 1966*, p. 3.

55. *Hsin-min wan-pao* (Shanghai), November 14, 1963. It was ironic that Liu Shao-ch'i was accused in 1967 for having advocated the "theory of docile tool" to the Party.

56. JMJP, November 4, 1965; *Ta-kung pao* (Peking), November 25, 1965.

57. *Issues and Studies*, no. 11 (August 1969), p. 93. For this aspect see chapter 10.

58. For these two methods of control, see Samuel Huntington, *The Soldier and the State*, pp. 80-97; also see Philip Selznick, *TVA and the Grass Roots*.

CHAPTER 7
POLICY INNOVATIONS AND CONFLICTS

1. For lack of a better term, *tang-ch'uan-p'ai* will be called the "Party establishment" hereafter. Mao formed this concept in the Twenty-Three Points of December 1964. See Baum and Teiwes, *Ssu-Ch'ing*, p. 120.

2. "Let the Radiance of the Thought of Mao Tse-tung Forever Shine over the Road of Agricultural Mechanization," *Nung-yeh chi-hsieh chi-shu* [Agricultural machinery and technology], no. 4 (July 8, 1967), in SCMM, no. 600 (1967), p. 5.

3. SCMM, no. 610 (1968), p. 19.

4. Ibid., pp. 10-22.

5. Li She-nan, "A Few Problems on the Lowering of Operational Cost of Agricultural Mechanization," JMJP, June 30, 1964.

6. SCMM, no. 610, pp. 16-26; ibid., no. 613 (1968), p. 21; "Letter to the People of the Whole Country," *P'i-t'an chan-pao* (Peking), June 1, 1967.

7. SCMM, no. 610, pp. 16-26.

8. KJJP, October 10, 1964.

9. SCMM, no. 610, p. 29.

10. JMJP, October 15, 1964, editorial.

11. Barry M. Richman, *Industrial Society in Communist China*, p. 676.

12. "Expose a Big Plot for Capitalist Restoration," *Wen-hui pao* (Shanghai), April 29, 1967.

13. Richman, *Industrial Society in Communist China*, p. 642.

14. Ching Hung, "The Plot of the Top Ambitionist to Operate 'Trusts' on a Large Scale Must Be Thoroughly Exposed," KMJP, May 9, 1967.

15. "Liu-Teng's Mad Ambition for Capitalist Restoration As Seen from Their Trust Plan," *Ch'iu-Liu chan-pao* (Peking), July 21, 1967.

16. *Wen-hui pao* (Shanghai), April 29, 1967; "Survey Report on Conditions in Tientsin People's Pharmaceutical Plant Since Trial Operation of Trust," *Ch'iu-Liu chan-pao* (Peking), June 21, 1967.

17. *Ch'iu-Liu chan-pao* (Peking), July 21, 1967.

18. Ibid.; *Wen-hui pao* (Shanghai), April 29, 1967. For an analysis of management of enterprises, see Stephen Andors, "Factory Management and Political Ambiguity, 1961-63," *China Quarterly*, no. 59 (July-September 1974), pp. 435-76.

19. *Ch'iu-Liu chan-pao* (Peking), July 21, 1967.

20. "Two Diametrically Opposed Lines in Building the Economy," *Wen-hui pao* (Shanghai), *Chieh-fang jih-pao, Tang chih-pu sheng-huo*, joint editorial, in JMJP, August 25, 1967; *Ch'iu-Liu chan-pao* (Peking), July 21, 1967.

21. *Wen-hui pao* (Shanghai), April 29, 1967.

22. *Ch'iu-Liu chan-pao* (Peking), July 21, 1967.

23. Richman, *Industrial Society in Communist China*, pp. 450-52.

24. *Wen-hui pao* (Shanghai), April 29, 1967; *Ch'iu-Liu chan-pao* (Peking), June 21, 1967.

25. "Drum-player of Revisionism, Outline of Li Hsien-nien's Black Remarks against the Thought of Mao Tse-tung," *Pei-ching kung-she* (Peking), May 26, 1967.

26. KMJP, April 22, 1967; ibid., May 9, 1967; "Only Socialism Can Save China," *Wen-hui pao* (Shanghai), April 29, 1967.

27. *Pei-ching kung-she* (Peking), May 26, 1967.

28. "Drag Out Liu Shao-ch'i and Show Him to the Masses," *Chingkang-shan* (Peking), April 18, 1967.

29. For details of this experiment, see John W. Lewis, "Commerce, Education, and Political Development in Tangshan, 1956-1969," in *The City in Communist China*, ed. John W. Lewis, pp. 159-69.

30. "Commodity Circulation Rationally Organized According to Economic Regions in T'angshan Area," *Ta-kung pao* (Peking), April 8, 1965.

31. Michel Oksenberg, "Communist China: A Quiet Crisis in Revolution," *Asian Survey*, vol. 6, no. 1 (January 1966), and in *Communist China*, ed. Franz Schurmann and Orville Shell (New York: Vintage Books, 1967), pp. 394-95.

32. Lewis, "Commerce, Education, and Political Development in Tangshan," p. 159.

33. NFJP, April 20, 1965.

34. See Oksenberg, "Communist China"; Lewis, "Commerce, Education, and Political Development in Tangshan," p. 162.

35. JPRS, no. 44052 (January 17, 1968), cited in Lewis, "Commerce, Education, and Political Development in Tangshan," p. 166.

36. Richman, *Industrial Society in Communist China*, p. 376.

37. Christopher Howe, *Wage Patterns and Wage Policy in Modern China, 1919-1972*, pp. 107-8.

38. *Chingkang-shan* (Peking), April 18, 1967; SCMM, no. 616 (1968), p. 24; ibid., no. 651 (1969), p. 5.

39. JMJP, September 3, 1964; SCMM, no. 653 (1969), pp. 24-26.

40. SCMM, no. 653 (1969), pp. 24-26; *Chingkang-shan*, February 1, 1967; ibid., February 8, 1967; NCNA (Canton), August 30, 1964.

41. "Two Instances of Liu Shao-ch'i's 'Two-Track System,' " *Kang pa-i chan-ch'i* (Canton), First Ten Days of December, 1967.

42. JMJP, August 20, 1964; for local variations, see ibid., from August 2 to September 14, 1964; NFJP, June 19, 1964.

43. SCMM, no. 653 (1969), pp. 21-25.

44. Ching Hung-chi, "Reactionary Nature of the 'Theory That Distribution Determines,'" JMJP, September 14, 1967.

45. "Is It a Reflection of Bourgeois Ideas to Wear Flowery Clothes and Buy Expensive Things?" *Pei-ching jih-pao* (Peking), April 16, 1965.

46. CB, no. 848 (1968), p. 12.

47. *Pei-ching jih-pao*, April 16, 1965.

48. SCMM, no. 616 (1968), p. 19; also see Howe, *Wage Patterns*, pp. 95-96.

49. "On Khrushchev's Phony Communism and Its Historical Lessons for the World," *The Polemic on the General Line of the International Communist Movement*, p. 475 (hereafter cited as *Polemic*).

50. *Chiao-hsüeh p'i-p'an*, no. 2 (1967); JPRS, no. 42887 (1967), pp. 22-25; for the contents of these documents, see above, chapter 5.

51. For some major problems of education seen in the light of Maoist egalitarianism, see Donald J. Munro, "Egalitarian Ideal and Educational Fact in Communist China," in *China: Management of a Revolutionary Society*, ed. John Lindbeck, pp. 256-301.

52. Interview Protocols nos. 43 (February 1970) and 53 (March 1970). Interviewees were graduates of Chungshan University in Canton.

53. "Draft Regulations on Secondary Education," *Shin-chūgoku nenkan, 1968* [New China yearbook 1968] (Tokyo: Chūgoku kenkyu jō, 1968), pp. 303-8.

54. Nishijima Atsuyoshi, *Proretaria kaikyū bunka daikakumei* [Great Proletarian

Cultural Revolution] (Tokyo: Shonen shuppan-sha, 1968), pp. 26-27.

55. Interview Protocols no. 43.

56. Chou Kuo-ying, "The Contention about Favoritism," *Wen-hui pao* (Shanghai), February 20, 1965.

57. *Wen-hui pao* (Shanghai), March 20, 1965.

58. Ibid., February 20, 1965.

59. "Black Commander Liu and Teng Are Backstage Bosses of Veteran Counter-revolutionary Fung Yu-lan," *Wen-hua ke-ming t'ung-hsün (Peking), no. 11 (May 1967)*; Chien Po-tsan, "Some Questions Found in Present Historical Research," *Wen-hui pao* (Shanghai), March 28, 1966; CB, no. 891, p. 51.

60. "Chronology of Important Events in the Struggle between the Two Roads in Higher Education," *Chiao-hsüeh p'i-p'an* (Peking), no. 2 (1967).

61. Wang Shu-chin, "Class Viewpoint Must Be Maintained," *Pei-ching jih-pao* (Peking), December 14, 1964.

62. Chia Ch'uan-kuei, "My View on the Question of Adhering to the Principle of Revolution at Home," ibid.

63. "A Few Examples of Crimes Committed by T'an Chen-lin against the Thought of Mao Tse-tung," *K'e-chi hung-ch'i* (Peking); March 26, 1967.

64. Marianne Bastid, "Economic Necessity and Political Ideals in Educational Reform during the Cultural Revolution," *China Quarterly*, no. 42 (April-June 1970), p. 18. The figures in Canton areas are based on interviews; see Interview Protocols no. 53 (March 1970). Interviewee was a graduate of Chungshan University.

65. SCMM, no. 616 (1968), p. 19.

66. JMJP, October 28, 1967, p. 1.

67. "Instructions Given at the Spring Festival concerning Educational Works" (excerpts), February 13, 1964; CB, no. 891, p. 43.

68. Ibid., p. 46; also see "Minutes of Spring Festival Talk," February 13, 1964, in *Mao, 1969*, JPRS, no. 61269-2, pp. 326-36.

69. *Chiao-hsüeh p'i-p'an* (Peking), no. 2 (1967).

70. CB, no. 891, p. 43; ibid., no. 888, p. 13.

71. Ibid., no. 891, pp. 42-43.

72. SCMM, no. 639 (1969), p. 11.

73. *Chiao-hsüeh p'i-p'an*, no. 2 (1967); *Mao, 1969*, JPRS, no. 61269-2, pp. 330, 335.

74. JMJP, July 30, 1964; ibid., August 18, 1964.

75. *Main Documents of the First Session of the Third National People's Congress of the People's Republic of China*, p. 31 (hereafter cited as *Main Documents of the Third NPC*).

76. *Chiao-hsüeh p'i-p'an*, no. 2 (1967).

77. CB, no. 891, p. 46.

78. *Mao chu-hsi chiao-yü yü-lu* [Chairman Mao's talks on education] in Nishijima Atsuyoshi, *Mō-takutō saikō shiji* (Tokyo: Sanichi shobō, 1970), p. 25.

79. *Chiao-hsüeh p'i-p'an*, no. 2 (1967); *Chiao-yü ke-ming*, April 16, 1967.

80. *Chiao-hsüeh p'i-p'an*, no. 2 (1967); *Chiao-yü ke-ming*, April 16, 1967.

81. CB, no. 891, pp. 51-55.

82. Interview Protocols no. 45 (February 1970). Interviewee was a middle-level cadre in the Kwangtung provincial government.

83. "Monstrous Crimes of Urban 'Lords' Health Ministry in Opposing the June 26 Directive," August 18, 1966, *Hung-i chan-pao* (Peking) and *Pa-i-pa chan-po*

[Battle bulletin], January 26, 1967. For an analysis of health care in 1958-60, see David M. Lampton, "Health Policy during the Great Leap Forward," *China Quarterly*, no. 60 (December 1974), pp. 668-98.

84. "Chairman Mao's Instructions on Health Work, 1928-1966," *Hsin jen-wei* (Peking), June 1967.

85. "Report of the Party Organization of the Ministry of Health to the Chairman," ibid.,

86. NCNA (Peking), February 15, 1965; ibid., February 19, 1965.

87. *Hsin jen-wei*, June 1967.

88. CB, no. 892 (1969), p. 20. This source put the figure at 50 percent but 15 percent was put by the following source: "Chairman Mao's June 26 Directive," *Hung-i chan-pao* (Peking) and *Pa-i-pa chan-pao*, June 21, 1967.

89. CB, no. 892 (1969), p. 20.

90. Ibid.

91. "Many Flies Lightly Plot to Topple Giant Tree," *Ch'üan-wu-ti* (Peking), June 26, 1967.

92. Ibid.,

93. "Letter of Instruction on Question of Agricultural Mechanization," March 12, 1966, *Mao, 1969*, JPRS, no. 61269-2, pp. 373-74.

94. These categories are defined by Theodore Lowi. See his "American Business, Public Policy, Case Studies, and Political Theory," *World Politics* 16 (July 1964): 677-715.

95. Michel Oksenberg, "Policy Making under Mao, 1949-68: An Overview," in *China*, ed. John Lindbeck, pp. 79-115.

96. For some of these tensions, see David E. Apter, *The Politics of Modernization*, pp. 72-72; also see John Kautsky, *Political Consequences of Modernization*.

97. Ralf Dahrendorf, *Class and Class Conflicts in Industrial Society*, pp. 214-15.

98. Ibid., p. 178.

99. For a study of Communist politics in this light, see Carl Linden, *Khrushchev and Soviet Leadership, 1957-1964*.

CHAPTER 8

POLICY CONFLICTS IN THE CULTURAL CIRCLE

1. For this relationship, see Byung-joon Ahn, "The Politics of Peking Opera, 1962-1965," *Asian Survey*, December 1972, pp. 1066-81.

2. Wu Wen-hui, "A Tentative Discussion on the Difference between So-called 'Middle Characters' and Characters of the Middle Status," *Hsüeh-shu yen-chiu* [Pedagogic research], no. 3 (May 5, 1966); *Wen-i pao* [Literature], no. 89 (September 30, 1964), pp. 15-20.

3. Yao Wen-yüan, *On the Counterrevolutionary Double-Dealer Chou Yang*, pp. 41-42; "Chronology of Events on the Cultural Front in Communist China," CB, no. 842 (1967), p. 7.

4. JMJP, May 29, 1967; CB, no. 842, pp. 7-8.

5. "New Arts of Socialism Occupy All Theaters," *Hung-she wen-i* (Peking), May 20, 1967.

6. Chiang Ch'ing, "Do New Service for the People," *Tungfang hung* (Peking), June 3, 1967; also see her speech in JMJP, December 4, 1966.

7. "Comrade Chiang Ch'ing's Outstanding Contribution to the Cultural Revolution," *Hsin Pei-ta* (Peking), May 30, 1967; also see *Hung-she wen-i* (Peking), May 20, 1967.

8. For details of this debate, see Joseph Simon, "Ferment among Intellectuals," *Problems of Communism* (September-October 1964), pp. 30-31.

9. Hsü Ch'i-shien, "Some Problems on Class Character and Moral Inheritance," KMJP, August 15, 1963; Wu Han, "More on Morality, Replying to Comrade Hsü Ch'i-hsien," ibid., August 19, 1963.

10. See articles in KMJP, October 6, 1963; for Wu Han's rebuttal, see JMJP, December 24, 1963.

11. According to this view, the Taiping rebels represented the peasants; Tseng Kuo-fan was a reactionary who suppressed them. The point at issue, then, was whether Li was really a traitor to the Taiping cause and hence was to be reviled or whether he only pretended to be a traitor and hence was a hero. For details of this controversy, see Stephen Uhalley, "The Controversy over Li Hsiu-ch'eng," *Journal of Asian Studies* (February 1966), pp. 305-17.

12. Ch'i Pen-yü, "On the Autobiography of Li Hsiu-ch'eng, in Discussion with Messrs. Lo Erh-kang, Liang Ku-lu, and Lü Chi-wen," *Li-shih yen-chiu*, no. 4 (August 15, 1963).

13. *Hsin Pei-ta*, May 30, 1967; also see CB, no. 842 (1967), p. 10.

14. Yao, *On the Counterrevolutionary Double-Dealer Chou Yang*, p. 44.

15. Ch'i Pen-yü, "Patriotism or Betrayal? Criticizing Reactionary Film *Secret History of Ch'ing Court*," *Hung-ch'i*, no. 5 (March 30, 1967), p. 22; *Wen-hui pao, Chieh-fang jih-pao, Chih-pu Sheng-huo*, August 9, 1967; "Attempting Betrayal against the Party Is the Usurpation of the Party," in JMJP, August 12, 1967, p. 4. Merle Goldman has offered a different interpretation. She suggests that Li Hsiu-ch'eng was depicted like P'eng Teh-huai as Li had courageously challenged Hung Hsiu-chuan who, like Mao, was portrayed as unwilling to listen to the advice of his associates. See Merle Goldman, "The Party's 'Cultural Revolution' of 1962-1964," in *Ideology and Politics in Contemporary China*, ed. Chalmers Johnson, pp. 219-56.

16. For Yao's view, see KMJP, September 24, 1963; for Chou's reply, see ibid., November 7, 1963; for Yao's revival of the debate, see ibid., May 10, 1964.

17. According to one source, Mao made this comment on September 23, 1963. See "Chairman Mao's Important Instructions on Literary and Art Work since the Publication of 'Talks at the Yenan Forum on Literature and Art' (1942-1967)," in *Survey of the Chinese Mainland Press*, no. 4000 (1967), p. 23 (hereafter cited as SCMP). Yao Wen-yüan claimed, however, that Mao made the comment "in the first half of 1963." See his *On the Counterrevolutionary Double-Dealer Chou Yang*, p. 43. It seems unlikely that Yao's misdating was an error in view of his relation with Mao. Perhaps he was implying here that he had started the criticism against Chou Ku-ch'eng in August 1963, with Mao's approval.

18. Yao, *On the Counterrevolutionary Double-Dealer Chou Yang*, p. 45.

19. SCMP, no. 4000 (1967), p. 23.

20. Ibid.; CB, no. 891, p. 41.

21. "Liu Shao-ch'i's Counterrevolutionary Revisionist Utterance on Culture and Art," *Hung-she hsüan-ch'uan-ping* (Peking), no. 4 (May 10, 1967); JMJP, April 23, 1967; Yao, *On the Counterrevolutionary Double-Dealer Chou Yang*, p. 46; CB, no. 842, pp. 11-12.

22. *Hung-she hsüan-ch'uan-ping* (Peking), no. 4 (May 10, 1967).

23. "List of Lin Mo-han's Crimes in Destroying Revolution in Literature and Art," JMJP, December 28, 1966.

24. Yao, *On the Counterrevolutionary Double-Dealer Chou Yang*, p. 43.

25. JMJP, May 22, 1963.

26. Yao, *On the Counterrevolutionary Double-Dealer Chou Yang*, pp. 43-44.

27. *Hsin Pei-ta* (Peking), May 30, 1967.

28. KMJP, September 9, 1963.

29. Chou Yang, "A Fighting Task Confronting Workers in Philosophy and Social Sciences," CB, no. 726 (1963), p. 2; also see Yao, *On the Counterrevolutionary Double-Dealer Chou Yang*, p. 45.

30. K'o Ching-shih, "Energetically Develop and Foster a Socialist Theatre, the Better to Serve the Socialist Economic Base," *Hung-ch'i*, no. 15 (August 15, 1964), in *A Great Revolution on the Cultural Front*, pp. 31-32.

31. Ibid., p. 31.

32. The Revolutionary Committee of the China Peking Opera Theatre, "Let Heroic Images of the Proletariat Shine on the Peking Opera Stage!" in Chiang Ch'ing, *On the Revolution of Peking Opera*, pp. 34-43; *Hsin Pei-ta*, May 30, 1967.

33. Chiang, *On the Revolution of Peking Opera*, pp. 40-55; *Hsin Pei-ta*, May 30, 1967; *Pei-ching kung-jen* (Peking), May 27, 1967, p. 4.

34. "Antirevolutionary Revisionist P'eng Chen's Crimes," SCMM, no. 639 (1969), p. 16; *Hsin Pei-ta*, May 30, 1967; Chiang, *On the Revolution of Peking Opera*, pp. 49, 1-11.

35. JMJP, April 28, 1967, p. 4; also see Huan Shih-chang, "Reactionary Movie *Blazing Field* and China's Khrushchev," *Hung-ch'i*, no. 7 (May 21, 1967), pp. 33-34. This movie depicted Liu's activities in Anyüan coal mines in the 1920s.

36. *Hsin Pei-ta*, May 30, 1967.

37. CB, no. 842, p. 20.

38. Chiang, *On the Revolution of Peking Opera*, p. 47.

39. CB, no. 842, p. 27.

40. *Carry the Great Revolution on the Journalistic Front Through to the End*, p. 60; "Big Political Struggle on the News Front," *Hsin-wen-hsien* [News front] (Peking), June 30, 1967.

41. This was a passage of her speech to the enlarged MAC made on April 12, 1967. See "New Arts of Socialism Occupy All Theaters," *Hung-she-wen-i* (Peking), May 20, 1967.

42. This was taken from another speech (or possibly the same speech as the one above) to the MAC made on April 13, 1967. See *Tung-fang hung* (Peking), June 3, 1967.

43. "Comrade Chiang Ch'ing and Peking Opera, *Sachiapang*," *Pei-ching wen-i* [Peking literature] (Peking), May 18, 1967. It is still unclear exactly when this group was formed, but it was definitely before July 1965. See JMJP, August 13, 1967, p. 4.

44. The Chinese Press has not reported the members of the Five-Man Group. This account was based on the following two Red Guard papers: "Take Out the Reactionary Program of Liu Shao-ch'i and P'eng Chen and Show It to the Masses," *Hsin kang-yüan* [New Steel Institute], May 20, 1967; The East Is Red Corps of the Peking Mine Institute, *San-fan fen-tzu Liu Shao-ch'i kui-e-shih* [The history of the three-anti element Liu Shao-ch'i's crimes], mimeographed (May 1967).

45. *Mao, 1969*, JPRS, no. 61269-2, p. 355; "A Great Revolution on the Cultural

Front," *Hung-ch'i*, no. 12 (June 30, 1964), editorial, in *A Great Revolution on the Cultural Front*, p. 86.

46. KMJP, June 5, 1967.

47. JMJP, July 31, 1964.

48. Chiang, *On the Revolution of Peking Opera*, pp. 1-7; CB, no. 842, p. 21.

49. Peng Chen, "Talk at the Festival of the Peking Opera on Contemporary Themes," *Hung-ch'i*, no. 14 (July 31, 1964), in *A Great Revolution on the Cultural Front*, p. 14.

50. *Peking Review*, no. 23 (June 2, 1967), p. 8; emphasis in original.

51. *Training Successors for the Revolution Is the Party's Strategic Task*, pp. 12-13; Chiang, *On the Revolution of Peking Opera*, p. 49; *Hsin Pei-ta*, May 30, 1967.

52. CB, no. 842, p. 23.

53. Li Chün, "Exposing Chou Yang's Various Crimes in Resisting Chairman Mao's June 27 Directive," *Wen-hsüeh chan-pao* (Peking), June 30, 1967; CB, no. 842, p. 16.

54. *On the Counterrevolutionary Double-Dealer Chou Yang*, pp. 47-48.

55. Ibid., p. 46; CB, no. 842, pp. 24-25.

56. Wang Chung and Kuo P'ei-heng, "Discussing the 'Two Combine into One' Question with Comrade Yang Hsien-chen," JMJP, July 17, 1964, p. 5; Lin Chieh, "Is the Theory of 'Two Combine into One' the Law of the Unity of Opposition?" KMJP, July 24, 1964; Kuan Feng, "Refuting Comrade Yang Hsien-chen's Theory of 'Seeking a Common Ground While Preserving Difference,'" ibid., October 16, 1964; Ai Ssu-ch'i, "Refuting Comrade Yang Hsien-chen's 'Theory of the Integrated Economic Basis,'" ibid., November 1, 1964; *Hung-ch'i* correspondent, "A New Debate on the Discussion of Comrade Yang Hsien-chen's Theory of 'Two Combine into One,'" in JMJP, August 31, 1964.

57. Ch'i Pen-yü, "On the Autobiography of Li Hsiu-ch'eng," JMJP, July 24, 1964; Ch'i, "How Should Li Hsiu-ch'eng's Surrender and Betrayal Be Treated?" *Li-shih yen-chiu*, no. 4 (August 31, 1964); Lo Erh-kang, "Loyal King Li Hsiu-ch'eng's Strategy for Helping His Troops by Suffering," ibid.; Chou Ku-ch'eng, "Unified Integral Whole and Differentiated Reflection," JMJP, July 18, 1964; Ch'ien Chung-wen, "On Chou Ku-ch'eng's Spirit of the Era," ibid., August 13, 1964; T'ien Ting, "The Era and the Spirit of the Era—Refuting Chou Ku-ch'eng's Reactionary View," ibid., September 10, 1964.

58. For details of these debates, see Merle Goldman, "The Party's 'Cultural Revolution' of 1962-1964," in *Ideology and Politics in Contemporary China*, ed. Chalmers Johnson, pp. 219-56.

59. *Wen-i-pao*, nos. 8-9 (September 30, 1964), pp. 15-20.

60. "On the Question of 'Writing on the Middle Characters,'—Selected Pieces," JMJP, November 17, 1964; Hu Ch'ing-chih, "What People Should We Put in the Main Position of Literature and Art," KMJP, December 18, 1964; Yao Wen-yüan, "A Theory Which Makes Socialist Literature and Art Degenerate," ibid., December 20, 1964.

61. SCMP, no. 3383 (1964), p. 10.

62. SCMM, no. 446 (1964), p. 8.

63. Chang En-tzu, "Exposing Comrade Feng Ting's Philosophy of Life," KMJP, November 7, 1964.

64. JMJP, September 9, 1964.

65. CB, no. 842, p. 15; ibid., no. 891, p. 41.

66. "The True Face of Hsia Yen Seen in the Light of the Struggle between the Two Commands," JMJP, August 23, 1967.

67. JMJP, June 4, 1967, pp. 3-4; "Antirevolutionary and Revisionist Movies Must Be Thoroughly Criticized," KMJP, June 2, 1967.

68. *Main Documents of the Third NPC*, p. 29.

69. CB, no. 842, p. 27.

70. JMJP, August 13, 1967, p. 4.

71. *Hung-she wen-i* (Peking), May 20, 1967.

72. "Hsiao Wang-tung's True Counterrevolutionary Face," JMJP, August 13, 1967; *Hung-she hsüan-ch'uan-ping* (Peking), no. 4 (May 10, 1967); CB, no. 842, pp. 29-30.

73. JMJP, August 13, 1967; this report was important in that it became the precursor to the February Outline of 1966 that turned the conflict between Chiang Ch'ing and P'eng Chen into the Cultural Revolution.

74. Yao, *On the Counterrevolutionary Double-Dealer Chou Yang*, p. 48.

75. JMJP, August 13, 1967, p. 4; CB, no. 842, p. 30.

76. *Circular of the Central Committee of the Chinese Communist Party*, May 16, 1966, p. 2; *Chingkang-shan* (Peking), April 18, 1967.

77. "Chairman Mao's Talk with Foreign Guests," August 31, 1967, in *Ming-pao* (Hong Kong), July 5, 1968; for a full text of Yao's article, see KMJP, December 2, 1965, p. 2.

CHAPTER 9

MAKING OF THE CULTURAL REVOLUTION

1. Chalmers Johnson, *Revolutionary Change*, pp. 99-100; Ralf Dahrendorf, *Class and Class Conflict in Industrial Society*, p. 178.

2. See, for example, Robert J. Lifton, *Revolutionary Immortality*.

3. James Rosenau, ed., *Linkage Politics* (New York: Free Press, 1969).

4. Donald Zagoria, "The Strategic Debate in Peking," in *China's Policies in Asia and American Alternatives*, ed. Tang Tsou, pp. 237-38; Uri Ra'anan, "Peking's Foreign Policy 'Debate,' 1965-1966," ibid., pp. 23-71.

5. Michael Yahuda, "Kremlinology and the Chinese Strategic Debate, 1965-66," *China Quarterly*, no. 49 (January-March 1972), pp. 32-75; also see the exchange of comments between Ra'anan and Zagoria on the one hand and Yahuda on the other in ibid., no. 50 (April-June 1972), pp. 343-50.

6. "Talk on the Third Year Plan" (June 6, 1964) and "Talk on Putting Military Affairs Work into Full Effect and Cultivating Successors to the Revolution" (June 16, 1964), in *Mao, 1969*, JPRS, no. 61269-2, pp. 356-60.

7. JMJP, August 27, 1967; *Sing-tao jih-pao* (Hong Kong), February 24, 1967; JMJP, June 18, 1964, p. 1.

8. "Report on the Question of the Errors Committed by Lo Jui-ch'ing," *Issues and Studies*, no. 11 (August 1969), pp. 2-3.

9. Ibid., p. 3.

10. Ibid., p. 95.

11. Ibid., pp. 93-99.

12. "Interview with Mao," in *Communist China*, ed. Schurmann and Schell, p. 373.

13. Ibid., pp. 370-71.

14. *Issues and Studies*, no. 11, p. 90.

15. Lo Jui-ch'ing, "Commemorate the Victory over German Fascism; Carry the Struggle against U.S. Imperialism Through to the End!" *Peking Review*, no. 20 (May 14, 1965), pp. 7-15.

16. Ho Lung, "The Democratic Tradition of the Chinese People's Liberation Army," JMJP, August 1, 1965. The three democracies refer to democracies in politics, economics, and military affairs.

17. Lin Piao, *Long Live the Victory of People's War!* For similar interpretations, see Zagoria's article and Ra'anan's article in *China's Policies in Asia and American Alternatives*, ed. Tang Tsou, pp. 237-68, 23-71.

18. *Mao, 1969*, JPRS, no. 61269-2, p. 327.

19. "On Khrushchev's Phony Communism and Its Historical Lessons for the World," July 14, 1964, in *Polemic*, pp. 417-67.

20. CB, no. 848, p. 17.

21. JMJP, August 15, 1967, editorial; *Hung-she hsüan-ch'uan ping*, no. 4 (May 10, 1967); *Main Documents of the Third NPC*, pp. 26-27; ''Self-Criticism," in *Collected Works of Liu Shao-ch'i, 1957-1967*, p. 361.

22. *Mao, 1969*, JPRS, no. 61269-2, p. 345.

23. *Polemic*, pp. 468-76.

24. JMJP, October 2, 1965; also see *Chūgoku jimmin kaihōgun*, p. 148; for Snow's report, see *New Republic*, April 10, 1971, p. 19.

25. Mao, "Talk at Enlarged Meeting of the Political Bureau," March 20, 1966, in *Mao, 1969*, JPRS, no. 61269-2, p. 375.

26. Wang Jen-chung, "Bring Politics to the Fore, Put the Thought of Mao Tsetung in Command of Everything," *Hung-ch'i*, no. 5 (April 5, 1966), in SCMM, no. 523, p. 14.

27. KMJP, December 2, 1965, p. 2; also see *Circular of the Central Committee of the Chinese Communist Party, May 16, 1966*, p. 2 (hereafter cited as *May 16 Circular*).

28. *Hung-ch'i* editorial, November 11, 1965, as trans. in *Refutation of the New Leaders of the CPSU on "United Action,"* p. 8.

29. Ibid., p. 14.

30. Ibid., p. 30.

31. For these steps, see Charles O. Jones, *An Introduction to the Study of Public Policy*, chap. 1.

32. "Counter-revolutionary P'eng Chen's Towering Crimes of Opposing the Party, Socialism and the Thought of Mao," SCMM, no. 640, p. 1.

33. The membership of this group were: P'eng Chen (head), Lu Ting-yi (director of the Propaganda Department), K'ang Sheng (secretary of the Secretariat), Wu Leng-hsi (director of *New China News Agency* and the *People's Daily*), and Yang Shang-k'un (director of the Secretariat office).

34. *Hung-ch'i*, no. 13 (August 17, 1967), editorial, p. 16.

35. Lin Li-hsin, "The February Outline Is the Black Program of the Bourgeois Dictatorship," JMJP, June 11, 1967; *Hung chan-pao* (Peking), January 6, 1967.

36. Reproduced in *Wen-hui pao* (Shanghai), December 6, 1965.

37. Ibid.

38. Ch'i Pen-yü, "Study History for Revolution," *Hung-ch'i*, no. 13 (December 6, 1965), pp. 14-22; SCMM, no. 640, p. 3; JMJP, May 12, 1967, p. 2; *Chingkang-*

shan, May 27, 1967.

39. "The Great Proletarian Cultural Revolution: A Record of Major Events," JPRS, no. 42349, p. 4.

40. "Talk at the Hangchow Conference," December 21, 1965, CB, no. 891, pp. 51-55; *Chingkang-shan*, May 27, 1967.

41. JMJP, December 30, 1965; *Chingkang-shan*, May 27, 1967.

42. JMJP, December 30, 1965; *Chingkang-shan*, May 27, 1967; for the debates, see *Pei-ching jih-pao*, January 12, 1966; JMJP, February 10, 1966; *Wen-hui pao* (Shanghai), December 17, 1965; ibid., February 13, 1966.

43. JMJP, August 13, 1966, p. 4.

44. Ibid.; also see *Chingkang-shan*, May 27, 1967; JPRS, no. 42349, pp. 7-8. The eleven participants were P'eng Chen, Lu Ting-yi, K'ang Sheng, Wu Leng-hsi, Hsü Li-chün, Hu Sheng, Yao Chen, Wang Li, Fan Lo-yü, Liu Jen, and Cheng T'ien-hsiang.

45. JPRS, no. 42349, pp. 7-8.

46. Ibid.

47. *Hsin-wen chan-pao* (Peking), June 1, 1967; *May 16 Circular*, p. 12.

48. "The February Outline," *Hsin kang-yüan* [New Steel Institute] (Peking), March 1968.

49. "The February Outline," *Hsin jen-ta* (Peking), May 1, 1967; SCMM, no. 640, p. 9.

50. *Summary of the Forum of the Work in Literature and Art in the Armed Forces with Which Comrade Lin Piao Entrusted Comrade Chiang Ch'ing* (hereafter cited as *Summary of the Forum*).

51. Ibid., p. 1; JPRS, no. 42349, p. 10.

52. "Two Diametrically Opposed Documents," *Hung-ch'i*, no. 9 (May 27, 1967), editorial, p. 25.

53. *Summary of the Forum*, p. 4.

54. Ibid., pp. 8-12.

55. Ibid., pp. 16, 11.

56. JMJP, November 27, 1965.

57. "Report on the Question of the Errors Committed by Lo Jui-ch'ing," *Issues and Studies*, no. 11 (August 1969), p. 88.

58. Ibid.; *Wu-ch'an chieh-chi wen-hua ta-ke-ming wen-chien hui-pien*, vol. 1 (May 1967).

59. *Issues and Studies*, no. 11 (August 1969), p. 88.

60. JMJP, March 29, 1966, p. 4.

61. *Hung-i chan-pao* (Peking), January 17, 1967.

62. CB, no. 894, p. 22.

63. "Counterrevolutionary Lo Jui-ch'ing Is Loaded with Crimes," *Chan-pao* (Peking), January 30, 1967.

64. "Deputy Commander Lin's Important Instructions," *Chu-ying tung-fang hung* (Canton), September 13, 1967.

65. JMJP, June 19, 1966, p. 1.

66. "Talk at Enlarged Standing Committee Meeting of the Political Bureau," March 17, 1966, in *Mao, 1969*, JPRS, no. 61269-2, p. 381.

67. *Chingkang-shan*, May 27, 1967.

68. For these charges, see JMJP, March 9, 1966; ibid., April 2, 1966; Ch'i Pen-yü et al., "Chien Po-tsan's Historical Views Must Be Criticized," *Hung-ch'i*, no. 4

(March 24, 1966), pp. 19-30; Kuan Feng and Lin Chieh, *"Hai Jui Deplores Emperor and Hai Jui Dismissed from Office* Are Two Anti-Party and Anti-Socialist Poisonous Weeds," *Hung-ch'i*, no. 5 (April 5, 1966), pp. 15-33.

69. SCMM, no. 640, p. 9.

70. Ibid.

71. Ibid., p. 11; also see *Chingkang-shan*, May 27, 1967.

72. SCMM, no. 640, p. 11.

73. "Crimes at the April Black Meeting Dash to the Sky," *T'i-yü chan-hsien* [Athletic line] (Peking), April 21, 1967.

74. SCMM, no. 640, p. 12.

75. JMJP, April 15, 1966, p. 1; ibid., April 28, 1966.

76. Reproduced in *Yang-ch'eng wan-pao* (Canton), April 30, 1966, p. 2.

77. *Pei-ching kung-jen* [Peking worker], May 27, 1967, p. 3.

78. SCMM, no. 640, pp. 14-15; JPRS, no. 42349, pp. 11-12; also see "Criticize P'eng Chen," April 28, 1966, in *Mao, 1969*, JPRS, no. 61269-2, p. 383.

79. *The Great Socialist Cultural Revolution* (1), p. 16; JMJP, May 7, 1967; CB, no. 891, p. 56.

80. Kao Chu, "Open Fire at the Black Anti-Party and Anti-Socialist Line," *Chieh-fang chün-pao*, May 8, 1966; Ho Ming [Kuan Feng], "Heighten Our Vigilance and Distinguish the True from the False," KMJP, May 8, 1966; Lin Chieh et al., "Teng T'o's *Evening Chat at Yenshan* Is Anti-Party and Anti-Socialist Double Talk," ibid.; Yao Wen-yüan, "On the Three-Family Village: The Reactionary Nature of *Evening Chat at Yenshan* and *Notes from Three-Family Village*," *Wen-hui pao* (Shanghai), May 10, 1966; Ch'i Pen-yü, "On the Bourgeois Stand of *Frontline* and the *Peking Daily*," *Hung-ch'i*, no. 7 (May 11, 1966), pp. 1-19.

81. "Striking Counterrevolutionary Cases," *Ch'üan wu-ti* (Peking), no. 9 (May 19, 1967); "Counterrevolutionary Revisionist Yang Shang-k'un," *Chan-pao* (Peking), February 24, 1967.

82. Mao, "Speech at Enlarged Work Conference of the Central Committee," 1966, CB, no. 891, p. 7.

83. "Lin Piao's Address at the Enlarged Meeting of the CCP Central Politburo," May 18, 1966, *Issues and Studies*, no. 2 (February 1970), pp. 82-83.

84. Ibid., p. 85.

85. Ibid., p. 96.

86. "Speech at a Report Meeting," October 24, 1966, CB, no. 891, p. 71; "Three Trials of Pickpocket Wang Kuang-mei," CB, no. 848, p. 23.

87. JMJP, June 4, 1966; ibid., June 7, 1966; ibid., July 2, 1966; "Criminal Records of T'ao Chu in Harming the Great Cultural Revolution," *Hung-wei ping* [Red Guard] (Canton), October 27, 1967.

88. The 38th Troops may have entered Peking. In 1968, this unit was hailed as the one that had performed the "glorious duty" of protecting Chairman Mao. In February 1967, Mao Li-shen, its commander, became director of the Peking Military Control Committee. See *Erh-ch'i kung-she* [February 7 commune] (Honan), no. 33 (March 1968).

89. JMJP, August 19, 1966; ibid., September 1, 1966; ibid., October 12, 1966; ibid., January 13, 1967.

90. Ibid., May 17, 1967.

91. CB, no. 891, p. 61.

92. "Chairman Mao's Talk with Foreign Guests," August 31, 1967, *Ming-pao*

(Hong Kong), July 5, 1968. The guests referred to here may have been a military mission from Albania that was in China at that time.

93. *May 16 Circular*, pp. 2-3, 13.

94. Ibid., p. 12; emphasis in original.

95. Ibid., p. 13; emphasis in original.

96. Ibid., pp. 8-9.

97. "What Have Sung Shih, Lu P'ing and P'eng Pei-yün Done in the Cultural Revolution after All?" JMJP, June 2, 1966, p. 2.

98. Ibid. The five assistants were Sung I-hsiu, Hsia Chien-ch'ih, Yang Ko-ming, Chao Cheng-yi, and Kao Yün-feng; the one student was Li Hsing-chen.

99. JPRS, no. 42349, p. 30.

100. JMJP, June 2, 1966, p. 2.

101. *Hung-ch'i*, no. 3 (February 3, 1967), editorial, p. 17; KJJP, June 4, 1966, p. 2; CB, no. 834, p. 27.

102. "Sweep Away All Monsters," JMJP, June 1, 1966; "A Great Revolution That Touches People to Their Very Souls," ibid., June 2, 1966; "Capture the Positions in the Field of Historical Studies Held by the Bourgeoisie," ibid., June 3, 1966; "New Victory of Mao's Thought," ibid., June 4, 1966; "Tear Off the Bourgeois Mask of 'Liberty, Equality and Fraternity,'" ibid., June 4, 1966; "To Be the Proletarian Revolutionary or the Bourgeoisie Royalist?" ibid., June 5, 1966.

103. "Self-Criticism," October 23, 1966, *Collected Works of Liu Shao-ch'i, 1957-1967*, pp. 357-58; "Teng Hsiao-p'ing's Self-Criticism," *Ming-pao*, May 20, 1969.

104. See Chiang Ch'ing's speech at a cultural forum on November 28, 1966, in JMJP, December 4, 1966, p. 1.

105. Ibid.

106. "Down with 'Three-Anti' Element and Big Renegade Po I-po," *Tung-fang hung* (Peking), February 15, 1967.

107. JPRS, no. 42349, p. 14.

108. *Ming-pao*, May 20, 1969.

109. JMJP, July 10, 1966, p. 1.

110. Liu T'ao, "Rebel against Liu Shao-ch'i, Follow Chairman Mao to Make Revolution for Life: My Preliminary Self-Examination," CB, no. 821, p. 3.

111. Commentator, "Bourgeois Reactionary Line on the Question of Cadres Must Be Criticized," *Hung-ch'i*, no. 5 (March 30, 1967), p. 24-25.

112. Liu T'ao, "Rebel against Liu Shao-ch'i," CB, no. 821, passim.

113. Ibid., p. 3.

114. Ibid.

115. Ibid., p. 6.

116. CB, no. 891, p. 63.

117. JMJP, August 24, 1966.

118. Ibid., August 19, 1966. At this occasion, Mao asked about her name. When she said "Pin-pin" (meaning "ornamental"), Mao said "How about Yao-wu?" (meaning "need martial spirit"). The next day she changed her name to Yao-wu. Yet in 1967 she also fell as a leader of the Lien-tung group.

119. "Li Hsüeh-feng Is the Executioner Suppressing the Great Cultural Revolution in Peking," *Hung-ch'i chan-pao* [Red flag combat news] (Peking), December 1, 1966.

120. *Hung-wei ping* [Red Guards] (Canton), October 23, 1967.

121. JMJP, June 18, 1966; ibid., August 24, 1966.

122. Hai Feng, *Kuang-chou ti-chü wen-ke li-ch'eng shu-lüeh*, pp. 31-32.

123. These interviews were conducted in Hong Kong in November 1969. For a similar interview, see Gordon A. Bennett and Ronald Montaperto, *Red Guard: The Political Biography of Dai Hsiao-ai* (New York: Doubleday and Company, 1971).

124. *Chūgoku jimmin kaihōgun*, pp. 169-70.

125. "Speech at a Certain Conference," July 21, 1966, CB, no. 892, pp. 35-37; also see "Address to Regional Secretaries and Members of the CRG under the Central Committee," July 22, 1966, ibid., no. 891, pp. 60-62; ibid., no. 892, p. 36.

126. CB, no. 892, p. 36.

127. JPRS, no. 42349, p. 28.

128. Ibid., p. 28; CB, no. 819, pp. 1, 4-7.

129. CB, no. 821, p. 4.

130. *Collected Works of Liu Shao-ch'i, 1957-1967*, p. 356; CB, no. 891, p. 63.

131. JMJP, August 19, 1966; *Yomiuri shimbun* (Tokyo), December 14, 1966, p. 1.

132. JMJP, August 19, 1966; CB, no. 891, p. 63; *Ming-pao*, January 5, 1967.

133. "Chairman Mao's Talk with Foreign Guests," *Ming-pao*, July 5, 1968; emphasis added.

134. "Decision of the Central Committee of the Chinese Communist Party concerning the Great Proletarian Cultural Revolution," in *Carry the Great Proletarian Cultural Revolution Through to the End*, pp. 1-2.

135. Ibid., article 4.

136. "Comrade Lin Piao's Speech at the Eleventh Plenum," JPRS, no. 49826, pp. 35-36.

137. *Communique of the Eleventh Plenary Session of the Eighth Central Committee of the Communist Party of China*, pp. 6-7.

138. For elements of the political process, see Hilsman, *To Move a Nation*, chap. 1; also see Etzioni, *The Active Society*, p. 317.

139. Huntington, *Political Order in Changing Societies*, p. 79.

CHAPTER 10
DYNAMICS OF CHINESE POLICY PROCESS

1. John Kautsky, "Comparative Communism versus Comparative Politics," *Studies in Comparative Communism* (Spring-Summer 1973), pp. 135-70.

2. A. Doak Barnett, *Uncertain Passage*, p. 4.

3. Richard Lowenthal, "Stalinism: One-Man Leadership vs. Institutional Control in Communist One-Party Regimes" (unpublished paper, Columbia University Seminar on Communism, The Research Institute on Communist Affairs, February 23, 1972).

4. Barrington Moore, Jr., *Soviet Politics*; Johnson, *Revolutionary Change*; Ted Gurr, *Why Men Rebel*.

5. Samuel Huntington, "Social and Institutional Dynamics of One-Party Systems," in *Authoritarian Politics in Modern Society*, ed. Huntington and Clement Moore, p. 24.

6. For "self-fulfilling prophecy" of Marxism and its "reality-testing," see Robert Merton, *Social Theory and Social Structure*, pp. 475-90.

7. See Chalmers Johnson, "Comparing Communist Nations," in *Changes in Communist Systems*, ed. Chalmers Johnson, pp. 28-32.

8. For the terms *revolutionary* and *managerial modernizers*, see John Kautsky, *The Political Consequences of Modernization;* for the political styles of Mao and Liu, see Lowell Dittmer, *Liu Shao-ch'i and the Cultural Revolution*, particularly pp. 179-213.

9. Solomon, *Mao's Revolution and the Chinese Political Culture.*

10. Richard C. Thornton, *China.*

11. Karnow, *Mao and China*; Rice, *Mao's Way;* MacFarquhar, *Origins of the Cultural Revolution;* for an analytical formulation of the factional approach, see Andrew Nathan, "A Factionalism Model for CCP Politics," *China Quarterly*, no. 53 (January-March 1973), pp. 34-66; Schurmann, *Ideology and Organization in Communist China;* A. Doak Barnett, *Cadres, Bureaucracy, and Political Power in Communist China;* William W. Whitson with Chen-hsia Huang, *The Chinese High Command;* Riker, *Theory of Political Coalitions.*

12. For this "factoring" process by organizations, see James G. March and Herbert A. Simon, *Organizations*, pp. 152-90.

13. Lin Piao, "Report to the Ninth National Congress of the Communist Party of China," *Peking Review*, no. 18 (April 30, 1969), p. 21.

14. Graham T. Allison, *Essence of Decision*, p. 68 and passim.

15. JMJP, August 2, 1966.

16. For these changes, see Byung-joon Ahn, "The Cultural Revolution and China's Search for Political Order," *China Quarterly*, no. 58 (April-June 1974), pp. 249-85.

17. For changes in communication patterns, see Michel Oksenberg, "Methods of Communication within the Chinese Bureaucracy," *China Quarterly*, no. 57 (January-March 1974), pp. 1-39.

18. JMJP, July 22, 1968.

19. JPRS, no. 61269-2, p. 470.

20. Whitson and Huang, *Chinese High Command*, chap. 8.

21. Dittmer, *Liu Shao-ch'i*, pp. 214-96.

22. Ying-mao Kau and Pierre M. Perrolle, "The Politics of Lin Piao's Abortive Military Coup," *Asian Survey* (June 1974), pp. 558-77.

23. JMJP, August 19, 1973; ibid., February 14, 1974; "Directive on Problems of Distribution in People's Commune," *Chung-kung yen-chiu*, September 1972, pp. 98-104.

24. *Outline of Education on Situation for Companies*, The Propaganda Division of the Political Department, Kunming Military Region (Taipei: The Institute of International Relations, 1974), p. 12.

25. Peter R. Moody, Jr., "The New Anti-Confucian Campaign in China: The First Round," *Asian Survey* (April 1974), pp. 307-24; KMJP, September 11, 1973.

26. *New York Times*, December 23, 1974.

27. Ch'u Lan, "Carry Out Deepgoing Criticism of the Bourgeois Theory of the Universality of Human Nature," *Hung-ch'i*, no. 4 (April 1, 1974); "Comments on Mr. Lu's Spring and Autumn," ibid.

28. *New York Times*, June 14, 1974; ibid., December 16, 1974.

29. JMJP, April 10, 1976; Kung Hsiao-wen, "Teng Hsiao-p'ing and 'Twenty Articles,'" *Hsüeh-hsi yü p'i-p'an*, no. 6 (June 14, 1976), p. 19.

30. Liang Hsiao, "Historical Experiences in Studying the Struggle between

Confucianism and Legalism," *Hung-ch'i*, no. 10 (October 1, 1974), pp. 56-62; Chi Heng, "Develop the Socialist New Things," *Peking Review*, no. 51 (December 20, 1974), pp. 9-11.

31. Chi, "Develop the Socialist New Things," p. 9.

32. *Chung-kung yen-chiu*, December 1974, pp. 95-96.

33. Chuang Yen, "On Capitalist Roader," *Hsüeh-hsi yü p'i-p'an*, no. 5 (May 14, 1976), p. 6.

34. *Peking Review*, no. 4 (January 24, 1975), p. 23.

35. JMJP, February 9, 1975, editorial.

36. Yao Wen-yüan, "On the Social Basis of the Lin Piao Anti-Party Clique," *Hung-ch'i*, no. 3 (March 1, 1975), pp. 20-29; Chang Ch'un-ch'iao, "On Exercising All-Round Dictatorship over the Bourgeoisie," ibid., no. 4 (April 1, 1975), pp. 2-12; *Peking Review*, no. 25 (June 18, 1976), p. 10.

37. *Hsüeh-hsi yü p'i-p'an*, no. 6 (June 14, 1976), p. 15; KMJP, June 28, 1976.

38. Professor Yang Chen-ning, the Nobel physicist, of the State University of New York, Stony Brook, identified this man as Hu. See *Hua-ch'iao jih-pao* (New York), August 23, 1976, p. 3.

39. Tso Ch'ing, "Reading an Unpublished Document," *Hsüeh-hsi yü p'i-p'an*, no. 4 (April 14, 1976), pp. 11-19; JMJP, January 31, 1976; ibid., March 25, 1976, p. 2.

40. KMJP, March 2, 1976; ibid., March 30, 1976; JMJP, February 1, 1976; ibid., February 24, 1976; *Peking Review*, no. 31 (July 30, 1976), p. 4; JMJP, November 30, 1975.

41. *Hsüeh-hsi yü p'i-p'an*, no. 6, pp. 14-19.

42. JMJP, July 14, 1975.

43. *Hsüeh-hsi yü p'i-p'an*, no. 6, p. 28.

44. JMJP, February 13, 1976; ibid., March 20, 1976.

45. *Hsüeh-hsi yü p'i-p'an*, no. 4, pp. 11-19.

46. JMJP, February 29, 1976; ibid., August 23, 1976.

47. Ibid., May 5, 1976.

48. *Hsüeh-hsi yü p'i-p'an*, no. 6, p. 9.

49. JMJP, September 4, 1975.

50. Ibid., October 10, 1975; ibid., October 12, 1975.

51. *Hsüeh-hsi yü p'i-p'an*, no. 6, pp. 9-11.

52. JMJP, November 22, 1975; ibid., March 4, 1976; ibid., October 29, 1975. The quoted passage appears in Confucius's Analects (*Lun-yü*), Kung-yeh Ch'ang 5.

53. JMJP, October 21, 1975.

54. Ibid., June 30, 1976.

55. Ibid., March 3, 1976.

56. Ibid., April 1, 1976; ibid., May 18, 1976.

57. *New York Times*, September 10, 1976, A 15.

58. JMJP, January 21, 1976.

59. Ibid., April 18, 1976; ibid., February 13, 1976.

60. Ibid., March 28, 1976.

61. *Peking Review*, no. 15 (April 9, 1976), p. 5.

62. JMJP, July 1, 1976, editorial.

63. Ibid., September 18, 1976; ibid., September 26, 1976.

64. Thomas W. Robinson, "Political Succession in China," *World Politics*, no. 1 (October 1974), pp. 1-38.

EPILOGUE

1. *Time*, September 20, 1976, p. 49.
2. *RF Illustrated*, The Rockefeller Foundation, July 4, 1976, p. 8.

APPENDIX 1
RURAL COMMUNE: 1958 AND POST-1962

1. For an analysis of the commune in 1958-74, see Byung-joon Ahn, "The Political Economy of the People's Commune in China: Changes and Continuities," *Journal of Asian Studies* 34, no. 3 (May 1975): 631-58.

2. JMJP, September 3, 1958, editorial; "Peitaiho Resolution," in *Communist China, 1955-1959*, p. 454.

3. Teng Tzu-hui, "Socialist Transformation in China's Countryside," JMJP, October 18, 1959.

4. See the charter of the Weihsing commune in JMJP, September 4, 1958; also see "Investigation Report of the East Wind Commune," *Journal of Hsi-pei University* (humanities), no. 3 (December 1958); Li Hsien-nien, "Views on People's Commune" (bulletin), *Hung-ch'i*, no. 10 (October 16, 1958), pp. 4-8.

5. *Communist China, 1955-1959*, p. 454.

6. Wu Ch'uan-ch'i, "Communism As Seen from People's Commune," JMJP, October 1, 1958.

7. Ch'en Po-ta, "Under the Banner of Comrade Mao Tse-tung," *Hung-ch'i*, no. 4 (July 16, 1958), p. 5; Chang Yu-san, "Report on Half-Study and Half-Work of People's Commune," ibid., no. 10 (October 16, 1958), pp. 28-30.

8. Chang Shih-hsing, "People's Commune and All People Armed," in *Lun jen-min kung-she* [On people's commune] (Peking: Ch'ing-nien ch'u-pan-she, 1958), pp. 108-13; *Hung-ch'i*, no. 7 (September 1, 1958), editorial, p. 15.

9. JMJP, September 3, 1958.

10. Ibid., November 29, 1958; *Liaoning jih-pao*, December 19, 1958.

11. *Communist China, 1955-1959*, p. 490.

12. KJJP, October 10-19, 1958; *Liaoning jih-pao*, December 16, 1958; ibid., December 24, 1958.

13. *Ta-kung pao* (Hong Kong), November 8, 1963, p. 1; JMJP, August 29, 1963; *Ta-kung pao* (Peking), March 11, 1966.

14. *Kung-fei nung-ts'un jen-min kung-she t'iao-li—hsiu-cheng ts'ao-an*, September 1963 (hereafter cited as *1962 Regulations*), see Art. 21; also see "Resolutions on the Further Strengthening of the Collective Economy of the People's Communes and Expanding Agricultural Production," ibid., September 1962.

15. Anna Louise Strong, *The Rise of the Chinese People's Communes—and Six Years After*, p. 202; also see *1962 Regulations*, Art. 21.

16. Chen, *Lien-chiang Documents*, pp. 62, 121.

17. Perhaps this result substantiates the validity of functionalism in social sciences in that there can be some alternative structures for the functional needs of society. For this school of thought, see Talcott Parsons and Edward Shils, eds., *Toward a General Theory of Actions*, pp. 53 ff.

18. *1962 Regulations*, Art. 13.

19. Ibid., Arts. 10, 15.

20. Ibid., Arts, 16-17.

21. Chen, *Lien-chiang Documents*, p. 167.

22. *1962 Regulations*, Arts. 19-20; "At Yangtan Commune," *Peking Review*, no. 12 (1966), p. 8; also see John C. Pelzel, "Production Brigade and Team Management" (Paper delivered at the Columbia University Seminar on Modern East Asia: China, February 16, 1966).

23. Strong, *Chinese People's Communes*, pp. 199-200; NFJP, September 19, 1965.

24. *1962 Regulations*, Art. 50.

25. For a theoretical explanation of these problems, see Etzioni, *Modern Organizations*, pp. 14-16; also see *The Case of P'eng Teh-huai*, pp. 3-4.

26. JMJP, December 12, 1964, p. 2; *1962 Regulations*, Art. 10; for details of this policy, see Carl Riskin, "Small Industry and the Chinese Model of Development," *China Quarterly*, no. 46 (April-June 1971), pp. 269-73.

27. KMJP, November 30, 1964; JMJP, October 20, 1964; Chang Ch'ing-t'ai, "On the Question of Strengthening the Operation and Management of Tractor Stations," *Chung-kuo nung-pao*, no. 11 (1963), in SCMM, no. 400 (1964), pp. 31-32.

28. Li Hsien-nien, "How Shall We Understand the Reform of Finance and Trade in the Countryside?" *Hung-ch'i*, no. 2 (January 16, 1959).

29. *Far Eastern Economic Review* (May 11, 1967), pp. 30-32.

30. This account of Chinese rural trade and what follows are based on interviews with a former cadre member who had had extensive experience in this field. The interviews were conducted in Hong Kong. Interview Protocols no. 4 (November 1969). Interviewees were middle-level cadres in Kwangtung provincial government.

31. Joan Robinson, *Notes from China*, pp. 30-32.

32. For this market system, see G. William Skinner, "Marketing and Social Structure in Rural China,"pt. 1, *Journal of Asian Studies* 24, no. 1 (November 1964):3-43; pt. 2, ibid., no. 2 (February 1965), pp. 195-228; pt. 3, ibid., no. 3 (May 1965), pp. 363-99.

33. "Summary of Revisionist Li Hsien-nien's Anti-Mao Remarks in Finance and Trade," *Pei-ching kung-she*, May 26, 1976; "Look at the True Face of Counterrevolutionary Ch'en Yün," *Ts'ai-mao hung-ch'i* (Peking), February 8, 1967.

34. Barnett, *Cadres, Bureaucracy, and Political Power in Communist China*, p. 73.

35. KMJP, December 1, 1961.

36. JMJP, April 5, 1965.

37. Ch'en Tsai-tao, "Investigation Report on Militia Work in Honan," *Kung-tso t'ung-shün*, no. 21 (May 26, 1961), pp. 9-16.

38. *Fei min-ping kung-tso t'iao-li* [Regulations concerning militia work] (Taipei: Nationalist Chinese Government, 1965).

39. Ts'ai Mao-wen and T'ang Ching-liang, *Nung-ts'un tang chih-pu tsen-yang chih-ch'ih pao-lu tso-yung*, pp. 12-15.

40. Interview Protocols no. 3 (November 1969), the same informant as no. 4.

41. JMJP, July 4, 1963.

42. Michel Oksenberg, "Local Leaders in Rural China, 1962-1965: Individual Attributes, Bureaucratic Positions, and Political Recruitment," in *Chinese Communist Politics in Action*, ed. A. Doak Barnett, pp. 159-71.

43. *1962 Regulations*, Art. 48; JMJP, April 21, 1965; ibid., May 27, 1965; for

leadership problems among the cadres, see Ronald C. Young, "Commitment among Cadres in Rural Communist China, 1960-1965."

44. JMJP, December 20, 1965, p. 3; ibid., November 12, 1965, p. 3.

45. Chen, *Lien-chiang Documents*, p. 150.

46. *1962 Regulations*, Art. 23; *Ta-kung pao* (Peking), September 19, 1965; *Szechwan jih-pao*, March 10, 1964; *Kiangsi jih-pao*, September 21, 1965.

47. "Yangpan Commune," *Peking Review*, no. 13 (March 25, 1966), p. 17.

48. Interview Protocols no. 6 (November 1969), the same informant as no. 4.

49. "Down with Counterrevolutionary Revisionist Ch'en Yün," *Tung-fang-hung* (Peking Mining Institute), January 27, 1967; "One Hundred Examples of Teng Hsiao-p'ing References against the Thoughts of Mao Tse-tung," *Chingkang-shan* (Peking), March 8, 1967; "Self Criticism," October 23, 1966, in *Collected Works of Liu Shao-ch'i, 1957-1967*, pp. 357-63; Chen, *Lien-chiang Documents*, pp. 104-5.

50. NFJP, February 1, 1963.

51. *Ta-kung pao* (Peking), October 10, 1963, editorial.

52. *1962 Regulations*, Art. 40.

53. Yi Fan, "Labor Management of Rural People's Commune," *Tsu-kuo* [China monthly], January 1969, p. 3.

54. JMJP, May 22, 1961.

55. For details of these aspects, see Andrew Nathan, "China's Work-Point System: A Study in Agricultural 'Splittism,'" *Current Scene*, no. 31 (1964), p. 11; Gargi Dutt, *Rural Communes of China, Organizational Problems*, p. 167; Hélène Marchisio, III, "Les Système de rémunération dans les communes populaires," in *La Construction du socialisme en Chine*, ed. Charles Bettelheim et al., pp. 71-99.

56. JMJP, March 22, 1966.

57. See Martin King Whyte, "The Tachai Brigade and Incentives for the Peasants," *Current Scene*, no. 16 (1969), pp. 8-9.

58. JMJP, October 18, 1959; *Kung-tso t'ung-hsün*, no. 17 (April 25, 1961), p. 3.

59. *1962 Regulations*, Art. 32.

60. NCNA, Peking, February 19, 1966, in SCMP, no. 3644 (1966).

61. *Peking Review*, no. 13 (March 25, 1966), p. 16; Jirō Nishikawa, "Traveling through the People's Republic of China," *Ajia keizai* (Tokyo), September 1965, pp. 113-19; Intervew Protocols no. 4 (November 1969); Chen, *Lien-chiang Documents*, p. 27.

62. NFJP, February 1, 1963; also see François J. Durand, *Le Financement du budget en Chine populaire*, pp. 245-69.

63. *1962 Regulations*, Arts. 34-36.

64. Ibid., Art. 34; *Ta-kung pao* (Peking), October 26, 1964, p. 1.

65. JMJP, April 10, 1965.

66. "A Survey of the Method of Setting Aside Reserve Fund in Commune," *Jen-min kung-she chien-che* [People's commune construction], no. 21 (November 5, 1964).

67. Strong, *Chinese People's Communes*, p. 196.

68. *1962 Regulations*, Art. 34; Chen, *Lien-chiang Documents*, p. 26.

69. Shahid Javed Burki, *A Study of Chinese Communes, 1965*, p. 27.

70. *Ta-kung pao* (Peking), September 4, 1964, p. 4.

71. Chen, *Lien-chiang Documents*, pp. 235-37, 196-98.

72. *Ta-kung pao* (Peking), October 21, 1965; NFJP, May 25, 1965.

73. *Chūgoku kenkyū geppō* (Tokyo), no. 244 (June 1968), pp. 1-32.

74. Hikotarō Andō, "The Great Cultural Revolution As Seen in Peking," *Kokumin* [Nationals], December 1966, p. 28.

75. *1962 Regulations*, Arts. 44-45.

76. See Burki, *A Study of Chinese Communes*, p. 37.

77. Lin I-Chou, "Commune Members' Sideline Occupations Are the Necessary Supplement to the Socialist Economy," *Hung-chi*, no. 17 (September 1, 1961), pp. 5-8.

78. *Ta-kung pao* (Peking), September 21, 1965. This report claimed that eighty thousand more branches of the SMC were set up in addition to the two hundred thousand existing branches in the countryside; Burki reports that this ratio reached 20 percent in the communes he visited. See Burki, *A Study of Chinese Communes*, p. 40.

79. *Selected Reading from the Works of Mao Tse-tung*, pp. 325-26.

80. *Kweichow Radio* (Kweiyang), June 28, 1967.

81. JMJP, November 1, 1965, p. 2.

82. *Yang-ch'eng wan-pao* (Canton), November 9, 1965, editorial.

83. See JMJP, January 27, 1972; also see Article 7 of the 1970 draft of the Constitution of the People's Republic of China in *Chung-yang jih-pao* (Taipei), November 5, 1970.

Bibliography

ENGLISH AND FRENCH

Agrarian Reform Law of the People's Republic of China. Peking: Foreign Languages Press, 1959.

Ahn, Byung-joon. "Adjustments in the Great Leap Forward and Their Ideological Legacy, 1959-1962." In *Ideology and Politics in Contemporary China,* edited by Chalmers Johnson, pp. 270-300. Seattle: University of Washington Press, 1973.

———. "The Cultural Revolution and China's Search for Political Order." *China Quarterly,* no. 58 (April-June 1974), pp. 249-85.

———. "The Political Economy of the People's Commune in China: Changes and Continuities." *Journal of Asian Studies* 34, no. 3 (May 1975): 631-58.

———. "The Politics of Peking Opera, 1962-1965." *Asian Survey,* no. 12 (December 1972), pp. 1066-81.

Allison, Graham T. *Essence of Decision: Explaining the Cuban Missile Crisis.* Boston: Little, Brown & Co., 1971.

Almond, Gabriel A., and Powell, G. Bingham, Jr. *Comparative Politics: A Developmental Approach.* Boston: Little, Brown & Co., 1966.

Along the Socialist or the Capitalist Road? Peking: Foreign Languages Press, 1968.

Andors, Stephen. "Factory Management and Political Ambiguity, 1961-63." *China Quarterly,* no. 59 (July-September 1974), pp. 435-76.

Apter, David A. *The Politics of Modernization*. Chicago: University of Chicago Press, 1965.

Barnett, A. Doak. *Cadres, Bureaucracy and Political Power in Communist China*. New York: Columbia University Press, 1967.

——. *Uncertain Passage: China's Transition to the Post-Mao Era*. Washington, D.C.: Brookings Institution, 1974.

——, ed. *Chinese Communist Politics in Action*. Seattle: University of Washington Press, 1969.

Bastid, Marianne. "Economic Necessity and Political Ideals in Educational Reform during the Cultural Revolution." *China Quarterly*, no. 42 (April-June 1970), pp. 16-45.

Baum, Richard Dennis. *Prelude to Revolution: Mao, the Party, and the Peasant Question, 1962-66*. New York: Columbia University Press, 1975.

——. "Revolution and Reaction in Rural China: The Struggle between Two Roads during the Socialist Education Movement (1962-1966) and the Great Proletarian Cultural Revolution (1966-1968)." Ph.D. dissertation, University of California, Berkeley, 1970.

—— and Teiwes, Frederick C. *Ssu-Ch'ing: Socialist Education Movement of 1962-1966*. China Research Monograph no. 2. Berkeley: University of California, 1968.

Ben-David, Joseph. "How to Organize Research in the Social Sciences." *Daedalus* (Spring 1973), pp. 39-52.

Bernstein, Thomas P. "Leadership and Mobilization in Collectivization of Agriculture in China and Russia: A Comparison." Ph.D. dissertation, Columbia University, New York, 1970.

Bettelheim, Charles, ed. *La Construction du socialisme en Chine*. Paris: François Mappero, 1965.

Bianco, Lucian. *Origins of the Chinese Revolution, 1915-1949*. Stanford: Stanford University Press, 1971.

Black, Cyril E. *The Dynamics of Modernization: A Study of Comparative History*. New York: Harper & Row, 1966.

Boorman, Howard L. "How to Be a Good Communist: The Political Ethics of Liu Shao-ch'i." *Asian Survey*, no. 8 (August 1963), pp. 372-83.

Braybrook, D., and Lindblom, C. *A Strategy of Decision*. New York: Free Press, 1963.

Brzezinski, Zbigniew K. *Ideology and Power in Soviet Politics*. New York: Praeger, 1962.

——. *The Soviet Bloc, Unity and Conflict*. Cambridge, Mass.: Harvard University Press, 1967.

—— and Huntington, Samuel. *Political Power: USA/USSR*. New York:

Viking Press, 1964.

Burki, Shahid Javed. *A Study of Chinese Communes, 1965*. East Asian Monograph no. 29. Cambridge, Mass.: Harvard University Press, 1969.

Carry the Great Proletarian Cultural Revolution Through to the End. Peking: Foreign Languages Press, 1969.

Carry the Great Revolution on the Journalistic Front Through to the End. Peking: Foreign Languages Press, 1969.

The Case of P'eng Teh-huai. Hong Kong: Union Research Institute, 1968.

Chang, Parris. "Pattern and Processes of Policy Making in Communist China, 1955-1962: Three Case Studies." Ph.D. dissertation, Columbia University, New York, 1969.

——. *Power and Policy in China*. University Park: Pennsylvania State University Press, 1975.

——. "Research Notes on the Changing Loci of Decision in the CCP." *China Quarterly*, no. 44 (October-December 1970), pp. 169-81.

Charles, David A. "The Dismissal of Marshal P'eng Teh-huai." *China Quarterly*, no. 8 (October-December 1961), pp. 63-76.

Chen, C. S., ed. *Rural People's Communes in Lien-chiang*. Translated by Charles P. Ridley. Stanford: Hoover Institution, 1969.

Chen Mai Fun. "Give and Take." *Far Eastern Economic Review*, May 11, 1967.

Ch'en, Jerome. "Commentary on 'Resolution of the Tsunyi Conference.'" *China Quarterly*, no. 40 (October-December 1969), pp. 1-38.

Ch'en Kuang-sheng. *Lei Feng, Chairman Mao's Good Fighter*. Peking: Foreign Languages Press, 1968.

Chiang Ch'ing. *On the Revolution of Peking Opera*. Peking: Foreign Languages Press, 1968.

Circular of the Central Committee of the Chinese Communist Party, May 16, 1966. Peking: Foreign Languages Press, 1967.

Collected Works of Liu Shao-ch'i, before 1944. Hong Kong: Union Research Institute, 1969.

Collected Works of Liu Shao-ch'i, 1945-1957. Hong Kong: Union Research Institute, 1969.

Collected Works of Liu Shao-ch'i, 1957-1967. Hong Kong: Union Research Institute, 1968.

"Communique of the Ninth Plenary Session of the Eighth Central Committee of the Communist Party of China." *Peking Review*, no. 4 (January 27, 1961), pp. 5-7.

"Communique of the Tenth Plenary Session of the Eighth Central Committee of the Communist Party of China." *Peking Review*, no. 39

(September 28, 1962), pp. 5-7.

Communique of the Eleventh Plenary Session of the Eighth Central Committee of the Communist Party of China. Peking: Foreign Languages Press, 1966.

Communique of the Enlarged Twelfth Plenary Session of the Eighth Central Committee of the Communist Party of China. Special supplement to *China Reconstructs*, 1968.

Communist China 1955-1959: Policy Documents and Analysis. Harvard East Asian Series, no. 10. Cambridge, Mass.: Harvard University Press, 1962.

Conquest, Robert. *Power and Policy in the USSR: The Study of Soviet Dynasties.* New York: Harpers Torch Books, 1967.

Constitution of the Communist Party of China. Peking: Foreign Languages Press, 1965.

Constitution of the People's Republic of China. Peking: Foreign Languages Press, 1961.

Dahl, Robert A. "The Concept of Power." *Behavioral Science* 2 (July 1957): 202-3.

———. *Modern Political Analysis.* Englewood Cliffs, N.J.: Prentice-Hall, 1963.

Dahrendorf, Ralf. *Class and Class Conflicts in Industrial Society.* Stanford: Stanford University Press, 1959.

Deutsch, Karl W. *Nationalism and Social Communication.* New York: John Wiley & Sons, 1953.

The Diary of Wang Chieh. Peking: Foreign Languages Press, 1967.

Dittmer, Lowell. *Liu Shao-ch'i and the Chinese Cultural Revolution.* Berkeley: University of California Press, 1974.

Documents of the National Conference of the Communist Party of China. Peking: Foreign Languages Press, 1955.

Domes, Jurgen. *The Internal Politics of China.* New York: Praeger, 1973.

Donnithorne, Audrey G. *China's Economic System.* London: George Allen & Unwin, 1967.

Doolin, Dennis J. "The Revival of the 100 Flowers Campaign: 1961." *China Quarterly,* no. 8 (October-December 1961), pp. 34-41.

———, trans. *Communist China: The Politics of Student Opposition.* Stanford: The Hoover Institution.

Dorrill, William. "Transfer of Legitimacy in the Chinese Communist Party: Origin of the Maoist Myth." *China Quarterly,* no. 36 (October-December 1968), pp. 45-60.

Downs, Anthony. *Inside Bureaucracy.* Boston: Little, Brown & Co., 1967.

Durand, François. *Le financement du budget en Chine populaire: Un exemple de développement fiscal dans une economie de croissance.* Hong Kong: Caritas Printing Training Centre, 1965.

Dutt, Gargi. *Rural Communes of China, Organizational Problems.* Bombay, New York: Asia Publishing House, 1967.

Eckstein, Alexander. *Communist China's Economic Growth and Foreign Trade.* New York: McGraw-Hill Books, 1966.

Eighth National Congress of the Chinese Communist Party of China. Vols. 1-3. Peking: Foreign Languages Press, 1956.

Eisenstadt, S. N. "Modernization and Conditions of Sustained Growth." *World Politics,* no. 4 (July 1964), pp. 576-86.

——. *Modernization: Protest and Change.* Englewood Cliffs, N.J.: Prentice-Hall, 1966.

Erikson, Erik H. *Young Man Luther: A Study in Psychoanalysis and History.* New York: W.W. Norton & Co., 1958.

Erlich, Alexander. *The Soviet Industrialization Debate, 1924-1928.* Cambridge, Mass.: Harvard University Press, 1960.

Etzioni, Amitai. *The Active Society: A Theory of Societal and Political Processes.* New York: Free Press, 1968.

——. *Modern Organizations.* Englewood Cliffs, N.J.: Prentice-Hall, 1964.

Fainsod, Merle. *How Russia Is Ruled.* Rev. ed. Cambridge, Mass.: Harvard University Press, 1963.

Feuerwerker, Albert; Murphy, Rhoades; and Wright, Mary C., eds. *Approaches to Modern Chinese History.* Berkeley and Los Angeles: University of California Press, 1967.

Field, Robert Michael. "Chinese Communist Industrial Production." In *An Economic Profile of Mainland China,* edited by Robert Michael Field et al. New York: Praeger, 1967.

Friedman, Edward. "The Revolution in Hungary and the Hundred Flowers Period in China." *Journal of Asian Studies,* no. 1 (November 1965), pp. 119-22.

Friedrich, Carl J. *Man and His Government: An Empirical Theory of Politics.* New York: McGraw-Hill Books, 1963.

Gittings, John. *The Role of the Chinese Army.* London: Oxford University Press, 1967.

Goldman, Merle. *Literary Dissent in Communist China.* Cambridge, Mass.: Harvard University Press, 1967.

——. "The Unique 'Blooming and Contending' of 1961-1962." *China Quarterly,* no. 37 (January-March 1969), pp. 54-83.

A Great Revolution on the Cultural Front. Peking: Foreign Languages Press, 1965.

The Great Socialist Cultural Revolution in China. (1)-(10). Peking: Foreign Languages Press, 1966-67.

Guillermaz, Jacques. *A History of the Chinese Communist Party, 1921-1949.* Translated by Anne Destenay. London: Methuen, 1972.

Gurr, Ted. "Psychological Factor in Civil Violence." *World Politics,* no. 2 (January 1968), pp. 245-78.

——. *Why Men Rebel.* Princeton, N.J.: Princeton University Press, 1970.

Harding, Harry. *Maoist Theories of Policy-Making and Organization: Lessons from the Cultural Revolution.* Rand Study, R-487-PR, September 1969.

Harrison, James. *The Long March to Power.* New York: Praeger, 1973.

Hilsman, Roger. *To Move a Nation.* New York: Doubleday, 1967.

Hinton, Harold C. "China and Vietnam." In *China's Policies in Asia and America's Alternatives,* edited by Tang Tsou, pp. 201-36. Chicago: The University of Chicago Press, 1968.

Hirschman, Albert O. *Journeys toward Progress.* Garden City, N. Y.: Doubleday Anchor Books, 1965.

Howe, Christopher. *Wage Patterns and Wage Policy in Modern China, 1919-1972.* London: Cambridge University Press, 1973.

Hsiung, James Chieh. *Ideology and Practice: The Evolution of Chinese Communism.* New York: Praeger, 1970.

Huntington, Samuel P. "Political Development and Political Decay." *World Politics,* no. 3 (April 1965), pp. 386-430.

——. *Political Order in Changing Societies.* New Haven: Yale University Press, 1968.

——. *The Soldier and the State: The Theory and Politics of Civil-Military Relations.* New York: Vintage Books, 1964.

——, and Moore, Clement, eds. *Authoritarian Politics in Modern Society.* New York: Basic Books, 1970.

Jacob, Philip E., and Toscano, James V., eds. *The Integration of Political Communities.* Philadelphia and New York: J.B. Lippincott, 1964.

Johnson Chalmers. *Changes in Communist Systems.* Stanford: Stanford University Press, 1970.

——. *Peasant Nationalism and Communist Power: The Emergence of Revolutionary China, 1937-1945.* Stanford: Stanford University Press, 1962.

——. *Revolutionary Change.* Boston: Little, Brown & Co., 1966.

——, ed. *Ideology and Politics in Contemporary China.* Seattle: University of Washington Press, 1973.

Jones, Charles O. *An Introduction to the Study of Public Policy.* Belmont, California: Duxbury Press, 1970.

Kalleberg, Arthur L. "Concept Formation in Normative and Empirical Studies: Toward Reconciliation in Political Theory." *American Political Science Review,* no. 1 (March 1969), pp. 5-25.

Karnow, Stanley. *Mao and China: From Revolution to Revolution.* New York: Viking Press, 1972.

Kautsky, John. "Comparative Communism versus Comparative Politics." *Studies in Comparative Communism,* Spring/Summer 1973, pp. 135-70.

———. *The Political Consequence of Modernization.* New York: John Wiley & Sons, 1972.

Kim, Illpyong J. *The Politics of Chinese Communism: Kiangsi under the Soviets.* Berkeley: University of California Press, 1973.

Klein, Donald W., and Clark, Anne B. *Biographical Dictionary of Chinese Communism.* Vols. 1-2. Cambridge, Mass.: Harvard University Press, 1971.

K'o Ch'ing-shih. "Energetically Develop and Foster a Socialist Economic Base." In *A Great Revolution on the Cultural Front,* pp. 21-77. Peking: Foreign Languages Press, 1965.

Kornhauser, William. *The Politics of Mass Society.* New York: Free Press, 1959.

Lampton, David M. "Health Policy during the Great Leap Forward," *China Quarterly,* no. 60 (December 1974), pp. 668-98.

Lee, Hong Yung. "Utility and Limitation of the Red Guard Publications as Source Materials: Bibliographical Survey." *Journal of Asian Studies* 34, no. 3 (May 1975): 779-94.

Levy, Richard. "New Light on Mao: His Views on the Soviet Union's Political Economy." *China Quarterly,* no. 61 (March 1975), pp. 95-117.

Lewis, John. *The City in Communist China.* Stanford: Stanford University Press, 1971.

———, ed. *Party Leadership and Revolutionary Power.* New York: Cambridge University Press, 1970.

Lifton, Robert J. *Revolutionary Immortality: Mao Tse-tung and the Cultural Revolution.* New York: Random House, 1968.

———. *Thought Reform and the Psychology of Totalism: A Study of "Brainwashing" in China.* New York: W.W. Norton & Co., 1960.

Lin Piao, *Long Live the Victory of People's War.* Peking: Foreign Languages Press, 1965.

———. "Report to the Ninth National Congress of the Communist Party of China." *Peking Review,* no. 8 (April 30, 1969), pp. 16-35.

Lindbeck, John, ed. *China: Management of a Revolutionary Society.* Seattle and London: University of Washington Press, 1971.

Lindblom, Charles. *The Intelligence of Democracy*. New York: Free Press, 1965.

——. *The Policy-Making Process*. Englewood Cliffs, N.J.: Prentice-Hall, 1968.

Linden, Karl. *Khrushchev and the Soviet Leadership, 1957-1964*. Baltimore: Johns Hopkins University Press, 1966.

Liu Shao-ch'i. *How to Be a Good Communist*. Peking: Foreign Languages Press, 1964.

——. *On Intra-Party Struggle*. Peking: Foreign Languages Press, n.d.

Lo Jui-ch'ing. "Commemorate the Victory over German Fascism: Carry the Struggle against U.S. Imperialism Through to the End." *Peking Review*, no. 20 (May 14, 1965), pp. 7-15.

London, Miriam, and London, Ivan. "The Other China, Hunger: Part 1 —The Three Red Flags of Death." *Worldview* 19, no. 5 (1976): 4-11.

Lowi, Theodore. "American Business, Public Policy, Case Studies, and Political Theory." *World Politics* 16 (July 1964): 677-715.

MacFarquhar, Roderick. *The Origins of the Cultural Revolution: 1. Contradictions among the People 1956-1957*. London, Kuala Lumpur: Oxford University Press, 1974.

Main Documents of the First Session of the Third National People's Congress of the People's Republic of China. Peking: Foreign Languages Press, 1965.

Mannheim, Karl. *Ideology and Utopia: An Introduction to the Sociology of Knowledge*. New York: Harcourt, Brace, 1946.

Mao Tse-tung. *Selected Readings from the Works of Mao Tse-tung*. Peking: Foreign Languages Press, 1967.

——. *Selected Works*. Vols. 1-4. Peking: Foreign Languages Press, 1965.

"Mao Tse-tung's Address at the Opening Session of the Ninth CCP National Congress," April 1, 1969. *Issues and Studies*, March 1970, pp. 92-93.

"Mao Tse-tung's Speech to the First Plenary Session of the CCP's Ninth Central Committee," April 28, 1969. *Issues and Studies*, March 1970, pp. 94-113.

March, James, and Simon, Herbert. *Organizations*. New York: John Wiley & Sons, 1958.

Merton, Robert K. *Social Theory and Social Structure*. New York: Free Press, 1968.

Miscellany of Mao Tse-tung Thought (1949-1968). Parts 1, 2. Joint Publications Research Service, 61269-1 and 2, February 20, 1974.

Moore, Barrington, Jr. *Social Origins of Dictatorship and Democracy: Lord and Peasant in the Making of the Modern World*. Boston:

Beacon Press, 1966.

——. *Soviet Politics—The Dilemma of Power: The Role of Ideas in Social Change*. New York: Harper & Row, 1965.

——. *Terror and Progress—USSR: Some Source of Change and Stability in the Soviet Dictatorship*. Cambridge, Mass.: Harvard University Press, 1966.

Nathan, Andrew. "China's Work-Point System: A Study in Agricultural 'Splittism.'" *Current Scene*, no. 31 (1964).

——. "A Factionalism Model for CCP Politics." *China Quarterly*, no. 53 (January-March 1973), pp. 34-66.

Nee, Victor, and Layman, Don. "The Cultural Revolution at Peking University." *Monthly Review*, July-August 1969.

Neustadt, Richard E. *Presidential Power, Politics of Leadership*. New York: John Wiley & Sons, 1964.

New China Advances to Socialism. Peking: Foreign Languages Press, 1956.

Oksenberg, Michel. "The Institutionalization of the Chinese Communist Revolution: The Ladder of Success on the Eve of the Cultural Revolution." *China Quarterly*, no. 36 (October-December 1968), pp. 61-92.

——. "Local Leaders in Rural China, 1962-1965: Individual Attributes, Bureaucratic Position, and Political Recruitment." In *Chinese Communist Politics in Action*, edited by A. Doak Barnett, pp. 155-215. Seattle: University of Washington Press, 1969.

——. "Policy Formulation in Communist China: The case of the 1957-8 Mass Irrigation Campaign." Ph.D. dissertation, Columbia University, New York, 1969.

——. "Policy Making under Mao: 1949-1968." *Comparative Politics*, no. 3 (March 1971).

Parsons, Talcott, and Shils, Edward A., eds. *Toward a General Theory of Action*. Cambridge, Mass.: Harvard University Press, 1953.

P'eng Chen. "Talk at the Festival of Peking Opera on Contemporary Themes." In *A Great Revolution on the Cultural Front*, pp. 1-20. Peking: Foreign Languages Press, 1965.

Perlmutter, Amos. "The Praetorian State and the Praetorian Army: Toward a Taxonomy of Civil-Military Relations in Developing Polities." *Comparative Politics*, no. 3 (April 1969), pp. 382-404.

Peterson, Joseph. *The Great Leap—China*. Delhi: B.I. Publications, 1966.

The Polemic on the General Line of the International Communist Movement. Peking: Foreign Languages Press, 1965.

Pye, Lucian. *The Spirit of Chinese Politics*. Cambridge, Mass.: Massachusetts Institute of Technology Press, 1968.

Ra'anan, Uri. "Peking's Foreign Policy 'Debate,' 1965-1966." In *China's Policies in Asia and America's Alternatives*, edited by Tang Tsou, pp. 23-71. Chicago: The University of Chicago Press, 1968.

Raid on the White Tiger Regiment. N.p.: Afro-Asian Writers' Bureau, 1967.

Ranney, Austin, ed. *Political Science and Public Policy*. Chicago: Markham, 1968.

The Red Lantern. N.p.: Afro-Asian Writers' Bureau, 1967.

Refutation of the New Leaders of the CPSU on "United Action." Peking: Foreign Languages Press, 1965.

"Report on the Question of the Errors Committed by Lo Liu-ch'ing." *Issues and Studies*, August 1969, pp. 87-101.

Rice, Edward. *Mao's Way*. Berkeley: University of California Press, 1972.

Richman, Barry M. *Industrial Society in Communist China*. New York: Random House, 1969.

Riker, William. *The Theory of Political Coalitions*. New Haven: Yale University Press, 1962.

Riskin, Carl. "Small Industry and the Chinese Model of Development." *China Quarterly*, no. 46 (April-June 1971), pp. 269-73.

Robinson, Thomas. "Political Succession in China." *World Politics*, no. 1 (October 1974), pp. 1-38.

——. "The Wuhan Incident: Local Strife and Provincial Rebellion in the Cultural Revolution." *China Quarterly*, no. 47 (July-September 1971), pp. 413-38.

——, ed. *The Cultural Revolution in China*. Berkeley: University of California Press, 1971.

Rosenau, James, ed. *Linkage Politics*. New York: Free Press, 1969.

Russian Institute, Columbia University, eds. *The Anti-Stalin Campaign and International Communism*. New York: Columbia University Press, 1956.

Rustow, Dankwart. *A World of Nations: Problems of Political Modernization*. Washington, D.C.: Brookings Institution, 1967.

Sartori, Giovanni. "Politics, Ideology, and Belief System." *American Political Science Review*, no. 2 (June 1969), pp. 398-411.

Scalapino, Robert, ed. *Elites in the People's Republic of China*. Seattle: University of Washington Press, 1972.

Schram, Stuart, ed. *Authority, Participation and Cultural Change*. London: Cambridge University Press, 1973.

——, and d'Encausse, Hélène Carrère, comps. *Marxism and Asia: An*

Introduction with Readings. London: Allen Lane, 1969.

Schurmann, Franz. *Ideology and Organization in Communist China.* Berkeley: University of California Press, 1968.

Schwartz, Benjamin I. *Chinese Communism and the Rise of Mao.* Cambridge, Mass.: Harvard University Press, 1951.

————. *Communism and China: Ideology in Flux.* Cambridge, Mass.: Harvard University Press, 1968.

————. "Modernization and the Maoist Vision—Some Reflections on Chinese Communist Goals." *China Quarterly,* no. 21 (January-March 1965), pp. 3-17.

————. "The Reign of Virtue: Some Broad Perspectives on Leader and Party in the Cultural Revolution." *China Quarterly,* no. 35 (July-September 1968), pp. 1-17.

Second Session of the Eighth National Congress of the Communist Party of China. Peking: Foreign Languages Press, 1958.

Selden, Mark. *The Yenan Way in Revolutionary China.* Cambridge, Mass.: Harvard University Press, 1971.

Selznick, Philip. *TVA and the Grass Roots.* Berkeley: University of California Press, 1949.

Simon, Joseph. "Ferment among the Intellectuals." *Problems of Communism* 13, no. 5 (September-October 1964): 29-37.

Skinner, William. "Marketing and Social Structure in Rural China." Parts 1, 2, 3. *Journal of Asian Studies* 24, nos. 1-3 (November 1964, February 1965, May 1965): 3-43, 195-228, 363-99.

Smelser, Neil J. *Theory of Collective Behavior.* New York: Free Press, 1963.

Snow, Edgar. *The Long Revolution.* New York: Random House, 1971.

Socialist Upsurge in China's Countryside (1956). Peking: Foreign Languages Press, 1957.

Solomon, Richard. *Mao's Revolution and the Chinese Political Culture.* Berkeley: University of California Press, 1971.

————. "On Activism and Activists." *China Quarterly,* no. 39 (July-September 1969), pp. 76-114.

————. "One Party and 'One Hundred Schools': Leadership Letharge, or *Luan.*" *Current Scene,* nos. 19-20 (1969).

Starr, John B. *Ideology and Culture: An Introduction to the Dialectic of Contemporary Chinese Politics.* New York: Harper & Row, 1973.

Strong, Anna Louise. *The Rise of the Chinese People's Communes and Six Years After.* Peking: New World Press, 1964.

The Struggle between the Two Roads in China's Countryside. Peking: Foreign Languages Press, 1968.

Summary of the Forum on the Work in Literature and Art in the

Armed Forces with Which Comrade Lin Piao Entrusted Comrade Chiang Ch'ing. Peking: Foreign Languages Press, 1968.

Sung, George C. S. "China's Regional Politics: A Biographical Approach." *Asian Survey*, April 1975, pp. 346-65.

Swarup, Shanti. *A Study of the Chinese Communist Movement.* London: Oxford University Press, 1966.

Taking the Bandits' Stronghold. Peking: Foreign Languages Press, 1968.

T'ao Chu. *The People's Communes Forge Ahead.* Peking: Foreign Languages Press, 1964.

Teiwes, Frederic C. "The Purge of Provincial Leaders, 1957-1958." *China Quarterly*, no. 27 (July-September 1966), pp. 14-32.

Ten Great Years: Statistics of the Economic and Cultural Achievements of the People's Republic of China. Peking: Foreign Languages Press, 1960.

Thornton, Richard C. *China: The Struggle for Power, 1919-1972.* Bloomington: Indiana University Press, 1973.

Townsend, James R. *Political Participation in Communist China.* Berkeley: University of California Press, 1968.

——. *Politics in China.* Boston: Little, Brown & Co., 1973.

Training Successors for the Revolution Is the Party's Strategic Task. Peking: Foreign Languages Press, 1965.

Tsou, Tang. "Revolution, Reintegration, and Crisis in Communist China: A Framework for Analysis." In *China in Crisis,* edited by Ping-ti Ho and Tang Tsou, 1: 227-377. Chicago: University of Chicago Press, 1968.

Tucker, Robert. "The 'Conflict Model.'" *Problems of Communism,* September-October 1963, pp. 59-61.

——. "Toward a Comparative Politics of Movement Regimes." *American Political Science Review*, no. 3 (June 1961), pp. 281-89.

Uhalley, Stephen. "The Controversy over Li Hsiu-ch'eng." *Journal of Asian Studies*, February 1966, pp. 305-17.

Vogel, Ezra F. *Canton under Communism.* Cambridge, Mass.: Harvard University Press, 1969.

Weber, Max. *The Protestant Ethic and the Spirit of Capitalism.* New York: Charles Scribner's, 1958.

Whitson, William W., and Chen-hsia Huang. *The Chinese High Command: A History of Communist Military Politics, 1927-71.* New York: Praeger, 1973.

Who's Who in Communist China. Vols. 1-2. Hong Kong: Union Research Institute, 1966-1968.

Whyte, Martin King. "The Tachai Brigade and Incentives for the Peasants." *Current Scene*, no. 16 (1969).

Wong, John. *Land Reform in the People's Republic of China*. New York: Praeger, 1973.

Yahuda, Michael. "Kremlinology and the Chinese Strategic Debate, 1965-66." *China Quarterly*, no. 49 (January-March 1972), pp. 32-75.

Yao Wen-yüan. *Comments on Tau Chu's Two Books*. Peking: Foreign Languages Press, 1968.

——. *On Counterrevolutionary Double-Dealer Chou Yang*. Peking: Foreign Languages Press, 1968.

Young, Ronald L. "Commitment among Cadres in Rural Communist China, 1960-1965." Master's thesis, Columbia University, New York, 1970.

Zagoria, Donald. *The Sino-Soviet Conflict, 1956-1961*. Princeton, N.J.: Princeton University Press, 1962.

——. "The Strategic Debate in Peking." In *China's Policies in Asia and America's Alternatives*, edited by Tang Tsou, pp. 237-68. Chicago: The University of Chicago Press, 1968.

CHINESE AND JAPANESE

Ajia kenkyūjō, *Jimmin kōsha sōran* [Survey of people's communes]. Tokyo, 1965.

An Tzu-wen. "Introducing the Good Experience of the Nanlin Party Branch Work." *Jen-min jih-pao*, March 29, 1965.

Andō Hikotarō. "The Great Cultural Revolution As Seen in Peking." *Kokumin*, December 1966.

Chang Ch'un-ch'iao. "On Exercising All-Round Dictatorship over the Bourgeoisie." *Hung-ch'i*, no. 4 (April 1, 1975), pp. 2-12.

Chang Shih-hsing, "People's Commune and All People Armed." *Lun jen-min kung-she* [On people's commune]. Peking: Ch'ing-nien ch'u-pan she, 1958.

Ch'en Po-ta. "Under the Banner of Comrade Mao Tse-tung." *Hung-ch'i*, no. 4 (July 16, 1958), pp. 1-12.

Ch'en Yun. "Some Important Problems in the Current Capital Construction Work." *Hung-ch'i*, no. 5 (March 1, 1959), pp. 1-16.

Ch'en Yung-kuei. "Self-reliance Is a Magic Word." *Hung-ch'i*, no. 1 (January 6, 1965), pp. 20-24.

Cheng-feng wen-hsüan [Selected documents of the rectification movement]. N.p.: Chieh-fang she, 1946.

Chi Ch'ün-yi. "People's Commune Is a Great Creation of the Masses in Our Country." *Hung-ch'i*, no. 5 (March 1, 1960), pp. 7-8.

Ch'i Pen-yü. "Commemorating the 25th Anniversary of Chairman

Mao's Talk at the Yenan Forum on Literature.' " *Hung-ch'i*, no. 8 (May 23, 1967), pp. 26-31.

——. *"Hai Jui Deplores the Emperor* and *Hai Jui Dismissed from Office*'s Reactionary Substance." *Jen-min jih-pao*, April 2, 1966.

——. "How Can Li Hsiu-ch'eng's Betrayal Be Treated?" *Jen-min jih-pao*, August 23, 1964.

——. "Patriotism or Betrayal? Criticizing Reactionary Film *Secret History of Ch'ing Court*." *Hung-ch'i*, no. 5 (March 31, 1967), pp. 9-23.

——. "Study History for Revolution." *Hung-ch'i*, no. 13 (December 6, 1965), pp. 14-22.

——. "What Class Stand Do the Editorial Departments of *Frontline* and *Peking Daily* Take?" *Hung-ch'i*, no. 7 (May 11, 1966), pp. 24-31.

——, Lin Chieh, and Yun Chang-kuei. "Chien Po-tsan's Historical Views Must Be Criticized." *Hung-ch'i*, no. 4 (March 24, 1967), pp. 19-30.

Chia Ch'uan-kuei. "My View on the Question of Adhering to the Principle of Revolution at Home." *Pei-ching jih-pao*, December 21, 1964.

Chien Po-tsan. "Some Questions Found in Present Historical Research." *Wen-hui pao* (Shanghai), March 28, 1966.

Ching Hung. "The Plot of the Top Ambitionist to Operate 'Trust' on a Large Scale Must Be Thoroughly Exposed." *Kuang-ming jih-pao*, May 9, 1967.

Ching Hung-chi. "Reactionary Nature of the 'Theory That Distribution Determines.' " *Jen-min jih-pao*, September 14, 1967.

Chou Yang. "Speech by Chou Yang at All-China Conference of Spare Time Literary Creation Activities." *Hung-ch'i*, no. 1 (January 1, 1966), pp. 8-26.

Chūka Jimmin Kyōwakoku soshikibetsu jimmeihyō [Who's Who in the People's Republic of China arranged according to organizations]. Tokyo: The Research Office of the Cabinet Secretariat, 1967.

Chūkoku jimmin kaihōgun [Chinese People's Liberation Army]. Tokyo: Asahi shimbun-sha, 1967.

Chung-kung chung-yang wen-chien hui-chi [Collection of CCP Central Committee documents]. Peking: Red Guard Liaison Post at Men-t'oukou ch'ü, 1967.

Fei min-ping kung-tso t'iao-li [Regulations concerning militia work]. Taipei: Nationalist Chinese Government, 1965.

Fei-wei nung-ts'un jen-min kung-she t'iao-li ts'ao-an [Draft regulations on Chinese Communist rural people's commune]. March 1961. Taipei: Nationalist Chinese Government, 1965.

Hai Feng. *Kuang-chou ti-chü wen-ke li-ch'eng shu-lüeh* [An account of the Cultural Revolution in the Canton areas]. Hong Kong: Union Research Institute, 1971.

Hsiao Hua. "How the Political Instructors of Our Army Study Mao's Works." *Jen-min jih-pao*, May 23, 1964.

——. "Several Problems on the Current Construction of Political Work within the Army." *Kuang-ming jih-pao*, January 22, 1964.

Hung-ch'i, Commentator. "Bourgeois Reactionary Line on the Question of Cadres Must Be Criticized." *Hung-ch'i*, no. 5 (March 30, 1967), pp. 24-25.

——. "Comrade Chao Yü-lu Is a Good Example of Studying and Applying the Thought of Mao Tse-tung in Living Way." *Hung-ch'i*, no. 4 (March 24, 1966), pp. 31-34.

——. "Ideological Work, Its Decisive Role." *Hung-ch'i*, no. 5 (March 17, 1964), pp. 14-20.

——. "Man's Role Is Decisive." *Hung-ch'i*, no. 10 (May 23, 1964), pp. 20-26.

——. "Ode to the Red Guards." *Hung-ch'i*, no. 12 (September 17, 1966), pp. 15-17.

——. "Political Work Is the Lifeline of All Work." *Hung-ch'i*, no. 6 (March 31, 1964), pp. 40-45.

——. "Protect the Great Result of the Four Cleanup Movement." *Jen-min jih-pao*, March 5, 1967.

——. "'Start from Practice' in Carrying Out Ideological Work." *Hung-ch'i*, nos. 7-8 (April 20, 1964), pp. 1-6.

I-chiu liu-chiu nien chung-kung nien-pao [Communist China yearbook, 1969]. Vols. 1-2. Taipei: Institute of International Relations, 1970.

Jen-min kung-ho-kuo fa-kuei hui-pien [Compendia of the laws and regulations of the People's Republic of China]. Peking: Legal Press, 1959-65.

Jen-min shou-ts'e [People's handbook]. Peking: Ta-kung pao, 1955-65.

K'ang Sheng. "Communist Party Member Must Be Marxist-Leninist, Not Fellow-Travelers of the Party." *Hung-ch'i*, no. 19 (October 1, 1959), pp. 51-55.

K'o Ch'ing-shih. "On the Whole Country as a Chessboard." *Hung-ch'i*, no. 4 (February 16, 1959), pp. 9-12.

Kuan Feng and Wu Ch'uan-chi. "Critique of Comrade Wu Han's Theory of Morality." *Jen-min jih-pao*, March 9, 1966.

—— and Lin Chieh. "*Hai Jui Deplores the Emperor* and *Hai Jui Dismissed from Office* Are Two Anti-Party and Anti-Socialist Poisonous Weeds." *Hung-ch'i*, no. 5 (April 5, 1966), pp. 15-33.

Kung-fei kung-yeh cheng-ts'e ch'i-shih t'iao chu-yao nei-yung [Main contents of the Seventy Articles on Industry in Communist China].

Taipei: Nationalist Chinese Government, 1965.

Kung-fei nung-ts'un jen-min kung-she kung-tso t'iao-li hsiu-cheng ts'ao-an [Revised draft regulations on Chinese Communist people's commune], September 1962. Taipei: Nationalist Chinese Government, 1965.

Kung-fei wen-hua ta-ke-ming chung-yao wen-chien hui-pien [Compendia of important documents on the Great Cultural Revolution in Communist China]. Taipei: Nationalist Chinese Government, 1968.

Li Fu-ch'un. "Report on the Draft Economic Plan for 1960." *Jen-min shou-ts'e*, 1960, pp. 175-76.

Li Hsien-nien. "Views on People's Commune." *Hung-ch'i*, no. 10 (October 16, 1958), pp. 4-8.

Liao Lu-yen. "The Whole Party and the Whole People Take Up Agriculture in a Big Way." *Hung-ch'i*, no. 17 (September 1960), pp. 1-7.

Liu Chih-heng, Ho Kui-ting, and Hsü Hsin. "The Relations between the Four Transformations and Economic Effects." *Ching-chi yen-chiu*, no. 2 (February 17, 1964), pp. 19-26.

Liu Jen. "On Several Questions of People's Commune." *Hung-ch'i*, no. 13 (December 1, 1958), pp. 25-27.

Lo Erh-kang. "Loyal King Li Hsiu-ch'eng's Strategy for Helping His Troops by Suffering." *Jen-min jih-pao*, July 27, 1964.

Mao Tse-tung chu-tso hsüan-tu, chia [Selected readings from Mao's works, A]. Peking: Jen-min ch'u-p'an she, 1964.

Mao Tse-tung chu-tso hsüan-tu, yi [Selected readings from Mao's works, B]. Peking: Ch'ing-nien ch'u-p'an she, 1964.

Mao Tse-tung Ssu-hsiang wan-sui [Long live Mao Tse-tung Thought]. 1967 edition; 1969 edition. Taiwan: Nationalist Government, 1974.

Meng k'ui and Hsiao Lin. "Comments on Sun Yeh-fang's Reactionary Stand and Economic Program." *Hung-ch'i*, no. 10 (August 10, 1966), pp. 26-37.

Nakagami Katsuji. "Trends in Labor Productivity and the Wage Differential between Industry and Agriculture in Communist China." *Ajia keizai*, no. 9 (1966).

Nishijima Atsuyoshi. *Mō-takutō saikō shiji* [Mao Tse-tung's supreme instructions]. Tokyo: Sanichi shobō, 1970.

———. *Proretaria Kaikyū bunka daikakumei* [Great Proletarian Cultural Revolution]. Tokyo: Shonen shuppan-sha, 1968.

Nishikawa Jirō. "Traveling through the People's Republic of China." *Ajia keizai*, no. 9 (1965).

Po I-po. "Steeling of Furnaces in Class Struggle." *Jen-min jih-pao*, May 5, 1964.

Shin chūgoku nenkan, 1968 [New China yearbook, 1968]. Tokyo:

Tōhō shoten, 1969.

Suganuma Masahisa. *Chūgoku no shakai-shugi* [China's socialism]. Tokyo: Ochanomizu shobō, 1970.

T'an Chen-lin. "Strive to Achieve Self-Sufficiency of Cloth and Food in Two or Three Years." *Hung-ch'i*, no. 6 (September 16, 1958), pp. 7-12.

T'ao Chu. "Compass for 500 Million Peasants in Following Path of Socialism." *Hung-ch'i*, no. 8 (July 31, 1965), pp. 16-30.

——. "Investigation Report of the Humeng Commune." *Jen-min jih-pao*, February 25, 1959.

——. "Refuting the Theory That There Is Limit in Grain Increase." *Hung-ch'i*, no. 5 (August 1, 1958), pp. 1-5.

——. "The Whole Country as a Chessboard, the Whole Province as a Chessboard." *Nan-fang jih-pao*, March 2, 1959.

Teng Tzu-hui. "Socialist Transformation in China's Countryside." *Jen-min jih-pao*, October 18, 1959.

——. "Speech at the National Democratic Youth League Conference." *Chung-kuo ch'ing-nien*, July 15, 1954.

Ting Wang, ed. *Chung-kung wen-hua ta-ke-ming tzu-liao hui-pien* [Compendia of materials on the Cultural Revolution in Communist China]. Hong Kong: Ming-pao yüeh-k'an. Vol. 1: *Tou-cheng chung-yang chi-kuan tang-ch'uan-p'ai* [Struggle against persons in authority at central organizations], 1967; vol. 2: *Teng T'o hsüan-chih* [Selected works of Teng T'o], 1969; vol. 3: *P'eng Teh-huai wen-t'i chuan-chi* [Special compilation on the question of P'eng Teh-huai], 1969; vol. 4: *Wu Han yü Hai Jui Pa-kuan shih-chien* [Wu Han and the *Hai Jui Dismissed from Office* incident], 1970; vol. 5: *Pei-ching shih wen-hua ta-ke-ming yun-tung* [Great Cultural Revolution movement in Peking], 1970.

Ts'ai Mao-wen and T'ang Ching-liang. *Nung-ts'un tang chih-pu tsen-yang chih-ch'ih pao-lu tso-yung* [How can the rural Party branch support the bastion function?]. Shanghai: Jen-min ch'u-pan she, 1964.

Wang Hsüeh-wen. *Chung-kung wen-hua ta-ke-ming yü hung-wei ping* [Great Cultural Revolution and Red Guards in Communist China]. Taipei: Institute of International Relations, 1969.

Wang Jen-chung. "Bring Politics to the Fore, Put the Thought of Mao Tse-tung in Command of Everything." *Hung-ch'i*, no. 5 (April 5, 1966), pp. 1-14.

Wu-ch'an chieh-chi wen-hua ta-ke-ming wen-chien hui-pien [Compendium of the Great Proletarian Cultural Revolution documents]. Vol. 1. N.p., n.d.

Wu Chih-p'u. "From Agricultural Producers' Cooperatives to People's

Commune." *Hung-ch'i*, no. 8 (September 16, 1958), pp. 5-11.

Wu Ch'uan-ch'i. "Communism As Seen from People's Commune." *Jen-min jih-pao*, October 1, 1958.

Wu Han. "Revolution or Inheritance? Self-Criticism on Moral Discussion." *Pei-ching jih-pao*, January 12, 1966.

Wu Wen-hui. "A Tentative Discussion on the Difference between So-Called 'Middle Characters' and Characters of the Middle Status." *Hsüeh-shu yen-chiu*, no. 3 (May 5, 1966).

Yao Wen-yüan. "Commemorate Lu Hsün and Carry the Revolution Through to the End." *Hung-ch'i*, no. 14 (November 1, 1966), pp. 4-10.

——. "Criticizing Counterrevolutionary Double-Dealer Chou Yang," *Hung-ch'i*, no. 1 (January 1, 1967), pp. 25-30.

——. "On the Social Basis of the Lin Piao Anti-Party Clique," *Hung-ch'i*, no. 3 (March 1, 1975), pp. 20-29.

——. "On 'Three-Family Village.'" *Chieh-fang jih-pao* (Shanghai) and *Wen-hui pao*, May 19, 1966.

——. "The Revolutionary Younger Generation Is Growing." *Hung-ch'i*, no. 6 (March 31, 1964), pp. 48-50.

——. "The Working Class Must Exercise Leadership in Everything." *Hung-ch'i*, no. 2 (August 25, 1968), pp. 3-7.

OTHER PUBLICATIONS USED IN THIS STUDY

Chinese Material Translated in English Periodicals

China News Analysis, Hong Kong.
Chinese Education, New York.
Chinese Law and Government, New York.
Current Background, Hong Kong: U.S. Consulate General.
Current Scene: Developments in Mainland China, Hong Kong.
Foreign Broadcast Information Service, Washington, D.C.
Selections from China Mainland Magazines, Hong Kong: U.S. Consulate General.
Survey of the China Mainland Press, Hong Kong: U.S. Consulate General.
Union Research Service, Hong Kong: Union Research Institute.
U.S. Joint Publications Research Service, Washington, D.C.

Chinese and Japanese Periodicals

Ajia keizai [Asian economy], Tokyo.
Ajia keizai jumpō [Trimonthly of Asian economy], Tokyo.

Chien-hsien [Frontline], Peking.
Ching-chi yen-chiu [Economic studies], Peking.
Chūgoku kenkyū geppō [Chinese studies monthly], Tokyo.
Fei-ching yen-chiu [Studies on Chinese communism], *Chung-kung yen-chiu* after 1969, Taipei.
Hsin-hua pan-yüeh-k'an [New China semimonthly], Peking.
Hsüeh-hsi [Study], Peking.
Hsüeh-shu yen chiu [Academic research], Peking.
Hung-ch'i [Red flag], Peking.
Kung-tso t'ung-hsün [Work bulletin], Peking.
Li-shih yen-chiu [Historical studies], Peking.
Ming-pao yüeh-k'an [Ming-pao monthly], Hong Kong.
Tsu-kuo [China monthly], Hong Kong.
Wen-i pao [Literature], Peking.

Chinese and Japanese Newspapers

Most of the Chinese local papers consulted in this study are from the Union Research Institute and the U.S. Consulate-General in Hong Kong.

Anhui jih-pao, Hopei.
Asahi shimbun, Tokyo.
Chekiang jih-pao, Hangchow.
Chieh-fang chün-pao, Peking.
Chieh-fang jih-pao, Shanghai.
Chung-kuo ch'ing-nien pao [Chinese youth paper], Peking.
Fukien jih-pao, Foochow.
Hopei jih-pao, Paoting.
Hsin hunan jih-pao, Changsha.
Hsin-min wan-pao, Shanghai.
Hunan jih-pao, Changsha.
Jen-min jih-pao, Peking.
Kiangsi jih-pao, Nanchang.
Kiangsu jih-pao, Nanking.
Kirin jih-pao, Kirin.
Kuang-ming jih-pao, Peking.
Kung-jen jih-pao, Peking.
Kwangchow jih-pao, Canton.
Kweichow jih-pao, Kweiyang.
Liaoning jih-pao, Shenyang
Mainichi shimbun, Tokyo.
Ming-pao, Hong Kong.
Nanfang jih-pao, Canton.

Nihon keizai shimbun, Tokyo.

Pei-ching jih-pao, Peking.

Pei-ching wan-pao, Peking.

Sansi jih-pao, T'aiyüan.

Sian jih-pao, Sian.

Sing-tao jih-pao, Hong Kong.

Szechwan jih-pao, Chengtu.

Ta-kung pao, Hong Kong.

Ta-kung pao, Peking.

Tang chih-pu sheng-huo, Shanghai.

Wen-hui pao, Shanghai.

Wen-hui pao, Hong Kong.

Yang-ch'eng wan-pao, Canton.

Yomiuri shimbun, Tokyo.

Red Guard Materials

Most of the Red Guard materials used in this study are from the Union Research Institute and the U.S. Consulate-General in Hong Kong.

Chan-pao [Combat news]. Peking: Detachment of Representatives from Universities and Institutes for Struggling against Counter-revolutionary Revisionist Clique of P'eng Chen, Lu Ting-yi, and Yang Shang-kun.

Chiao hsüeh p'i-p'an [Criticism and repudiation of pedagogics]. Peking: Cultural Revolution Committee of Peking University.

Chiao-yü ke-ming [Educational revolution]. Peking: Educational Liaison Committee of Peking Municipality.

Chin-chün pao [Marching army news]. Peking: Red Guard Unit of Mao Tse-tung Thought, Department of Philosophy and Social Sciences, Chinese Academy of Sciences.

Chingkang-shan, Peking: Chingkang-shan Corps of Tsinghua University.

Ch'iu-Liu chan-pao [Drag-out-Liu combat news]. Peking: Red Guard Fighting Detachment of the Peking Commune, Ministry of Higher Education.

Ch'üan-wu-ti [Entirely matchless]. Peking: Revolutionary Committee of Metropolitan Medical Circles and Health Bulletin, Yenan Command.

Chu-ying tung-fang hung [Chu-ying east is red]. Canton: Organs of Red Headquarters, Chu-chiang Movie Production Station.

Hsin jen-ta [New people's university]. Peking: New People's University Commune, Capital Red Guard Congress.

Hsin jen-wei [New people's health]. Peking: Liaison Office, Health Department, Peking Medical College.

Hsin nung-ta [New agricultural university]. Peking: Tung-fang hung Commune, Peking Agricultural University.

Hsin Pei-ta [New Peking university]. Peking: Peking University Cultural Revolution Committee, Chinese Department Combat Corps.

Hsin-wen chan-pao [News combat paper]. Peking: Metropolitan News Criticism Liaison Station, New China News Agency.

Hung chan-pao [Red combat news]. Canton: General Headquarters of Revolutionary Rebels of the Agencies Directly Attached to the Kwangtung Provincial Committee.

Hung-ch'i [Red flag]. Peking: Peking Aeronautical Institute Hung-ch'i Combat Team, Congress of Red Guards.

Hung-i chan-pao [Red health combat news] and *Pa-i-na chan-pao* [August 18 combat news]. Peking: Red Medical Battle Bulletin and August 18 Battle Bulletin, a tabloid published by the Revolutionary Committee of Peking Medical and Health Circle and Peking Medical College.

Hung-kung chan-pao [Red workers combat news]. Shanghai: General Headquarters of Red Workers Revolutionary Rebels.

Hung-she hsüan-ch'uan-ping [Red propaganda soldier]. Peking: The Data Processing Groups of Capital Revolutionary Literary and Art Rebel Headquarters, Yenan Red Flag General Corps of Organs of Ministry of Culture, Revolutionary Committee of Publishing Sys-tem of the Capital, and Cultural Revolution Committee of Peking University.

Hung-she tsao-fan-tse [Red rebels]. Canton: Canton First Middle School, Chinang-men Editorial Department.

Hung-she wen-i [Red literature and art]. Peking: Metropolitan Literary Art Circles, Red Rebel Headquarters.

Hung-wei chan-pao [Red Guard combat news]. Peking Foreign Affairs Institute Revolutionary Rebel Corps.

Hung-wei pao [Red Guard news]. Peking: Red Flag Combat Brigade of Peking Institute of Foreign Languages.

Hung-wei-ping pao [Red Guard news]. Peking: Red Guard Revolutionary Rebel Headquarters, Chinese Academy of Sciences.

Kang Pa-i chan-ch'i [Steel August 1 combat flag]. Canton: Steel August 1 Middle School Headquarters, Secondary Schools Hung-ch'i Headquarters, and Workers Revolutionary United Committee.

K'e-chi hung-ch'i [Science and technology red flag]. Peking: Joint Committee of Revolutionary Rebels of Metropolitan Science and Technology Units.

Ke-ming kung-jen pao [Revolutionary workers news]. Peking: August 8 Combat Headquarters, Central Institute of Finance and Banking.

Ke-ming tsao-fan pao [Revolutionary rebellion news]. Paoting: Provincial Editorial Team of *Ke-ming tsao-fan pao*.

Kung-jen p'ing-lun [Workers forum]. Canton: Red General Headquarters of the "Red Workers" and Construction Command of Red General Headquarters.

Kwangchow jih-pao hung-ch'i [Canton daily red flag]. Canton: *Kwangchow jih-pao hung-ch'i* Editorial Department.

Liu Shao-ch'i wu-ko tzu-liao [Five materials on Liu Shao-ch'i]. N.p., n.d. A xeroxed copy available at the East Asian Institute, Columbia University.

Pa-i-san hung-wei-ping [August 13 Red Guard]. Tientsin: Tientsin University *Pa-i-san hung-wei-ping* Editorial Department.

Pei-ching kung-she [Peking commune]. Peking: Peking Commune August 8 Combat Brigade, Central Finance Institute, Congress of Red Guards.

P'i-T'an chan-pao [Combat news of criticizing T'an Chen-lin]. Peking: Liaison Center of the Revolutionary Rebels of the Agricultural Department and Liaison Center for Criticizing and Repudiating T'an Chen-lin.

Shou-tu hung-wei-ping [Capital city Red Guards]. Peking: Congress of Red Guard Universities and Colleges in Peking.

T'i-yü chan-pao [Athlete combat news]. Peking: Sheng-huo-she, Maoism Corps of Athlete Institute of Workers, Peasants and Soldiers.

Tou-p'i-kai [Struggle-criticism-transformation]. Peking: Chinese People's University Three Red Corps, Red Guard Congress.

Ts'ai-mao hung-ch'i [Finance and trade red flag]. Peking: Rebel Liaison Committee of the Finance and Trade System.

Tsao-fan yu-li [Rebellion is justified]. Peking: September 16 Revolutionary Rebel Corps of the Seventh Machine Building Ministry.

Tung-fang-hung [East is red]. Peking: Peking Mining Institute Tung-fang hung Commune, Congress of Red Guards.

Tung-fang-hung [East is red]. Peking: Peking Normal College Tung-fang hung Commune, Congress of Red Guards.

Tung-fang-hung chi-ta hung-ch'i [East is red, Chinan University red flag]. Canton: Chinan University Tung-fang-hung Headquarters.

Tung-fang-hung pao [East is red news]. Peking: Peking Institute of Geology.

Wei-tung [Defend the East]. Tientsin: Branch of Nank'ai University's Weitung Economic Research Institute.

Wen-hsüeh chan-pao [Literature combat news]. Peking: Rebels Corps of All China Writers Association.

Wen-hua ke-ming t'ung-hsün [Cultural Revolution bulletin]. Peking: Revolutionary Committee of Metropolitan Publications System.

Wen-i hung-ch'i [Literature and art red flag]. Peking: Literature and Art Commune of Workers, Peasants and Soldiers.

Yeh-chan pao [Field combat news]. Shanghai: Revolutionary General Headquarters of Shanghai Workers.

Yu-t'ien chan-pao [Post office combat news]. Peking: Propaganda Team, Joint Committee of Revolutionary Workers in .the Peking Post and Telecommunication System.

Index

and Documents. Vol. 1: *History.* 1966. 256 pp., maps, index. Vols. 2 and 3: *Documents and Comments.* 1971. 756, 1,107 pp.

15. Vincent Y. C. Shih. *The Taiping Ideology: Its Sources, Interpretations, and Influences.* 1967. 576 pp., bibliog., index.

16. Nicholas Poppe. *The Twelve Deeds of Buddha: A Mongolian Version of the Lalitavistara.* 1967. 241 pp., illus. Paper.

17. Tsi-an Hsia. *The Gate of Darkness: Studies on the Leftist Literary Movement in China.* Preface by Franz Michael. Introduction by C. T. Hsia. 1968. 298 pp., index.

18. Tso-liang Hsiao. *The Land Revolution in China, 1930-1934: A Study of Documents.* 1969. 374 pp., tables, glossary, bibliog., index.

19. Michael Gasster. *Chinese Intellectuals and the Revolution of 1911: The Birth of Modern Chinese Radicalism.* 1969. 320 pp., glossary, bibliog., index.

20. Richard C. Thornton. *The Comintern and the Chinese Communists, 1928-31.* 1969. 266 pp., bibliog., index.

21. Julia C. Lin. *Modern Chinese Poetry: An Introduction.* 1972. 278 pp., bibliog., index.

22. Philip C. Huang. *Liang Ch'i-ch'ao and Modern Chinese Liberalism.* 1972. 200 pp., illus., glossary, bibliog., index.

23. Edwin Gerow and Margery Lang, eds. *Studies in the Language and Culture of South Asia.* 1974. 174 pp.

24. Barrie M. Morrison. *Lalmai, A Cultural Center of Early Bengal.* 1974. 190 pp. maps, drawings, tables.

25. Kung-chuan Hsiao. *A Modern China and a New World: K'ang Yu-Wei, Reformer and Utopian, 1858-1927.* 1975. 669 pp., transliteration table, bibliog., index.

26. Marleigh Grayer Ryan. *The Development of Realism in the Fiction of Tsubouchi Shōyō.* 1975. 133 pp., index.

27. Dae-Sook Suh and Chae-Jin Lee, eds. *Political Leadership in Korea.* 1976. 272 pp., tables, figures, index.

28. Hellmut Wilhelm. *Heaven, Earth, and Man in the Book of Changes: Seven Eranos Lectures.* 1976.

29. Jing-shen Tao. *The Jurchen in Twelfth-Century China: A Study of Sinicization.* 1976. 206 pp., map, illus., appendix, glossary, bibliog., index.

30. Byung-joon Ahn. *Chinese Politics and the Cultural Revolution: Dynamics of Policy Processes.* 1976.

31. Margaret Nowak and Stephen Durrant. *The Tale of the Nišan Shamaness: A Manchu Folk Epic.* Forthcoming, 1977.

32. Jerry Norman. *A Manchu-English Lexicon* Forthcoming, 1977.